India's Forests, Real and Imagined

India's Forests, Real and Imagined

Writing the Modern Nation

Alan G. Johnson

BLOOMSBURY ACADEMIC
LONDON • NEW YORK • OXFORD • NEW DELHI • SYDNEY

BLOOMSBURY ACADEMIC
Bloomsbury Publishing Plc
50 Bedford Square, London, WC1B 3DP, UK
1385 Broadway, New York, NY 10018, USA
29 Earlsfort Terrace, Dublin 2, Ireland

BLOOMSBURY, BLOOMSBURY ACADEMIC and the Diana logo are trademarks of Bloomsbury Publishing Plc

First published in Great Britain 2023
This paperback edition published 2024

Copyright © Alan G. Johnson, 2023

Alan G. Johnson has asserted his right under the Copyright, Designs and Patents Act, 1988, to be identified as Author of this work.

For legal purposes the Acknowledgments on pp. vii–viii constitute an extension of this copyright page.

Series design by Charlotte James
Cover image © Andrew Aitchison / In pictures via Getty Images

All rights reserved. No part of this publication may be reproduced or transmitted in any form or by any means, electronic or mechanical, including photocopying, recording, or any information storage or retrieval system, without prior permission in writing from the publishers.

Bloomsbury Publishing Plc does not have any control over, or responsibility for, any third-party websites referred to or in this book. All internet addresses given in this book were correct at the time of going to press. The author and publisher regret any inconvenience caused if addresses have changed or sites have ceased to exist, but can accept no responsibility for any such changes.

A catalogue record for this book is available from the British Library.

A catalog record for this book is available from the Library of Congress.

ISBN: HB: 978-0-7556-3410-1
PB: 978-1-3503-5392-3
ePDF: 978-0-7556-3412-5
eBook: 978-0-7556-3411-8

Typeset by Newgen KnowledgeWorks Pvt. Ltd., Chennai, India

To find out more about our authors and books visit www.bloomsbury.com and sign up for our newsletters.

Contents

List of Figures	vi
Acknowledgments	vii
Introduction: Imagining India's Forests	1
1 Moral Kingship, Forest Dwellers, and Epic and Vernacular Forests	51
2 Colonial History, Home Forests, and Mother India in Bankim's *Anandamath*	79
3 Premchand's Forest, Bibhutibhushan's *Aranyak*, and the Progressive Era	117
4 History, Nation, and Forest in Salman Rushdie and Amitav Ghosh	131
5 Indigeneity, Forestry, and the State in C. K. Janu, Mahasweta Devi, and Easterine Kire	153
Conclusion: The City in the Forest	181
Notes	191
Bibliography	235
Index	257

Figures

0.1	Banyan tree, St. Thomas Mount, Chennai	15
0.2	Shola forest, Palni Hills	19
0.3	Radha and Krishna painting	31
0.4	Ajmer Dargah tree	38
0.5	Sacred tree, Tezpur	47
1.1	Sadhu in Corbett National Park	52
1.2	Areca nut palm	52
4.1	Sundarbans mangrove trees in tide	132
4.2	Bon Bibi figure	139

Acknowledgments

This book has been incubating for several years, and I am grateful to all the people, institutions, and organizations who have helped see it through to completion. My home institution, Idaho State University, has offered invaluable intellectual, administrative, monetary, and library support. A sabbatical and an Idaho Humanities Council Research Award helped jump-start the project, as did an Office of Research travel award. The College of Arts and Letters funded a research assistant, two course releases, and three conference travel awards. A Fulbright-Nehru award in 2016–17 enabled the final research phase. I am fortunate to be in a collegial department, English and Philosophy, that provides intangible networks of support and opportunities to develop and share research ideas.

Parts of the project, in various stages of development, were presented at the following conferences and institutions: Association for the Study of Literature and Environment (ASLE); CMS College, Kottayam; Dwellings of Enchantment Conference—Université de Perpignan; Forest and Literature Conference—Challakudi (Kerala); Department of Humanities and Social Sciences—IIT Madras; Golden Jubilee/UGC Conference—Berhampur; University of Gour Banga—Malda, West Bengal; Department of English—National University of Singapore; Northeast MLA; Rocky Mountain MLA; ASEAN-ASLE—Manila; Assam University—Diphu; Study Centre for Indian Literature in English and Translation (SCILET)—American College, Madurai; the USIEF Fulbright offices in New Delhi and Chennai; Osmania University; Zakir Hussain Delhi College; National Seminar on Women in Indian Knowledge Tradition—Kamala Nehru College, University of Delhi; Central University of Karnataka; and the Idaho Environmental Humanities Symposium.

I thank the many scholars, colleagues, co-panelists, and hosts who have been vital interlocutors, listeners, and supporters of this project, among whom are the following: Nobel Ang, Brian Attebery, Jennifer Attebery, Patrycja Austin, Ralph Baergen, Meera Baindur, Isabel Banzon, Jacob Berger, Amit Bhattacharya, Sivasish Biswas, Sravani Biswas, Alan Blackstock, Adam Bradford, Tera Cole, Sri Craven, Shruti Das, Coralynn Davis, Asis De, Carlen Donovan, Will Donovan, Ebenezer, Jennifer Fuller, Priyanjana Ghosh, Sushilla Gopaul, Susan Goslee, John Gribas, Adam Grotsky, Brandon Hall, Monirul Haq, Hal Hellwig, Bethany Schultz Hurst, Adeline Johns-Putra, Margaret Johnson, Gurpreet Kaur, Hameed Khan, Tom Klein, Pradip Krishen, Mathangi Krishnamurthy, T. Vijay Kumar, Joy Landeira, Dawn Lattin, Sonja Launspach, Dave Lawrimore, Matt Levay, John Lourduswamy, Kim Madsen, Bill McCurdy, Kanchana Mahadevan, Barb Mayfield, Shelley McEuen, Bénédicte Meillon, Minakshi Menon, N. Nagaraja, Lalitha Nagesvari, Geetesh Nirban, Melissa Norton, R. P. Nair, Joji John Panicker, Premila Paul, Cathy Peppers, Ruth Pison, Tom Pfister, Madhu Ramnath, Giri Rao, Manohar Rao, Usha Devi Rao, Sura Rath, T. Ravichandran,

Liz Reiman, Ignasi Ribo, Mike Roche, Evan Rodriguez, Susmita Roye, Chitra Sankaran, Roger Schmidt, Hansda Sowendra Shekhar, Ruchi Singh, Murali Sivaramakrishnan, Brian Skerratt, Jim Skidmore, Scott Slovic, M. Somasundaram, Michael Sowder, Mike Stubbs, Mali Subbiah, Maya Sundararajan, R. Swarnalatha, Aleena Teny, Lily Rose Tope, Jyoti Tripathy, Kandi Turley-Ames, Matt VanWinkle, Rob Watkins, Russell Wahl, Teresa Warren, Curt Whitaker, Lydia Wilkes, Jessica Winston, Brent Wolter, Michael Wutz, Zainor Zainal, Bonnie Zare, and Amanda Zink.

Parts of Chapter 5 previously appeared in different forms in *ISLE: Interdisciplinary Studies in Literature and Environment* 23, no. 2 (Summer 2016), 506–25, as "Sacred Forest, Maternal Space, and National Narrative in Mahasweta Devi's Fiction"; and in *Dwelling in Enchantment Writing and Reenchanting the Earth*, edited by Bénédicte Meillon (Rowman and Littlefield, 2020), 277–308, as "Shadows of Enchantment in Indian Forest Fiction: Mahasweta Devi's 'The Hunt' and Hansda Sowvendra Shekhar's *The Mysterious Ailment of Rupi Baskey*."

Special thanks to my editors at I. B. Tauris-Bloomsbury Academic, David Avital and Olivia Dellow, for their kind attention to and interest in the manuscript, and to the copy editor.

Finally, I am grateful to Margaret and Shirin, Nishant and Roshin for their unending love and support over the years.

I must end by acknowledging the rich corpus of texts that make such a study not only possible, but also delightful. I am profoundly aware that many of India's great ancient and medieval works have sustained communities of faith for centuries, and I engage them, in translation, with humility and an acute sense of my own interpretive limitations. As will be clear, I approach these works not, as my friends of faith do, on devotional terms, but on their extraordinary literary merits and social–historical roles. Although I sincerely hope my literary and cultural interests are clear, if any should feel a stirring of displeasure, please know that my intentions are entirely opposed to any such effect. These works are gifts to the world; my respect for them has only grown over the decades.

Introduction: Imagining India's Forests

Environments, Metaphors, Texts

A bird's-eye view of India's plains three millennia ago, moving south from Himalayan valleys dotted with oak,[1] would have revealed dense forests of sal, sandalwood, teak, neem, banyan, champa, and other trees. Some of these may have been part of the legendary Naimisha, a dry deciduous forest described in many ancient and medieval Sanskrit texts, but which has now vanished. To the west, our aerial vision would have taken in thorny, dry jungle. Toward the Eastern Ghats and extending down to central India would have been the Dandaka Forest (*Dandakaryana*), described by the poet-sage Valmiki in his Sanskrit *Ramayana*, which covered an area straddling several modern states. Remnants of it still exist: further west our eye might pick out a section of it called *Panchavati*, literally "five banyans." It, too, has disappeared, though the area has remained an important pilgrimage center. Further south still, our flight would bring into view the Western Ghats, a mountain range that extends from roughly the midpoint of India's western coast down to the country's very tip. The rainforest and moist, tropical deciduous forest that thickly cover these hills still harbor, as they did long ago, one of the earth's most biodiverse regions. Still in the south but eastward, we might spot the *mullai*, or forestland, one of the seven (though in practice, mainly five) fabled landscapes, or *tinai*, described in ancient Tamil Sangam poems. Together with the mountainous *kurinji* regions, the *mullai* boasted (as some areas still do) jasmine and *kurinji* flowers, thickets of bamboo, and thick forests of sandalwood, teak, and areca palm.[2]

The interplay between ecology and legend in this imagined flyover illustrates the subject of this book, which is the depiction of forests in modern Indian fiction. I argue that the forest, a long-standing motif in Indian cultural history, has been a crucial image in modern Indian writing.

The forest afforded India's early nationalist novelists a means of reconciling ancient and modern values in their efforts to forge a new national consciousness. It did so because, as a site that traditionally accommodated a wide variety of opposing forces and beliefs—danger and refuge, authenticity and deceit, mystery and transparency, innocence and depravity, action and contemplation—it seemed capable of accommodating an analogous range of differences, both perceived and lived, among modern Indians, including linguistic, religious, gender, and class differences. In nineteenth-century nationalist writers' hands, the forest stood, in this sense, for the nation, and has for this reason been an integral part of evolving, and often conflicting, ideas about nationhood. As Jennifer Wenzel has observed, although India can be characterized as a "forest culture," it is one "that has been defined, throughout its long history, as much by *contests* over its forests as by peaceful existence within them" (original emphasis).[3]

Another reason Indian writers have turned to forest imagery is because colonial modernity in India, which forged many of the categories and metaphors that continue to inform narratives of national development, was infused with a rhetoric of "loss and recovery."[4] On a governmental level, this outlook assumed that degraded landscapes must be either rejuvenated, such as by reforestation, or turned to uses for so-called improvement. But in the imaginative realm of Indian literature, "recovery," as Ashis Nandy has asserted in his analysis of the psychological damage of colonialism, means enabling a self that can enact "an alternative mythography of history."[5] At its best, the literary forest thus affords a space in which to present alternative visions to both the physical and the psychological "rhetoric of progress" that continues to frame national development.[6] Long after India's independence in 1947, writers have continued to draw on the forest images described above, though they have elaborated on and added to them in a variety of ways, often as a means of critiquing national policies and social injunctions.

Indian narratives are not the only ones, certainly, to depict the forest in terms of oppositions like danger and refuge, innocence and deceit. Many of these oppositional features are familiar across cultures. Worldwide, writers have variously depicted the forest as both fecund and barren, innocent yet dangerous, rejuvenating as well as enervating, beautiful and damned. It harbors heroes and demons alike, and is in every way distinctly different from the settled life of towns and cities. Forests are therefore both isolating and social, a polarity that the language and structure of a text sometimes mirrors. Individual trees frequently stand in for individual humans, both rooted to a common soil.[7] (Happily, scientists have lately found a basis for this arboreal image with the discovery that trees are, in fact, "social" and "care for each other" through biochemical communication.[8]) The forest can be an arena in which ascetics commune with one another and with nature; or a place that accentuates human community by virtue of the latter's conspicuous absence; or a stage for a warrior-king's nonascetic epiphany. The anthropologist Mary Douglas has described the "immense prestige of the forest" for the Lele people of central Africa, who "often contrast the forest with the village." A common saying, therefore, is that "Time goes slowly in the village, quickly in the forest." For the Lele, as with all forest dwellers, the forest is the source of all "good things," including "clean [food]."[9] Perhaps, as Elias Canetti maintains in *Crowds and Power*, this ambivalent regard is built into the forest's physicality. "Man stands upright as a tree and he inserts himself amongst the other trees. But they are taller than he is and he has to look up at them. No other natural phenomenon ... is invariably above him and, at the same time, so near and so multiple in its formation as the concourse of trees ... none is as perpetually near him as the forest." This dense and immovable entity, Canetti believes, made the forest "the first image of awe" for humans.[10] Canetti and Douglas echo other commentators in further noting that the forest is usually opposed to its other natural surroundings, such as the grasslands in which the Lele also habitually moved, and that it has tended to be a primarily male sphere.[11]

In more-specifically literary terms, Robert Pogue Harrison, in *Forests: The Shadow of Civilization*, his oft-cited study of the forest in Western literature, has described the many ways in which forests, as depicted in both ancient and modern texts—*Gilgamesh* and the Bible, Grimm's folktales and Thoreau—have been used to constitute both religious and secular definitions of what it means to be a civilized human. In human storytelling, as Harrison persuasively, if sometimes too sweepingly, claims, forests have since the remote past seemed to be "archaic" and "antecedent to the human world."[12] Partly for this reason, Harrison emphasizes, the forest served as "*an indispensable resource of symbolization in the cultural evolution of humankind*" (original emphasis).[13] Harrison calls forests the "shadow of civilization" to mean that in the physical as well as (and primarily) symbolic forest, apparent dualities "[go] astray."[14] Using a phrase that characterizes his study and that will very broadly serve mine as well, Harrison examines the long-standing use of "the forest as a metaphor for human institutions."[15] Harrison illustrates his broad conclusions by ranging, in nuanced discussions, from the Sumerian epic *Gilgamesh* and Dante to Giambattista Vico and Joseph Conrad. As humans everywhere consumed more and more trees for shelter and food and ornamentation, they increasingly lamented their loss and invested forests with ever more powerful—and often contradictory—meanings. Harrison uses "shadow" in a double sense: to describe how "Western civilization ... project[s] into the forest's shadows its secret and innermost anxieties" and to characterize the ways in which forests have "cast their shadow" on us. Forests are, in other words, both agent and receptacle.[16]

Harrison argues that it was in the early modern period, when the sway of religion began to ebb, that forest settings in literature began to dramatize the world's adoption of an ironic view of the past. In Europe, this change not coincidentally accompanied the enclosure of common lands, meaning more and more privatization of property in the hands of the wealthy and greater restrictions to its access by commoners, a process that in Britain was already underway by medieval times.[17] Ironically, some Enlightenment thinkers, like natural historian John Williams, who advocated the planting of oak trees in Scotland, argued that private property owners—which in the 1770s meant the upper classes—were solely capable of safeguarding these plantations from lower-class tenants.[18] For European romantics in the late 1700s and early 1800s, like the Grimm brothers, the loss of forests translated into the loss of a mystically imagined, open-access human collectivity on both a global and a national scale.[19] Harrison's poetics of the forest therefore crystallizes a profoundly influential development in European national cultures. As forests increasingly fell to create clearings for human settlement and to provide wood for people's needs, settled society grew nostalgic for these forests. Forests eventually came to represent all that urban life lacked: mystery and magic, wildness and deep time. The very density of forests, Harrison argues, came to symbolize a realm "where the logic of distinction goes astray," where the world is always upside down.[20] We might say that the city, broadly speaking, consists of classifications and exteriorities, the forest of murky essences. Yet however much the city displaces the forest, a vestige of the forest's primordial "grounding" remains,[21] allowing a few—artists, thinkers—to glean something existentially valuable from that groundedness.

To some degree, as the destruction of sacred cedars in the epic of *Gilgamesh* illustrates, this development seems to have been universal and to have begun very early on, as Harrison usefully reminds us. Ancient Rome, for instance, legally labeled any uninhabited forest *res nullius*, "belonging to no one," and therefore regarded the edges of such forests as marking the "natural boundaries" between the lawless wilds and the *res publica*.[22] The root of "forest," after all, is *foris*, or "outside," giving early modern Europeans the late Latin term *forestem silvam*, or "outside woods."[23] Europeans likewise coined "savage" from *silva*, meaning woods.[24] *Silva* is likely cognate with the Greek *hyle*—that is, forest—which, Harrison informs us, Aristotle used to mean "matter."[25] Ancient Indian texts, as we will see, similarly distinguish forest dwellers from city dwellers. The very interest of cities in forests and forest dwellers, however, shows that they mattered greatly to city dwellers. And, indeed, we find that ancient and medieval writings, whether in Sanskrit or Latin or Tamil, demonstrate that settled societies the world over have long recognized that their cultural vitality is inseparable from their proximate natural environments.

The globally shared opposition between city and countryside does not, however, tell us very much about specific literary works or the particularities of the cultures that produced them. The Sanskrit terms for forest, chiefly *aranya* and *vana*, do echo some features of the Latin *silva*, such as the inference that forest dwellers are crude and urban dwellers, civilized. Yet forest settings in Sanskrit literary works, not to mention those in Tamil and other classical languages, are filled with astonishingly detailed and accurate botanical references, which are used to convey very particular sensibilities that no generic term (or translation of a term) can do. Nuanced associations of regional flora, for example, infuse a plant with particular ceremonial and poetic, juridical, and medical usages. Taken together, these infuse a character's outlook, which may differ from that of another persona. The description of a plant or tree, in other words, metonymically carries cultural meaning, which in turn interacts with an individual character's mood, personality, and societal (moral) obligation.[26] When the fifth-century Sanskrit playwright Kalidasa, for instance, references the *nava-mallika*—literally, in Vinay Dharwadker's translation of Kalidasa's *Shakuntala*, "nine-petalled jasmine"—he means the "genus *Jasminum*," and more specifically the *sambac* variety of *Jasminum*, which is different from, and more valued than, the more-common "five-petalled [*Jasminum officinale*]." Both are fragrant climbing vines, and so either one would seem to serve Kalidasa's poetic identification of the character Shakuntala with jasmine. Why, then, choose *sambac*? One reason, undoubtedly, is the latter's varied colors, its petals either "white or yellow,"[27] which partly accounts for its comparatively greater value. Its nine petals suggest greater efflorescence and are said to have a reenergizing aroma.[28] *Sambac* is also more distinctively native to South Asia, as compared to the much wider distribution of *officinale*, another reason for its value among classical authors.[29] The *sambac* variety is therefore the more appropriate metonym for Shakuntala. But in the context of the play, it also functions metaphorically to evoke the constellation of moods and images associated with Shakuntala's forest home, as distinct from King Dushyanta's court.

Both Shakuntala and the forest are presented as bringing an essential moral balance to the royal capital.

Such examples reconfirm the insights of linguistics, that "the conceptual systems of various cultures partly depend on the physical environments they have developed in."[30] Making meaning is a transactional process, in that every culture "project[s]" its spatial metaphors onto its environment. If ideas and environments shape one another, it follows that everyday concepts will differ substantially among cultures and geographical regions. We may thus perceive a copse of trees as forming "a natural boundary" (as the Romans did), or we may "impose boundaries" by constructing, say, a "wall."[31] For India, the story of literary forests is considerably longer and more varied than Europe's, as this book aims to show. The subcontinent's immense linguistic, religious, and topographical diversity ensures this. Yet because of British colonialism, depictions of forests by Indian writers since the early 1800s also informed developing ideas of modern nationhood, perhaps most notably the trope of regenerating a lost unity through the language of the sciences. Ideas of nationhood involve both people and land, and for many Indians under the yoke of colonialism, the uneven access to land naturally became a unifying rallying point—sometimes against the British, as when rebellious Indian soldiers in the service of the East India Company joined hands with certain Indian landowners in 1857, and sometimes against the Indian landowners, or *zamindars*, themselves.[32] In England at this time, "commonable land" had long since been converted to "exclusively owned parcels," with "the concomitant extinction of common rights," particularly open pasturing.[33] But in this case, law followed practice, as in the use of hedges to mark property boundaries, which only later became codified and abstracted.[34] In nineteenth-century India, however, the reverse seems to have occurred, as Siraj Ahmed argues: British philologists and legal scholars underwrote British land acquisition and taxation by translating and interpreting classic Sanskrit and Arabic texts to serve their interests.[35] Nineteenth-century Indian writers who wanted to elicit nationalist sentiment in their readers clearly had a daunting task. Besides colonial censorship and a charged atmosphere of emotive and often polarizing popular symbols, they had to contend with uneven literacy, unpredictable dissemination, and religious and linguistic sensitivities.

What Indian writers did have in their quiver, however, was a vast, multitudinous corpus of cultural texts, in which representations of the forest figure prominently. This rich storehouse of narratives has arguably afforded modern Indian writers unparalleled access to images and associative meanings with which to inform their writing. At the same time, the very breadth of this repertoire has meant that it can inform any kind of meaning. Some of these narratives were restricted to elite readerships, but most have long been enmeshed in the country's popular, mainstream imagination. The forests in these stories—epics and folktales, poems and dramas—variously connote the following, to cite only a few possibilities: a realm of spiritual rejuvenation, where ascetics can meditate to channel cosmic energy; a setting for the refinement of moral kingship, aided by self-discipline and divine intervention; incivility and wildness, especially when a forest is inhabited by demons; a material resource, with the ever-present potentiality for both abundance and scarcity, refuge and labyrinth, and so a resource of game and a place for hunting and learning to hunt, but also for learning to live abstemiously; the interface between the natural and supernatural, and so the proper place for sacrifices to the gods; a site of spiritual and erotic play, sometimes questioning normative gender roles and societal strictures; and, at the edges of forests, a space in which to hear exciting new, and potentially heretical, ideas, such as the Buddha preached 2,500 years ago. To these arboreal characteristics we must add the later European descriptions of India's forests with which modern Indian writers had to contend. In European eyes, the subcontinent's forests were alternately beautiful and diseased, abundant with game but also with bandits, and disordered and wasteful but, with "proper"—that is, European—stewardship, potentially "useful" and marketable.[36]

Forests of Continuity and Change

A broad theme that cuts through the myriad narrative treatments of forests in India, from ancient epic traditions to the modern novel, is the tension between the preservation of tradition and the promise of change. For instance, India's great hero-epics, the *Mahabharata* and the *Ramayana*, which have been told and retold in many languages, each contain a Forest Book, or *Aranyaka*, that describes specific woodlands in which the royal warrior protagonists refine their moral compass so that they can then refine their societies. A correlate of this theme is that life is at once ephemeral (for individuals) and unceasing (for communities). But unlike European understandings of the forest as primarily a place for individuals to evade (if also to critique) societal obligations and responsibilities, Indian forests have traditionally been settings in which one learns to take those communal responsibilities to heart.[37] The forest in precolonial India, in other words, was not conventionally the site of abrupt breaks with a monolithic and universalized past, but instead signified a multilayered past that simultaneously accommodated a variety of group identities in the present. It was in the nineteenth century, with the growth of nationalist, anti-British sentiment, and talk of how to enact such a break, that Indian writers began to dramatize the forest as a place of immutable regional and national affiliations and associated values. For example, in the ancient Tamil epic *The Cilappatikaram*, the wedded protagonists, Kovalan and Kannaki, must traverse thickly forested countryside between their home city, the ancient port of Pukar (also styled Puhar), and their destination, sacred Maturai (Madurai), in order to escape social stigma. For R. Parthasarathy, the epic's most authoritative translator, the narrator succeeds in "ground[ing] the poem in the actual"—that is, the sensible and material world of ordinary people—"by invoking a specific place." The forest is an identifiably physical realm in "Tamil country" and also, at the same time, a symbol of cultural initiation.[38] It is clearly not a habitat aligned with a single group or ideology, in the way that modern writers would come to interpret them.

The fate of trade cities like Pukar, which for millennia depended on its lucrative production of forest products, is apropos of the changes wrought by European colonialism. In fact, historians have turned to *The Cilappatikaram* to mine its detailed descriptions of Pukar's long-standing international trade. Europe was a latecomer to the subcontinent's robust maritime trade and remained an economic toddler throughout the 1500s and 1600s, even after Vasco da Gama's arrival on the western coast, its endeavors dwarfed by Indian and Chinese production and maritime prowess.[39] Later Indian writers knew this history well: their knowledge of Europe's violent wresting of trade from India both on sea and on land in the 1700s, and its subsequent transformation of landscapes, shapes the tone of numerous modern works, which alternate between mourning for lost vistas and adulation of regional landscapes or their future possibilities. In wresting control of this preexisting trade network, European nations eventually fractured it and then fought over the pieces. They established a different kind of commerce, based not on the free flow of goods but on the selective restriction of them by monopolizing trade. Philip Curtin notes, for example, that the Dutch East India Company, or VOC, "created a genuine monopoly over nutmeg and cloves production" in Southeast Asia "by controlling production itself," thanks to soldiers sent from the Netherlands to chop down healthy trees and so confine production to a smaller, controllable number to raise prices.[40] It is no wonder, then, that da Gama's 1498 entry into South Asia's sea trade is retrospectively seen to be the historical hinge that ushered in monopoly capitalism's effect on the natural environment.

By the early 1800s, when British management of Indian topographies intensified, along with their concerted aim of educating, as Thomas Babington Macaulay advocated, "a class of persons Indian in blood and colour, but English in tastes, in opinions, in morals and in intellect" to serve colonial interests, change had long since become the leitmotif of Europe's grand narrative of progress.[41] Certain momentous developments—the Portuguese circumnavigation of the globe, for example—were plotted in a purposeful sequence of human perfectability, with Europe, naturally, in the lead. Such developments were seen to betoken breaks with a stultified past, one that Europeans believed they had made with the aid of Reason and, in Macaulay's view, "the languages of western Europe." Only by instructing Indians in the virtues of English, he concludes, can their "prejudices" be "overthrown" and true "knowledge diffused."[42] This grand narrative seduced many of India's leading intellectuals, including polymathic reformer Rammohun Roy and pioneering Bengali writer Bankimchandra Chattopadhyay (or Chatterji,[43] and commonly referred to as Bankim), who believed that "British rule was a necessary period of tutelage that Indians had to undergo to prepare precisely for what the British denied but extolled as the end of all history: citizenship and the nation-state."[44] This acceptance helped early nationalists reconcile the European articulation of history as such with Indian pasts that, retrospectively, are seen to presage the modern Indian state—a dilemma Sudipta Kaviraj calls the "double nature of the imagined community" that these early advocates of pan-Indian nationalism understood.[45]

Of course, the truth was not so simple: Macaulay, and most Europeans, remained excessively fond of their own "traditions." Even Marx, as Dipesh Chakrabarty notes, worried about the past's hold on revolutionary ideas.[46] What interests me about this narrative of historical progress is that the forest in modern times became for European nations a powerful symbol of their own distinctively glorious past. The tropical forest, meanwhile, became in European eyes—especially when characterized as jungle—a foil for the notional European forest and frequently a metonym for savagery. For instance, British politician Samuel Romilly could not help describing the French revolutionaries as "a republic of tigers in some forest in Africa"; and William Wordsworth compared revolutionary Paris to "a wood where tigers roam."[47] Similarly, when enlightened Europeans of the time condemned the rapacity of European colonialism, they resorted to metaphors still used today: Denis Diderot's eighteenth-century characterization of the colonial settler as a dehumanized, avaricious "tiger returning to the forest" is seconded by twentieth-century historian Fernand Braudel, who describes European global capitalism as a realm in which "predators roam [and] the law of the jungle operates."[48] Nineteenth-century Indian writers, who were conversant in both European and traditional Indian arboreal motifs, had to contend, therefore, with myriad, often conflicting, forest images as they forged possible futures for a country steeped in both ancient and modern iconographies. We will see how, for example, Bankim chose to juggle these various, often competing, symbolizations of forests in the context of national aspirations in his influential, though controversial, 1882 novel *Anandamath*. Bankim's strategy will be more understandable if we look into this colonial context a little more closely.

Indexical Forests, Liminal Forests, and *Darshanic* Vision

India's modern nationalist writers, to reiterate my argument, were burdened with having to create idioms that were suitably modern, in the European sense, and yet distinctively Indian. Since European colonialist tropes, as the examples above illustrate, spoke so often of the tropical forest—in part because it served as a foil to both European forest symbolism and mercantile interests—a prime strategy of Indian writers was to counter these European tropes by drawing on their own rich corpus of forest narratives and images. Because both Indian and European nationalists were sometimes drawn by their passions into narrowly bounded ideas of nationhood, such as the concept of a singular Teutonic race that certain nineteenth-century German writers espoused or the idea of India as being essentially Hindu that influential Bengali activists proclaimed—a tendency whose current hardline expressions in India scholars term "neo-traditionalist"[49]—it will be helpful, before moving forward, to identify the structural components of such a tendency. The key concepts in this regard are those of the index, a part standing for a broadly cultural whole, and the singular, or imagery that contests the strong tendency in modern systems to generalize. A discussion of how these structuring concepts have shaped both forest symbolism and national narrative, in particular a variety of historical romance that enabled powerful and influential expressions of Indian nationhood, will help guide our circuit of modern forest fictions.

In neo-traditionalist narratives, observes Dipesh Chakrabarty, both modernity and tradition are represented as homogeneous and self-evident, ignoring the particularity, or "singularity," of peoples and beliefs that cannot be subsumed within the "generality"—the "grand narrative"—of modern history.[50] Chakrabarty uses "singularity" to mean beliefs and practices that "def[y] the generalizing impulse" underlying our conventional tools of interpretation.[51] Generality depends on categories and regularities, which is how we usually make sense of the world. Modern biology relies, for example, on grouping creatures according to their successive degrees of likeness: species, genus, and so on.[52] By contrast, something is singular if it seems to be unique, and so less susceptible to the duplication that modern disciplines treat as part of universalized time and space, which in the national imaginary takes the form that Walter Benjamin notably termed "homogeneous, empty time."[53]

These points remind us that the forest is not, and never was, a free-floating signifier, as my own frequent use of the word's singular form might suggest. If the word "forest" seems freighted with associations that seem archetypal, we need to keep in mind that each of the many forests described in literary works across the world retains its ecological as well as literary specificity, as indicated by my previous comments on forests' bioregional particularity, their overlapping but situational distinction from the concept of jungle, and their ecological diversity. A particularly helpful way to compare forest imagery in India's wide variety of works is to see them as indexical. This is philosopher Charles Sanders Peirce's term for the ability of sign, whether a textual description or an event, to convey to an observer "a connection" between one event, such as the sound and action of a falling tree, and some other potential event. The index can do so because of the world's "semblance of regularity."[54] As A. K. Ramanujan puts it, each version of a well-known Indian epic "is embedded in a locale, a context … and would not make much sense without" this rootedness.[55] A forest is thus indexical of its author's milieu, just as a tree can be indexical of a particular forest and its context. These, in turn, provide the framework for the text's ideas.

Conventionally, a specific event or thing is not at all unique, but instead part of a meaningful pattern. If something does not fit into a pattern, it does not mean that it is nonsensical. But as Ranajit Guha has shown with regard to British misinterpretations of events leading up to the 1857 war that very nearly drove them out of India, it is easy for outsiders to mix up the visible signs of an impending event. In this case, when the colonial government was informed of the passing of a chapati (unleavened bread) from one village to another in the north-western provinces, it was befuddled. After the war began, however, the British decided that the chapati was a definitive signal to rebel—in other words, a signal that fit with conventional notions of how rebellion (in Europe) was incited.[56]

With the concept of singularity, Chakrabarty tries to find a way of seeing the circulated chapati for what it is, a symbol that makes sense to its handlers—perhaps in accordance with supernatural forces—but that cannot be assimilated into modern colonial schemas. For those who created it, the chapati as communicative symbol was, like "gods, spirits and other spectral … beings," an interpretive "part of a network of power and prestige within which both the subaltern and elite operated in South Asia." Gods and goddesses were not, therefore, representations "of some deeper and 'more real' secular reality."[57] They *are* reality. To try to understand such symbols on their own terms requires not just an unusual degree of sympathy, as Hamish Dalley observes, but also, as a preliminary step, a conscious resistance to the tendency to typify.[58] To shoehorn a symbol like the chapati into patterns and types is to strip it of its singular quality. But if this singularity is not simply uniqueness, what is it? If we were to claim that the circulated chapati is a metonym for the scarcity of food, say, or a metaphor for regional unity, we would fail on both counts. The chapati is not exactly what we expect of either a metonym or a metaphor in the conventional sense. In fact, the very inclination to find in the itinerant chapati a particular meaning betrays the generalizing impulse Chakrabarty wants to avoid. To the degree that supernatural or mythic qualities attach to it—to the degree, that is, that its significance is wrapped in its local cultural context rather than determined by British administrators—the chapati resists being entirely one or the other. Above all, if we accord the chapati this singularity, it cannot be abstracted, or generalized. It is not substitutable with any other chapati at any other time, yet it is still an identifiable item belonging to a food group called chapati. To grasp something of the untranslatability of the circulated chapati, we must at minimum try, Chakrabarty argues, to hold onto its "uncanny" figuration, so that it is both familiar and entirely strange.[59] We must allow the chapati to elicit, in Guha's words, "a vagueness of meaning" deriving from its "polysemy."[60]

The forest, like the chapati circulated by villages in the nineteenth century, is both a generalizable object and a singular entity, depending on who is observing it or relating to it. We must scrutinize our concepts further, however, if we want to tease out the many ways in which forests can be viewed. My reference to the chapati's supernatural elements, for instance, suggests (as the conventional use of supernatural implies) that the realm of the gods is distinct from, or beyond, nature. One could argue that in many literary works, whether of the "West" or the "East," nature is clearly infused with divinity, as for example English Romantic poetry frequently emphasizes. But here, too, an interpretive limit obtains since each romantic poem, as a product of European modernity, is understood to be a reflection of an individual and self-consciously reflective mind. As moderns, in other words, these poets bring to their craft a particular worldview that thinks in categories and that has the privilege of being able to take the nation-state, as a historical and political entity, for granted.[61] This is why, as we will see, current writers of historical fiction like Amitav Ghosh create singular characters whose perceptions are neither exclusively ocular nor purely visionary, in the manner of disembodied mystic apprehension, but rather a combination of the two. Each of these characters' bifocal, idiosyncratic outlooks challenge conventional ways of seeing and of expressing what we see. And it is the forest, and imagery evocative of the forest, that, to reiterate, affords writers the relatively indistinct, or liminal, spaces that can best contextualize and communicate such double-sightedness to modern readers.

Gayatri Chakravorty Spivak has amplified our understanding of the value of singularity with the phrase "ethical singularity," meaning an honest relationship between individuals in which each acknowledges the other in the humility of accepting that neither of them can fully know, or control, the other. In this two-way (and admittedly rare) exchange, each person retains their integral persona, along with the many cultural, historical, and environmental layers that compose that persona. This is why Spivak sees ethical singularity as the first, indispensable step in trying to achieve an "ecologically just world."[62] Readers can enact a notional kind of ethical singularity if they approach a particularly sensitive, nuanced literary work with a like openness and humility. Several of Ghosh's characters, for example, exemplify a multifaceted vision that neither the prose of conventional realism nor of magic realism can credibly express. Their uncanny perceptions of both everyday life and portents of larger, globally inflected changes must be described with a similar openness to multilayered sight.

My uses thus far of the word "vision," though not semantically identical in each instance, invoke a concept concerning perception in the Indian context that importantly underlies my discussions of fictional works that reimagine history from a South Asian, rather than European, standpoint—a strategy Dipesh Chakrabarty has termed "provincializing Europe."⁶³ This modern reimagining of received histories draws, as I have said, on a multifarious corpus of texts whose leitmotif is the Indian forest, a setting that, together with its associated images, interconnects ecological and social environments that would otherwise seem to be unrelated and even, as mentioned, in tension with one another: land and sea, the natural and the supernatural, and eroticism and asceticism. The forest's liminality often, in fact, provides writers with a context in which to envision, and to show, the fluidity between these apparent oppositions. Of particular help in representing these layered interconnections is the perceptual concept, and practice, of *darshan*, the traditional Indian term for apprehending a correspondence between ocular and divine (or pseudo-divine) vision. Traditionally, *darshan*'s effect builds on a culturally shared knowledge of not only its practice, but also of what is being viewed, whether a revered person or the iconic manifestation of a deity. Gandhi, for example, was approached daily in this way by crowds of people.

Darshan is "a form or knowing,"⁶⁴ but not in the purely subject-oriented, individual, and Western sense that John Berger, for instance, has enlighteningly examined.⁶⁵ It is instead "both a subject-centered and a subjectless practice," as Chakrabarty observes (in his discussion of Bengali nationalism), in part because in this practice, the viewer is also the viewed.⁶⁶ *Darshan* is a dialogic mode of devoted seeing in which a sacred aura attaches to the visible object, eliciting an emotional response that is almost tactile; for to see is also to touch and be touched.⁶⁷ This kind of seeing is arguably a more far-reaching apperception than that afforded by empirical observation. In a later chapter, for example, we will see that Amitav Ghosh's 2008 novel *Sea of Poppies* opens with the character Deeti perceiving the "apparition" of "a tall-masted ship" even though she is "four hundred miles from the coast" at the time.⁶⁸ The ship, the *Ibis* is a portent of momentous changes in the lives of Deeti and many other key characters, amplifying the weight of her vision. Even the "light grey" of her eyes makes Deeti "seem at once blind and all-seeing."⁶⁹ We read her instances of second sight, or what we might call *darshanic* vision, in the same vein in which the narrator tells us the specific distance of Deeti's village "from the coast"⁷⁰: two ways of perceiving the world offered up in one breath, as it were. The reader in this way apprehends something of what Deeti senses when she "sees" the *Ibis*. Ghosh's narrative strategy is, for these and other reasons that I will later discuss, more convincing and ethical—in a word, more successful—than Bankim's earlier, more narrowly construed manner of countering colonialist history through an innovative combination of historical romance, realism, and mythic tropes.

Modernity, Romanticism, and Nationalist Fiction

Despite the innovative and influential narrative strategies developed by Bankim and others, nineteenth-century novelists in India could not overcome the intrinsic unfeasibility of having a single geographical and linguistic region speak for all other regions of the subcontinent. But this did not prevent numerous writers from trying. In *Anandamath*, as I mentioned, Bankim wishes for Bengal's forests and histories to represent India as a whole. In the context of modern nationalist movements, this desire is understandable, and perhaps even laudable. But if the effort is ultimately unachievable, the strategies that writers fashioned in the process have had lasting effects on later narrative innovations, on ideas of nationhood, and, as this book shows, on representations of forests. Here, to convey a sense of this challenge, we may note that one way Bankim addresses this is by conjoining epic forest tropes and ecological details. But even these epic tropes, familiar across India, have distinctively regional assignments, such as in Tamil Sangam literature's *tinai* landscape conventions. And when we factor in narrative treatments of forests by Adivasi (indigenous), Muslim, and other non-Hindu mainstream writers, the possibilities quickly multiply.

Besides the representational effects of writers who sought to express nationwide coherence beginning in the modern period, the tendency to homogenize national culture can have, as noted above, real and serious consequences for the natural environment. Indeed, the efforts to forge a modern culture distinct from European culture may ironically come to mirror, in the postcolonial period, Europe's acquisitive habits, as Frantz Fanon cautioned.[71] This means that we must not only critique the homogenizing tendency whenever we detect it in literary works, but also identify and commend the singular features of a text that challenge this tendency. Broadly speaking, this tension is obviously not unique to Indian literature. For example, Ngũgĩ wa Thiong'o refers to the British devastation of Kenyan forestland in his novel *Petals of Blood*, about the 1950s Mau Mau rebellion, when he has an elderly character recall that the forests that once covered the land, bringing rain and shade, have been "eaten" by the railway.[72] In Gabriel García Márquez's *One Hundred Years of Solitude*, as family patriarch José Arcadio Buendia attempts to forge a path through thick Colombian rainforest, "that paradise of dampness and silence," he and his men are "overwhelmed by their most ancient memories."[73] And Tayeb Salih, in *Season of Migration to the North*, has a Sudanese emigrant tell an Englishwoman who has exoticized him the "fabricated stories about … jungles" with "non-existent animals" that she wants to hear.[74] The examination of forests in modern literature also, therefore, requires a consideration of how these depictions have mediated imagined pasts, presents, and futures. Forests and jungles may be allegorical settings for cultural and political conflict, or they may serve as metonyms for specific forms of environmental, and so cultural, degradation.

What makes India's literary treatments of forests stand out among those of other parts of the world, however, is the country's distinctive role in the development of European romanticism, a movement that is inseparable from expressions of modern nationalism. A paradoxical feature of this entangled history is that it is dependent on expressions of singularity as it is on ideas of generality. The notion of singularity is literally grounded in materialities—woods, rocks, rivers—that distinguish a region and that are believed to long antedate the present. To illustrate singularity in modern European works, for example, Harrison reaches as far back as Plato, who, in *Critias*, contrasts the considerable and ongoing deforestation in contemporary Greece with the "abundance of wood" in the not-so-distant past. The trees were cut, Harrison tells us, mainly to satisfy "the Athenian navy's need for wood."[75] Because Plato's story reflects his Athenian loyalty, his lament for trees lost to ship making points the finger at the enemies of Athens, whose attacks on the city necessitate the maintenance of an able fleet. The particularity of this fact contrasts with Plato's own writing method, which (to use today's genre categories) favors allegory in the service of political-philosophical arguments. This illustrates Harrison's point that the loss of forests haunts not just modernity, but also the classic texts that ground that modernity. A similar tension, as I have noted, can be seen in Bankim's *Anandamath*, in which Bengal's forests serve the practical need of concealing an insurgent army while also functioning as mythic and allegorical frames for the expression of modern national piety.

The words I have used here—"practical," "mythic," "modern"—are freighted with presumptions and connotations that reveal their European provenance. These are also words used by nineteenth-century writers like Bankim, who called for his compatriots to learn the British aptitude for "outward" and "practical" forms of knowledge, such as modern science and political action.[76] However, determining the degrees to which such ideas influenced nineteenth-century Indian intellectuals is, as we will see, complicated by the country's different relationships to forests on both practical and religious grounds. These relationships were shaped by the mix of European and Indian attitudes, which produced the tensions that persist to this day. An especially potent strain of European literary visions of nationalism in the nineteenth century was romanticism, whose influence on India's contemporary elites has been well-documented.[77] By the late 1700s, Europe's pillaging of American and Asian lands, combined with a growing distaste for urban sprawl, generated the romantic attitudes to nature that are so familiar in European literature.[78] Romantic poets, as we know, resisted Europe's commoditization of nature, which had been a powerful ideological motivator, and a colonialist trope, since at least the early 1600s. Katie Trumpener, Ian Duncan, and Beth Fowkes Tobin, among others, have detailed the effects of these attitudes on European authors of the period, from Aphra Behn to Walter Scott, and through the nineteenth century.[79] In his first published work of fiction in 1842, Gustave Flaubert has the narrator describe his coming-of-age as being "like an immense Indian forest where life throbs in every atom" and where "the mysterious and unformed gods were hidden in the hollows of caves amid huge piles of gold."[80] These romantic attitudes inevitably influenced, in turn, those educated in the colonial system, especially the nineteenth-century Bengali writers I discuss, though the effects were often contradictory. Romanticism's influence could not but be contradictory in light of its colonialist heritage, which was at odds with the movement's revolutionary idealism. For instance, some Indian writers who espoused this idealism nonetheless accepted, and at times even endorsed—in the name of development—British colonialism's extraction of resources at the expense of natural environments.[81] Indian writers were painfully aware of the irony of British colonialists mouthing democratic ideals while ravaging the subcontinent, especially its forests, just as they were aware of their own elite and conflicted status in this milieu.[82]

A broader context for such ironic awareness is the fact that modernity is steeped in irony, whose leitmotif is the vanishing forest. Echoing Heidegger, Harrison says suggestively that in the modern era, "We dwell not in nature but in the relation to nature" and that "We dwell not in the forest but in an exteriority with regard to its closure" for "the forest remains an index of our exclusion."[83] One consequence of this exclusion for Europeans, Harrison argues, has been the development of a deep sense of irony, an awareness of the loss of forests and the innocence they signified.

Yet this innocence was, according to Enlightenment thinkers, really a symptom of past societies' naïveté and irrationality: their very absorption in nature obstructed critical thinking. "Irony," concludes Harrison, "is the trope of detachment," for the post-Enlightenment critique of the past is also inescapably marked by our separation from that past. A potent emblem of this self-awareness is the loss of forests, which generates a sense of perpetual "longing" for the "loss" of a past "plenitude."[84] If, to use a well-known example, we apply Harrison's points to romantic poet William Blake's lines "Tyger tyger burning bright/In the forests of the night," we could say that the poet understands that the material, elemental space of woodland is inseparable from its spiritual mystery. Such a reader might answer the speaker's question about what kind of awesome "art" can create the tiger's "fearful symmetry" by saying that it is the poet's very craft that produces a discursive, and still powerfully resonant, tiger. The poet's art thus mirrors, however weakly by comparison, the cosmic artistry that has produced the awe-inspiring, sublime tiger and its sylvan habitat.

This familiar reading of Blake's poem is an apt illustration of forest imagery because it connects to India by way of cultural-historical context and does so in ways that crystallize key strands of this study. Yet the poem and its context reveal some significant absences in Harrison's analysis. We should note, first of all, the provenance of the tiger image. Blake published the original poem along with his own, colored intaglio drawing of a tiger standing beside a tree, which represents the poem's "forests of the night." Tigers had long been, as Blake's intentionally archaic spelling indicates, a familiar ingredient in European lore. But it was only after Britain's violent insertion into Indian affairs starting in 1757 that European artists began to exhibit their on-site drawings of India to London audiences, particularly in the 1770s. Before this time, which saw the emergence of public zoos, hardly anyone had seen images of India or its flora and fauna.[85] Indian trees, too, were soon in vogue, especially those conjoining religious sites. Edmund Burke based part of his 1757 thesis on the sublime on the prints he had seen in the English translation, published in the 1730s, of Bernard Picart's influential *The Ceremonies and Religious Customs of the Idolatrous Nations of the World*.[86] Burke is particularly drawn to a plate in this book that shows Hindu devotees in various postures of worship beneath a banyan tree that has spread expansively around an ancient temple. For Burke, as Srinivas Aravamudan explains, the banyan and the worshippers represent immense "*vacant spaces*" (original emphasis) that provide no familiar reference points to the European eye, no ready means of making meaning.[87] In Burke's sublime, such vast and penumbral spaces, when viewed either in situ or, less effectively, as a representation, overload the senses and induce terror at the recognition of one's comparative insignificance. The pleasure derived from such scenes, according to Burke, is, in effect, relief—the relief of returning to the world of familiar perspective.[88] Although the temple-and-banyan image Picart ostensibly documents (though he never visited India) is not beautiful—the Burkean sublime is distinguished from this—it apparently gratified its viewers nonetheless.

Both Blake's poem and his accompanying painting, part of his "Songs of Experience" cycle, aim to evoke just this kind of sublime pleasure, one that is amplified when contrasted with the poet's "Songs of Innocence." The tree in his painting, with its tendriled branches forming a border for the words, is likely meant to be a banyan. As the popularity of Picart's engraving suggests, the banyan became for Europeans "one of the most celebrated tropes of the Indian geography," as Romita Ray informs us.[89] Romantic poet Robert Southey's Orientalist narrative poem of 1810, *The Curse of Kehama*, dotes on the vast spread of a "venerable [Banian]" in a forest's "sunny glade." In the shade of this "temple"-like tree, which Southey's protagonists worship, they build a shelter of "jungle-grass" and "lithe creepers."[90] A member of the fig family, the banyan shoots branches down into the ground to create new trunks (Figure 0.1), so that a single tree can cover acres of land, effectively creating a kind of forest—a feature that beguiled the ancient Greeks no less than modern Europeans.[91] (David L. Haberman surmises that this feature may explain why the banyan is today a common "metaphor for Hinduism—simultaneously singular and vastly divergent."[92]) Describing the banyan's depiction in well-known drawings made in India by Johan Zoffany in the 1780s, Ray says the tree fascinated Europeans because of "its embodiment of the strange and unusual," key constituents of the Orientalist outlook.[93] The banyan, just as in Picart's and Blake's representations, "is the threshold at which the gaze converges and diverges, registering asymmetry as a form of cultural/visual 'in-between-ness' shaped by the multiple realities of India."[94]

Blake and other European romantics maintained an abiding interest in Indian flora and fauna, which they took to be emblematic of an inchoate, primeval originality that served as atavistic source for, and foil to, European modernity.[95] If the banyan could be classified and described, they surmised, so could Indian society, for as Ray puts it, the banyan represented "the primeval as a desirable threshold of Otherness."[96] Romanticism and modernity would not, in fact, exist without European colonialism, since the latter was the violent means by which Europe, through "war-driven capitalism" (rather than abstract capital) became modern.[97] I will have more to say about the connections

Figure 0.1 Banyan tree, St. Thomas Mount, Chennai
Source: Photo by author.

between romantic and Indian writers, but here I want to comment on Harrison's important point that the romantics turned to the natural world, rather than to the civic, in part because they believed nature's primordiality to be a source for renewal, for a genuine (often national) essence that could "liberate the past from the grand narrative schemes of classical" thinking that were stifling people's "spirit."[98] The forest, as the Brothers Grimm famously proclaimed (having in mind the Black Forest), is the wellspring of a people's physical as well as spiritual authenticity.[99] Because it was the commons of ordinary folk, the forest was a space that, unlike cropland, "cannot be owned" by individuals, as Harrison says of the contemporary romantic view.[100]

This last statement presents problems, for although Harrison pinpoints many of the effects of romanticism on European nationalism, he does not consider the role that non-European cultures played in this development and, more importantly, in offering alternative considerations of forestland. This oversight may be because, as Partha Chatterjee has observed, European nationalism, which has shaped modern considerations of forests for centuries, has been accepted as the model for all other regions, rather than one of many possible versions of collective identity (which it was).[101] The British did, in fact, declare their ownership of forests in India, basing this claim on the idea of commercial, rather than autochthonous, rights, which in turn rested on the pretense of responsible stewardship (as opposed to indigenous "wastefulness"). Among the most important, and contentious, of these claims were the rights to the forest, which in colonial modernity meant that those with power—namely, British administrators—were within their "rights" to control woodlands. In other words, colonial ideology defined legalisms like "land rights" so as to serve their commercial interests. Harrison's tendency to universalize Europe's relationships with forests[102] overlooks non-European ways of imagining and inhabiting forests, which the representative modern Indian texts I examine variously describe. Although very different from one another, these texts "fashion alternative narratives"[103] more suited to the times, peoples, and places—especially forests—that they depict.

These political and cultural contexts obviously made it immensely challenging for nineteenth- and early twentieth-century nationalist writers to craft a vision of the country that could effectively balance a variety of perspectives. Influenced partly by the European constructs they had imbibed and partly by their own urban preconceptions, writers regarded the jungle as simultaneously holy and profane, spiritual and demonic. Consider, for example, the modern association of the popular, or the folk, with nature in the evocation of national consciousness. National spirit is frequently identified with its "heartland," the countryside, including its woods, as the beating pulse of a transcendent community. The Grimm brothers, Wilhelm and Jacob, "famously declared 'Old German forests,'" including the Black Forest, to be the nation's heart, its locus of origin.[104] Seeking narratives for a country that was "divided" and besieged, and inspired by compatriot Johann Gottfried Herder's celebration of an idealized *Volk*, or common people, the Grimms turned to the forest as a space that was, as Jack Zipes puts it, "unconventional, free, alluring, but dangerous."[105] In the Grimms' eyes, the forest space was not inherently "enchanted," as in the folk tales they collected, but instead "*allows* for enchantment and disenchantment" (original emphasis).[106] As the main proponent of linking romantic ideals to ancient India, Herder viewed human civilization as growing from its "one old ... trunk," spreading forth its "boughs and twigs." He believed that the Vedic peoples represented the best of human societies, "the gentlest branch of humanity."[107] For Schlegel, too, India was "the eternal home [of the soul]," fulfilling the Enlightenment's yearning for a place of unspoiled "origins."[108]

Herder, as it happens, had also championed Kalidasa's *Shakuntala*, which was first translated into English by William Jones in 1789 and into other European languages soon after. The play, much of which is set in a forest, was celebrated by adherents of the budding romantic movement, including Friedrich Schiller, for extolling nature, and likely influenced the Grimms—probably alongside Schiller's hugely popular play *The Robbers*, which had appeared in 1781. In 1790, Schiller published, in his journal *Thalia*, part of a German translation of Jones's English rendition of *Shakuntala* by Georg Forster.[109] The irony for nineteenth-century Indian intellectuals who were educated in colonial institutions was that *Shakuntala*, like most Indian literature, was deemed by the British to be too indecent for instruction.[110] *The Robbers*, on the other hand, was judged to be consonant with colonial enculturation.[111] The greater irony, then (as I discuss more fully below), is that while early Indian nationalists were inspired by the ideas of European romantics, the latter had been energized by the works of ancient India, which they believed to be the cradle of humanity and a model of nature devotion.[112]

Although these cultural intersections might have generated mutual admiration between European romantics and Indians in the early 1800s, and a shared perception of nationhood, this did not happen. German romantics, in particular, believed they had found in ancient Sanskrit literatures a model of societal harmony that could help alleviate their own region's modern fragmentation.[113] The paradox was that whereas German romantics sought inspiration for cultural awakening and unity from ancient India, Indian intellectuals were at the same time trying to graft a form of European modernity onto their rapidly changing society in order to unify their own compatriots.

Not surprisingly, given the complexities sketched out here, Indian nationalists articulated a wide range of ideas as they tried to find a common narrative for the country's diversity of cultures and terrains. For example, in his famous 1946 tribute to a still-colonized India, *The Discovery of India*, India's first prime minister, British-educated Jawaharlal Nehru, identified his compatriots as the true manifestation of nationality, as opposed to the country's topographical features. "You," he declared to audiences, "are ... yourselves this Bharat Mata [Mother India]." Environmental historian Ajay Skaria cites this example[114] to underscore the paradox of the construct, whose appeal to the new nation-state is premised on the primitivism which, even as it looks forward to industrialized progress, was Nehru's particular interest (as opposed to Gandhi's agrarian vision). The modern Indian nation-state, in other words, carried forward colonial policies rooted in utilitarian science, but at the same time invoked an ostensibly folk-based geographical romanticism that was in many ways opposed to such utility. Nehru's impossible task was to somehow balance three different outlooks: an ancient Vedic ethos, a non-Vedic folk perspective, and a modern scientific interest. This amalgam continues to characterize India's evolving social and political idioms, and, more pertinently, its literary expressions. (I follow common usage in using the adjective Vedic to refer to the four ancient and canonical Hindu scriptures, written in Sanskrit, called the Vedas: the *Rigveda*, the *Yajurveda*, the *Samaveda*, and the *Atharvaveda*. The Vedas, like the epics, advocate moral behavior, but with far more detailed injunctions about how to do so in a social system whose hierarchical categories descend from Brahmins, the priestly caste, to cities, villages, animals, and forests.[115])

One writer, for instance, might allude to the association of Sita with a grove of Ashoka trees, as in the epic *Ramayana*, in order to highlight a present-day woman character's devotion to her husband. Another writer might make the same comparison, but in an ironic sense. A single novel, in fact, may contain both of these depictions (and more) and may even set these off against yet another one, such as a forest tended by an indigenous people who call it home and speak a different language. These differences exemplify an undercurrent of tension in nationalist novels especially, but also in many postcolonial ones, between regional and cross-regional identities. Bengali writers, who were in the vanguard of Indian nationalism in the nineteenth and early twentieth centuries, famously extolled (with what Western readers may consider to be a romantic eye) their region's natural beauty, in part to rebut colonial British disparagement. Where a colonial agent saw only diseased jungles, for instance, Rabindranath Tagore appreciated the open countryside's "unobstructed sky ... filled to the brim, like an amethyst cup."[116] Tagore and most other Bengali writers of the time represented Bengal's natural environment as representative of India as a whole, which Bankim incorporated into the influential image of Mother India in *Anandamath*. Although this prioritizing of Bengal served a wider patriotism, which Julius Lipner calls "the cultivation of a certain lifestyle that focuses on service to the motherland,"[117] it is important to consider, as this study does, how this maternal image's grounding in a localized environment—and more specifically a forest—can conflict with images arising in other regional environments. For example, a national motherland premised on Bengal's forests, both actual and imagined, collides with an idea of nationhood derived from writers in Tamil Nadu, India's southern-most state, whose forests have provided equally fertile grounds for imagining the nation.

This variance among writers should not surprise us, given that physical forests differ greatly from region to region across the vast subcontinent, from the mangroves of the Sundarbans in Bengal, on India's northeast coast, to the rainforests (*shola*) of Tamil Nadu's hill ranges (Figure 0.2). At the same time, Bengali and Tamil writers (to continue with this example), although geographically distant, share a rich inheritance of Sanskrit epics, Puranic legends, folktales, and, beginning in the early twentieth century, nationalist media. Nationalist writers in particular, such as Raja Rao, thus drew on both regional and cross-regional tropes of landscape to capture local idiosyncrasies while also appealing to a nationwide readership. This can result, at times, in a writer displacing forests geographically, as it were, as when a South Indian novelist uses an epic trope based on northern Indian forests to illuminate his southern setting and characters. This occurs in older works, too. For example, classical Tamil texts describing Shiva's adventures in the Darukavana (or Daruvana) Forest of the western Himalayas, which is made up primarily of a cedar called the deodar, transplant the forest wholesale to the Tamil region, or "Tamil country," which has no such trees, in order to lend the region a textual sanctity befitting its immanent holiness.[118] A nineteenth-century Tamil poem by Nellaiyappa Pillai is, indeed, "the most elaborate version of the Daruvana

Figure 0.2 Shola forest, Palni Hills
Source: Photo by author.

story."[119] This may seem surprising, since ancient and medieval Tamil poets have long been noted, as A. K. Ramanujan has observed, for accurate descriptions of their physical surroundings. "These poets knew their fauna and flora," he says, for "their botanical observations … are breathtakingly minute and accurate."[120] Though their descriptions of natural environments work as symbols, they are "half-motivated by botanical facts" and so "never lose sight of the "real world." Ramanujan uses American poet Marianne Moore's line to characterize these Tamil poets as "literalists of the imagination."[121]

The imaginative relocation of epic forests makes more sense, however, in the context of a specifically Tamil nationalism, which since the nineteenth century has accentuated a sacred Tamil geography distinct from northern India's Sanskrit-inflected landscapes.[122] As Sumathi Ramaswamy makes clear in her 1997 book *Passions of the Tongue: Language Devotion in Tamil India, 1891–1970*, Tamil has increasingly come to denote ethnic, linguistic, and geographical identity all at once.[123] What has not changed significantly in these constant retellings and relocations of ancient stories, however, are some central tropes, the most important of which is, as we will see, the hero's transformational passage through the forest. The latter's liminality—the sense of in-betweenness conditioned by the forest's assemblage of beings, moral choices, and sacred and profane spaces—tests the hero so that he can grow into the fullness of his expectant kingship.[124] These examples illustrate two often conflicting authorial motivations in the context of local and national identity formation—namely, to emphasize a distinctly regional space while, at the same time, connecting that space to the wider world of the subcontinent and beyond.

Region-specific texts are not alone in displaying such motivational conflict. Cross-regional fiction can do so as well, such as by placing a particular forest tree in an ancient setting, despite the fact that this tree was brought to India during the relatively recent period of British colonialism. A topical example appears in Book One of a popular novelization of the *Ramayana*, Ashok K. Banker's *Prince of Ayodhya*, which describes "a small grove of eucalyptus" in ancient northern India—an impossibility.[125] The British imported eucalyptus trees from Australia in the mid-1800s as their need for timber grew.[126] Not only did the fast-growing eucalypts provide wood for the expanding railway system's sleeper cars and fuel for stoves, they were also thought (mistakenly) to keep diseases like malaria at bay.[127] Eucalypts demand lots of water, so the British chose the Nilgiri Hills of southern India, with their abundant rainfall, for new plantations of the tree (along with acacia).[128] But the trees soon crowded out native species, and their shallow roots caused them to topple easily in monsoon storms and the soil to erode, problems that continue to this day. (Underscoring the shortsightedness of ecological imperialism is the fact that in the 1960s, a century after the British imported eucalypts for their ostensibly fast growth, researchers found that the tree did not, after all, grow any quicker than a number of native Indian species.)[129]

Eucalyptus plantations also took an immediate toll on local indigenous communities, especially Adivasis (the preferred name in India today), whose livelihoods and cultures, such as those of the Badagas in the Nilgiris, were forever changed.[130] Local indigenous folklore, religions, and customs were, and in some instances still are, entwined in forest habitat, which were shaped by these communities, who for centuries before Europeans arrived had resisted encroachments of land-hungry pastoralists.[131] But although forest-dwelling groups had managed to hold onto parts of their environment in the past, such as when Mauryan kings of the third through first centuries BCE had maintained forest reserves,[132] Europeans quickly began to loosen this control. It was largely the scale of European forestry, along with an idea of private property that was intolerant of "itinerant groups," that "unleashed changes with no precedent."[133] One outcome of these changes is that although Banker's fictional placement of the eucalyptus is factually wrong, his choice likely stems from the tree's importance in India today, where its famously salubrious oil is extracted from its leaves and then sold across the country. (In a neat bit of recycling, dried eucalyptus leaves provide fuel to boil down the oil.) The tree, having taken its place alongside native species like neem as part of modern India's social–cultural–economic web, lends Banker's scene an aura of authenticity for his modern readers. It is possible, in this sense, that to remark on Banker's isolated anachronism is to miss the point of both the novel's epic context and its modern form.

Yet if we survey the ideological landscape surrounding Banker's text, this anachronism becomes more problematic, for it points to a more overtly politico-religious tension in India today, which conditions attitudes to forests and their regional and national representations. Both sides (if I may grossly simplify, for the moment, a complex reality) of this tension are obliged to find ways of balancing regional and national outlooks that are largely conditioned by language and territory. On one side is the political Hindu Right's insistence that epic Sanskrit texts be treated as the historically factual and original basis of India as a unified Hindu-centered nation. On the other side is the belief among more regionally minded and minority communities that Sanskrit epics are purely poetic, not historical. The political-religious Right advocates Hindutva, a political concept propagated by V. D. Savarkar in the 1920s to mean an essential "Hinduness"—what he called "Hindutva"—of India as a nation. Nehru was calling for the nation's multireligious, secular "oneness," a vision he would present most fully in the aforementioned *The Discovery of India*.[134] Savarkar, influenced by Bankim's concept of the "Mother India" goddess and nationalist activist Bipin Chandra Pal's development of this (in which he emphasizes the Vedic idea of nature, *prakriti*, as an attribute of the goddess), championed the country as an everlasting geographical unity made coherent by the Vedas. He consciously uses the loose colonial label "Hindu" to demarcate this Vedic political constituency "through the language of primordial identity." He prefers the term "Hindusthan" to emphasize that "this land ... stretches ... from the Indus to the Seas," an ageless realm "more closely marked out by the fingers of nature as a geographical unit" than any other country.[135]

This is a vision of the whole of India as a primordially Vedic, ethnically Aryan country, termed *bharatavarsha*. The name, meaning "land of Bharat" and derived from ancient texts, had been used in the early nineteenth century by the great Bengali religious and educational reformer Rammohun Roy, who began a work addressed to "authorities in England" by describing the geographical reach of "India, anciently called the 'Bharat Varsha.'"[136] Other notable writers expressed visions of an age-old, geographically demarcated country, such as Michael Madhusudan Datta, or Dutt, who in an 1850 English poem extols a land, "Indus," composed of ancient kingdoms mentioned in epics like the *Mahabharata* as well as his home region of "Bengala."[137] In

1909, the nationalist philosopher Aurobindo Ghose, impassioned by Bankim's Mother India ideal, penned a loose English version in which the Mother's "lands" are "clothed beautifully with her trees in flowering bloom."[138]

Forests and Historical Romance in Nineteenth-Century India

Romanticism's influence on colonial Indian writers was arguably most notable in the movement's approach to historical fiction, with Scott the primary model. Following Scott, who was influenced by German romanticism,[139] the historical romance, so crucial to national narratives, has mostly echoed modern nationalism's homogenizing urge.[140] In Georg Lukács's influential theorization, the historical novel domesticates both geography and time to make them align with national prerogatives.[141] It does so by depending on characters who reflect typified—which is to say, generalized—features of national culture, even if the characters are represented as individuals in historical settings.[142] But these individual characters are usually men, with the privilege of mobility, in contrast to the domesticated and more-typified women characters.[143] Hamish Dalley points out that the male protagonists Lukács posits as "neutral," or "middling," in fact only seem so because they are from, or close to, metropolitan—and incipiently national—culture. The further one moves away from the metropolitan center, the more one moves "backward in time."[144] Nineteenth-century Calcutta viewed rural peoples in similar ways. (I use the anglicized colonial-era spelling of the city name for historical context, rather than today's more accurate Kolkata.) But Calcutta itself, like India, was viewed by Europeans as peripheral to their (European) centers, in this case London. Early Indian national-historical novelists were initially painfully self-conscious of this attitude, going so far as to write (as Bankim did) novels in English, thinking that this was the price of a ticket to enter the world of serious fiction. It was Bankim, according to most critics, who eventually sought to write fiction in his own language of Bengali to avoid imitating escapist romance in the vein of the very popular contemporary English novelist G. W. M. Reynolds. Nor could Bankim turn to European historical fiction like Scott's, for he saw that the characters in Scott's novels, being ordinary individuals in a modern historical framework, could only observe events unfolding around them, rather than directly shape those events. In *Waverley* (1814), for instance, the protagonist is "startled, and even alarmed," to find himself amidst the political and military activities surrounding the 1745 Jacobite uprising.[145] He is the "average English gentleman" whom Lukács believed necessary to the realist effects of Scott's historical romance, a man who is mostly reactive rather than proactive.[146] Bankim found such middling heroes entirely unsuitable to a nationalist fiction that emulates radical change. He instead turned to the Indian epic for heroes of proper heroic "stature" so that they could upend "social order," as Priya Joshi argues. Bankim similarly selects a narrator who, as in the Indian epic, "repeatedly elucidated, explained, commented upon, offered sermons, edited, and judged the events under his purview"—although by the time he wrote *Anandamath*, the omniscient narrator had dropped out, and a protagonist of change himself (Satyananda, leader of the *santan* rebels) had become a narrator.[147]

As mentioned, however, nineteenth-century Indian nationalist writers faced the additional challenge of making their own distinctly regional cultures representative of India as a whole—a task that was not, as we will see, entirely successful. In other words, these writers were compelled to balance, as best they could, the aforementioned tendencies of generality and singularity. Like their European counterparts, Indian writers often underwrote this with the allegory of loss and revival—except that they obviously experienced loss much more intensely. Speaking of the postcolonial novel generally, and without reference to India, Dalley similarly argues that, because non-European colonized countries are figured as peripheral to European history (which is naturalized as universal, global, and linearly advancing), writers from these regions aim at "interrupting" this history. One way in which they do this is by conjoining speculative, nonlinear time and historical time, thereby generating "alternative" frames of reference that circumvent European historicity. Dalley further argues that postcolonial realist fiction is for this reason best characterized as having an overriding allegorical structure, but one in which singular (as opposed to typological) characters effect change in the present.[148] We can productively adapt, or flip, Dalley's argument to say that in the colonial-era Indian novel, such as in Bankim's *Anandamath*, imagined character types directly act upon singular events of the past in order to make room for the imagined consequences of those actions—that is, to speculate on alternative futures. As Joshi remarks, "these novels provided not simply a perspective on the present, as Lukács has suggested à propos of novelists such as Scott, but a version of the past itself that was usable in the present."[149]

Realism, Reality, Habitus

Indian writers, as mentioned, had a considerably expansive "usable [past]" on hand in the country's rich repertoire of imaginative resources, the most notable and frequent of which are forest settings, referents, and metaphors. In India, the forest's imaginative and existential associations alike afforded writers more intense, more multidimensional contexts in which to articulate both regional and national affiliations. Scott's historical romances were certainly powerful treatments of national histories, with his quotidian details of past lives activating readers' "powers of visualization," with "constant shifts in focalization, distance, and tempo," as Ina Ferris argues.[150] But if Scott thereby "produced a quasi-physical impact, inducing a sense of reading as an embodied experience," this effect was, it seems to me, "new" for European readers, but not for Indian readers.[151] Long before Scott's depictions of modern actors in their physical surroundings, classic Indian works had emphasized a similar kind of "embodied experience." The *Aranyakas* (Forest Books) in the *Mahabharata* and *Ramayana* play vital roles in these epic universes. Valmiki's Sanskrit version of the *Ramayana* describes the god-king Rama entering a "a grove of pepper plants" in a "forest clearing" that also boasts "many flowers and fruits," and "resound[s] with the cries of different birds," including "geese" and "sheldrakes." "Here and there," the delighted Rama says to his younger brother

Lakshmana, "you can see piles of logs heaped up and, along the way, the sheaves of darbha grass the color of cat's-eye beryl."[152] (Darbha, mentioned in the *Rig Veda*, is a holy grass in Hinduism.[153])

Valmiki's *Ramayana* is, in fact, remarkable for its attention to forest ecology. As ecologist David Lee notes about the epic (with reference to Pollock's translation of Valmiki's version), "Few of the plants named during Rama's sojourn in the forest are cultivated species; almost all are wild forest trees."[154] The fauna of the Dandaka Forest, a tropical deciduous forest that "spans much of India," are described by Valmiki and named by Rama. They represent "virtually all the trees" of this vast region, which Lee lists.[155] Clearly, the epic's author and his society knew a lot about their natural surroundings. Among the trees Rama names are sal, teak, and sandalwood, all still important and familiar in India despite ongoing deforestation (with teak suffering the most). These are trees that grow in different regions—a fact that is unsurprising, given the epic's geographical sweep, but that is notable, again, for reflecting the northern author's ecological knowledge. Robust ancient trade and travel, including pilgrimages, as well as the accompanying movement of oral tales undoubtedly helped spread such knowledge.

Valmiki's knowledge of geography matches the sweep of events in the *Ramayana*, which begin in the north (Ayodhya and its vicinity) and move steadily southward, with the demon king Ravana residing in today's Sri Lanka. On the one hand, Valmiki's narrative reflects his location in the foothills of the Himalayas, as when he describes snow in the forest, which cannot occur in the tropical Dandaka.[156] On the other hand, Valmiki is "consistent" in placing particular trees in their ecological niche, such as when Rama encounters sandalwood as he moves southward, an accurate description. Valmiki is also fairly consistent in correctly placing animals in their native ecosystems.[157] He similarly matches water bodies with these forest descriptions, for water is vital to "the ecology of the tropical deciduous forest" to which Rama, Lakshmana, and Sita have been exiled and where much of the epic is set.[158] Valmiki is acutely aware, writes Lee, of the intimate connections between the forest ecosystem and the water on which it depends, from the "dramatic changes in the forest after the monsoon" to its role as a "conserving element in the hydrological cycle, ensuring that streams continue to flow during a dry season, that they run more clearly during the heavy rains."[159] Lee's ecological analysis makes clear that India's ancient forests are, as Valmiki and Rama appreciate, a dynamic and wondrous system.

Even in Valmiki's time, however—and, indeed, millennia earlier—humans shaped and reshaped forestlands, as Michael R. Dove has found.[160] For example, starting around 2000 BCE, the remnant population of the Harappa civilization arrived at the foothills of the Himalayas, and a combination of climate change and human activity, such as the burning of forest cover, led to a "decline of oak, alder and pine forests."[161] By circa 1000 BCE, "people of the Painted Grey Ware (PGW) culture brought large-scale cultivation to the upper Jamuna–Ganges valley" as well as "iron smelting," developments that some scholars judge to have had slight impact on forests,[162] but that, given the need for a great deal of charcoal for iron casting, must have had considerable effect. Oak forests had mostly "recovered [after]" circa 480 BCE and remained in place until about 1050 CE, when pine, alder, and other deciduous trees, as well as shrubs, had colonized much of the oak, due again to a mix of human intervention and natural occurrences.¹⁶³ Knowing this history, we can better appreciate the irony of previously cited comments by early-nineteenth-century European visitors to the region, who fawned over the vistas of "noble" forests of pine and felt that a bit of Europe had been recreated in the Himalayan foothills, unmindful that the pines were relatively new arrivistes as compared to the oak. A further irony, of course, is that even in Europe, forests had long been shaped by human hands, all the more intensively in the nineteenth century. And as scholars as various as Raymond Williams and Keith Thomas have pointed out, the very sentiment these vistas afforded was a product of urban-dwelling Europeans who romanticized the "country" (or "countryside").¹⁶⁴

This mythic particularity, as we might call it, afforded modern writers a bioregional setting whose familiarity could be relied on to elicit in readers a degree of awe and emotion that suited a particular plot's nationalist themes. Even setting aside for now the ancient concept of *rasa*, which theorizes the sensory and emotional responses of a cultivated audience, it is clear that we are in a particular wood that is present to the reader, both materially and temporally. This temporality is not, to be clear, that of history in Scott's modern sense, which is peopled by relatively ordinary actors involved in everyday acts. Rama is a royal, as well as an avatar of the god Vishnu, and this clearing is where the mythic sage Agastya resides. The forest's temporal presence has to do, instead, with its ecological immediacy for the reader (or listener), regardless of when or where that reader encounters the narrative. The forest is timeless, but not for that reason distanced, as Homer's "luscious forest" (in Emily Wilson's translation) on Calypso's island seems to readers today.¹⁶⁵ The classical Sanskrit and Prakrit inheritance was complemented by an equally ancient, and influential, classical Tamil legacy, which, along with noted vernacular works in later centuries, afforded modern writers across India a repertoire of multilingual richness and polysemy. Equally important were these writers' reflections on modern history, which supplemented, and sometimes even transformed, the aforementioned mythic temporality. A modern political leader is still frequently judged, in the popular Hindu imagination, by the standard of epic heroes Rama and Arjuna, who owe much of their moral centeredness to their forest journeys.

We can see, to reiterate a point made earlier, that classical literary works,¹⁶⁶ despite their great influence on writers' representations of nature, were not the only cultural toolkit at hand for modern novelists, nor were their tropes and themes adopted wholesale. To express local values along with aspirations for national autonomy, nineteenth-century writers like English-language poet Henry Derozio, aforementioned bilingual Bengali dramatist Michael Madhusudan Dutt, Tamil poet Subramania Bharati, and Bankim experimented with combining epic, classical, and folk traditions in a form that would appeal to their readers' growing sense of individual as well as cross-regional identities. The classical heritage was, however, available only to readers steeped in Sanskrit, a situation paralleled in other parts of India at the time. A. R. Venkatachalapathy notes the popularity, in the late 1800s and early 1900s, of colloquial Tamil chapbooks of ballads about "everyday life of the common folk," "social bandits," popular Hindu deities, and (Muslim) Sufis.¹⁶⁷ Among the most popular themes were nationalism and the challenges of modern life.¹⁶⁸ However, elites considered the topics and presentation to be "morally suspect" and thus unfit for nationalist expression¹⁶⁹—not only because the narratives frequently ventured into ostensibly illicit topics like crime and sexuality, but also because of the intrinsic mixing of subjects, religious beliefs, and linguistic styles in chapbooks.

Despite the vibrancy of inexpensive and popular publications across India at this time, their dismissal by elites, nearly all of them men from predominantly Hindu families, had tremendous repercussions for Indian historiography and fiction. Among the most significant of these consequences, in literary and political terms, was the supposed adulteration of traditional styles and topics, which incited fierce debates about the respective roles of classical and vernacular languages and cultures.[170] This supposition reflects the idealized and primarily Hindu vision of language and society held by many nationalists, who—taking their cue, ironically, from European Orientalists who had since the late 1700s extolled a lost golden age of Vedic civilization—spoke increasingly of this loss and of the need to revive it in modern form.[171] In many nationalist writers' hands, Indian history was coded as purely Hindu and, in reflecting a European historiographical "template," was seen to trace a line from original glory to decline at the hands of Muslim and British invaders, with the qualification that European science—including, unfortunately, the "science" of race theory—was a favored tool for Vedic revival.[172] Central to this perceived template of historical decline, victimhood, and revivalism was the epic forest, which, as mentioned, was reworked and repositioned to suit each particular (modern) writer's ends. This is much the same dilemma as that of following a European teleological template of nationhood, which depends on the sense of newness and of a break with a stultified past, but also depends on continuity with that past. No wonder nineteenth-century novelists' emphasis on national history made them feel obliged "to prove their [genre's] linear descent and legitimacy by establishing links with ancient texts."[173] The forest setting offered them a way to accommodate both newness and antiquity within modernity.

These various significations of forestland continue to have powerful resonance in Indian literature, whether or not a particular narrative is defined as a variety of "forest fiction," as the works of Bengali writer Mahasweta Devi are often described, or as a cosmopolitan novel, such as by Anuradha Roy. While one can speak, then, of today's "hegemonic project of nationalism," to use Partha Chatterjee's phrase,[174] one can also point to numerous imagined communities within India, such as the one C. K. Janu, a Tamil indigenous rights activist, describes in her autobiography *Mother Forest*. Such imagined communities, despite strategic affiliations with the modern state, and despite the unraveling of their habitats, maintain cultural sensibilities very different from the mainstream. The tensions at play in these significations exemplify the many forms of power that intersect each narrative, particularly those embedded in hierarchies of class, caste, gender, education, and language, which can determine whether an author uses an "elite" language like Sanskrit (or, in the modern period, English) or the local vernacular.[175] For these reasons, I treat figurative forests as intersectional spaces. This intersectionality, common in classical Sanskrit and Tamil Indian texts, for instance, also encompasses formal intersectionality, or more accurately, the inclusion of different forms within a single text. Classical authors do so in order to create not verisimilitude in classical European usage—that is, "the 'illusion of reality' happening in 'real time'"—but instead, as Phillip B. Zarrilli puts it, "opportunities for elaboration of states of mind/being/doing appropriate to the dramatic circumstances of a particular narrative."[176]

To put this another way, literary forests intersect with the "real" forests an author is presumed to have in mind, with the accent on "presumed," since premodern ideas of reality in India often seem more impressionistic to European—and, indeed, to most modern Indian—audiences. For example, a dancer of the Kerala-based (and entirely male) dance drama called Kathakali works within a tradition that is among "the farthest from earthly reality and humanism. There is no attempt at representing the mundane world in any manner." Rather, Kathakali strives to remove the viewer from "the transient worldly experience of pleasure to one of transcendental entrancement."[177] In an ideal context, a viewer of Kathakali possesses a repertoire of epic narratives, an appreciation of the art's particular gesture language (which ancient *rasa* theory encodes), and an understanding of the figurative contexts to which these gestures allude. But even nonspecialists can appreciate something of the drama's figurative language (with translations of the accompanying musical narration, if needed), such as when a performer's body language and choreographed movements bespeak the abrupt move from a court to a forest setting. The performance's aim for nonspecialist Western or modern Indian viewers, argues Zarrilli, should be to preserve key features of local settings and narratives while also providing, for example, nutshell plots and explanations of gestures so as to maintain "an active tension" between the two different traditions.[178]

Although this holistic practice of art may be familiar to modern writers and readers, the Aristotelian idea of mimesis continues to burden interpretations of texts—especially realist texts—that consider the natural world. Most readers understand that fiction's work is not to record natural "reality" as a camera seems to do, but instead to "produce an imaginative experience."[179] As Ursula K. Heise notes, there is no "outside" of nature in a strict sense since we project our desires and thoughts onto "nature."[180] Fictional forests are in effect indices of these projections, mediating a given culture's often contradictory views of woodland. Yet presumptions about fictional verisimilitude, such as the demand governing nineteenth-century realism that a good writer must be as faithful to the "real" world as possible, recur frequently enough to warrant caution, as the aforementioned practice of *darshan* illustrates. A critical-historicist lens therefore seems to me to be an especially effective approach for a study of literary forests, by which I mean paying attention to the ecological, historical, and cultural contexts in which imaginative narratives are produced so as to show, as far as possible, how their depictions of forests are inseparable from their particular ethos and their aesthetic visions. This multilayered approach compels me to draw on scholarship in a number of disciplines.

A particularly provocative recent example of an anthropological approach is Eduardo Kohn's effort to understand how Ecuador's indigenous Runa see their Amazonian forest environment. Kohn says that he had to first appreciate that all "life is, through and through, a product of sign processes."[181] One way to perceive this semiosis is to find the "regularity," or "habits," around us and in the words we use to articulate our surroundings.[182] Kohn's use of Peirce's idea of "habit" echoes sociologist Pierre Bourdieu's concept of "habitus," which describes a combination of habitation and habit in a given community. Habitus suggests the sense of inhabiting a modern, changing world, and of inheriting, at the same time, particular social practices in much the way that one inherits money. Language in particular invests a person with "schemes of thought and expression" that seem perfectly natural, producing, in concert with economic networks, "symbolic interests" that generate "symbolic capital."[183] Indian nationalism in the nineteenth and early twentieth centuries understandably struggled to find ways of accommodating regional differences within the rubric of nationhood. Even within each region, differences of language and religion, caste and class, and social conventions regarding women and education (to name just a few) present, as they still do, complex challenges in the national context. The forest, essentially a shorthand term in this study to mean both a generalized trope and a collective noun for a wide variety of wooded landscapes, is an index of these differences and the social complexities they incur. But precisely because there are a great many types of forest, their representations—legal, cultural, religious, and, as this study shows, literary— powerfully influence a modern nation's many efforts to define itself.

Vernacular Forests, Colonial Boundaries, and Tensions of Play

Although they had a repertoire of ancient and medieval forest tropes to which they could turn, the reality for Indian writers in the nineteenth century was that forests throughout the subcontinent were being systematically razed or transformed by the British colonial administration's extractive technologies. Under British rule, villagers and "tribal" communities—that is, noncaste indigenous peoples—whose livelihoods were tied to forests, and who had for centuries lived far beyond the purview of urban administrative centers while also trading with those centers, found their lands the object of colonial envy. The great economic, social, and ecological transformations of the Indian countryside have a complex history. What stands out in this story is that by the mid-nineteenth century, British rule had accelerated these transformations to such a degree that the trees that generated a substantial portion of India's economy were fast disappearing.[184] Forests became less and less porous, and their boundaries more fixed to facilitate state administration, which the Indian Forest Act of 1865 made clear. Pallavi V. Das, for example, describes how the British expansion of the railways between 1869 and 1884 led "not only to the depletion of the Himalayan forests," but also to "the denudation of the plains forests in the Punjab." Forests thus bore the brunt of nineteenth-century colonialism's "unprecedented" acquisitive aspirations.[185] As one British administrator declared with regard to a prized northern region, "all the forests are the property of Government, and no general permission to cut timber therein will be granted to anyone."[186] At the same time, however, the introduction of modern technologies, ideas, and forms of expression, especially the spread of vernacular publishing and literacy, helped Indians initiate novel-writing and national alliances. The spread of deforestation—in order to create more arable, and thus taxable, land— and the consolidation of an Indian class of urban elites, whose nationalist sentiments grew in the telling, generated an awareness of nature besieged. It is not surprising that Nobel Laureate Rabindranath Tagore (on whom more below) poeticized the chief virtue of his family's famous school, Shantiniketan, far from Calcutta, as being the opportunity to congregate "in the shadows of her trees" and idyllic "groves," "in the freedom of her open sky."[187]

Urban intellectuals, farmers, and Adivasis alike understood the political realities of colonial rule, which, like the nation-state, relies on fixed boundaries and is avowedly intolerant of porosity. By contrast, the Indian forest's inclusiveness, as represented in a number of traditions, entertains a variety of nomadic and pastoral lifestyles. In Hindu traditions, Lord Krishna, who became hugely significant for Indian nationalists, was himself a cowherd, and his forest home of Vrindavan, though bereft of the original forest, is still a pilgrimage center. Krishna, avatar of Vishnu and one of India's most popular deities, famously inhabits the sacred forest of Vrindavan, literally "forest of Vrinda" (or Brinda, meaning *tulsi*, or holy basil).[188] Vrindavan is unique among Hindu sacred pilgrimage centers, or *tirthas*, because it *is* a forest. "It simply doesn't belong in their company," John Stratton Hawley observes, for "forests have no concourse with cities, and Vrindavan, the forest *tirtha*, does not speak the same language as the others." It is no Banaras or Prayag, but merely a forest—precisely the reason Krishna makes it "his home."[189] Krishna bucks tradition by forsaking the usual trappings of kingship and order, choosing instead "a place where every advantage of hierarchy is sacrificed to the joys of intimacy," where "insults" are preferred to ornate "praise" because they are genuine and spontaneous rather than mannered, and where one comes to "forget the world's concerns."[190] Jayadeva's twelfth-century CE lyric Sanskrit narrative poem *Gita Govinda* richly describes these natural surroundings. Drawing on the rhythms of folk music,[191] Jayadeva invites us into the Vrindavan Forest: "See the clove-tree with its creepers," he writes, characterizing the forest as, among other terms, *vana-bhuvah* ("forested earth") and *vraj* (originally "cow shelter," and by extension the birthplace of Krishna). While the poet's Sanskrit pedigree is reflected in his use of received arboreal tropes like "creepers," his distinctive vision and voice vivify the "shadows" on the forest floor made by "blackish tamala [bay leaf] trees" and Radha's yearning for "Krishna's forest haunts" as he first frolics with the *gopis* before returning to her.[192]

Forests, as well as other natural ecosystems, have therefore always been "the central focus of Krishna worship," with the famous *Ban* (or *Van*) *Yatra* (forest pilgrimage) continuing to be a favored journey for Krishna worshippers, even more so than temple visits.[193] (The current impulse to fix sacred forest sites is therefore ironic in light of Krishna's boundary crossing.) The suffix of the Sanskrit word *Vrindavan, vana* (or *bana*), means forest, as it does in a number of famous names, including Ravana and the aforementioned Daruvana, the forest of Shiva's wandering. *Vana* has traditionally been represented not as entirely wild, but rather a forest suitable for restorative human retreat, as indicated by *vanavasa*, the word for exile. In the *Bhagavata Purana*, Krishna declares, "The birth of trees is truly the most blessed in the world, for they contribute to the well-being of all creatures," and offers a sample list of arboreal attributes: "leaves, flowers, fruits, shade, roots, bark, wood, fragrance, sap, ashes, and charcoal."[194] Krishna himself has traditionally been seen to embody a sacred landscape, with "fifty-five forests, groves, and villages" comprising his "limbs."

Yet the forest is also, as Krishna's teasing of the *gopis* illustrates, a realm for mischievous humor and playfulness, or *lila*, where spontaneity and desire trump custom and discipline. It is a kind of sacred commons, where hierarchies are inverted. The forest is a sanctuary from worldliness (figured in ashrams and sleep, for example) and blurs normative boundaries. Yet forest ashrams are also, at the same time, embodiments of divine order that keep shape-shifting evil at bay—evil exhibited most often by *rakshasas*, the demon deities. In their forest exile, Lord Rama, his peerless wife Sita, and fiercely loyal brother Lakshmana are embodiments of hierarchy itself. However deeply they traverse the forest, their divinely ordained status is recognized. Their exile itself is understood to be a fixed period of time that will end with their return to the city of Ayodhya, which Rama will govern as the rightful king. These otherwise oppositional themes of order and disorder, urbanity and wildness, the sacred and the profane thus coexist within forests. In fact, these dualities sometimes seem to break down altogether in the deep woods, presenting us with a liminal space where events and dialogue are open to interpretation.[195] It is this tension, as we will see, that animates many of the novels examined in this book.

Another commonly used Sanskrit word for forest is *aranya*, which tends to be more suggestive of remote wildness in which demons dwell. In Sanskrit texts, the *aranya* is opposed to the *gramya*, or village; each conditions the other, although settled society—city and village—is always the central concern. But characterizations like these should be treated as broad, even tentative definitions since the *aranya*, too, is frequently a place for ascetic renunciation and enlightenment. In ancient literary works, *aranya*, *vana*, and *jangala* (whence the English word jungle) settings evoke a range of particular emotions, depending on characters and contexts. These features confirm Romila Thapar's observation that human treatments of Indian forestland have been "neither static nor uniform."[196] A notable example is that in sixteenth-century Braj, Krishna's homeland and the location of the Vrindavan Forest, *jangala* referred to the region's "political and administrative milieu." By the following century, however, as deforestation accelerated in the realm, making pilgrimages to the many forest sites harder and harder, artists and writers began to depict these as idealized garden-like settings in the manner of the *kunja*, "verdant bower," that earlier works, including Jayadeva's famous *Gita Govinda*, had visualized.[197]

The Indian forest has, in short, been an ambivalent locus of disguise, doubleness, indiscipline, and violence as well as purity, moral contemplation, and rejuvenation. These features echo the idea of nationality as an ambivalent incorporation of its supposed mystic origin, on the one hand, and its modern, historical being on the other. The purposeful constitution of a new nation must therefore be read in light of "the large cultural systems that preceded it."[198] The traditional life story of Krishna presented an especially acute dilemma for nationalist writers. For many Hindu leaders, Krishna embodied the forthright qualities that could model active resistance to colonialism, while the rich legacy of Krishna devotion could appeal to a broad cross-section of society, from villagers to urbanites. Krishna's naturalistic, spontaneous, and loving behavior had for centuries been a beloved font of mystical devotion and art. But Krishna's famously playful dalliances with Radha (Figure 0.3) and with the young cowherding women, the *gopis*, in the twin Nidhuban and

Figure 0.3 Radha and Krishna painting
Source: Public domain.

Nikunjaban forests were too erotically charged for many of these Victorian-minded intellectuals, including Bankim.

Part of this ambivalence has to do with historical and regional shifts in people's attitudes to woodland and the consequent changes in terminology. For example, we can reach back to Kautilya's coldly pragmatic treatise on statecraft, the *Arthashastra* (from roughly the second century BCE), which is interested, for strategic and tax purposes, in forests that are relatively close to agricultural communities. These include *aranya*—in this case, wild forest, sometimes imprecisely characterized as wilderness—as well as *vana*, less-intimidating groves that invite either exile or meditative retreat.[199] (The Buddha preached one of his first sermons in the Simsapa Grove, near today's

Allahabad.[200]) Modern politics adds more layers to this complex picture. The English term forest and its cousin, jungle, began to acquire new meanings in India with the advent of colonialism, whose systemization of forestry and perception of certain jungles as "waste" generated deleterious tropes that supplement, and sometimes supplant, the terms' older meanings. These supposed waste lands became foils for the legalized idea of the "propertied" self.[201] This underscores how the semantic and ideological slippage between forest and jungle in modern literary works renders the terms ambiguous, allowing them to underwrite modernity's "fable" of "liberation from wildness," but also sometimes allowing them to undercut that very fable.[202] The terms are, in short, politicized.

This political context is arguably the reason that Adivasis and forest-dwelling Dalits (literally "broken," used as a self-affirming label by those excluded from India's caste system) have chanted slogans like "*Van vibhag jangal chhode!*" ("Leave the jungle, Forest Department!"), where forest is explicitly associated with a government institution, and jungle is the protestors' home.[203] The activists were calling on the government to honor the official transfer to their people of voluntary gifts of privately owned land made to them during Vinoba Bhave's 1950s Bhoodhan ("land gift") movement.[204] At other times, however, *van* (forest) and other Sanskritic words for woodland are acceptable to these groups, demonstrating their savvy strategic use of terms to suit political circumstance. (The groups' very politicization depends, of course, on new alliances and new forms of collective self-identification, in contrast to what Sudipta Kaviraj has called their "fuzzier" precolonial ideas of group identity.[205]) As Anand Vaidya remarks, the two broadly labeled groups, Adivasi and Dalit, are not easily distinguished from one another in rural areas, with many calling themselves Dalit Adivasis[206]—as against mainstream society's (and the law's) insistence on identifying Adivasis as tribals and Dalits as non-tribal "scheduled caste" peoples, though they represent a range of faith traditions besides Hinduism. Their frequent self-identification (as in the above example) as Dalit Adivasi exposes the brittle artifice of modern designations and the piquant irony that these labels were, and are, necessary for the groups' political efforts.[207] These examples illustrate how the political uses of "forest" and "jungle" mostly depend on the normative valuations of the terms, even when the words are used by subaltern groups who relate to forests in far more multidimensional ways than moderns do. The irony, in short, is that although the two English terms, which dominate the language of bureaucracy and law, often gloss over the nuances of forest dwellers' interactions with forests, their distinctions can be politically vital. In this light, the continued "forest/jungle" slippage by both mainstream urban society and scholars can be hazardous.

Vrindavan's importance in India is reflective of Hindu concepts of sacred space that today contend, as never before due to conservative strands of Hindu revivalism, with the concepts of cartographic space that govern the nation-state. Generally speaking, sacred space, partly as a consequence of nation-making, has ironically come to mirror the nation-state's exclusiveness. In India, this mixing of modern and traditional geographical representations is a product, as Sumathi Ramaswamy has argued, of the combination of three vital components: "geo-piety," a worshipful reverence for the country in terms of geography; the "geo-body," the notion that national territory, because scientifically mapped, is visually identifiable; and, embodying both geo-piety and geo-body, the mother goddess as both "form and presence."[208] India as geo-body was conceivable because of the colonial state's cartographic measuring of the subcontinent, which for the first time "enable[d] the whole country to be seen at one glance in its entirety and synoptically," giving ordinary citizens the sense of landed inhabitance.[209] This landscape includes, as has been said of South India, "the two most [celebrated places]" in literature, farmland and forest[210]—to which we should add, if extending this claim to literatures of other regions, rivers and mountains. Of these, forests are the most symbolically laden[211] and the most ecologically manipulated. Although they have been measured and labeled for millennia, it was the scientific surveying initiated by the East India Company that allowed most of India's forests, along with other topographies, to be mapped so as to standardize and control them. Thus "homogenized" and ostensibly demystified, forests became more amenable to state interests.[212]

This means that as a measured entity, each forest was (and is) now circumscribed on two counts, religious and colonial or national, qualifications that are frequently conjoined. Forest-dwelling communities in the measured forest are now doubly suspect, their heterodox religious practices and nomadism at odds with the powers that be, whether British or Indian. When postcolonial writers critique the nation-state, therefore, as many of them do, they are often compelled to also critique, even if implicitly, the modern consolidation of sacred Hindu space, including Hindu conservatism's current tendency to exclude from its idea of nationhood other, particularly Muslim, sacred spaces. The forest in these cases is presented as a contested site, with different constituencies and worldviews pitted against one another. An important point in this regard is that Adivasi rights and anti-caste activists, beginning with nineteenth-century Dalit social reformers Jyotirao Phule and his wife Savatribai Phule, have reenvisioned denigrating tropes for forest-dwelling peoples found in Sanskrit epics to argue that these peoples are, in fact, the true inheritors of India's forestlands. Phule famously wrote that the Sanskrit word for demon, *rakshasa*, in fact identifies the "original inhabitants" of forests, the true "protectors of the land" whom Aryan settlers chose to demonize.[213]

Tagore's Loss, Atavistic Forests, and Mother India

Perhaps the most famous rendering of India in terms of geography besides Bankim's is the 1911 Bengali poem by Rabindranath Tagore that became, soon after India's independence in 1947, the national anthem "Jana Gana Mana."[214] Tagore is an especially apt figure to look to as an exemplar of what we might call a mainstream Indian regard for forests because he not only inhabits a prominent role in India's national consciousness (as a nonsectarian universalist), but is also regarded as a shaper of modern Bengali literature. His 1922 essay "The Religion of the Forest" encapsulates his belief that the Vedic form of contemplative forest retreat is the best model for the new nation, for it harmonizes moral consciousness and the purity of the natural world. The essay is still frequently cited in publications across the globe as a call for an urgently needed environmental and egalitarian vision in the Anthropocene.[215] In

"Jana Gana Mana," Tagore avoids the Mother India image (which he refuses to deify[216]) by invoking, in the first line, "the minds of all [of India's] people." The pulsing litany of regional names—"Panjaba-Sindhu-Gujarata-Maratha Dravida-Utkala-Banga"—lends itself to song, as do the alliterative rhymes identifying mountains ("Vindhya-Himachala"), rivers ("Yamuna-Ganga"), and sea ("jaladhi-taranga"), all of which form Bharat. Of these topographies, the forest, though only implicitly invoked in the anthem by association with mountain ranges, is repeatedly celebrated in other Tagore poems, and in his essays, as the "heart" of India. For example, early in his 1922 essay "The Poet's Religion," Tagore notes that Wordsworth "complained" in a famous sonnet that

> The world is too much with us; late and soon,
> Getting and spending, we lay waste our powers.
> Little we see in Nature that is ours.

In a signature move that undercuts Wordsworth's implication that the modern world is irredeemably changed, Tagore, writing in an essay for a global audience, says that while this may be true of Europe, India retains a closeness to nature that is a beacon for the world. "But it is not," Tagore affirms, "because the world has grown too familiar to us; on the contrary, it is because we do not see it in its aspect of unity, because we are driven to distraction by our pursuit of the fragmentary." This is because, he says (both in this and other essays), India has not forgotten that it was "the peace of the forest" that led its great philosophers to their "best ideas." Living within, and in communion with, "the living forest," rather than "being caged in" cities of "brick, wood and iron," India's sages recognized that their wooded abode, with all its resources and life, was the true "source of knowledge." "Indian civilization," Tagore declares to both his Indian and Western readers, has been "distinctive in locating its source of regeneration, material and intellectual, in the forest."[217] Like his elite Hindu peers, he opines that the "ideal of perfection" attained by ancient Vedic sages in forest retreats—whom he calls "forest-dwellers"—"runs through the heart of our classical literature and still dominates our mind." It is they, "in the seclusion of the primaeval forest," who apprehended "Brahma-vidya—the knowledge of Supreme Truth," the ostensibly untouched forest having provided the only setting in which "the human mind could intensely concentrate itself in the depth of things and the reality of spiritual existence."[218] So taken is Tagore with this arboreal motif that it permeates his evaluation of India's ancient past. He writes, "We have seen how, after the decline of Buddhism, a path had to be cleared through the jungle of rank undergrowth which had been allowed to run wild during the prolonged inaction of the Brahmanic hierarchy."[219]

The vitality of the forest in Indian culture explains, says Tagore, why the great epics "cluster under the forest shade bearing ... the message of [these] forest-dwellers" and a sense of the "purity of the forest hermitage." He contrasts this ancient heritage with Europe's, declaring that although "the history of the Northmen of Europe is resonant with the music of the sea," these peoples saw only "danger" in the sea: they did not commune with it in the way that "Northern" Indians did with forests, which offered "no barrier" between ancient Indians' everyday "lives and the grand life that permeates the universe."[220] In short, Europe merely conquered nature, whereas India learned to live with and through it. To illustrate the lasting influence of this ancient sensibility to nature, Tagore describes the importance of trees in his own upbringing:

> I remember, when I was a child, that a row of cocoanut trees by our garden wall, with their branches beckoning the rising sun on the horizon, gave me a companionship as living as I was myself. I know it was my imagination which transmuted the world around me into my own world—the imagination which seeks unity … this companionship was true.

He fondly recalls that not far from the coconut trees "stood an immense banyan tree," whose evening "shadows" captivated

> my whole attention. Some of its aerial roots … had formed a dark complication of coils at its base. It was as if by some sorcery this obscure corner of the world had escaped the regime of natural laws, as if some improbable dreamworld, unobserved by the Creator, had lingered on into the light of modern times … It was of this banyan tree I later wrote:
>
> > Day and night you stand like an ascetic with matted hair.
> > Do you ever think of the boy whose fancy played with your shadows?
>
> That majestic banyan tree is no more, alas, and neither is the tank that served as her mirror … And the boy, grown older, has put down his roots far and wide and now contemplates the patter of shadow and sunlight, sorrow and cheer, cast by the tangled skein.[221]

Tagore's sense of personal loss hints also at the larger process of speedy urbanization that Calcutta witnessed during his lifetime. This comes up again when he comments upon what formerly used to be the house's garden and likens this childhood's garden with paradise, whereas now he sees "the absolute defeat of village life in Kolkata."[222] Although Tagore, like many of his Hindu intellectual peers, maternalizes these natural attributes in the figure of Mother India, whose purity has been preserved by the lessons of ancient forest ascetics, he condemns the appropriation of this legacy by nationalists with a martial bent.[223] We can see this in a song addressed to "my motherland," in which Tagore celebrates these ascetics for the "forest chants" and "first epics of wisdom and faith" they composed in their "forest retreat." Addressing his arboreal land, he writes: "Hail, mother of abiding beauty,/sustainer of millions at home and abroad." But in another song, he criticizes the self-described "pious [soldiers]" who cry "Kill! Kill!" in the name of nationalism.[224] Yet despite his celebration of Vedic *ashramas*, he is keen to distance himself from outward forms of piety, to avoid "becom[ing] entangled in the usual convictions and rituals," which he thought too frequently resulted in factionalism. It is his personal attachment to the countryside, he claims, that enabled him to be "the first to introduce the land of Bengal to Bengalis as a subject fit for literature—neither Michael nor Nabin Sen nor Bankim did that." (He credits Bankim, however, for "usher[ing] in an age in which Bengalis felt pleased and proud to speak and write in their own tongue.")[225]

In some ways, Tagore's sentiments about the role of forests in Indian society are unimpeachable. Believing forests (and nature, more generally) to be a still-vital force for Indians, his tone is buoyant and aspirational, as opposed to the mournful tone in Wordsworth. He is also refreshingly less sententious than the German nationalist Riehl, and exhibits none of the latter's racially charged jingoism. Troublingly, however, Tagore mentions in passing that the philosophers he extols owe their environmental abode and enlightenment to the displacement of the forest's original inhabitants—who, ironically, are the true forest dwellers: "just as the European colonists in America, while cutting down its forests, had to contest every step with the aborigines, who depended on the chase for their living, so also in India the pioneers of agriculture encountered the opposition of the non-Aryans living in its wildernesses, whose fierce onslaughts made their task far from easy." As in British colonial hands, non-Aryan aboriginals are styled as rude inhabitants of "wildernesses" who fortunately gave way to Vedic "forest-dwellers"—never mind that forest wilderness in Sanskrit texts differs from the American trope.[226] "India," he wrote, "is the one country in the world where the Aryan colonisers had to make constant social adjustments with peoples who vastly outnumbered them; who were physically and mentally alien to their own race; who were for the most part distinctly inferior to the invaders."[227] Whereas Tagore criticized certain compatriots for wanting to champion modern, European-style industry, which he believed was disrespectful to nature, he accepts with Nehru and most other elites the civilized–primitive polarity, inherited from Europe and still alive in India today, in which indigenous communities equate to crude and uncivilized, counterbalancing the supposed sophistication of settled society.

These examples illustrate the greater challenge that Indian writers in the colonial period, especially, faced as they reflected upon the potency of the forest image in popular as well as orthodox cultural traditions. They had to reckon with the legacy of India's own long and complicated treatments of forestlands as well as with recent, and more consequential, European practices. Although British colonizers introduced the European notion of the noble savage, India's own Brahminical heritage evoked a similar civilization/wildness split. On the one hand, the British emphasized, almost to the point of fetish, the idea of "taming" India's wildness, in part by cataloguing and enumerating tribes and castes and by assigning them labels that the Indian government continues to use: scheduled tribes, backward castes, other backward castes, and so on. On the other hand, even as British administrators tried to "extinguish wildness," as Skaria puts it, they retained, and even encouraged, its "celebration"—an example of European modernity's ambivalent regard for the natural environment.[228] India's modern rhetorical landscape is still laden with tropes generated by this mélange of outlooks, which, given India's complex social strata and its diversity of languages and religious practices, complicate considerations of the jungle–city nexus. As we will see, Indian novelists like Amitav Ghosh are acutely aware of the contradictions on which a new-old country like India has based its national aspirations. As the out-of-place eucalypt in Banker's novelization of the *Ramayana* illustrates, the visualizing of India as simultaneously modern and timeless—as a nation at once ready-made and in the making—incurs pressures that are hard, if not impossible, to reconcile. Banker's arboreal anachronism is a symptom of this challenge, one that has been expressed in a variety of interwoven modes, as I aim to show.

Forest India: Hindu, Muslim, Modern

The influential invocations of arboreal India by Bankim, Tagore, and others underscore that however varied nationalist treatments of the forest are, it has proved to be an irresistible image through which to explore the intersections of regional and national identities. It bears repeating that the potency of this image is not surprising. Whether secular or religious, all of these representations take their cue from India's "sacred geography," as Diana L. Eck calls it, an awareness of which goes back millennia in accordance with the subcontinent's intricate network of pilgrimage routes, which stitched together cities, towns, villages, and remote shrines.[229] In the Sanskrit epics as in the *puranas*, to visit a pilgrimage center is to undertake a "spiritual [crossing]," or *tirtha*, with the compound term *tirthayatra* designating this journey (*yatra* meaning journey).[230] Sites of pilgrim devotion were, and are, associated with topographical features, principally rivers, hills, and forests. The subcontinent was essentially mapped in this way to create "deep traditions of geographical awareness," a landscape "overlaid with layer upon layer of story."[231] It was possible to undertake, as some kings and nobles did, a *pradakshina*, or circumambulation of a specific site, such as a city or mountain, or even to make a *tirthayatra* around the subcontinent, as the five Pandava brothers do in the *Mahabharata*.[232]

But in the millennia before the term "Hindu" existed, this geographical conception was far more heterogeneous than it is today. Besides numerous religious sects, each with their own shrines and philosophies, not to mention differences between the views of settled societies and indigenous peoples, the advent of Islam in the subcontinent led to an additional overlay of sacredness. Although Turkish and Afghan rulers who swept into northern India in the eleventh century attacked certain Hindu temples, these were geographically and strategically "selective" targets intended "to delegitimize … defeated ruling houses."[233] In the succeeding centuries of rule by various Muslim dynasties, while some segments of the lower-caste population converted to Islam, Sufi poet-saints proliferated. Their tombs became shrines, or *dargahs*, which intersected with the existing network of sacred centers dotting the subcontinent.[234] Among the great Sufi poet-saints of India was Amir Khusrau, who in the late 1200s and early 1300s produced Persian poetry and prose that is still read and sung. A follower of Mu'in al-Din (or Moinuddin) Chishti, whose *dargah* in Ajmer (Figure 0.4) has ceaselessly drawn pilgrims of all faiths since his death in 1236, Khusrau famously called India a "paradise on earth" (*firdaus*). He extolled India's flowers, trees, and spices as well as betel leaf (*paan*), "a marvelous accompaniment of food." "There is nothing in the world like a good Betel-leaf," he writes.[235] Khusrau's implicit association of betel leaf (and its areca nut and pepper leaf ingredients) with India's arboreal richness is a metonym favored by many writers, both before and after Khusrau. To make *paan*, betel leaves—which are, like pepper, part of the *Piperaceae* family—are wrapped around the areca nut, a fruit of the areca palm, mixed with a few other ingredients, and then chewed

Figure 0.4 Ajmer Dargah tree
Source: Photo by author.

as a mild stimulant and digestive. And as the Scottish physician and botanist Francis Buchanan-Hamilton observed in the record of his travels in Malabar in 1801, betel leaf is always cultivated next to pepper.[236]

Like other Persian-language Islamic poets, Khusrau favors gardens, which were seen to mirror the heavens (medieval Delhi being likened, for this reason, to "the garden of paradise"[237]), and his poems are sprinkled with tree imagery: a princess is a "young cypress" and a "rose" in a "garden," and a couple's hug is rendered as, "He took her in his embrace so tightly that/The white poplar sapling turned into a redwood."[238] His storehouse of images not surprisingly included conventional set pieces from Persian and Arab landscapes, as his use of "cypress" and "garden" indicates. But Khusrau's relish for Indian flora is clear from its greater detail, as in the following, which describes a man's search for a princess: "On that spot was a large *pipal* tree, forming a canopy [of such extent], that if a thousand horsemen sheltered themselves under its wide-spread branches, they would be protected from the sun and rain."[239] This intermixing of natural imagery from different locales, like Khusrau's multilingualism, reflects Sufism's nonsectarian outlook, as when he says, "The Brahmans of India have greater wealth of philosophical thought than what Rumi had revealed to the World."[240]

Sufism later intersected, as well, with the similarly nonsectarian *bhakti* movement that spread across India between the fifteenth and seventeenth centuries, which emphasized emotional devotion centered on love for god. Both movements emphasized song and dance as expressions of this devotion, which were performed without discrimination in small towns, pilgrim centers, and cities.[241] This does not mean, however, that religious-poetic imagery and everyday lives reflect one another. Muzaffar Alam tells us that a seventeenth-century work in Persian by the Mughal Sufi writer 'Abd al-Rahman Chishti, *Mir'āt al-makhlūqāt*, draws on Islamic and Sanskrit sources to describe "the origin of the world" in the context of India.[242] The text exhibits "[familiar] toponyms," such as the city of Kannauj, which are depicted as distinct from "the world of forests and mountains."[243] Settled society is favored by God, whereas rebellious *jinns* (spirits) are banished to forests. But this is a rhetorical distinction in support of the author's argument and clearly not to be taken literally, as his pragmatic patron, Emperor Akbar, well knew. Mughal Delhi boasted both groves and flowering plants, and Mughal kings were as fond of hunting in forests as were Hindu rajahs. Illustrative of this city–forest convergence is a biography of Akbar's Rajput general Man Singh by 'Abd al-Rahman's contemporary, Amrit Rai. Written mainly in Sanskrit, in the genre called *nagaravarnana*, "description of the city," this text, the *Māncarit*, is also noteworthy for its occasional interjections of Persian and other non Sanskrit diction as a means of extolling both Man Singh's Rajput culture while also signaling his "service in a Persianate imperial order."[244] In the poem, clustered names of trees in and around Man Singh's home city of Amber, near present-day Jaipur, bear this out, as Allison Busch presents them:

Many varieties of gardens could be seen,
>dense with flowers, fruits, and fine trees.
There were champa and jasmine flowers of magnificent form,
>groves of pines,

Clusters of ketaki blooms, water lilies, screwpines, grand trumpet flowers,
Lovely coral trees, basil, and jewel-bright jasmine.

Dense orchards of myrobalan, mangoes, pomegranates,
    tamarind, neem, lemons, and oranges.
Delectable citrus fruits, excellent betel nut, apples, and plums flourished.
Jamuns, limes, figs, and copious orange apricots,
Jackfruits, corindas, coconuts, large bels, and barhal trees.[245]

After naming even more trees, including the *pipal*, Rai exclaims, "countless in number are the varieties!/I joyfully describe all the types of gardens and groves/on the outskirts of the city," evidently using the Sanskrit for forest, *vane*, for "groves."[246] Although appearing in a biographical work, these alliterative lines and the piling up of arboreal images are textual correlatives of improvisational Mughal court recitations. Even stories that were written down were recited to audiences, not all of whom could read (likely true of Akbar, as well).[247] Mughal-era literary culture was thus "both orally transmitted and literate at the same time," encompassing a variety of performers—an "oral-literate" environment.[248] Because this culture encouraged vernacular compositions, rather than only those in Persian or Sanskrit, literatures in regional languages like Brajbhasha and Bengali began to proliferate in the late sixteenth century.[249] Texts in several genres appeared, including the "immensely popular" Bengali *mangalkavya* (or *mangalkabya*), fabular tales that describe how a "previously unknown" god or (more commonly) goddess "establishes his or her cult" of devotion in a particular place.[250] This and other popular genres greatly influenced nineteenth-century writers, including Bankim.[251] What is especially noteworthy for my discussion, besides the *mangalkavya* genre's improvisatory provenance, is that each composition was not expected to be "wholly original"; it instead reworked one or more previous works, not only in the genre as a whole, but in the tradition devoted to the particular deity being described. For example, the hugely influential *Chandimangal* by Kavikankan Mukundaram Chakravarti was not the first tale in this genre about the goddess Chandi when it appeared in the late 1500s: there were many Chandimangal *mangalkavyas* both before and after it.

These examples underscore the significant point that a work like Banker's, which retells the *Ramayana*, is part of a long and vibrant tradition of reworking core stories—in this case, a Sanskrit epic—to provide fresh perspectives and interpretations. To put this another way, Banker's retelling reflects a very long tradition of robust debate, skepticism, and change within India's many Hindu faith communities, as Amartya Sen has observed.[252] Why, then, have some political conservatives advocated literalist interpretations of Sanskrit works, an approach that began in the nineteenth century but that some mainstream political parties actively encourage today? One answer is that this outlook is, ironically, an outgrowth of the modern European obsession with textual authenticity, which began with William Jones's pioneering philological endeavors in the late 1700s. In extolling the juridical authority and historical veracity of ancient Sanskrit texts, Jones and others evoked a romanticized Vedic past in which adherents of the Vedas were believed to practice a harmonious relationship with nature. One modern scholar who advocates this view recently declared that the Hindu golden age ended with the "700 years of foreign"—primarily Mughal and British—"cultural domination."²⁵³ This supposed golden age is also frequently said to have developed a knowledge system that anticipated modern scientific empiricism.²⁵⁴ This anachronistic outlook is decidedly modern in its juxtaposing of different historical times and ideas to suit its purpose.²⁵⁵ These examples underscore the influence of European modernity on Indian nationalist writers, not the least of which was the very notion of a geographically unified nation-state and the associated idea of the city–country divide. Raymond Williams has thoroughly examined these changes with regard to England, and his conclusion applies here: the "powerful myth" of modern industrial (and, we can add, postindustrial) society is to retrospectively imagine "an 'organic' or 'natural' society," uncontaminated by the very modernity that creates this myth.²⁵⁶ In India, as mentioned, Hindutva nationalists have retrospectively constructed an imagined countrywide Hindu polity that encompasses the nation from the forests of the Terai, in the Himalayan foothills, and the Sundarbans in the east to the Nilgiris in the south.

A Note on the Concept of Modernity and the Paradox of Representing Past and Present

My understanding of modernity follows scholarly consensus in seeing it as a habit of being in a highly technologized world. More specifically, it is the inhabitance of a world of global capital, with a complementary social dimension that is governed by the contract of private property, individual possession, scientific knowledge, and all the institutions that support these, from schools to militaries. Possession here means not just the parcel of land a single person owns but humanity's command of the earth.²⁵⁷ The act of possessing either land or knowledge informs the conventional twentieth-century notion of development, a discourse meaning both infrastructural and cultural "improvement" that not only "helped colonial consolidation" but was "a rallying cry for independence movements."²⁵⁸ Modernity also means, then, an approach to writing the nation, with an acute consciousness of this as a historically grounded process requiring a break with the past, but also, paradoxically, selective remembering. In fact, given the innumerable incarnations of such an outlook, scholars have been advocating "multiple," "alternative," "hybrid," and "regional" modernities.²⁵⁹ These terms contrast with the very logic of modern "development," which assumes a temporal and teleological movement from so-called premodern to modern stages of demystified self-awareness.²⁶⁰

A paradox soon becomes evident in this conceptualization of the planet, however. In the classic Lockean idea of civic society, the past holds no power over the newly propertied individual: he (this being a male prerogative in Enlightenment thought) is freed of useless traditions and can look to the future. Yet, as Dipesh Chakrabarty points out, this newness "can be imagined and expressed only through a language made out of the languages already available," which are still dominated by a European rhetoric of modernity.²⁶¹ We are constantly urged to remember the past lest we repeat its mistakes: good. But in European modernity's march into the future, the supposed lessons from such mistakes are meant for non-European cultures that are "*not yet civilized enough to rule themselves*" (original emphasis).²⁶² These competing claims to national narratives inescapably condition fictional depictions of forests in the modern period. These representations are for this reason, as my example of Banker's reference to the eucalyptus indicates, often contradictory, since they simultaneously rehearse and resist the biases built into mainstream modernity. In other words, references like Banker's derive from the historical, ecological, and cultural processes that condition this modernity. But at the same time, processes and tropes from beyond this matrix, such as Banker's allusions to sacred banyan trees or to the chewing of *paan*, trouble mainstream modernity's air of self-assurance. At stake in these representations is the treatment of India's environment. Banker's novel is, on the one hand, a material artifact: published in English, widely marketed, and avidly read by members of the upper middle class; on the other hand, as a cultural artifact, it also illustrates the conjunction of seemingly antithetical values, a secularized retelling of incidents of a great and polysemous epic, which revisionists, as noted, are customizing to fit increasingly narrow meanings. The popular appeal of epic narratives has been especially useful for the revisionist idealization of a past in which members of Hindu faith communities, retrospectively pooled into a single group, are said to have maintained a harmonious relationship with nature. Yet in true modern fashion, this neo-traditionalist version of the past has at times served "as a template for alternative development policy" that ignores environmental concerns.²⁶³

Revisionism and Indigenous Forests: Visualizing Mother India

The aforementioned V. D. Savarkar's notion of Hindutva would prove to be the most politically influential of the many nineteenth-century responses to colonial rule that fused modern cartographic and mythic perceptions, shaping the views of today's Hindu conservatives. These views exemplify the intersection of rhetoric (in a variety of media), nationalism, modernity, and politics, a combination that has been severely consequential for forests and that informs aesthetic expressions as well. As in nationalist expressions worldwide, novels, poems, and songs lyricize India's landscapes, providing powerful emotional registers in the public sphere. In these registers, too, modern cartography played a key role; even Tagore's generally nonsectarian vision of the country, as Ramaswamy observes, "seems to follow the outline map of India."²⁶⁴ Broadly, all of these expressions of India as a geographically bounded and primarily (even if nominally) Hindu nation would seem to reflect Bankim's rendering of Mother India in *Anandamath*. In the novel, this vision of the land is presented as a song called "*Vande Mataram,*" or "Praise to the Mother," sung by one of the *santans,* Bankim's name for the ascetic patriots of Bengal who seek to purify the motherland by battling its alien occupiers. This land is "rich in waters, rich in fruit/Cooled by the southern airs,/Verdant with the harvest fair." The land is a mother "radiant with foliage and flowers in bloom/Smiling sweetly, speaking gently,/Giving joy and gifts in plenty." A manifestation of this "spotless" Mother is the goddess Durga, to whom one stanza is addressed, and whose form, like the Mother's other forms, is expressed as "this ever-plenteous land of grace." But it is this very bounty that has made her the envy of rapacious invaders, against whom the song asks Bengal's "seventy millions" to raise "sharpened swords."[265] The inclusion of these song lyrics in the novel illustrates how Bankim and other late-nineteenth-century Hindu revivalists experimented with a variety of narrative devices to disseminate nationalist ideas that combined Hindu traditions and European science.

The strand of scientific method to which nineteenth-century Hindu nationalists like Bankim were drawn was the Enlightenment turn to a "historicist" and "comparative method" of language studies, which we today call sociolinguistics, a primary basis for the humanities.[266] Before Jones's efforts, and laying the groundwork for this analytical climate, there was Giambattista Vico's 1725 multidisciplinary work *The New Science*. This text, notes Harrison, influenced the period's contrastive definitions of "civilized" and "primitive" peoples, the latter supposedly conditioned by humanity's original residence in forests, and the civilized becoming so by clearing away forests, as depicted in the earliest known epic text, *Gilgamesh*.[267] As forests were cut, they were imbued with a profound symbolism, as Harrison observes in his analysis of Vico. This idea is part of the historicist turn, since forests can be understood as "lost" only in linear time.[268] Modernity accentuates this feeling of loss and indeed depends on the idea of loss. Yet neo-traditionalists in India troublingly place this modern allegory of loss and revival, figured as a revival of natural (as opposed to commercially planted) forestland, within narratives of national history and national religion. This move is troubling because it attempts to graft the logos (reason and linear history) of European modernity onto Vedic religious traditions. This inevitably means, to borrow from Chakrabarty's discussion of the concept of an "Indian people," that neo-traditionalists try to shoehorn particular "antihistorical" Vedic beliefs into a unified idea of modern India, with a "secular, linear calendar," by appropriating non-Vedic traditions, such as those of indigenous groups.[269] This maneuver makes the supposed unity of Vedic traditions, conceived retrospectively, the analogue of modern national unity, whose leitmotif is the idealized forest setting of ashramic retreat. This conclusion is partly the outcome of early Hindu nationalists' absorption of the European assumption that civilization began when humans left the woods and partly the projection of nationalist ideals onto the classical, primarily Sanskrit representations of forests. Ironically, on the other hand, eighteenth-century British intellectuals like Edmund Burke believed it was India's ancient peoples who, "whilst we were yet in the woods," had great cities in which they cultivated "all the arts of polished life."[270]

The greater irony of neo-traditionalist narratives is that they belie the very traditionalism they claim to uphold by ignoring its history of pluralism. They overlook, for example, the rights of indigenous groups, like the forest-dwelling Dhurwa (also spelled Duruva), as well as a range of more-pluralistic Hindu belief systems and texts—what Amartya Sen has called India's "argumentative heterodoxy"—all of which call attention to the very problem of defining Hinduism. Even in the time in which Bankim's *Anandamath* is set, the late 1700s, Indians identified themselves "on the basis of locality, language, caste, occupation, and sect," rather than on broad "religious beliefs or practices." Vasudha Dalmia tells us that in his award-winning 1966 Hindi novel *Adha Gaon* (Half the Village), Rahi Masoom Raza describes his identity as being inextricable from his "home" village, both of which are composed by "thousands" of nuanced factors. It was Europeans who started to bracket groups according to "religions." Many groups, in fact, continue to see themselves according to the older, less-homogenized identities, though modern media are increasingly funneling these groups into more monolithic categories.

Indigenous communities, in particular, have had to contend with the consequences of neo-traditionalism's rise. The Forest Service is a case in point. During colonial rule, the service, intent on securing forestland for the British government, greatly eroded indigenous rights. It was the governmental arm indigenous communities knew best, and feared most. Today, ironically, Adivasis still tend to denounce the Forest Service, whose practices are seen as supporting national "development" with empirical and infrastructural methods—precisely the formula that neo-traditional governance advocates. Attesting to the power of institutional culture, the Forest Service has not only persisted in planting harmful eucalyptus trees, it has also ignored the effects on Adivasis whose water resources have been sucked dry by the thirsty eucalypts—a crisis that noted Bengali writer and activist Mahasweta Devi, whom I consider in a later chapter, highlighted long ago.[271] As in other countries, these cases illustrate the intersection of indigenous and environmental rights, on the one hand, and the modern state's economic and ideological interests on the other. Thus, the Chattisgarh Bachao Andolan (Chattisgarh State Defense Movement) advocacy for indigenous rights clashes with the move by the right-leaning government to open the state's Hasdeo Arand Forest, "one of the largest contiguous stretches of very dense forest in central India," to coal mining—a move largely supported by mainstream society.[272] Neo-traditionalism can thus facilitate the exploitation of those very forests it claims to protect. The impulse to homogenize versions of the past and project them onto the present rides roughshod over the numerous regional identities in India that writers have long espoused.

About the Book

This book is not a study of India's biological forests, nor does it pretend to touch on all of India's regional literatures and fictional forests, which would, in any case, be an implausible goal. Instead, I have selected what I take to be some representative texts from across India published between the 1880s and the present to illustrate the importance of forest imagery in Indian critiques of colonialism and conceptions of nationhood. In the pages that follow, I begin with a discussion of how ancient and medieval classics have described forestland and how nineteenth-century novelists adapted these depictions for their own aesthetic, nationalist, and regional purposes. I then compare these to some classic twentieth-century novels before considering, in concluding sections, more recent fiction. My method is broadly cultural and historicist, though not because this is the only or the best approach. As Chakrabarty, among many others, has observed, it was historicism that "enabled European domination of the world in the nineteenth century," for as a measurement of industrial "development," its naturalized temporal "structure" amounted to "first in Europe, then elsewhere."²⁷³ Not surprisingly, Eurocentric historicism was nonetheless what early Indian nationalists had in mind, whether as a form to be emulated or one to be resisted. Historicist models are at the heart of most Indian novels beginning in the late nineteenth century, which invites us to critique their aspirational, formal, and thematic concerns. Yet as I have noted, in having recourse to a rich cultural mythos of the forest, these writers could imaginatively place history as such in "suspension"²⁷⁴ in order to question the dominant presumption that historicism—the consciousness of modern history—alone determines nationhood.

The pages that follow examine these nuances in works I have taken to be fairly representative of certain regions, outlooks, and styles. Ancient and medieval texts demonstrate, however, that while a sense of regionalism has clearly obtained for centuries, the forestlands taken to represent each region changed over time. We will want to consider, therefore, which particular ideas and images of the forest modern writers chose to adapt for their own aesthetic and regionalist–nationalist purposes. For example, ancient Indian settlers appear to have distinguished between two broad types of forestland on which they relied for everyday sustenance: *jangala*, which was applied to dry lands of "thorny shrubs" and arid forests as well as to plains rich in grains and game, and *anupa*, "marshy lands," malarial and generally unhealthy.²⁷⁵ *Jangala*, being salubrious and productive to the Aryan settlers, thus connoted "civilization," whereas *anupa* referred to unhealthy wetlands and forests into which they pushed the "wild," indigenous inhabitants from any purchase on the plains.²⁷⁶

Why, then, did *jangala* eventually come to mean "wild?" And how did *vana* and *aranya* forestlands acquire their different values? *Anupa*, too, could mean both wetlands and "riverside lands," which at one time were associated with illness and incivility.²⁷⁷ These semantic shifts have had significant consequences. All of the terms were used in compound nouns referring to types of settlement, such as *Jangal Desh*, Hindi for "jungle country," to describe an area northwest of Delhi, or *Kurujangala*, "jungles of the Kuru," a fabled kingdom mentioned in the *Mahabharata*, and *anupagrama*, a riverside village.²⁷⁸ Francis Zimmermann has shown that for ancient Indians, *jangala* was in fact infused with "*all the values of civilization*" (original emphasis).²⁷⁹ However, as Michael R. Dove has shown, the eventual transformation of *jangala* into wildness was not a "one-time" occurrence but instead followed a gradual and "dialectical" relationship between early pastoralists and the land. In other words, jungle and forest lands, and human attitudes to them, have neither remained static over time nor have they followed a predictable trajectory. The caution here is that our interpretation of ancient Sanskrit or Tamil texts according to later understandings of jungle and forest can lead to erroneous conclusions.²⁸⁰

Let us glance, for prefatory purposes, at an example of the ambivalence with which ancient and medieval metropolitan cultures regarded indigenous communities and their environs. In the accounts of medieval-era Tamil Chola kings, we hear of "primitive tribal groups" who, forced to earn a living as itinerant musicians and dancers, visit the king's court, where their unsophisticated ways are the butt of jokes.²⁸¹ Yet these were the very people who inhabited—and continued for some centuries to inhabit, though in ever-diminishing numbers—lush "forest belts" of mountain ranges and whose forest homelands were—we can surmise—among those whose "reclamation and settlement" the Chola kings periodically sought, leading to the groups' displacement and destitution.[282] At the same time, certain forests in the region were considered the proper place for spiritual retreat, such as the one that legendary Tamil Jain ruler-saint Jivaka is described as embracing, after renouncing the throne, in Tiruttakkadevar's great tenth-century poem the *Jivakacintamani*.[283] These examples of semantic slippage, instances of which I will return to, persist in most accounts of forests and jungles.

These conceptualizations of forest and jungle, which overlap with the veneration of individual sacred trees (Figure 0.5) continue to inform depictions of forests in Indian texts, even guiding state policies. For example, the word "jungle" to mean wild and uncivilized is still used in Hindi, just as the primitive-uncivilized polarity, accentuated by British colonialism, is still used by the central government as part of its characterization of forest-dwelling communities, whose mineral-rich land it covets. In whichever ways these terms are used, it is clear that they have always done double duty, referring to specific ecologies as well as to social principles. Especially illustrative of this is the term *sadharana*, which referred to lands between *jangala* and *anupa*, and so avoiding the latter's "extreme climates."[284] As a region of moderate climate, *sadharana* therefore also came to mean moderation in spiritual and somatic life.[285] The constellation of meanings attached to "forest" and "jungle" will appear in various narrative incarnations in the chapters that follow.

Chapter 1, Moral Kingship, Forest Dwellers, and Epic and Vernacular Forests, discusses key perspectives on forest symbolism from different disciplines, including the following: the forest as a liminal rite of passage, according to Thomas Parkhill's sociological study[286] of Sanskrit epic (following Victor Turner's *The Ritual Process*); a "zone of tension" between pastoral and forest-dwelling communities, in Dove's words; a refuge for social (i.e., those considered morally just) outlaws; a spiritual retreat, as in Buddhist, Jain, and Hindu *ashramas*; an enchanted realm, whether good or ill; a resource for raw materials; a womb-like and moral home space, as both Sanskrit texts and nationalist writers espouse; a liminal, threshold space for personal moral transformation, especially of kings, which includes both exile and hunting as rites of passage; and, as I argue, a space for the democratizing play of voices. These are strategies, as later chapters discuss, that representative modern literary works draw on and revise to express ideas of nationhood and national belonging.

Chapter 2, Colonial History, Home Forests, and Mother India in Bankim's *Anandamath*, closely examines Bankimchandra Chattopadhyay's iconic and controversial 1882 novel, originally published in Bengali, to demonstrate the significance of its forest setting for the period's evolving nationalism and for the modern Indian novel. The novel's unique combination of classical and vernacular idioms (resembling in this sense Luís Vaz de Camões' strategy in his 1572 Portuguese nationalist epic poem on da Gama), and of romanticism and realism, proved to be a winning formula for advocating a mythic-historical—which is to say, Indian and mostly non-European—ethos to urban readers. The novel's influence on both nationalist sentiment and literary style was profound and complex, as the chapter shows. It forged a modern idiom in which to express national belonging and topographical form by reactivating forest motifs, by figuring the country as a maternal goddess, and

Figure 0.5 Sacred tree, Tezpur
Source: Photo by author.

by selectively drawing on British histories of Bengal. Yet the novel has rightly been criticized for excluding Bengali Muslims from the imagined community, which is embodied by a company of ascetic Hindu warriors who gather in a Bengal forest to plan their fight for freedom.[287] The novel also ignores indigenous forest dwellers, which a number of later novelists would seek to counterbalance. However, the goddess-as-nation whom Bankim's rebels worship, as invoked in the famous "*Bande Mataram*" ("Hail to thee, Mother"[288]) song lyrics, shares some features common to folk deities of the forest, as I show. In exemplifying these and other conjunctions, the novel reflects the ethos of Bengali Hindu intellectuals like Bankim who were experimenting with ways of representing India in terms of its forestland.

Chapter 3, Premchand's Forest, Bibhutibhushan's *Aranyak*, and the Progressive Era, turns to forest imagery in two well-known early twentieth-century novels, Premchand's Hindi classic *Godaan* and Bibhutibhushan Bandyopadhyay's Bengali *Aranyak: Of the Forest*. Like many literary works in the years preceding independence, these novels consider, in very different ways, what it means to be Indian in a modern era, when nature is besieged and poverty plagues rural areas. Both writers sought to address the social ills they believed the nation had to resolve if it was to be morally viable. The forest episode I focus on in Premchand's novel illustrates, through its use of familiar classical tropes, the hollowness of urban upper-class sensibilities that rely on such tropes as well as the author's problematic perpetuation of those very tropes. In loving, sometimes romantic detail, Bibhutibhushan describes Bengal forestlands of the early 1900s, which his urban readership had hitherto viewed mostly through the prisms of British history and legend. His portrayal of the hardship of indigenous forest dwellers, like Premchand's depictions of rural poverty, indicts both the colonial state and the Indian landowning class for their responsibility in this development.

In Chapter 4, History, Nation, and Forest in Salman Rushdie and Amitav Ghosh, I show how these well-known authors in their own ways turn to arboreal images in order to decenter dominant worldviews. The ostensibly "historyless" Sundarbans forest that Rushdie describes in a chapter of *Midnight's Children*, and in which the narrator Saleem Sinai and his three fellow battle-scarred soldiers wander confusedly during the 1971 Bangladesh War, invites us to interpret the episode in several ways simultaneously, much as the forest itself seems to continuously "change its nature." The mangrove forest in this way reflects the novel's rendering of subcontinental history as multiply told, multiply imagined, and kaleidoscopic, as befits its cultural intermixing. I then turn to another, more substantive representation of the Sundarbans, Ghosh's novel *The Hungry Tide*, which conveys the wide variety of interpretations that the region has elicited, as displayed in colonial history, folk songs, scientific data, social activism, religious fable, and memoir. A consideration of Ghosh's subsequent novel *Sea of Poppies*, shows how, through a central character's *darshanic* visions, Ghosh captures the polyglot and creole subcultures resulting from early nineteenth-century maritime trade. Metonyms of forests, which were central to this colonial period, are indexical of forests, both real and imagined. Each of these perspectives responds in its own way to an environment increasingly scarred by anthropogenic activities. The novel urges its readers to see that these worldviews cannot be understood independently of each other and that such an understanding is essential for the region's survival.

Chapter 5, Indigeneity, Forestry, and the State in C. K. Janu, Mahasweta Devi, and Easterine Kire, examines works by three writers and activists. C. K. Janu's *testimonio* recounts her ongoing activism on behalf of her Kerala-based Adivasi community and their rapidly shrinking forestlands. Mahasweta Devi's stories describe the exploitation, as well as individual agency, of Oraon and other Adivasi women in the forests of Bihar and West Bengal. Easterine Kire's folkloric account of a Naga man's journey through a forest in India's Northeast intimates, through his eyes, the transactions of corporeal and supernatural states in his encounters with were-tigers. These works describe the particular predicaments faced by indigenous communities in today's India and depict endangered modes of forest inhabitance. The narratives thereby counter mainstream forest tropes that associate indigenous groups with wildness and incivility.

In the Conclusion, my subtitle, The City in the Forest, signals the increasing economic and cultural power of cities in an increasingly globalized Indian economy. I first briefly consider why two noteworthy novels by writers representing India's first and second post-independence generations, Sunil Gangopadhyay and Upamanyu Chatterjee, choose forest settings in which to critique the views of self-absorbed city dwellers. I close by touching on some recent works—by Aravind Adiga, Karan Mahajan, Indra Sinha, Arundhati Roy, and Anuradha Roy—that invoke arboreal motifs to expose the pressures of a globalized, urban-centered era. In ways that resonate suggestively with the works discussed in previous chapters, these younger writers show that the forest is not a self-contained and distant realm, but is instead part of the city, both ecologically and imaginatively.

A Note on the Use of Translated Texts

My determination of what texts are representative has depended on a mix of received scholarship and my own judgment. For this reason, I have had to leave out some notable works and have missed noticing others. There will inevitably be critical gaps and some broad conclusions, though the works I discuss and my evaluations of them provide, I trust, a fruitful introduction to this important but neglected topic.

The subject matter has also required me to use translated works in addition to those composed in English. Although it would be ideal to read and evaluate them in their original forms, the sheer number of languages—India has 22 official ones, not to mention ancient tongues—makes this prohibitive. Where possible, I use translations that have earned an authoritative imprimatur among available versions, though in many cases, there exists just one translation, rendering my choice moot. This dependence may weaken the ability to fully catch linguistic nuance and cultural uniqueness, but the advantages of being able to draw on, and compare, a variety of significant non-English works far outweigh this limitation. Without translation, such a study would be impossible—just as, conversely, it would be foolhardy to extrapolate conclusions on a topic of this breadth based on a single region and language.

Two other dimensions of translation are worth noting, and pertain to virtually every literary work in India. The first is the representation, implicit or explicit, of characters whose speech and cultures are understood to be different from that of the authorial voice or the focal characters, or both. Mahasweta Devi, for instance, transliterates certain English loan words into Bengali to indicate when her characters are using them, a device that one of her English translators, Gayatri Chakravorty Spivak, indicates by italicizing the words.

The other dimension involves the paradox that although the motivation to translate regional literary works into English reflects the latter's continued, perhaps neocolonial, global dominance, this move is inseparable from the conventional idea of modernity. As Pascale Casanova remarks, the translation of James Joyce's seminal works from English to French in the 1920s was vital to the dissemination of "literary modernity."[289] In other words, a work's translation into one of the world's dominant languages (all of European origin) is still seen to be a necessary precondition for the consecration of literary, which is to say modern, worth. At the same time, a writer like Joyce, who lived in France in self-exile from Ireland, was (and is) seen to be quintessentially Irish. For writers in all but a handful of dominant languages, in other words, the stamp of national essence is possible only, paradoxically, by a move into global (European) modernity.

In India, the situation is, for several reasons, more complex, a point worth repeating. English-language publication continues to act as a centripetal force in an industry with publishers in all regional languages. Increasingly, however, translation into English does not aspire to, or "require," a concomitant recognition abroad, since the national boundary has become a large enough tent. Indian readers' multilingual capacity and shared cultural idioms also mean, generally speaking, that when they read a translated work, they are more attuned to its cultural codes. As Anjali Narlekar observes in her study of modernist poet Arun Kolatkar, who wrote in both Marathi and English, translation in India always incurs a regional component that readers judge on a kind of authenticity scale. At the same time, writers rightly worry about the erosion of their home language in the face of English and other language dominance.[290]

1

Moral Kingship, Forest Dwellers, and Epic and Vernacular Forests

About two thousand years ago, in what is today the southern state of Tamil Nadu, a young married couple is fleeing their famed home of Pukar, the eastern port city, to start a new life in the sacred inland city of Maturai (Madurai). Halfway to their destination, but unsure of the route, they enter a forest grove, where they meet a Brahmin ascetic and ask the way (Figure 1.1). He warns them that their journey to Maturai in this hot season will be hard, taking them through dangerous and deceptive forests. But if they make it to where the path splits into three, they must look for certain telltale trees that mark the correct one: trees like *cadamba*, bamboo, *ukaay* (miswak), and *serissa*. After a time, they will see a hill adorned with fruit trees (jackfruit, plantain), spice plants (turmeric), and areca palms (Figure 1.2). Keeping the hill to their left, they will eventually arrive at the great city.

This journey is a small section of the great fifth-century Tamil epic *The Cilappatikaram* (also sometimes rendered in English as *Silappatikaram* to reflect the sibilant), which describes the misfortunes that befall our wedded protagonists, Kovalan and Kannaki, after they reach Maturai. The forests they traverse and the arboreal motifs that fill this paragon of Tamil literature, together with the minutiae of life in Pukar and Maturai at this time, roughly the first through fourth centuries CE—a period broadly labeled Sangam—have provided us with a wonderfully detailed view of ancient Tamil cultures. Sangam poems are especially famous for their astonishingly familiar and earthy language. In particular, the elaborate treatments of landscape in *The Cilappatikaram* and other Sangam-era poetic works reflect both sophisticated aesthetic theorizations and comprehensive ecological knowledge. Forests in these texts therefore evoke both their material values—such as the practical and economic importance of fruits—and their symbolic significance, which may be strictly literary or principally religious, or a combination of the two.

This combinative, intersectional quality matters greatly to this study of how forests characterize regional self-perceptions in the modern era because these classical forest signifiers, especially those in *The Cilappatikaram*, have directly informed modern Tamil nationalist evocations of landscape. This is problematic, since nationalist movements—especially under colonialism and especially when their adherents simultaneously try to articulate their regional distinctiveness—are often pressured to narrow their membership criteria. The dilemma facing Indians across the country, as I noted in

Figure 1.1 Sadhu in Corbett National Park
Source: Photo by author.

Figure 1.2 Areca nut palm
Source: Photo by author.

my introduction, was how to preserve features of the past while looking to the future, which usually entailed a melding of select regional and trans-regional tropes—mainly classical-literary and religious, such as Mother India—with a historical consciousness that advocates industrial "development."[1] The price of this modern political devotedness has, however, been a sharp narrowing of the richly suggestive meanings of past forest images, a development that prevailed in most regions of the country as nationalists concentrated their vision to more effectively oppose colonialism and, after independence in 1947, to advance particular political aims. I should reiterate that my interest is in the literariness of these images and how writers respond to them, rather than in national political movements. Nineteenth-century writers, in other words, were often intentional in drawing on classical literary images of region and nation, even as they sought to enlist more vernacular traditions, such as folk songs and other widely popular expressive modes, in their historically minded texts. By historically minded, I mean the ways in which these modern works redirected classical motifs, especially the attributes of moral kingship, toward concepts of national development, including criteria for proper leadership. *The Cilappatikaram* thus becomes, for twentieth-century Tamil nationalists, a cautionary tale about the dire consequences of poor kingship, for the tragic ends of our two ordinary—rather than heroic or semidivine—protagonists are due to the failure of a leader who has forgotten the geographical and arboreal virtues of his realm, signified by his tutelary scepter wrought from the local *cadamba* tree. Never again, modern nationalists avow, should Tamil leaders forget this, for only by appreciating their custodial responsibilities toward the land do they earn the right to govern. The essential features of this land have, for Tamil nationalists, been clearly articulated in *The Cilappatikaram*. For although in their journey from a coastal city (Pukar) to an interior, sacred one (Maturai), Kovalan and Kannaki must pass through disorienting forests and dangerous rivers, these topographies constitute an avowedly Tamil ecumene. Yet in regarding Tamil country and language as singularly and self-evidently virtuous, modern nationalists have had to overlook those features of the forest that trouble this narrowed outlook—namely, its indigenous inhabitants who called it home and displayed a measure of autonomy from the city. In reality, as *The Cilappatikaram* itself shows, forests and forest dwellers exhibit features that to urban dwellers may seem shadowy and strange, but which, besides helping to sustain the city, show urban life to be no less shadowy and no less perplexing.

To better understand why and how Indian nationalists have at times celebrated the intersectional richness of forest motifs in ancient and medieval works while also editing them to fit their views of proper national leadership, this chapter turns to select translations of Tamil and Sanskrit classics. I begin with *The Cilappatikaram*, contextualizing its setting and looking closely at some of its many forest representations, and then follow with a brief consideration of other Sangam-era Tamil texts. These Tamil works' indictment of amoral leadership and their comparatively egalitarian representations of human agency exemplify the classical models, of both northern and southern India, that nationalists could turn to as inspiration for models of leadership.[2] I then provide an overview of how and why other culturally influential works, including the *Ramayana* and Kalidasa's drama *Shakuntala*, accentuate the roles played by real and imagined forests in the tutelage of moral kingship. Yet while these arboreal signifiers of proper governance have provided guidance for nationalist writers, they perpetuate the denigration of ostensibly wild forest-dwelling communities, much as the British did in the course of their two centuries of rule. I conclude the chapter with a brief overview of the eventful political and economic changes, primarily centered on forest products, that followed the entry of Europeans into South Asia's long-standing trade networks and that would be consequential for modern literature. The ensuing cultural interactions influenced portrayals of local landscapes by Indian writers, who, as subsequent chapters show, tailored classical depictions of forests to the specifications of modern nationalism.

The Cilappatikaram and Tamil Country

The Cilappatikaram[3] recounts that a few years after Kovalan and Kannaki's festive wedding, Kovalan has an affair with a courtesan, repents, and leaves with Kannaki for Maturai, where they plan to pawn her jeweled anklets to start a new life. After their aforementioned trek through ostensibly treacherous woods to the capital of the Pandyan kings, they need cash to survive, and so Kovalan attempts to sell one of Kannaki's anklets. It so happens that the king's wife has had her ankle bracelet stolen, and someone—a goldsmith—mistakes the one Kovalan is carrying for the purloined anklet. Kovalan is arrested and summarily executed—ensuring that the goldsmith, who is the true thief, will never be caught. But a distraught Kannaki confronts the king and proves Kovalan is innocent. Here the poet presents Kannaki as being so wild with grief that, "Like a forest, her dark hair spread about her"—an image that not only causes the Pandyan king to die "of terror" but that foreshadows other arboreal omens. For the still-enraged Kannaki curses Maturai, tears off her "left breast," and flings it at the city. Agni appears, and at his instigation, Kannaki sets fire to Maturai, a conflagration the poet likens to Krishna's incineration of the Kandava Forest. Kannaki "ordered the god of fire" to "spare" the virtuous and destroy the "wicked"—including the Pandyan king's family and palaces.[4] The goddess of Maturai herself then appears before Kannaki and tells her to journey westward, to a hill located in the neighboring Chera kingdom—which, along with the now-headless Pandya kingdom and the Chola kingdom to the east, make up *Tamilakam*, realm of the Tamils. From atop this hill, as witnessed by the forest-dwelling Kuravas, Kannaki is carried by Indra into heaven.[5] The Kuravas report this to the Chera king, Cenkuttuvan, who, wishing to erect a memorial to Kannaki using Himalayan stone, travels northward, which provides an excuse to defeat the Arya kings of the north, who disrespected *Tamilakam*.

A variety of nature motifs help constitute this Tamil landscape in *The Cilappatikaram*. Areca palms, cadamba and jackfruit trees, turmeric plants—the signposts that Kovalan and Kannaki must watch for on their way to Maturai, as recounted in the epic—are among the clear indicators that we are in what was called *Tamilakam*, or, as the epic's most authoritative translator into English, R. Parthasarathy, renders this word, "Tamil country."[6] It is telling that the word's suffix, *akam*, means the "inner world" of individual emotions as distinct from *puram*, the "outer, heroic world" at large. Sangam-era poetry oscillates between expressions of *akam* and *puram*, which are usually signified by conventional associative images and an elaborate, unique poetics, unaffiliated with that of Sanskrit, that is tied to seven (in practice, mainly five) regional landscapes, called *tinai*. *Mullai*, for instance, refers to forested land, and is typically invoked by its namesake flower, a type of jasmine.[7]

These organic signifiers of a distinct region do not merely adorn the epic, therefore, but play crucial roles in the two protagonists' actions and in the work's multilayered significance. This is not unique to *The Cilappatikaram*: together with other Tamil works, it comprises a corpus of what Sumathi Ramaswamy aptly calls Tamil "place-making imaginations," or the imaginative crafting of a regional identity that is equal parts linguistic, geographical, and mythic. Especially intriguing in *The Cilappatikaram*'s poetic crafting of precolonial signifiers of Tamil country is how the forest links together the text's compositional parts. As in other classical works in both Tamil and Sanskrit, *The Cilappatikaram* renders the forest in various ways: sometimes metonymically through its products (sandalwood, pepper), sometimes metaphorically (wilderness as heroic test), or yet again through tropes (women likened to elegant forest creepers,[8] for instance) that variously signal physical beauty, spiritual purity, natural bounty, or all at the same time. These assignations frequently intersect in a text to evoke a complex play of emotional responses in the epic's contemporary reader. Twentieth-century Tamil nationalists, as mentioned, turned to these rich literary images in order to distinguish, often in stridently passionate voices, their linguistic-geographical identity from the Sanskritic markers of affiliation that prevail in northern India.[9] Canto 25, "The Choice of the Stone," encapsulates the arboreal associations of Tamil country, such as when the Chera king—whom tradition holds to be Ilanko's older brother—brashly voices Tamil pride from his position of power. Accepting his counselors' recommendation to honor the late Kannaki with a statue carved of Himalayan stone, thereby conjoining the holy Kaveri River of his land with the source of the holy Ganga, the king boasts that if the "[northern] king of the mountains refuses us the stone," he, the righteous Chera king and his forces, "with garlands of willow around our necks … will rob the Himalaya/ Of his [the northern king's] crown." Besides the garland of Indian willow, a poetic metonym for the Chera king's diadem,[10] he will, he says, wear "a wreath of mantāram [*Hibiscus rosa-sinensis*] flowers strung together with/Kino blossoms."[11] Both the kino tree and *mantāram* shrub, like the willow, signify a distinctly southern landscape, as do a number of other flowering trees and vines. Importantly, the "hill dwellers" (forest peoples), in their praise songs to Kannaki in the previous Canto (number 24), accentuate her goddess status by describing her as "the woman who stood in the shade/ Of the fragrant kino of the forest," one whom the very "gods of heaven praised/And worshipped."[12] The arboreal splendor that distinguishes Tamil country from northern lands is further signaled by the name of the Chera king's fabled port city, Vanchi, named after the willow. *Vanchi* is also the name given to this final book of the epic.

Equally important in *The Cilappatikaram*'s evocation of a Tamil landscape are, as I briefly noted in the book's introduction, the roles that the two legendary southern cities play in the fateful forest journey of our protagonist couple. Kovalan and Kannaki's peregrination effectively conjoins their home city of Pukar (where today's Poompuhar stands) and Maturai, as Parthasarathy styles it to effect phonetic contemporaneity, which I also use here. Apart from their already legendary status at the time the epic was composed, the cities represent two sides of what was perceived to be a broadly Tamil ethos: the sacred (Maturai) and profane (Pukar). *The Cilappatikaram* extols the merits of both cities, thus conjoining the demotic space of littoral Puhar with the orthodox and riverine Maturai, signifying the two cities' symbiotic relationship. Maturai's sacred status is effectively even greater than that of Banaras, the traditional center of Hindu devotion far to the north of India. Of particular interest to my discussion is that the epic evokes the two cities' mutually dependent qualities through forest motifs. These precolonial signifiers were taken up, Ramaswamy informs us, by modern champions of Tamil, for whom *The Cilappatikaram*'s language itself embodies the rootedness of their identity. This outlook is expressed by another Tamil word (besides *Tamilakam*), *Tamilpparru*, roughly "Tamil-centeredness," a "devotion" reflective of "those networks of praise, passion, and practice centered on Tamil" and which cannot be subsumed under the monolithic concept of nationalism.[13]

Yet although land and language are tightly woven together in the Sangam writings of generations of scribes in Maturai, who may be credited with shaping a Tamil ethos, the constituent threads of this conceptual interweaving are more mutable, less restrictive than the modern pronouncements of regional identity would have them be—hence the allowance for a play of emotional responses to these images, as mentioned above. To put this differently and more broadly, forest images in classical Sanskrit and Tamil works signify orthodox as well as vernacular outlooks, conservative as well as transgressive. These varied forest images together evoke a sense of regional identity that is identifiable but nonetheless fuzzy around the edges. In the *Cilappatikaram*, for example, Pukar and Maturai are defined not solely by their distinctive reputations as, respectively, commercial and sacred centers. Even in their worldly bustle, residents of Pukar take time to sing "hymns to Vishnu,"[14] just as Maturai, too, boasts a vibrant "marketplace" laden with everything from "leather shields" to "black pepper."[15]

These attributes, and other examples I will shortly examine, certainly evoke the "specific" natural locale of the Tamil region, as R. Parthasarathy observes in his authoritative 1993 English translation of the epic, as I also noted in this book's introduction. It is equally true that Pukar, Maturai, and the forested country in between also function as symbols that inform the epic's major themes, including the interplay of agency and fate exemplified by the two protagonists. It is harder, however, to interpret these three spaces, as Parthasarathy does, as primarily serving the protagonists'—Kovalan and Kannaki's—"rite of transition" between "preliminal" Pukar and "postliminal" Maturai, with the forest "represent[ing] a descent ... into the unknown," and so effectively the liminal phase (in Arnold van Gennep's terms) on the path to self-awareness and societal reintegration.[16] This reading, though helpful, is limited for several reasons, in my view. It requires Pukar, first of all, to be the city that must be left behind and Maturai to be the favored embodiment of the couple's reincorporation into normative society. This reading also plays down the story's most terrifying episode, in which Kannaki, outraged at the king's execution of her innocent husband Kovalan, "wrenched off her left breast," "hurled it" at Maturai, and then asks Agni, the god of fire, to burn the renowned city.[17]

Finally, and most importantly, Parthasarathy's reading of the epic's cities and the forest as primarily serving the social-psychological development of its mythic characters misses the critical role, I believe, of the inhabitants of the forest, the "hill dwellers"—the Kurava people—to whom the author grants the honor of witnessing Kannaki's hilltop ascent to heaven.[18] These indigenous forest dwellers are described in detail that is every bit as "actual" as the detailed characterization of Pukar, Maturai, and the Tamil landscape as a whole. One cannot, in other words, accept that the forest plays an incidental role in an ostensibly more meaningful and substantive story, as implied by Parthasarathy's otherwise excellent interpretation of the epic. The hill- and forest-dwelling Kuravas, accorded their own Canto—number 24, "The Round of the Hill Dwellers"—anchor the epic's commentary on the importance of virtuous kingship, and, conversely, the penalty—death, in this case—for one who fails in this role, as the Pandyan king of Maturai does. In fact, then, it is Maturai that is shown to have become morally decadent, while Pukar is extolled, as Parthasarathy notes. Kovalan and Kannaki are clearly not fleeing a symbolically primordial realm for one that is more culturally and morally advanced—quite the reverse. But this reversal is neither permanent nor even, in my reading, a necessary dualism. Rather, the epic shows us that each city contains a range of behaviors and practices. Most importantly, they equally evoke a "Tamil" ethos that is actualized to a great degree through arboreal motifs, arguably anticipating an arboreal urban sensibility in current cultural texts.

Forest Communities, Urban Trade, and Moral Order in Tamil Country

The honored role that the author gives to the hill dwellers in his epic is notable not only for acknowledging the significance of a forest community, whom city dwellers historically (as today) tend to denigrate. Hill—which is to say, forest—peoples were typically judged to be rough-cut "jungle-folk," with the word forest shading into jungle, illustrating once again the semantic slippage between the terms.[19] The community's depiction is also significant because it illuminates their historically vital role in sustaining the cities to whose kings they had sworn allegiance. For example, the inhabitants of forests in the Western Ghats of southern India had long exchanged goods with coastal cities like Calicut, the historically great entrepôt in the Malabar region of present-day Kerala. Just as Ilanko depicts Pukar and Maturai as exemplifying different but equally valuable constituents of Tamil country, so does he show that the region's cities cannot exist without their hinterlands. The accounts of visitors to medieval Calicut, as well as local *puranas* and poems,[20] attest to the bountiful and well-managed forests surrounding, and sometimes abutting, the city. Hill dwellers in Ilanko's time had been trading their goods with coastal kinds for "generations."[21] The dominant image in all of these reports is that of a thriving, enlightened port, much like ancient Muziris—the fabled port further down the western coast that was first excavated only in the twentieth century—and which was famous across the ancient Mediterranean for its prized commodities: pepper, of course, but also teak, glass beads, gems, tortoiseshell, and ivory.[22] These coastal cities owed their fortune to astute commerce not just with foreign merchants, but also with the forest communities who harvested and transported their products to cities for both domestic consumption and international trade.[23]

Even centuries later, in the years immediately before Vasco da Gama's consequential 1498 arrival in Calicut, every year "ten to fifteen ships" (K. S. Mathew informs us) departed the city "loaded with pepper, ginger, cinnamon, cardamom, myrobalans, tamarinds, canafistula, precious stones of every kind, seed pearls, musk, ambergris, rhubarb, aloes-wood, great store of cotton cloths and porcelains," sailing "to Aden and Mocha."[24] The goods listed here denote the sophisticated, millennia-old network of trade across southern India in natural tree products, whose cultivation served both international and local needs. For example, the *canafistula* tree, also called *Cassia fistula* in English (Indian laburnum), has long been closely tied to local cultures, both urban and indigenous. Its yellow blossoms are still prized in the South for the annual Vishnu festival, and it provides vital shade, along with several other tree species, for the cultivation of cardamom, which together "flourish wild in the jungles."[25] *Cassia fistula* also supplied timber for ships, as indicated by the discovery on the Kerala coast, in the 1990s, of a "sailboat" dating to between the twelfth and fifteenth centuries. Culturally, this and many other trees linked to cities today retain, in everyday life, a large measure of their multilayered value.

It is not only in India, of course, that forests and cities have long been entwined, as the Sumerian epic *Gilgamesh* illustrates. But in India, as we have seen, this linkage continues today, at least notionally. Banaras and Maturai, Hinduism's most sacred cities, are associated with specific forests: The Forest of Bliss for Banaras, and the Kadamba Forest for Maturai, named for the sacred *cadamba* tree (whose spelling varies in English). The forest names are still in currency, and although the original forests are severely depleted—a recent report tells us that only twenty *cadamba* trees remain in today's Maturai, for instance[26]—their religious symbolism and iconography maintain a powerfully felt presence for devotees. This is entwined, as well, in mythohistorical accounts, such as in the *Madurai Sthala-purana*, which tells of a tradesman in ancient times who finds a Shiva lingam in the Kadamba Forest and rushes to tell the region's Pandyan king. The king, recognizing the site as holy, orders a city to be built around it, which he calls Madura, "sweetness."[27] The *Madurai purana* illustrates how the intersection of physical origin, sacred meaning, and ceremonial power characterize many of India's sacred sites: each of these dimensions requires the other. Certain trees, too, can signify whole forests. In the seventh-century CE Sanskrit prose romance *Kadambari*, for example, author Banabhatta compares a huge, wizened *calmali* (cottonsilk) tree to a "temple" and its limbs to the "thousand arms" of Shiva "outstretched in his wild dance at the day of doom." The tree's "many boughs" seemingly "embrace … the whole Vindhya Forest."[28] In Sanskrit and Tamil literatures, such intersections amplify a particular forest's sacred aura, even if that forest has disappeared, as in Vrindavan, or nearly so, as in Maturai.

To see more clearly why *The Cilappatikaram* eulogizes hill dwellers and their forestland while also extolling the virtues of cities in Tamil country, let us return to Pukar, where we first meet our protagonists, Kovalan and Kannaki. On most days at this time, the city's merchants and dock workers scanned the ocean's horizon for the masts of ships arriving from Rome, Athens, and other far-off cities. After unloading their goods—olive oil and Tuscan wine, or copper and glass—the ships filled their holds with pepper and cinnamon, sandalwood, beryl, and ivory. Pukar, also called Puhar, or Kaveri Poompatinam—today's Poompuhar—was the Chola dynasty's primary sea port, which flourished for centuries until its demise around the third century CE. The place of Pukar in the epic, and its ground-level descriptions of the city, is revealing, for this conveys not a city-state centrality, such as contemporary Athens possessed, but instead a regional—that is, Tamil—outlook. *The Cilappatikaram*, which grew out of an existing oral tradition, is said to be the work not of a Pukar (Chola) resident, but of a Jain Chera (or Cheral) prince named Ilanko Atikal, younger brother of the Chera king at the time, whose capital city was the port of Vanchi, on the opposite—western—coast.²⁹ Pukar and the comparably illustrious Vanchi—which some argue is a local name for fabled Muziris (or Muciri, which may be the site of today's Kodungallur)³⁰—together with Maturai, are the keystones of Tamil country, representing, in turn, the Chola, Chera, and Pandya kingdoms. The three powers, despite tense relationships at times, shared the same Tamil language and culture.

The Cilappatikaram describes Pukar with self-evident pride, a city resplendently robed by the "billowing" waves of the Bay of Bengal, its markets bursting with foods—fresh appam, wine, and meats—and the choicest silks, pearls, and sandalwood, with merchants "from distant/ Lands" mingling with throngs of customers, entertainers, "harlots," and artists (Canto 5, line 90, pp. 46–8). Even Vidyadhara, a winged attendant of Lord Shiva, cannot help but marvel at this most "prosperous city."³¹ In Ilanko's epic, Pukar's carnal pleasures, dependent on trade with foreigners, or "Yavanas," counterpoint the holy pilgrimage city and classical Tamil hub of Maturai, far from the coast and in which much of the story is set. In between the two cities lie hills, rivers, and a forest "wilderness" that "confuse[s]" travelers.³² As members of the thriving merchant class of Pukar, the journey that Kovalan and Kannaki (also transliterated as Kannagi) undertake serves, in part, to interlink seemingly bewildering forestland with southern cities that, in equal measure, constitute Tamil country. Pukar, not unlike the reputed author's home of Vanchi, thus contrasts with the "moral order" of the pilgrimage city of Maturai—a contrast that "is an essential element in the theme and structure of" the epic.³³ Both Pukar and Vanchi/Muziris were, the epic tells us in characterizing the lovers' home, universally "envied" for their "rare objects and diverse/Merchandise," which "Ships/And caravans from foreign lands" brought "in abundance" (Canto 2. 3–7). Ilanko tells us of the "hill dwellers" who, living in the forest, produce the "cardamom and pepper," ivory and "sandalwood," and "areca nuts" and fruits that are in such demand (25. 44–53). Historical documents, such as a second-century Alexandrian papyrus, confirm this fact, listing textiles, spikenard (muskroot), ivory, and betel nut as well as the ever-coveted pepper.³⁴

But why should Maturai, however morally degraded, have to burn? Fire in most classical Indian texts traditionally represents ritual purification, whether in the circling of a flame in wedding ceremonies, or, in the *Mahabharata*, the violent but ostensibly necessary burning of the Khandava Forest (more on which below), or, yet again, in the *Ramayana*, the "test" of fire (*agnipariksha*) that, in some versions of the *Ramayana*, Rama orders Sita to undergo to prove her faithfulness to him. It is clear in Ilanko's epic that a corrupt Maturai must be razed in order to allow fresh moral roots to grow. But to have Kannaki be the agent of this is striking. Her act echoes the many variants of Sita's response to Rama's injunction, in some of which she defies his request and leaves—though many interpret even the account of her consent to the trial by fire as an act of dissent that throws shade on her otherwise virtuous and just spouse.³⁵ Kannaki's ordeal echoes, as well, the forest setting associated with Sita's ordeal in several ways: it is from the forest that Sita is abducted by Ravana; Rama banishes her, in most versions of the epic, to the forest even after regaining his kingdom due to a perceived slight; and, in a variant circulated among Maithil communities in the north, Rama is scolded for forcing Sita to "walk barefoot in the forest."[36] Sita's ordeal in the forest is, indeed, often likened by Maithili storytellers to the ordeal of every woman's marriage because, as Coralynn V. Davis puts it in her study of Maithil women's stories, "like a forest, a new marital home is a strange and inhospitable territory with unknown inhabitants and dangers and unknown means for survival."[37] By extension, Sita—like all women—is accorded her own forest exile, in contradistinction to Rama's.[38] This is doubtless why the story of Krishna's playfulness with free-spirited *gopis* in the Vrindavan Forest has remained so popular: it stands as a possible alternative to Sita's tribulations.

Like the admiration for Sita these tales express, Kannaki in *The Cilappatikaram* is pitied by a motherly "herdswoman," Matari, for having had "to walk through forests" to reach Maturai. In this pivotal episode, recounted in Canto 16: "The Scene of the Murder" (i.e., Kovalan's killing), a number of lines seem to portend a Sita-like trial by fire for Kannaki. These lines are rendered ironic by imminent events, an irony that, as I read it, serves to undercut the ideal wife trope that Kannaki has thus far generally seemed to embody. In a few short pages, the poet forecasts Kannaki's incineration of the city, sets in motion Kovalan's fateful decision to obtain much-needed money, and seals the fate of the city's selfish Pandyan king. The arboreal images that characterize these narrative seeds rely for their power, to some degree, on similar images in countrywide stories of Sita. But in localizing these images and portraying Kannaki as having a mind of her own, one that dares to transgress societal norms, the Tamil narrative itself stands as a rhetorical riposte to the epics of "northern countries" that would presume to speak for every region.[39] In Canto 16, portentous images set these events in motion, such as when, while helping Matari and her daughter prepare food, Kannaki's "slender fingers/ Turned red" and "Blood rushed to her fair eyes." Over a "fire ... she cooked a good meal/For her husband," and "As if to remove/The heat of Mother Earth, she sprinkled water on the floor." Kovalan, his stomach full and admiring his wife's faithfulness to him, calls her "purest gold,/Vine, girl with fragrant locks of hair!" It is at this point that he cements his fate—and Kannaki's and Maturai's—by asking for her gold anklet so he can pawn it. The comparison of Kannaki to a vine, or creeper, is a trope for natural feminine beauty familiar in Sanskrit works as well, such as in *Shakuntala*. But the Tamil poet ironizes the image by having Matari describe Kovalan, seated before a "plantain leaf" laden with a freshly cooked dinner, as "Krishna himself" because, like the Lord of the northern forest, the man from Vanchi takes equally great pleasure in "good food" (Canto 16, lines 43, 48, p. 161). Krishna's "village of cowherds" (Canto 16, line 50, p. 161), as Matari calls his maternal home, elicits the image of unabashed consumption, quite at odds with the Brahminical ascetic traditions associated with forest groves. In fact, a grieving, enraged Kannaki, with her forest-like hair, embodies the unpredictability of the ostensibly wild woman whom kings fear, a veritable "outlaw," as Parthasarathy aptly describes her.[40] This outlaw characterization is all the more apt for its historical association with forests as beyond the law, a realm that rulers wished to control but often could not.

The fiery fate of a morally lapsed Maturai, when it actually occurs in Canto 22, about two-thirds of the way into the narrative, is not entirely surprising to the reader given the buildup: the clear injustice of an innocent Kovalan's execution, Kannaki's justified rage, and the accretive details about Maturai's worldly pursuits—courtesans adorned with "fragrant mullai blossoms" to attract "their lovers," alluring women "delicate as vines" of "the matavi plant," together producing a bouquet that "fills woods and groves" (Canto 14, lines 91–2, pp. 142–5). These pleasure groves, like the city's copious merchandise, have filled Kovalan with admiration and delight—perhaps suggestive, as well, of the appetitive, life-affirming spirit of Krishna's Vrindavan Forest. But as Kovalan leaves the heart of the city, "emerg[ing] from among the vines"—figuratively, its material resplendence—he "entered a grove/On the outskirts" to seek the counsel of the renowned ascetic Kavunti. The wooded ashram, given its own canto—number 15, "The Refuge"—clearly stands as a rebuke to the city's epicurean pursuits. The poet further underscores this contrast and explicitly foreshadows Maturai's conflagration, when, in the midst of describing the city's carnal excesses, he (if we accept Ilanko's authorship) marks the shift from "cold" to hot seasons with this portentous, arboreal double entendre: "The fierce heat/Spread everywhere as if the forest itself was on fire."[41] It is as if the twin possibilities of a forest, the one orthodox and the other transgressive, are at war. This is arguably why, when modern writers turned to classical forest imagery, their representations were similarly conflicted, as in Bankim's *Anandamath* (the subject of the next chapter).

This conflict, however, is due not only to the tension between perceived propriety and violation, but also to the inherently fuzzy contours of each of these cultural and material entities. The denotative senses of each characterization of the forest in the epic—whether as a sacred grove or as a pleasure garden—conflict with their connotative and contextual implications. The forest sometimes appears as a "wasteland" (when Kovalan and Kannaki cross through them on their journey) and sometimes as a "vast grove" inhabited by ascetics;[42] and, as we saw, the city's courtesans in a similarly "spacious grove" are adorned with *mullai* blossoms, the same flowers that, back in Pukar, Kovalan's courtesan lover Matavi wore.[43] *Mullai*, as mentioned, is one of the five *tinai*, or traditional landscapes of Tamil country—in this case representing the forest. Yet even this usage often leaks into the *kurinji* landscape, which designates forested hills. The interpretive meanings of these natural images arise from their layered narrative contexts as much as from their biotic attributes.

The reader recognizes, for instance, that however withering the seasonal sun of Maturai may be, it is the same heat that "burnt … the fertile mountain regions"—the forested hills whose products are tied to these seasonal turns and whose life is entwined with the city's. Even the sensation of burning, in other words, is relative, discomforting certain human and nonhuman animals, but enabling the florescence of Tamil country, a feature the poet mirrors with his profusion of detail. This detail invokes figurative heat as well, with couples engaged in "the joy of lovemaking in pleasure gardens" even as "spotted bees" are "hovering over them." The land and its inhabitants are clearly not burdened by the hot season, a fact that undercuts the poet's intermittent pronouncements of the city's sensual release being a symptom of its immorality—pronouncements that seem to pay lip service to societal and religious convention. An example of the latter is the sage Kavunti's caution to Kovalan that only "Those who observe celibacy" are untouched by "the torments of love" (Canto 14, lines 44, 48, p. 141). But as we have seen, the many images of pleasure and verdure that follow, which catch Kovalan's eye, are the very attributes that signify the pride of *Tamilakam*. The poet does not controvert Kavunti's point, but instead lets the rich imagery speak for itself, enabling both viewpoints to coexist. He presses this point by beginning the following canto, number 15 ("The Refuge"), in which Kovalan revisits Kavunti, by extolling the virtues of the Pandyan king, "the Kauriyan," as a man "renowned for his upright scepter/His cool, royal parasol and his heroic spear." As we presently discover, however, the Pandyan king is very far from "upright," his parasol suggestive of his unease in the bright sun and his ego-driven condemnation of Kovalan an insult to the *cadamba*-wood scepter bequeathed to him by his paternal predecessor. The indictment of the king that eventually follows this obligatory tribute, chiefly at the hands of Kannaki, ironizes the presumptive rectitude of Maturai's male potentate.[44]

The epic is therefore not a fable of religious immorality, as the conventional roles of revered sages might lead a reader to believe, but instead a tale that alerts us to the danger of narrowly determining what attributes inform a culture and its ecological inhabitance. This ecology, as I have said, is equal parts forest and city, which is why our protagonists are obliged to visit and revisit each space. Just as the fertile "mountain regions" depend on the hot season as much as on the cool, so do hill-dwelling Kuravas depend on both, for their livelihood is entwined with that of their urban compatriots. The poet for this reason celebrates the community by awarding them the vital role of witnessing a vindicated Kannaki as "she ascended/to Heaven" from their hilltop forest (Canto 25, lines 64–5, p. 221). As noted, they report this to the Chera king, Cenkuttuvan, in Muziris, where he has come to take charge after the Pandyan royal's death. The primacy ascribed to indigenous forest dwellers is an implicit rebuke to metropolitan arrogance. This indictment is arguably reflected in the text's very composition: it is a rare nonreligious epic, contains a female lead, does not mirror Sanskrit classics, and, more pertinently, incorporates features of oral folktales that are replete with forest motifs. Parthasarathy observes, for example, that the epic includes a story from the ancient Sanskrit *Panchatantra* collection of animal fables in order to elucidate Kovalan's "nobility."[45] The narrative's recourse to orality, or what Parthasarathy calls its oral "residue," recalls the similar conjunction of vernacular and mainstream currents in *Shakuntala*, which, as noted in the introduction, has its women characters use the more colloquial Prakrit rather than the comparatively more literary Sanskrit, a move that arguably threatens to undercut both the Kshatriya (warrior) king's status and, in a form of metacommentary, the Sanskrit play itself.[46] No wonder the forest, with its accommodation of vernacular, nonliterary traditions and transgressive possibilities, is the heartbeat of these narratives, offering a corrective—and, as noted, identifiably local—vitality to the city's tendency to pretension. It is also why many modern writers have viewed the forest as the ideal setting for their expressions of regional and national aspirations.

The Cilappatikaram, as I have said, elects to have the forest inhabitants of Tamil hill country, who call themselves "people of small huts" (Canto 24, line 18, p. 211) embody the arboreal vitality that symbolizes a restorative moral order. Ilanko signals their generosity of spirit—and so their significance as agents in a grand, unifying narrative of Tamil country—by telling us that they have no ulterior motives in their plea to the Chera king on her behalf. The poet magnifies their moral stature by underscoring their forest provenance. Immediately before their report and plea, the poem describes in detail the "Overflowing ... profusion of riches" the forest dwellers have offered the king, among them "white tusks," "whisks/Of deer hair, pots of honey, sticks/Of sandalwood, lumps of sindura, kohl/And orpiment, stalks of cardamom and pepper," "Clusters of areca nuts," as well as a variety of fruits, animals, and birds (Canto 25, lines 43–59, p. 220). The illustrious Chera warrior-king, who himself once ritually "tore apart the cadamba oak" (Canto 25, line 3, p. 219), is in this way explicitly allied with the forest dwellers and their products, which indeed his kingdom and its capital of Muziris rely on for their power. In fact, the Kuravas' eyewitness report opens the epic, setting the stage for Cattan (or Chattan), "poet of exquisite Tamil"—and, notably, a "grain dealer of Maturai" (Prologue, line 102, p. 22)—to summarize Kannaki's story (which is the anklet tale); for Ilanko Atikal to summarize its lesson that "even kings, if they break/The law, have their necks wrung by dharma (Prologue, lines 62–3, p. 21); and for Chattan to then beseech Ilanko to "write it yourself,/Since it relates to all three kings" (Prologue, lines 70–1, p. 21), that is, the kings of Maturai, Pukar, and Muziris. These interconnections are illustrated, too, when the hill people's "songs" mingle with the "hymns" of the Brahmin priests as they welcome the Chera king to their hill country (Canto 25, lines 30–1, p. 220).

The poem in this way asserts the combined importance of ascetic devotion (embodied by the Jain monk and traditional author Ilanko), commerce, and proper kingship, all of which, as mentioned, are intimately tied to practical and sacred attributes of forests. The forest dwellers mediate not only the vital commodities that undergird the king, but also his *dharmic* duty to honor, with a stone sculpture, a selfless woman whose associations with forest purity echo author Ilanko's renunciation of worldly things. Kannaki's "hair adorned with flowers" echoes, within a few lines, the forest folk's "hair adorned/With flowers dripping honey" (Prologue, lines 86, 97–8, p. 22), which in turn echoes the images of forest ascetics sprinkled throughout the poem, from Ilanko himself to those in "the vast grove/Near Arankam" (present-day Srirangam; Canto 11, lines 8–9, p. 110). These accretions inform Kannaki's later "transform[ation] ... into a force of nature," when, enraged by the king's awful "murder" of her innocent lover Kovalan, she sets fire to Maturai, "her dark hair" is "spread about her [Like a forest]"—a sight that instantly kills the Pandyan king (Canto 20, lines 105–6, p. 190). Kannaki thus, according to our translator Parthasarathy, embodies the forest as a site of "uncontrolled" life forms[47]—as well as, we should add, the forest's paradoxical association with virginal purity.

The Cilappatikaram thus straddles the land of the Tamils, which, though not a unified nation in the modern sense, is clearly distinguishable from regions further north. In Tamil country too, Maturai, figuratively purified so it can be reborn in the epic, would continue historically to sustain its religious centrality and continue to be a foil of sorts for the commercial port of Pukar, though now with the humility necessary in order for different urban centers to uphold regional integrity. In the third-century Tamil idyll *Maturaikanchi*, Maturai is described as being "located in the center of a realm which comprises all five of the landscapes or ecological zones into which the South Indian world was divided: mountains, seashore, jungle, desert, and riverine tracts. The "setting suggests that the city ... is symbolically, the center of the world."[48] Its walls are guarded by "Yavanas," "either Greek or Roman mercenaries" (and sometimes meaning any foreign presence), and the king's sacred symbol is a "tutelary tree."[49] When, in *The Cilappatikaram*, Kovalan is struck down by a sword for the presumed theft of the anklet, his blood "rushed in a tide over Mother Earth" and the "king's scepter turned crooked" (Canto 16, lines 224-7, p. 168)—tragically fulfilling the Pandyan Queen's premonition. The bent scepter, as Holly Baker Reynolds points out, symbolizes royal rule gone wrong.[50] The scepter's association with the city's tutelary tree, the *cadamba*, recalls Maturai's arboreal founding, as recorded in the medieval *sthala-purana*s, the traditional, mostly vernacular stories about sacred sites in Tamil country. The story goes that Indra, suffering "from the sin of having killed a Brahmin," comes to the holy Kadamba Forest, where he is immediately cleansed. Seeing that he owes his release from sin to "the presence of a Shiva *lingam*," Indra dedicates a shrine to Shiva that comprises a kadamba tree, a bathing pool, and "two sancta." In time, a city forms around this.[51] Later still, the city, and its surrounding area, produced the great tradition of Tamil Sangam literature (c. 300 BCE–300 CE), which includes *The Cilappatikaram*, the *Maturaikanchi*, and the *Pathupattu* collection of poems.[52] No wonder Kannaki ascends to heaven from the hill forest with Indra himself. And yet Maturai's claim to arboreal provenance is, in practical terms, no greater than that of Pukar.

Tamil Country and Twentieth-Century Tamil Nationalism

Since *The Cilappatikaram*'s rediscovery in the 1880s by U. V. Swaminatha Aiyer, who first read it as a palm leaf manuscript before publishing it in print, its iconicity has grown steadily.[53] The poem's print edition and revived influence is a prime example of how, in Ramaswamy's words, "print helped in the standardization and homogenization of Tamil, and granted it a visible continuity with an ancient remote past that it resurrected."[54] The modern politicization of Tamil devotion, Ramaswamy explains further, "has to be located within new regimes of imagination, institutional practices, and technologies of meaning production that were ushered in, however skewed, with colonialism and modernity." (Today's occasional preference for the word "Tamizh" rather than "Tamil" is an effort to better exhibit the word's actual pronunciation to non-Tamil speakers and an outgrowth of the modern Tamil-devotion movement.) Chief among these new forms of meaning-making was that "language [is] personal property," a notion that had been enabled by a combination of print culture, comparative philology, and romantic nationalism and that began to take hold among Tamil scholars in the nineteenth century, following the arrival of the printing press in the 1830s.[55] What is distinctive about modern Tamil devotion even in India—with the arguable exception of Bengali devotion—is the fusing of this modern conception of language as property to be owned, with its embodiment as a goddess demanding reverence, as Ramaswamy shows in *Passions of the Tongue*. It is this two-fold proprietary sensibility, I suggest, that helps explain the reimagining of classical-literary and precolonial forests—forests, that is, in their figurative, metaphysical, and functional senses—in the service of early national ideals, such as by poetically locating mythic forests in Tamil country, as mentioned in the previous chapter. Devotion to the Tamil language, in other words, includes devotion to Tamil landscapes, a feature that *The Cilappatikaram* illustrates and that adds to the epic's luster, as well as devotion to a pantheon of artifacts prized for Tamil-ness, particularly Sangam poetry and the poet Thiruvalluvar's great classic *Tirukkural*, or simply the *Kkural*.[56] The Tamil devotional movement's "apotheosis of the language as" both "mother and maiden" in the form of the goddess Tamilttay has had to contend carefully, explains Ramaswamy, with the pan-Indian (but largely northern-led) advocacy of the Mother India (Bharat Mata) figure. Where Bharat Mata embodies, for instance, Bengal's forests, Tamilttay is frequently depicted as "carrying a sheaf of cadjan [cocoa-palm] leaves in her left hand"[57] to represent her identity with age-old palm leaf books of classical Tamil poetry.[58] The leaves appear to do double duty by signifying both literature and distinctively regional trees. Tamil's literary as well as oral importance is clear from both the references to palm leaf writing and books in Tamil literature and to the preservation of *The Cilappatikaram* itself on such books.[59]

We can see in Tamilttay's iconography the coalescence of physical artifacts, sacrosanct literary texts, and landscape metonyms as the embodiment of regional identity. It is also clear, however, that despite her southern distinctiveness, Tamilttay seems to closely resemble Bharat Mata's northern heritage in her role as both "mother and maiden." Ramaswamy describes in this regard the intense politicization of Tamil in modern politics, such as the DMK (Dravida Munnetra Kazhagam) Party's championing of "a new pantheon of secular icons surrounding the presiding deity, Tamilttāy" (sometimes rendered as Tamil Thai), chief among whom are Thiruvalluvar, the great Tamil poet of the ancient period, and Kannaki, promoted as the "ideal Tamil woman." Tamilttay, Ramaswamy informs us, whose name literally means "Mother Tamil," is "the apotheosis of the language as goddess, queen, mother, and maiden."[60] Her embodiment of the mother tongue is, like the Mother India image, a recent construction, consciously politicized by rival parties in post-independence Tamil Nadu as a means of unifying their constituents.[61] Like nineteenth-century Bengal's maternal-national figure Bharat Mata, Tamilttay is visualized cartographically as Mother Tamil, fusing maternal language, in this case, with the modern map. In fact, Tamilttay is sometimes imagined as displacing Bharat Mata to represent all of India, echoing how Bengali nationalists construed pan-Indian nationalism through their regional lens.[62] The twentieth-century exponent of Tamil, G. Devaneyan, believed that Tamil Nadu had, in fact, spawned all of humanity and devoted his life to "rescuing … Tamil from the subjugation to Sanskrit."[63] These dual, and dueling, icons of nationhood have inevitably added to the political tensions between Tamil and Sanskrit-based Hindi. Like the depiction of King Cenkuttuvan in *The Cilappatikaram* as willing to battle northern rulers to preserve *Tamilakam*, Tamilttay has therefore been styled as a firm resistor of northern peoples and languages, a goddess armed with palm leaves to evoke a distinctly Tamil landscape.

The geographical location and primacy of Tamil country is never in doubt in Tamil literature, nor is its defense by heroic figures like Cenkuttuvan, who, as we saw, equates the sanctity of the Kaveri River with the Ganga. Some poets, especially of the Sangam era, go further by imaginatively transposing sacred northern landscapes, including forests, to the south, as mentioned in my introduction. This poetic strategy is not unique to Tamil authors, of course. In India (as elsewhere, generally speaking), forests in the public imagination and in literature are often conflations of their everyday use and their mythic-religious associations. We might look, for instance, to the classical Tamil narrative translated as "Forest of Pines," a retelling of an episode in which Shiva wanders in the Himalayan Daruvana (or Darukavana) Forest disguised as a mendicant, in part to test the faithfulness of the forest's sages. Scholars of Tamil observe how the narrative relocates this sacred northern forest in the south, despite there being "no Himalayan pines" in the region.[64] To account for the environmental ethos of such texts means that interpreters need to "foreground the poetics of creativity and the politics of imagination in place-making."[65] Formal poetics play a vital role in these evocations: both ancient and medieval Tamil poetry developed, and ascribed to, literary conventions that pertain as much to topographical contexts as to linguistic ones. David Shulman calls this a "patterned semiotic map of the Tamil country" that readers would have been familiar with. In the Sangam era, prominent genres like war poetry, or *puram*, and love poetry, or *akam*, variously evoked the five aforementioned poetic ecoscapes, or *tinai*, of Tamil country to convey particular moods that were conventionally associated with them.[66] The five primary toponyms, we may recall, are riverine plains (*marutam*), coastal areas (*neytal*), desert (*palai*), forest (*mullai*), and hills, which are often forested as well (*kurinji*).[67]

These *tinai* evoke a Tamil homeland without dwelling on Vedic traditions. Sangam love poems, like Ilanko's Sangam epic, are notable for their comparatively secular, nonreligious topics, such as the very human emotions elicited by lost love, grief, and separation. A later (eighth- or ninth-century CE) Tamil prose treatise, the *Grammar of Stolen Love*, that consolidates this poetics is notable for its rich descriptions of *tinai* flora, and although the work is couched in more explicitly religious language—it is said to be written by no less than Lord Shiva[68]—the arboreal details reflect a decidedly sensorial attentiveness. Some of these references are to trees and forests native to southern India, while others refer to those found throughout the subcontinent, as if these worldly poets want to signal the regional as well as subcontinental affiliations that are more common in outwardly religious narratives, like those recounting Shiva's Daruvana Forest episode. In one Sangam poem, for example, a couple meeting in a forest is aware of the myriad particular trees and their fragrances:

> All about … are sandalwood trees, champak trees, sweet mango trees, sweet jackfruit …
> Trees, breadfruit trees, asoka trees, caung trees, kino trees, and ipecacunaha trees. Gamboge, barbadoes pride, crocus-vines, copperleaf, delight-of-the-woods, jasmine, and Arabian jasmine combine their fragrances. Trumpetflowers, screwpine, and fresh laburnum burst open; water-thorn, purslane, and lemon flowers blossom.[69]

The lovers take in the southern jackfruit and as[h]oka trees, and the southern jasmine (*kurinji*) as well as the champak that grows throughout India.[70] Here, the ecology expressed in *kurinji*, or forested mountain, is unique to Tamil Nadu, with its *shola*, a now-endangered variety of tropical rainforest. Sangam poems conventionally use this motif to express the secret, premarital meetings of lovers. At the time of the poems' writing, and sometimes even now, the *kurinji* flower recalls romance, without any necessary resonance with, say, Krishna's Vrindavan dalliance, or even with Shiva's adventures in the Daruvana. As Ramanujan puts it in commenting on the Sangam poems he translates so wonderfully, "the actual objective landscapes of Tamil country become the interior landscape of Tamil poetry."[71]

For example, in the poem "What Her Girl-Friend Said," the female speaker accuses the "white moonlight" of "do[ing] him"—that is, her lover—"no good at all/ as he comes stealing/through the night in the forest," on whose floor flower petals fall.[72] The darkened forest floor is barely lit—and yet the flowers soften the man's step. Western readers often assume that the personal voice here points to autobiography, but as Ramanujan notes, poetic convention dictated that, for example, a speaker's greater range of motifs reflects both gender (a man's is wider) and class (the higher-class heroine usually having less experience and mobility in the world than her "girl-friend").[73] These are not meant to be "realistic": Sangam poets relied on these and other dramatic conventions, including those governing social roles and, as noted, topographical associations.[74] In Ramanujan's words, "The poet's language is not only Tamil; the landscapes, the personae, the appropriate moods, all become a language within a language."[75] Sangam poetic landscapes are a product, then, of the symbolism of particular geographies in which the poet is nurtured, with the aim of evoking a credibly sincere sentiment. These are sentiments that any reader today can recognize, even if the landscapes are unfamiliar. Another way to say this is that one's reading of these poetic landscapes generates a compensatory reality, in the way that Ramaswamy suggests. This is especially true of exilic or anachronous voices, where the displacement of peoples, whether geographic or cultural, is expressed as loss.

These multilayered expressions of local and countrywide affiliations through organic motifs, which simultaneously reflect poets' everyday world and mythopoetic traditions, inevitably invite contradictions. For instance, some Tamil writers of the early twentieth century—Ramaswamy notes in her study of the fabled lost land of Tamils[76]—sought to celebrate the fabled "lost land" of the Tamils, Lemuria, by drawing on both *tinai* conventions and modern science.[77] Ramaswamy observes that sustaining these in both the popular and literary imaginations, regardless of their apparent cognitive dissonance, was important for Tamils since colonialism's "disciplinary geography" had "generally disavowed native categories and spatialities as so many ... 'seas of treacle and seas of butter,' in the words of one Englishman."[78] To these syncretic practices, we must add the syncretism of the language itself. Shulman, among others, reminds us that multilingualism was, and is, a prominent feature of subcontinental cultures and literatures. It was likely "the linguistic norm in the south for most of the second millennium," so that the early-modern explosion of semantically dense texts in Tamil is a veritable "Republic of Syllables."[79] In this context, polyglossia is also frequently, and inevitably, religiously ecumenical. Shulman writes, for instance, of the "two new languages" that global maritime trade in southern India has ushered in "by the late seventeenth century," Arabic and Persian, resulting in polyglossic, cross-cultural works like *The Cirappuranam* by the seventeenth-century Tamil Muslim poet Umaruppulavar, who "exemplifies the mixed cultural world of the southern Tamil country."[80] The work is a biography of the Prophet Muhammad, an influential and popular genre long known across the Muslim world, but rendered in Tamil for the first time after the coastal Muslim community became acquainted with the genre.[81] Shankar Nair describes the text as being "in the language and literary conventions of a 'Hindu' Tamil Purana"—and hence also a *Mahatmya*, we could add—so that "the Arabian desert is reimagined as a lush South Indian jungle."[82] This illustrates how "in many cases, certain boundaries taken for granted today simply did not exist prior to the modern period." Nair reminds us that Hindu–Muslim intellectual and cultural exchanges were common in this medieval Mughal period, "spanning both elite and vernacular literary registers."[83]

Vasuda Narayanan shows us how Umaru worked with conventions of Tamil literature, including the *tinai* landscapes that evoke specific emotions, which readers in Tamil Nadu would have expected. The reimagined Arabian desert, for example, takes its cue from Kampan's classic ninth-century Tamil rendering of the *Ramayana*, which similarly transposed the landscapes of northern India described in Valmiki's Sanskrit Ramayana to Tamil Nadu.[84] Kampan describes distinctively southern Indian waters

> Carrying the pearls, gold, peacock feathers,
> beautiful white ivory from an elephant, aromatic akil wood,
> sandalwood, matchless in fragrance.[85]

Umaru's ostensibly Arabian streams similarly cross landscapes that are cast in the Tamil poetic tradition of *tinai*, so that they flow through the forested hills of the *kurinji* flower. These stand-in Tamil streams are "laden [with] rich bamboo" as well as with "fallen sandalwood, branches from the dark/*akil* tree," and "pearls from the broken elephant's horn, white ivory."[86] The effect, Narayanan observes, is to domesticate otherwise unfamiliar Arab topographies, making Tamil readers and listeners more receptive to the Islamic content and thereby accommodating "identities that were simultaneously Muslim and Tamil."[87]

Moral Kingship, Vernacular Traditions, and the State

These cross-pollinating, heterogeneous traditions of South Asia would, as I noted in the introduction, be challenged by British colonialism starting in the late 1700s, which crafted laws—most consequentially, land laws—technologies, and "scientific" pedagogies in order to "naturalize colonial state-space."[88] These functional, ostensibly rational devices, as Manu Goswami observes, pointedly condemned traditional customs and narratives, such as Puranic tales, as being obfuscating "fictions."[89] It was in these "fictions," however—epics, folktales, legends, and spiritual teachings, all articulated in both oral and literary traditions—that local communities could voice their cultural sensibilities and stake claims to their local lands. Ironically, as we know, it was in the context of the rationalist Enlightenment that many Europeans turned to their own folklore, particularly having to do with forests, as a means of shoring up an increasingly nation-minded identity, as mentioned in the introduction. This occurs most famously in eighteenth-century Germany, when the Grimm brothers' collections of folktales came to be valued as expressions of a deep-rooted national spirit tied to topography, particularly the Black Forest. True products of the Enlightenment, the Grimms exercised a systematic, "historical-philological" approach to their enterprise, which idealized ordinary people (*volk*) in the countryside in support of "a monarchical constitutional state."[90] This strand of romanticism would exert an influence on nineteenth-century Indian nationalists.

Yet long before the Grimms, a variety of Indian language communities produced vernacular—usually meaning, in this context, non-Sanskrit—narratives expressive of regional sensibilities that were rooted in particular topographies, yet still within the purview of a regional state—narratives in which the state had a vested interest, but not complete control. A rich vein of recent scholarship has demonstrated increasing use, in the postclassical, medieval period—broadly, the sixth through sixteenth centuries—of regional languages over Sanskrit, with Sheldon Pollock and Christian Lee Novetzke, for example, probing the intersection of state power and language use to see how courts jostled for control in a changeable environment.[91] Novetzke shows how in medieval Maharashtra, the famed *Lilacaritra*, a fourteenth-century biography of the *bhakti* spiritual leader Chakradhar, expresses—notably in the locally spoken Marathi language—"a [carefully] outlined geography that will later become a sacred geography," and one that traces the interconnections among forests, cities, military settlements, and other topographical and social features in the context of the Brahmin Yadava dynasty.[92] Because royal courts *were* the state, medieval kings were, like their classical counterparts, the patrons of official narratives, just as they are the frequent subjects of those works, from the *Lilacaritra* to Kampan's Tamil *Ramayana* and even Abu'l Fazl's sixteenth-century Persian *Akbarnama*. On the one hand, these and other works explore the quality and role of kingship in the public sphere, and the "dynamic relationship" between kingship and literary arts, in ways that echo classical models as a means of establishing their authoritative pedigree. On the other hand, medieval vernacular works voice a distinctive regional cultural identity.[93]

Popular folk narratives and the demotic cultures that produced them were similarly important to nineteenth-century writers as they variously tried to develop the idea of collective national identity, which, to be politically viable, would need to attract a wide readership. Fortuitously, most Indian communities had (and have) a ready-made figure whose popular stories exemplify a moral connection to the land, and this is the hero-king. An essential point of both elite and folk narratives is that the hero-king, not unlike historical kings, is required to demonstrate his prowess by hunting in a dangerous forest.[94] Although almost always male, the hero-king sought the aid of forests goddesses in this effort. And like these goddesses, the hero-king appealed to a wide variety of social groups. Shiva's many manifestations, or *Bhairavas*, include both indigenous deities, like Mailar (or Malhar), and Brahmin ones, in order to appeal to farmers and warriors alike. This is vital, since these groups were mutually interdependent. For instance, in village communities until the late nineteenth century, a "mystique of kingship" prevailed, which reflected long-standing societal structures on which both the king and his subjects had to rely. This is also why, according to C. S. Bayly, the Mughal emperor "continued to be a fount of authority" for ordinary people "throughout India" even after the British had muted his power in the later 1700s. As an authority who both depended on and encouraged long-held customs, the Mughal figurehead was essential to the symbolic capital—which is to say, the local trust—which assured the viability of British rule.[95] Mughal accounts describe the royals' favored hunting grounds as *shikargah*, or reserved hunting places, which allowed the king "to project … good governance."[96]

In most stories about moral kingship, the kingly forest hunt conveys multiple meanings. One obvious aim, as in the epics, is to "evoke the aesthetic mood of *virya* ('heroism')" to characterize a particular king, as Philip Lutgendorf reminds us.[97] In the *Mahabharata*, King Dushyanta and his troupe travel through "a wood like Indra's paradise," where he slaughters numerous tigers and other animals.[98] Another function of these literary hunts is to illustrate the forest's fecundity and, by extension, the king's natural ordination. The Mughals likewise took hunting seriously, seeing it as a way to model strong kingship. Mughal writers, for instance, describe the royals' favored hunting grounds as *shikargah*, which they sometimes developed into elaborate way stations.[99] In many folk legends, kings must not only hunt in the forest, but they must also draw on its power by coupling with a forest "huntress," usually a goddess, and often one who represents indigenous forest dwellers. In Sanskrit classics, the erotic forest also conveys to readers and listeners the aesthetic "mood" of *sringara*, one of the nine aesthetic *rasas*, or "flavors," used to elicit particular emotions in enculturated audiences. This eroticism may celebrate natural efflorescence, as by naming forest fruits, trees, flowers, and vines, which typically stand for the natural purity of the king's love interest. By association, he must learn to balance his warrior, Kshatriya ethos, which reflects the prerogatives of settled society, with an appreciation for nature and a measure of wildness. Wildness here, in the form of a suitably pious heroine, is not typically the sort associated with demons and outlaws, as we have seen, but instead a form of nature untainted by petty urban considerations, an unworldly retreat in which the hero-king can sharpen his moral discernment.

The duty of good warrior kings is to embody all these traits, which they are fully able to do only by spending time in the forest. Lutgendorf takes his cue from Michael R. Dove's finding that ancient human settlers set fire to jungles to clear more space and so came to see jungles as antagonistic, producing an "active zone of tension between society and nature."[100] Lutgendorf proposes that the two Sanskrit epics constitute a narrative ecosystem where inherent tensions between the warrior's social prerogative to kill when expedient and the warrior-king's duty to preserve life—in short, the epics' depictions of violence and nonviolence, and of the different duties of castes—are "balanced."[101] The transactions between moral ideals and realpolitik are, Lutgendorf observes, enacted through the countless retellings and rereadings of the stories.[102] I would add that it follows that these forest settings and their associated events also exemplify the tension between the two forms of justice described in Sanskrit jurisprudence, the *niti*, or good conduct, as well as *nyaya*, the operation of justice in everyday life.[103] Although kings in this warrior context are men, women as consorts sometimes remind their royal husbands that they have lapsed in this duty, as Draupadi does with Yudhishthira in the *Mahabharata*.[104] Significantly, Draupadi's scolding of Yudhishthira for not taking action against their Kaurava cousin Duryodhana, who is chiefly responsible for the Pandava brothers' exile, occurs in the forest. "There is," she tells Yudhishthira, "no *ksatriya* without *manyu* [justified anger]—this saying is well known in the world. In you, however, I now see a *ksatriya* who is (acts) like the opposite." She laments her husband's (and his brothers') un-kingly existence: the "rags" they wear and their rough forest provisions.[105]

The theme of a hero-king tested and ultimately strengthened by forest encounters, sorceresses, and principled women (or goddesses) recurs in various forms, as we will see, in modern fiction—such as, to name only those pre-independence works I discuss in subsequent chapters, in Bankim's *Anandamath* (1882), Premchand's *Godaan* (1936), and Bibhutibhushan Bandyopadhyay's *Aranyak* (1939). When these writers echo classical forest tropes in modern society, they do so with mixed results. At times, especially in works published in the first decades of the twentieth century, a classical trope helps sharpen the author's criticism of certain classes and their presumptions. Premchand's landowning character Rai Sahib, for instance, despite being personally decent, is unable to see the systemic injustices that sustain his class. Yet when Mehta, the young professor who dares to point out these injustices to Rai, encounters a young woman of the "jungle," he cannot help naturalizing her, thereby preserving the essential difference between his liberal-humanist outlook and her Adivasi one—the same difference we see echoed by Draupadi, an otherwise understandable model of female agency, when she echoes the conventional city view of jungle primitivity. In other cases, as in Bibhutibhushan's novel, the male first-person narrator's encounters with local women in the forest he is sent to manage causes him to reconsider his conventional ideas about class, leadership, and labor. While each of these three male writers glosses over the theme of moral leadership in his own way, they all seem to feel obliged to invoke a goddess figure—as maternal deity, or forest nymph, or folk rebel—whose arboreal sensibility echoes the trope's classical provenance and whose presence shapes the work's commentary on modern leadership. Bibhutibhushan's citified narrator likens certain Adivasi women to forest goddesses, exposing his unselfconsciously masculine treatment of that trope, for although he intends thereby to grant them the agency they are usually denied, he does so with the same kind of romantic vision as Premchand's Mehta. In enlisting classical tropes in their novels, however, modern writers tend to lose a sense of the broader "narrative ecosystem" that the epic affords, rendering themes of justice in less-nuanced, more two-dimensional ways.

I have been using "classical" fairly generically here, which may imply a primarily elite audience. But in fact, all of these narratives, including the *Mahabharata* and the *Ramayana* have been, and continue to be, immensely popular across classes and peoples, who distil them in their own distinctive ways. Throughout India to this day, in towns and villages, reenactments of key scenes from the *Ramayana*, called *Ramlilas*, reflect local flavors and preferences. Although performances retain the core story's main topographical references—Ayodhya, Lanka, Rameshvara—these are inflected with local signposts and sensibilities.[106] Popular songs, too, convey regional flavors, as well as gender and caste differences, such as in the Telugu *kolatam*, which Velcheru Narayana Rao informs us is a song-and-dance genre of "narrative songs … sung by [low-caste] women when they are working in the fields, grinding flour," with the women "mov[ing] in circles as they hit wooden sticks held in each other's hands." The songs depict a degree of freedom from the conventions of domesticity common to upper-caste women, sometimes even expressing the wish that the gods themselves would "work for us as slaves" and "[cook] in our kitchen." They also sing of the "fine *ponna* tree[s] all around," referring to the *Calophyllum inophyllum* tree, also called Indian laurel (among other names), which is native to southern India and used medicinally as well as for shipbuilding.[107] Likewise, in Tamil traditions of the epic, Ravana, the demon king of Lanka characterized in Valmiki's Sanskrit telling as the dastardly nemesis of Rama, is a heroic and worshipful being, and his sister Shurpanaka is the "ruling queen of the forest."[108] The sacred status of the core *Ramayana* story—which is also regarded by devotees as history—clearly does not prohibit its geographical or ecological recontextualization.

Stories from the *Mahabharata* are also retold across India, although because its characters are regarded as being relatively more historical—as *itihas*—than the idealized, mythic figures of the *Ramayana*, it offers up more typically human and morally complex characters.[109] As Meenakshi Mukherjee succinctly puts it, the astonishingly multilayered world presented in the *Mahabharata* revolves around "a fratricidal battle in a royal clan" and is filled with "tales of deceit, aberration, transgression, deviant morality, greed, treachery, and lust, thereby problematizing the relationship between statecraft and ethics."[110] Owing partly to the *Mahabharata*'s greater historical charge, and despite encompassing the entire subcontinent, from north to south and east to west (with references to the great pilgrimage points, or *tirthas*), the epic's setting is more clearly tied to northern India. "There is no doubt," Eck observes, "that the bards of the *Mahabharata* knew the plains of north India and the mountains of the Himalayas far better than they knew India south of the Narmada River."[111] This is, after all, a tale of the northern Kuru peoples, who flourished beginning around 1200 BCE, among whom are the five heroic Pandava brothers and their one hundred cousins, the Kauravas.[112]

Details of the Pandava brothers' exilic travels in the southern Dravida regions are scarce, in contrast to the detailed topographies they traverse in the northern half of the country, from Saurashtra in the west to the fabled Badrinath perched at 3,100 meters in the Himalayas.[113] It is nonetheless important to keep in mind that in these epics, the Dravida and Himalaya regions signify the country's geographic poles that bracket a large midsection in which, as Shulman advises, linguistic division is not the rule. Instead, a "complex dynamic of Sanskrit-in-Tamil and Tamil-in-Sanskrit" that characterized the medieval period echoes an earlier linguistic interpolation that is represented by the Vedic (thus originally northern) sage Agastya's iconic role as Tamil's first grammarian following his migration south. Kalidasa, in his narrative poem *Raghu-vamsa*, describes Agastya officiating at the inauguration of the Pandyan king of ancient Maturai, and he legendarily resided in his forest retreat in the Western Ghats.[114] The use of cardinal points to differentiate regions of ancient and medieval India in this way is a retrospective imposition on what was a dialectical cultural-linguistic relationship.[115] It follows that the landscapes described in period texts are frequently laden with values rooted in two or more different topographies, whose references can seem, to modern eyes, displaced or anachronistic, as I noted previously with regard to Ashok Banker's novel. In effect, as with the multiplicity of *Ramlilas* performed every year, each description of a landscape in the retelling of these core stories is a reinterpretation of not only topographical detail, but also of that environment's emotional and spiritual power. Devout listeners and viewers who experience such oral, imagistic, and theatrical renderings of the *Ramayana* in the form of *darshan*—which, as noted in the introduction, is an Indian viewer's sense of being in the auspicious or divine presence of a deity's image or of a great person—can thus bring the epic's landscapes to life. In this sense, India's many sacred epics and legends sustain a living vibrancy that the Western epic has long since abandoned.

These powerful, ancient, and complex narratives inevitably invite, as mentioned, a wide range of interpretations. The forest setting accommodates the male hero-king's violent, sometimes questionable acts, as well as his need for meditative renewal. The forest also offers comparatively greater latitude for female agency, as Sita's remonstrations illustrate. The hero's moral lapses are not always resolved, but, somewhat like Greek mythic heroes' tragic flaws, these lapses do not define the full person. It would seem that a degree of monstrous wildness does, in fact, cling to the hero-king even after his emergence from the forest. This is why, we recall, King Dushyanta's love interest (and later wife), Shakuntala, has been raised entirely in such a forest *ashrama* (hermitage) by her sage-like father and is therefore the corrective to her husband's urban hubris, which lasts for a significant period and is never downplayed. In some cases, an epic hero acts in even more outwardly cruel ways, as in the notorious *Mahabharata* episode when Krishna and Arjuna help the god Agni incinerate the Khandava Forest, whose human forest dwellers, figured as woodland animals, are either killed or must flee, leaving their deforested land to the usurping Aryans.[116] The epic does not, however, characterize this self-evidently brutal behavior as damnatory—just as his and his four brothers' pitiless pawning of their common wife Draupadi in the dice game does not void their heroic stature. In holding their spouses to account, Draupadi and Shakuntala, and—in her holding of the Pandyan king to account—Kannaki achieve a moral stature that, although it does not displace male-ordered rule, sustains a measure of feminine, and sometimes even transgressive, agency. This agency is, in fact, explicitly upheld in many tales, such as those told by Maithili women, in which the forest affords female characters the mobility and emotional expressivity normally denied to them.[117]

Kalidasa's works, with their rich arboreal motifs, such as the creeper vines that variously signal feminine beauty, floral efflorescence, and wildness, have influenced northern pre-independence writers' explorations of leadership. It is no accident that Bankim was enamored of the classical Sanskrit texts and epics: *Anandamath*'s dedication page even quotes from an epic poem by Kalidasa.[118] In *Shakuntala*, King Dushyanta's entry into the forest to hunt is paradigmatic of traditional Hindu kingship, the proper expression of which, as depicted in the *Mahabharata* and *Ramayana*, requires the king to manage the otherwise murky world of the forest by "cull[ing] the big game."[119] Yet these forests are relatively tame compared to other, more dangerous forests populated by demons, or *rakshasas*. On the one hand, the epic forest, like the Dandaka Forest in the *Ramayana*, is "wilderness" lorded over by creatures like the bloodthirsty Viradha, "as terrifying to all creatures as Death."[120] Yet the forest, as we have seen, harbors the "gardens" created by Brahmin sages in their tranquil *ashramas*. The forest is itself, in fact, frequently styled as a veritable garden:[121] Krishna's home forest of Vrindavan is often called this.[122] One of the names for this idealized forest, *goloka*, or realm of cows, reflects its pastoral provenance, emphasizing Krishna's playful resistance to societal and topographical boundaries.[123] In Tulsidas's great poetic narrative of Rama's life in Hindi, the *Ramacharitmanas*, Rama and Sita first meet in a *phulwari*, or flower garden; and garden groves, or *kunj*, are popular meeting places for Krishna and Radha and the *gopis*.[124]

Knowledge of the peaceful garden, then, is as important to the tutelage of Hindu leaders as is a familiarity with the frequent dangers of forests. If the forest is a garden, however, then knowledge itself is implicitly prone to dangerous processes, represented as moral lapses and meandering journeys. As in *The Cilappatikaram*, arboreal motifs in Sanskrit and popular narratives like that of Tulsidas invite a range of concurrent interpretations, depending on their contexts—a feature of the literary forest that early nationalist writers exploited, but usually to serve their particular objectives. Lutgendorf argues compellingly that in the epics, royal excursions into forests offer an imaginative means of "resolv[ing] the dialectical tension between" kingly rule and forest wilds (sometimes designated as jungles), not least because these Kshatriya rulers must contend with the charisma of their realm's Brahmin sages.[125] (Even once back in the polis, according to some Sanskrit texts, various representations of forests, such as a freshly-cut tree, might be used in ceremonies to reauthorize the king's rule.[126]) Vishnu, especially in his Krishna avatar, plays a "mediatory role" in the epics, attracting the devotion of both Kshatriya and Brahmin.

This overview of the literary valuing of forests in ancient and medieval works illustrates how forests have been viewed as alternately revitalizing and stifling, bountiful and austere. But by virtue of appearing in textual form, even positive representations of forests may ultimately elide oral folk traditions that voice alternative ways of inhabiting the forest, such as when indigenous groups understand their arboreal homes to include a wide range of "selves," human and nonhuman alike, as Kohn observes. The publication process of narrative elision and splicing means that particular ecologies and their inhabitants may be subsumed into the mythic domains of the authors and their patrons. An example of such elision is that of the indigenous Kol community, who occupy forests in the Kaimur Hills of the eastern Vindhya Range, in today's Uttar Pradesh, which in ancient times was part of the fabled Kashi Kingdom.[127] The Kols' own stories, like the *kolatam* songs of Telugu women fieldworkers, have been especially muffled by the modern privileging of print and containment, a reality that activists, folklorists, and writers are trying to change. The plight of the Kol illustrates the interdependence of story and landscape, with power over the latter translating to power over narratives about that landscape. When modern writers draw on such narratives, therefore, they inevitably imbibe many of the texts' typifying tendencies even as they revise others. Taken together, these examples show that while the forest's changeability makes it an ideal space for explorations of leadership and character, this very mutability in space and time also nurtures non-elite actors and ideas, which kings—that is, kings from cities outside the forest—must either subdue or accommodate.

Forests of Modern Myth: Legacies of British Colonialism

With the arrival of Europeans in the early modern period, however, opportunities for producing and sharing such eclectic outlooks began to diminish. Da Gama's arrival on the Malabar coast in 1498 was consequential on both economic—which is to say, material—and cultural grounds, with reverberations that would touch Bankim in nineteenth-century Bengal. To begin with, the Portuguese, recognizing the superiority of ships made of teak that grew along the southwestern coast, and which Indian boats had long used, were soon (following da Gama's bloody incursion) sectioning off teak plantations. The Portuguese king declared teak a royal commodity and prevented local traders from dealing in the wood, which the Europeans prized nearly as much as the black pepper that lured them there.[128] As I mentioned earlier in this chapter, Calicut had long been among the planet's "best centres for shipbuilding," with "good timber in great abundance surpassing the supply of timber in Italy." Forests inland from Calicut boasted a wide variety of trees for this purpose (in addition to the growing of spices), and the timber was conveyed to the city by an intricate river system.[129] In taking control of Malabar's timber growth, the Portuguese set in motion the systematizing of plantations that would become in British hands, beginning in the early 1800s, a central plank of their empire building.

An equally consequential result of Portuguese colonialism was the 1572 publication, by a Portuguese of noble but impecunious birth named Luís Vaz de Camões (who worked briefly for his country's Viceroy in Goa), of what was arguably the first modern national epic, *The Lusiads* (*Os Lusiades*). This narrative poem, which proved to be immensely popular and influential, providing tropes of eastern conquest to writers like Milton, mythifies da Gama, muting the mariner's violence to extol Portuguese virtue. Camões' time in Goa had introduced him to the Jewish physician and naturalist Garcia d'Orta, who within a few years of meeting Camões would publish, in Goa's Jesuit printing press, his famous compendium of Indian medicinal plants, *Colóquios dos simples e drogas he cousas medicinais da Índia*,[130] in which he extols the ameliorative properties of, among other products, pepper, nutmeg, and cloves.[131] Camões would later address an ode to d'Orta praising his botanical learning and drawing on the *Colloquia* for the final cantos of his epic.[132]

Just as Camões allegorizes da Gama's conquest of nature, so do British narratives in later centuries allegorize colonial rule.[133] Such national allegory was, as I discuss in Chapter 2, one narrative tool available to Indian nationalist writers, notably Bankim, in their search for methods of accommodating their sometimes competing ideals and conveying these to their urban compatriots. European accounts of the Portuguese arrival in Malabar were influential, in part, because they were widely disseminated through the relatively new technology of print, attracting a variety of European visitors. Among these was the aforementioned Francis Buchanan-Hamilton, who, traveling through Malabar in 1801, reported that he "passed through a stately forest, in which the pepper-vine grows spontaneously" amidst "some teak." He goes on to describe the rotational harvesting in the same forest of "plantain trees" and "cardamoms," always mindful as he does so of the market value of the spices. "We may," he concluded, "from the price given at this place, judge of the practicability of the [East India] Company's taking at a low rate of all the pepper in that country."[134] Buchanan-Hamilton's narrative, commissioned by Lord Wellesley, Governor General of India, bespeaks the chief interest of the East India Company, describing in detail how the timber and produce from these forests can increase the company's revenue.

Buchanan-Hamilton's use of "stately" to characterize Malabar forests echoes the descriptions of his contemporary compatriots in the north, who fawned over Himalayan pines. The emphasis in these accounts is on forest rather than on ostensibly unworthy jungle, for whereas European forests boasted "noble" oak, larch, and pine, the forests of acacia and banyan on the Indian plains were seen to be either inherently "wasteful" or troublingly mysterious. The notable exception was the Himalayan foothills, whose pine and birch could make European travelers think they had been "transported by some good genii from India to Europe," evoking nostalgia for "home."[135] In these alpine tracts, trees were seen not as inherently wasteful, but wasted, their unhampered growth taken as proof of local inhabitants' habitual inability to properly care for and use them. In the early 1800s, Scotsman James Baillie Fraser bemoaned the "waste of noble timber" as these "grand trees … flourish and decay!"[136] A tree's perceived usefulness was, on this view, inseparable from its perceived beauty. It was not, in other words, untended nature that must be prized, but nature nurtured by appropriately moral hands. Even woods designated as forests, then, were not perceived as inherently "stately": they required the kind of careful tending that Buchanan-Hamilton saw in Malabar and that (in European eyes) could imbue even Indian forests with nobility. This nineteenth-century rhetoric of improvement, which in Europe had underwritten a redemptive view of (elite) forest management, was prepped by earlier European tropes of tropical forests. Whereas Europe's temperate climes invited amelioration and served as touchstones for concepts like the sublime, India's tropicality was believed by Europeans to be lethally deceptive.[137]

These views of forests, screened through notions of racial and cultural hierarchies, buttressed colonialist presuppositions. Pine and teak became indexical signifiers of the kind of cultural and infrastructural "improvement" that the British claimed they would bring to India.[138] The particularly consequential notion of Indian "waste" forests in need of redemption, for example, was an idea that had been first applied in Europe. Romantics in England had been urging just such improvement of their own landscapes for decades. The agriculturalist Arthur Young exhorted his compatriots to redeem "the waste lands of the kingdom" by "cover[ing] them with turnips, corn and clover, instead of ling, whims and fern."[139] These perceptions of Indian woodland as alternately noble and wasteful resulted in part from the combination of utilitarian and romantic ideals that predominated among the British in the early 1800s. Systematic management of India's forests, which continues to shape the Indian state's approach today, was enabled by the actions of Governor General of India James Ramsay, Earl of Dalhousie, who during his eight years in India (1848–56) established "the administrative and legal structures that became the Indian Forest Department and the model of forestry for the empire" to bring order to unregulated deforestation resulting from *laissez faire* policies.[140] A linchpin of this development was Dalhousie's aggressive annexations of northern Indian lands for the colonial state. A self-described utilitarian and imperialist, he viewed India's forests as purely commercial resources to facilitate state operations.[141] He initiated, "for the first time in India, a centrally organized and policed forest system" under the tutelage of German foresters like Dietrich Brandis and Berthold Ribbentropp, a development that would lead to the momentous 1865 Forest Act.[142]

Ironically, it was Dalhousie's annexation of Oudh, an important princely state in the region of Awadh (whence the anglicized Oudh), just three weeks before his departure that helped stoke the resentment among Indians that would erupt in the 1857–8 war, which the British later dubbed the Great Mutiny and which independent India calls First War of Independence.[143] With Britain's eventual victory and the Crown's takeover of the East India Company came "a far more centralized regime" that had "profound implications for the [country's] environment."[144] Ironically, the conflict led directly to more widespread deforestation and elicited vigorous countermeasures as officials became aware of the war's deleterious effects on their colonial practices.[145] Perhaps the most lasting result of Dalhousie's measures and the aftermath of the war was the drafting of the aforementioned Forest Act, which set out the legal definitions of types of forest and then outlined people's rights to these forests.[146] A number of refinements to this original document followed in subsequent decades and continued after India's independence, with the latest iteration being the controversial 2006 Forest Act, whose official lengthy title reflects its colonial inheritance: the Scheduled Tribes and Other Traditional Forest Dwellers (Recognition of Forest Rights) Act.[147]

A further, more lasting irony of British forestry was that Brandis, dubbed the Inspector General of Forests and a man who shared Dalhousie's utilitarian outlook,[148] would unwittingly help facilitate the creation of India's geographically "natural" borders. It was these surveyed borders that, beginning in the same time period, helped inspire writers like Bankim and, a bit later, painters like Abanindranath Tagore (nephew of Rabindranath) to perceive India in its modern cartographic form.[149] Brandis saw the practical value of maintaining local forest rights in India, recognizing that those who had long lived in forests knew best how to manage them; this view was directly at odds with his own belief that only state control of forestland had the means to ensure a judicious allotment of lands, including forest reserves.[150] As Ramachandra Guha observes, "In Brandis's larger vision for Indian forestry, a network of state reserves would run parallel to a network of village forests."[151] However, the state, in Brandis's view, was a beneficent steward and the only entity equipped to oversee a natural environment integrated with modern commerce, in which forests were the vital part of a network of everything from rivers to fields and gardens—the "household of nature."[152] According to this view, the state should control all access to forests, which were still being carefully recorded and mapped, a process that had begun in 1802 with the vast, ultimately successful "Great (trigonometric) Survey" of the subcontinent. This resulted in distinct forest boundaries that come to be seen as natural in the same way that India's international boundaries came to be—and are still—seen.[153] Yet it was Brandis, whose approach was pragmatic rather than ideological, who insisted on establishing "protected," "reserved," and "village" forests as a means of addressing local, including "tribal," rights while maintaining state control.[154] His view inevitably clashed with that of hardliners like Lord Baden-Powell, who advocated absolute state control of forests, leading to a watering down of local forest jurisdiction policies detailed in the 1878 Forest Act.[155]

Ironically, too, this Act's enforcement of state restrictions on village and indigenous foresters fomented anti-colonial resistance, which often dovetailed with nationalist activities.[156] The Forestry Department's energetic planting of commercially viable trees, such as teak in the south and sal and pine in the north, often crowded out species that were vital to local livelihood and culture, such as the sacred mahua tree, a source of nutrition, medicine, and alcohol for forest dwellers, but which the state found "less valuable."[157] The state's exclusionary role was clearly not just about commerce, but also about political culture.[158] Indigenous and peasant groups who resisted the new forest regulations became, according to state logic, "criminals."[159] Gadgil and Guha describe an instance of resistance in the Himalayan foothill region of Kumaon, when, in 1915, a local temple priest urged his fellow villagers to ignite a pine forest, as they had done in times past in order to "get rid of both the dry grass and the insects it harboured." Prosecution proved impossible since practically every person in the region refused to cooperate with state agents.[160] In many cases, indigenous communities had no choice but to sidestep colonial laws, as the Badaga peoples of the Nilgiri Hills in southern India did. Having been displaced by eucalyptus and other plantations introduced by the British, they were obliged to log trees in the new enclosures, which were officially off-limits, simply to survive.[161]

These examples illustrate how nineteenth-century colonial forestry, for all its self-avowed scientism, was shot through with its own mythic ideas and civilizational hierarchies. The difference between the colonial approach to forests and the approaches that preceded it, such as that of the Mughals, is the ratcheting up of systematization and scale, which were enabled partly by technological developments (including in weaponry), globalized trade, and the exploitation of local hierarchies. Modern colonial forestry reshaped the land, while also generating ideologies couched in mythifying rhetoric, on display in administrative records, advertising, and European literature,[162] to undergird this enterprise. These ideas partially conditioned the views of Indian writers of the period, as I have argued. But these writers also took note of the physical transformation of their lands and cities by the British, prompting their search for places, especially forests, that embodied their own ideals and that could serve as imaginative alternatives—even resistance—to colonial rule. These arboreal alternatives were often, in these writers' hands, a mix of idealized and historicized representations that they hoped would accommodate a modern Indian nationalism.

2

Colonial History, Home Forests, and Mother India in Bankim's *Anandamath*

In 1882, Bankimchandra Chattopadhyay—whom I refer to as Bankim, for reasons explained in the Introduction—published what is arguably the first successful novel in modern India, *Anandamath*.[1] Abandoning his attempts at English-language novels, Bankim hit upon a combination of stylistic and formal innovations that saw the novel become part of a popular idiom of nationalism, which by this period was very much in the air.[2] A number of scholars have demonstrated how Bankim's skillful interweaving of mythic and historical, and colloquial and "high," Sanskritized Bengali, produced a new style of communicating with his nineteenth-century readers in a manner that was at once modern (which at the time meant European) and local.[3] This, in Priya Joshi's estimation, "created imaginary pasts in which his characters portrayed a range of values desirable in the contemporary world." *Anandamath* manages to nimbly conjoin historical and re-imagined pasts to provide "a version of the past … that was usable in the present."[4] By "desirable," Joshi implicitly means the wishes of Calcutta's *bhadralok*, or urban Hindu elite, who were Bankim's readers. This is a relatively small group on which to confer a generalized Indian motivation for *Anandamath*'s region-specific— that is, Bengali—ethos. This specificity includes the Bengal forests in which Bankim sets his story, and which are blessed and sanctified by the patron goddess of the land.

How, then, did the novel's distinctive Bengali language and ethos produce images and words that spread across the subcontinent, in tandem with the growth of nationalism? In many ways, as we will see, the text exhibits a tension between its regional and national visions of nationhood, a tension that in modern Indian history has tended to parallel the tension between India's many vernacular literary cultures and its English literatures, which Tabish Khair has respectively labeled "Babu" and "Coolie" fictions.[5] Bankim eschewed English, in which he had produced his first fiction, partly because Bengali understandably served to evoke more suggestively and credibly his urban milieu's cultural sensibilities and partly because this supplied a sense of "Indianness" that English could not. But an idea of Indianness refracted purely through a Bengali *bhadralok* sensibility could not easily appeal to a pan-Indian nationalist movement, and the novel, despite classical Sanskrit allusions that were widely known, was indeed limited by its regional scope—except for the song "*Bande Mataram*" (the Bengali transliteration of "Vande Mataram," "Hail to Thee, Mother"), whose lyrics appear early in the book and, when set to music some years after its publication, would become a popular nationalist anthem. More significant for the novel's context, as I show, is the relationship between its forest setting and the representation of Mother India (though Bankim did not actually use this term).[6] This relationship is significant because the forest is taken to represent both an essential Bengaliness and an essential Indianness. But an Indian—which in Bankim's view meant Hindu—authenticity represented by forests invites contradictions on several levels. These may be heuristic, such as the inherent contradiction of Bankim's attempt to reconcile modern history and mythic traditions, resulting in a productive horizon of future possibilities for the book's readers. Another contradiction arises from the novel's particularizing as well as universalizing of the forest setting, with the latter described both figuratively and factually. Perhaps the most noteworthy contradiction stems from the novel's essentializing of Indianness as Brahminical, which is reflected in select images of the classical forest and espoused by the ascetic rebels, but which conspicuously excludes Muslims—overlooking both India's and the forest's syncretic realities. This is an especially significant move given that the depiction of Muslims in the novel adversely influenced, and continues to influence, relationships between Hindus and Muslims in India today.[7]

Before examining how these threads of influence, innovation, and motivation weave through the novel and its forest-world, it will be helpful to summarize the story. Bankim's story unfolds against the backdrop of the devastating Bengal famine of 1770–1, which British mismanagement had exacerbated, and which elicited a rebellion led by both Hindu and Muslim ascetics. A young married couple, Kalyani and Mahendra, a now-impoverished landowner, and their infant daughter are forced, like everyone else in their rural village, to migrate in search of food. Separated from her husband along the way, Kalyani and her child are seized by rapacious, hungry bandits, who carry them into a thick and forbidding jungle—or is it an enchanting forest? Bankim, as we will see, intentionally employs both words. Kalyani is able to slip away with her child, and, having fainted at the side of a river, is discovered by a *santan*, the name the author uses for the Hindu ascetics, or *sannyasis*, who live in the forest and have taken up arms against the British. The forest sanctuary, or abbey—*math* in Sanskrit, whence the book's title "Abbey of Bliss" (*ananda*) serves these rebel monks in both spiritual and practical ways. A *santan* named Jiban, who is married to Shanti, entrusts Kalyani and her daughter to the nurturing care of his sister. Meanwhile, Mahendra comes across other members of this cohort, who take him to their forest sanctuary, where he is given a tour of their underground temple and an audience with their leader, Satyananda. It is here we first encounter the song *Bande Mataram*, rhapsodically sung by one of the monks. Despite being reunited with his family, Mahendra is so impressed with the rebel monks that he starts to consider joining their fold (which he does, later becoming a *santan* leader). In this pivotal episode, we learn about their righteous mission to battle the East India Company and about their devotion to the Goddess Kali, who is described in language suffused with images of a womb-like earth.[8] The rebel ranks grow, with Shanti disguising herself as a man to spy for the *santans*. The latter eventually confront the company army (aided by the regional Muslim king), and battles ensue. Despite facing the more-powerful weaponry of the British, suffering many casualties, and having their leader captured, the *santans* manage to snatch a victory, which inspires them. The novel concludes with the main characters—Shanti and Jiban, Kalyani and the leader Satyananda—in the presence of the Mother Goddess's forest temple, where, listening to the sage counsel of the deity-like Healer, they renew their dedication to a better future for their country.

Bankim thus projects onto a historical setting—the famine that was still, in the author's lifetime, a traumatic generational memory—concepts of patriotism, Hindu devotion, and the primacy of homeland. Classical forest images in *Anandamath* serve this purpose by helping to create an ethos of naturalized morality. But because Bankim was steeped in European literature, he also relies on that indispensable quotient of modernity, the idea of primitivism. For European romantic nationalists, as I noted in the Introduction, the forest primeval may have been wild, but it was also for that reason uncontaminated, a fertile place of pure racial origins and a realm of enchantment that must be appreciated anew. Hence the vogue among German romantics to see the Black Forest as the provenance of national essence. Bankim goes one up on his German counterparts by pointing out that India's inheritance of forest lore is far older than Europe's. "It is impossible," Bankim declares in a famous satirical work, "for one whose ancestors were only the other day barbarians roaming the forests of Germany to accept the realities of India's glorious past."[9] The clear implication is that Europe's relatively recent emergence from a primitive state means that its civilization pales in comparison to India's. This may not seem controversial, since European romantics viewed ancient India as the "cradle" of all civilization, but Bankim's narrative removes from European hands the presumption to be the sole interpreters of this past and speak on behalf of all Indians. Bankim does not see Europeans as the inheritors of this past, but only its expedient witnesses since they lack that necessary quotient, *dharmic* devotion. For Bankim, consequently, it stands to reason that India's—which is to say, Bengal's—forests host all of the elements required of a true Indian nation: divine intervention, which in the novel often takes the form of a sagacious disembodied voice speaking to a character;[10] principled actions based on such counsel;[11] and the Comtean positivism that he advocated and that was in vogue among Bengali intellectuals of his time because it was seen to accommodate scientific progress as well as a Brahminical social order.[12]

One indispensable feature of the modern forest for Bankim, which happily combines romantic and Vedic requirements, is that it is an ideal domain for fellowship. The Grimm brothers had adduced that the German forest was the necessary site for a national fable of fraternal bonding: the cementing of a spiritual tie to the woods and to one's confreres with the aim of reviving cultural unity.[13] This fraternity would most effectively be achieved by the righteous outlaw, who with his (always male) band inhabits a forest that exists, like the bandits themselves, on what the corrupting society deems to be its fringes. The very presence of the outlaw band therefore "challenges the law on its own terms, exposing its inherent contradictions."[14] Bankim's rebel protagonists, the patriotic Hindu ascetics (*santans*) who call themselves "children" of Mother India, do exactly this by battling the colonial lawgivers, the British, for future—not current—control of the wider realm (since British rule was seen as a necessary step in the process of forging the nation and since this rule was, of course, in force when Bankim wrote). The *santans*' real foes are Muslims, the supposed outsiders whom British colonialist historians described as intellectually "inferior" to Aryan Hindus, who had prevented the wider world from learning the glories of ancient Sanskrit law texts, such as the *Laws of Manu*. William Jones, its first English translator, called it one of the most "celebrated" works ever written and that it was his "good fortune to restore" it to the world.[15]

The influence of Jones's translations, including Kalidasa's *Shakuntala*, on Indian nationalists is, as I noted in the Introduction, part of the ironic circuit of European ideas linking back to Sanskrit source materials. Jones's interpretations, including his passing conjectures about ethnic and cultural links between ancient Aryans and Europeans (such as the suggestion that Manu was the Greek Minos),[16] fired the imagination of both Hindu nationalists and European romantics, including the Grimms, who, as Jack Zipes puts it, sought "to preserve the *pure* sources of modern German literature." [17] The philological revolution that Jones helped launch, and that sought to preserve the supposedly pure bases of Hindu—actually, Brahminical—society, provides one strand of influence on Bankim's thinking about Bengali and thus Indian identity (since in his mind the essence of Bengal equated to that of India as a whole). It is this strand of influence that the rebel monks in *Anandamath* display. The forest evokes the notion of essential purity, which European romantics viewed as part of an Aryan golden age, a view Bankim's *santans* similarly reflect. But Bankim goes further than European romantics by having his *santans* seek to revive features of that past age in the present, with an eye to a future emancipation from foreign rule.

Among the European literary works that shaped the Bengal intelligentsia's ideas about nation-making were, besides those of the romantic movement,[18] Shakespeare's plays, Milton's *Paradise Lost*, and, as noted in the preceding chapter, the translation from the Portuguese of Luís Vaz de Camões 1572 epic about Vasco da Gama, *The Lusiads* (*Os Lusíadas*). The Portuguese poet had managed to reclaim the epic form for modern nationhood by preserving a past (an idealized one) while also inaugurating a new, unscripted future in which that nationhood could imaginatively fulfill its potential—a strategy of Camões that earned Milton's admiration. In a characteristically colonialist move, Camões depicts da Gama's voyage as at once historically original and, through the retrospective ploy of prophesy, an event that transcends history by entering into myth.[19] As Shankar Raman puts it, allegory was in this way used "to legitimate colonial history."[20] It is almost certain that Bankim—given his deep knowledge of European writers, *The Lusiads*' publication in colonial Goa, and the epic's renown—knew of *The Lusiads*. Like Camões, Bankim understood that if he were to succeed in mythifying his subject matter (which both their works do quite effectively), his characters would have to contend with both natural and supernatural forces and would have to be aided in their actions by supernatural intervention. Again like Camões, Bankim does this in *Anandamath* through varieties of classical rhetoric and symbolism.

Both writers run into irresolvable contradictions with this strategy, though it leads to very different outcomes. Camões' poem exhibits a "tension" between the mythically selfless da Gama who heroically "conquers nature" to reach Calicut, and who reassures the Samudri Raja that the Portuguese intend peaceful trade, and the historical da Gama, who, as Camões well knew, would soon belie this supposed virtue.[21] Bankim's own rhetorical contradiction is evident in wishing for an idealized, unadulterated form of Krishna worship, via the Mother India Goddess, while at the same time wanting this worship to transcend religious differences—a contradiction that haunts his portrayal of Muslims in the novel. The ascetic rebels in *Anandamath* embody a similar contradiction, for they are at once violent and reposed. It is possible, in fact, that Bankim found the combination of romanticism, history, and national mythmaking irresistible precisely because he himself was conflicted. He admired "western historical writings" because "he recognized" that a "memory of past glory ... was an essential component of a nation's greatness." He excitedly read Scott's *Waverley* novels and other historical romances and knew his *Paradise Lost* (though he complained of Milton's unconvincing characters).[22] At the same time, he understood the self-serving nature of these subjective histories, and, though his writings are justly famous for brilliantly satirizing both colonial policies and the Indian *babus* who imitated English mannerisms, he earned his living, after all, as a bureaucrat in this establishment and believed that science and infrastructure were as important for a modern nation as an intimate knowledge of Indian literatures and history.[23]

The often conflicting tendencies in Bankim had several Indian precursors. Take, for instance, Tarinicharan Chattopadhyay's nationalist *The History of India*, first published in 1858 (in Bengali), which Partha Chatterjee calls "probably the most influential textbook read in Bengali schools in the second half of the nineteenth century."[24] Chatterjee cites the book as a prominent precursor of the "Hindu-extremist political rhetoric current in postcolonial India," a rhetoric that extols an idealized Bharatvarshya, the putative "Land of Bharat," the legendary king of northern India who appears in the *Mahabharata*. My interest is in Tarinicharan's use of both forest and jungle, unremarked by Chatterjee, to distinguish and contextualize his ideological points. Tarinicharan states (in Chatterjee's English translation), "In very ancient times, there lived in India two very distinct communities," whose "descendants are" the Hindus—those who "resembled us in height and other aspects of physical appearance" and a "short, dark and extremely uncivilized" group of "primitive [jangla *[sic]*, 'of the bush'] jati" ("*jati*" generally meaning caste). The Hindus, Chattopadhyay continues, eventually moved to the south, a region "covered by forests and inhabited by non-Hindu and uncivilized *jati*. Ramacandra was the first to hoist the Hindu flag in that part of India."[25] Chatterjee shows how Tarinicharan's influential history was part of a nationalist project of historiography, informed by religious symbolism, that directly influenced the rhetoric of today's brand of Hindu conservatism. Chatterjee also observes, however, that this was one among several other treatments of national history at the time, including what he sees as Bankim's more fluid, less monolithic approach. Tarinicharan's conservative version, which infuses its eminently "modern, rationalist, and historicist" outlook with sacred symbolism, and which was part of a larger movement, happened to win out.[26] Bankim's history is more fluid because while it nods to symbols of a unified national identity, such as Mother India, it is clearly rooted in Bengali cultural and geographical identity, as both his contemporary and current readers have recognized. *Anandamath* is thus indexical of the author's nineteenth-century social and environmental milieu, which lends the story some of its credibility.

Yet *Anandamath* is also, like Tarinicharan's *History of India*, deeply imbued with particular religious motifs that have had lasting and deleterious effects. Like Tarinicharan's *History of India*, Bankim wishes to have his Bengali rebels, specifically, be representative of all Indians. The aforementioned projection of regional topographies onto far distant ones by classical authors like Valmiki and Ilanko is also a tendency many modern nationalist texts display, as indicated by Tarinicharan's denigration of *"jangla"* peoples in the north and "[uncivilized] non-Hindu[s]" in the south, in contrast to the author's own upper-caste community. This community was Bengali cosmopolitan, an outlook that further complicates the picture, since so-called *jangla*— or, in common usage, *jungli*[27]—peoples inhabit Bengal's own forests, not just those far away. The irony is that like this term itself, which says more about those who use it than about the people it describes, the physical proximity of jungles to cities points to their ecological interdependence, a relationship that, as we will see, fascinated twentieth-century Bengali novelists. These ideological convolutions turn indices into icons, to use another of Peirce's terms, meaning signs that reflect the same qualities as the objects they represent. An icon is a value-laden object, such as a painting, that makes the viewer blind to the "distinction of the real and the copy."[28] A particular forest, whether it appears in epic or historical form (or both, since the genres are often conflated), can thus become iconic, feeding into an increasingly inflexible political– religious project. The frequent result of these novelistic predilections for both indexical and iconic forests is a dissonant representation of the natural environment, a vision that is at once richly dialogical and perilously narrow.

Reality and Realism

Bankim had at his disposal, then, a range of strategies and motifs from which to select the ones that he felt were best suited to the evocation of essential regional and national affiliations. These strategies and motifs were the tools he needed to depict an unspoiled inheritance, and he saw that the forest was the perfect space, at once analogical and physical, in which to combine Hindu revivalist and modern iconography. As he wrote shortly after the *Anandamath*'s publication, "The passionate yearnings of the heart for the Ideal in beauty, in power, and in purity, must find an expression in the world of the Real."[29] By "real," Bankim means the natural world (*prakriti*) and its "force," feminized as *shakti*, both of which derive from Hindu belief systems.[30] Reality, in other words, assimilates to the neo-Hindu outlook espoused by Bankim, in which schema it is natural that the patriotic *santan* ascetics, and no one else, should be the forest's guardians. Indigenous forest dwellers, Muslims, and even the British, with their ostensibly necessary but terminal rule, are all intruders onto a sacrosanct domain. For Bankim, a balanced *prakriti* is needed in order to ameliorate the modern, instrumental attitude to nature.[31] Tagore, however, saw no such struggle since he believed a subject's inner life, if pure, would always supersede outward temptation.[32] Although I find Dipesh Chakrabarty's explication of these ideas about interior and exterior *prakriti* to be somewhat nebulous—partly because this ancient concept has always been interpreted in a variety of ways[33] and partly because "spirituality" is notoriously hard to define—he helpfully identifies how, in these writers' hands, *darshan* conveys the suggestive richness of a widespread approach to reality in the lives of modern Indian subjects, while also exposing the limitations of Western notions of mimesis. As Rashmi Bhatnagar and Rajender Kaur observe, works by nineteenth-century Indian novelists therefore compel their readers to consider "how we know objective realities" in a colonial setting "and how we constitute the social world and subjective interiority of characters."[34]

This assortment of possible approaches to fiction writing was a resource all the more important to the situation India's first novelists faced since they could not take available European mimetic forms for granted in the way that, for instance, French realist novelists of the period or Scott's earlier historical romances could do. But Indian writers could draw on a rich subcontinental repertoire of narrative traditions, and not only those of classical Sanskrit or Tamil. European realism and historical romance were not, in any case, the only models on offer in nationalist writers' efforts to accommodate a modern present.[35] For example, although we hear an echo of *Shakuntala*'s setting and story in the hugely popular and influential Hindi novel *Chandrakanta*, by Devaki Nandan Khatri, the author also uses Urdu words that had not until then been mixed with Hindi in popular narrative form.[36] First serialized in 1888 before being published in a single volume, Khatri drew on classical Sanskrit motifs, Bankim's works, and the Urdu romance genre of *dastan*. His aim was, indeed, to render the latter genre in the form of a modern novel.[37] Chandrakanta, the protagonist, whose love for the prince Virendra Singh is obstructed in various ways, is introduced to us much as Shakuntala is, a beautiful woman enjoying with her close female companions a variety of trees and flowers. Although not in a forest, Chandrakanta is, like Shakuntala, associated with fragrant and beautiful creepers (*lata*, *bela*), jasmine (*juhi*), and rose (*gulab*) as well as fruitful trees (such as mango). Her face is, in classical convention, compared to a lotus (*kamal*). From the *dastan* romance tradition Khatri borrows, among other devices, the *tilism*, a magical world that certain characters can create to entrap others (whence the word "talisman").[38] Khatri's liberal use of Urdu words and storytelling traditions and his use of motifs from Sanskrit romance settings, especially jasmine creepers, offer a snapshot of the ways in which nineteenth-century novelists turned to an eclectic range of sources as a means of reflecting their regional, and Indian, time and place.

The novel form was ideal for such expression for several reasons. In her study of how nineteenth-century Urdu novels contributed to the genre's development in India, Jennifer Dubrow illustrates how "the novel ... arose in colonial India because of its ability to hold divergent points of view and to subtly critique the British government."[39] It did so, in part, by mixing both demotic and formal styles, whether in English or Hindi, Tamil or Telugu, Bengali or Odia. Dubrow could also have pointed to the inherent syncretism of Urdu, having been formed from a mix of languages, as the great nineteenth-century Urdu poet Ghalib observed.[40] Some of the available demotic styles and forms, which Meenakshi Mukherjee, Rumina Sethi, A. R. Vekantachalapathy, and others have discussed, include those conventionally associated with oral traditions, such as in Raja Rao's evocation, in his classic 1938 novel *Kanthapura*, of *sthala-puranas*, the palimpsestic local legends that tie people to land, usually at the village level.[41] Such legends also appear in folk songs, another stylistic device novelists employed in attempting to give their texts a sense of local authenticity. Early fictional experiments of this kind were not too successful, in part because, as Priya Joshi suggests, the European-realist mode in which novelists felt obliged to frame their text jarred with these local genres and worldviews.[42] In nineteenth-century Europe, as Mukherjee has observed in her pioneering study *Realism and Reality*, the realist mode assumed that individual characters could roam and grow at will, open to possibilities being created by industrialization. This became increasingly unavailable to Indians restricted at every turn by the colonial system, which treated mobility with suspicion.[43] This fact, together with the strictures of a "tradition-bound society" that frowned on protagonists who broke sacrosanct rules,[44] conspired to limit the free and unmonitored movements of the Indian middle classes. Writers had to find ways, then, as they started to do with Bankim's *Anandamath* and other novels,[45] to accommodate dissimilar views and narrative modes, along with colonial critique. It is not coincident to these strategies that Bankim's novel centers around a forest.

History and Myth in *Anandamath*'s Vision of Nation

It seems likely that one reason Camões, in *The Lusiads*, chose to focus on an individual like da Gama for poetic and patriotic inspiration was because the author felt a connection to the mariner as a result of their shared knowledge of Portuguese India. In *Anandamath*, however, Bankim chooses not to turn to a like historical individual for inspiration. In what ways, then, does Bankim draw on historical events for his nationalist novel? More specifically, what was it about the 1769–70 calamity that motivated Bankim to set his novel at that time and in forests that are, as mentioned in my opening chapter, at once ecologically credible and, in terms of the sacred national space he invokes, suitably epic? It is important to address these questions about historical, narrative, and critical contexts in order to understand not only Bankim's influential critique of European modernity, but also his choice of forest setting, which suits the righteous rebellion he imagines, or rather what Sudipto Kaviraj calls the rebellion's "nonactualized possibility."[46]

As Bankim's use of counterfacts indicates, his narrative approach to modernity, like his use of language, is intentionally mixed. His primary historical resource was the 1868 British account of the 1769–70 famine by Scottish historian W. W. Hunter, *Annals of Rural Bengal*, whose authoritative voice presumes to speak for the "sufferings" of northern India's "ancient rural society" and to detail British East India Company administrators' mismanagement.[47] To cement the pretense of evenhandedness, Hunter acknowledges East India Company's administrative missteps leading up to the famine. He even acknowledges as understandable the resentment that motivated the ensuing rebellion of Majnu Shah, a Muslim *fakir*, or religious ascetic, who had instigated other *fakirs* as well as Hindu *sannyasis* to jointly rise up against the company's army, a rebellion that is the historical counterpart to Bankim's fictional uprising.[48] But as Upamanyu Pablo Mukherjee points out in his analysis of *Anandamath*'s famine motifs, Hunter predictably defends British rule as a "progressive, distinctly modern system"— the necessary and self-correcting guardian—against the "arbitrary powers of nature" that overwhelm a seemingly passive peasantry.[49] Hunter naturalizes the rural poor in the same way that he tries to naturalize the famine—an unwitting contradiction, as Mukherjee observes, given that the British missteps leading to famine that Hunter has admitted are decidedly not natural. Hunter's view of Indian landscapes, like his representation of Majnu Shah, is characteristically ambivalent—an ambivalence that derives from his strained effort to endorse colonial modernity while also exoticizing India, both its peoples and landscapes. In other words, Hunter presumes to speak in the manner of a disinterested observer, but couches this voice in Orientalist tropes that belie this disinterest.

This contradiction, I suggest, also partly informs Bankim's depiction of forests in *Anandamath* as well as his depictions of the women protagonists who venture into those forests and of the men they encounter there. There are several dimensions to these representations that we need to examine. It is important at the outset, however, to address the novel's most salient contradiction, mentioned earlier: its denigration of Indian Muslims. For so resolutely nationalist a novel, this depiction is, ironically, lifted directly from British colonial discourse, which styled all past Muslim rulers, regardless of their diversity, as alien invaders of a once-great Hindu country. This trope is premised on the colonialist objectification of landscape that Hunter's works epitomize—a premise Bankim strains to evade. The rhetorical effect is telling. Whereas Bankim's rendering of Muslims as enemies of his *sannyasi* protagonists, the *santans*, serves his purpose of naturalizing Hindu indigeneity, which he underscores by having the rebels reside in a forest hermitage, Bankim's forest itself undercuts this purpose through its liminality.

A further irony behind this stereotype of Muslims is that it was Britain's obsessively sectarian ethno-historicizing that had required the trope of Islamic invader.[50] Until early in the nineteenth century, revolutionary Bengali intellectuals like Rammohun Roy had prized the rich Persian-Islamic traditions of the Mughals. But as elite, high-caste intellectuals (including Roy) sought to craft a more localized identity distinct from either Persian or European traditions, there began, as Sudipto Kaviraj writes, "a slow but decisive equation of the modern Bengali self with a cultural gestalt associated with Hinduism," which "was a fundamental reason for the gradual alienation of Muslims."[51] Bengali intellectuals thus styled the true inheritors of Bengali soil in tropes of classical Hinduism, so that forests, along with the open countryside and villages, become aestheticized ideals. This idealized landscape, with "birds, trees, and goddesses" reflecting "an eternal Bengal," was, as Dipesh Chakrabarty observes, "a purely nationalist construction," emptied of Muslims, a construction that would feature in Bengali literature well into the twentieth century.[52] Even Tagore, whose nationalism was otherwise resolutely inclusive, voiced his peers' general skepticism of received history (though not of history as such). "Whatever historical records exist from Mahmud's invasion to the arrogant imperial pronouncements of Lord Curzon, these constitute a strange mirage for India," he wrote, for it is a history "that hides the essence of [our] land from us."[53] Bankim and other Hindu intellectuals concluded that history would have to be rewritten, but in light of classical Hindu ideals. This context suggests some of the reasons why Bankim's novel is unable to settle on what exactly the forest represents and what role it should play in the national imagination. To state my claim another way, if this idea of Indianness is flawed to begin with, so will the idea of its topographical integrity be flawed. Whereas Bankim's ability to combine history with counterfactual possibility has rightly been called an ingenious rhetorical strategy, his reliance on a colonial religious stereotype muddles his national arboreal ideal.

Yet the contradictions that Bankim's competing aims incur cannot be collectively characterized as a simple opposition between modern historicizing and mythic possibilities, since the colonialist history on which he relies is itself obviously conflicted. The historical event Bankim takes for his fictional model is principally the *Sannyasi Rebellion* of 1770–1, which was sparked by the terrible famine but rooted in disputes over land ownership and taxation that had flared in the previous five years.[54] The East India Company exerted its new power by increasing taxes, greatly straining an already-burdened system that, in turn, interfered with adequate food distribution.[55] The Hindu *sannyasis* (traditional renunciates), like some Muslim *fakirs* (ascetic mendicants), had previously benefited from pilgrimage and other religious fees collected from traditional landowners (*zamindars*) in Bengal. According to David N. Lorenzen, in the late 1760s, the *zamindars*, betting their future on the British, elected to start paying taxes to them rather than pay anything to the ascetics, leaving the *sannyasis* and *fakirs* to fume and, eventually, join hands to rebel. Company officials tagged such eclectic rebel consortiums "lawless banditti."[56] Bankim's focus on forestlands conveys something of this backdrop, for he has his fictional rebels seek refuge in woods, just as the historical ones did. But in his version of the rebellion, *fakirs* and other participants, including hungry and disaffected villagers, are second-tier *santans*, useful to the rebellion's moral goal but not true renunciates devoted to the Mother India Goddess.[57] The leader of Bankim's *santans*, Satyananda, accounts for the rebel collective's use of excessive violence by telling Mahendra,

> There are two kinds of *santan* … Those who have been initiated and those who have not. The latter are either householders or beggars. They appear when it's time to do battle, and after they've received their share of the loot or some other reward, they go away. But those who are initiates have renounced everything. (178–9)

Although Bankim does not mention *fakirs* by that name, his use of "beggars" suggests a broad collective designation for those, including (as Bankim knew from historical accounts as well as social memory) Muslim mendicants, who participated in this resistance. (Ironically, some historical *sannyasis* actually joined forces with Muslim rulers, even when the latter battled Hindu kings.[58]) Yet Satyananda characterizes the "uninitiated" as motivated by greed and therefore prone to the violent excess that the gentlemanly Mahendra frowns upon.

The novel's acknowledgment of this moral lapse, Satyananda's unpersuasive explanation, and the vague appellation "beggars" all point to Bankim's complicated view of Indian Muslims. On the one hand, Bankim, like many of his Bengali Hindu peers, chooses to adopt the British stereotyping of Muslim rulers as ruthless invaders disdainful of their Hindu subjects.[59] In this scenario, the land has been figuratively raped by Muslim invaders and must now be rescued by armed Hindu ascetics—figures whom Bankim calculatedly espoused at the risk of alienating his more devout contemporary readers, for whom true renouncers are never violent and the very idea of a rebel monk is an oxymoron. On the other hand, in his own essays, Bankim describes Bengali Muslim peasants (as distinct from Muslim rulers) as products of the same soil as their Hindu compatriots and therefore essentially the same.[60] This contradictory treatment of Muslims is characteristic of both the novel and Bankim's developing Hindu revivalist philosophy, as Lipner observes.⁶¹ Figured as maternal in Bankim's novel, the land is shown to be victimized by Muslim invasion, its beautiful forests ravaged. At the same time, the alien British, despite their imperious attitude, are shown by Bankim to be the arbiters of a necessary modernity that India must imbibe. This is why, in the novel's concluding scene, the disembodied Healer tells his listeners—Kalyani, Shanti, and Satyananda—that India must for a time learn "outward knowledge" (modern science) from the British, a knowledge he says "has been lost in this land" and must be relearned (229).

Bankim's scapegoating of Muslims in the novel appears to be due to a combination of expediency and ideology: expediency in that scapegoating the Muslims provides a "foreign" foe for the *santan* rebels without having to name the real enemy, the British, and so avoid colonial censorship, and ideology in that Bankim, adopting (as previously noted) European typologies, views Muslims as usurping the land's true Aryan inheritors. Bankim also, as mentioned, wishes to historicize the recent past— that is, the eighteenth-century famine—for his readers, who can potentially achieve the national spirit that the novel's eighteenth-century protagonists have imagined. They can achieve this, the novel submits, only by plotting their future in historical time while simultaneously drawing on their ancient, timeless Vedic inheritance, which the forest embodies. The forest is, in other words, both atavistically Aryan and historical, which means the spirit of that past era of nobility can be recouped only by actors who embody a similar dualism. Muslims, because they pay no heed to cosmic Vedic time, and are therefore unable to transcend history (just like the British, the text implies), are destructive interlopers in the forest.

This two-pronged outlook, representative of Bankim's revivalist, neo-Hindu philosophy,⁶² finds echoes in the novel's figurative language, in particular Bankim's recourse to classical forest imagery. Ironically, some of the same images appear in Hunter's history. Paul Greenough, commenting on Hunter's essay on the Sundarbans, Bengal's forbidding expanse of mangrove forests, shows how his writing embraces the colonial aesthetic treatment of Indian landscapes, which were variously deemed sublime and picturesque. The reasonable tone in which Hunter describes the Sundarbans— the same authoritative voice he employs in his history of the famine—allows him to slip in an exotic, picturesque portrayal of the area.⁶³Hunter sees no contradiction in mixing empirical data with romance, as when he characterizes the region as the antithesis of the sublime⁶⁴—a method that happens to echo, though for different purposes, Camões' conjoining of history and myth. Hunter uses, sometimes in the same sentence, words that evoke timeless romance, tropical danger, and utilitarianism. In his history of the Birbhum (or as he styles it, "Beerbhoom") region of Bengal, he describes "turbid cataracts [that] leap down the valley" and "gorgeous creepers" that "strangle their parent stems." Yet these are forests that boast "noble timber" and "fruit-bearing groves."⁶⁵ The Birbhum forests, he is careful to note, have also been the stage for "rebellion[s]" by their indigenous inhabitants, the Santals, who have had to be put under the "direct administration" of the British.⁶⁶ I say "careful to note" because wherever recorded history comes into Hunter's purview, so do the British and their eye for the forest products he deems useful to modern society. But because most areas of Birbhum are, he says with "regret," "primitive [jungle]," "without any record of the past," they are assumed to be timeless and in need of proper cultivation. It also happens that Hunter—and here we can most visibly see the influence on Bankim—sees these "primitive" Birbhum jungles as having long been an "ethnical frontier" between "aborigines" and the "[noble] Aryan civilisation."[67]

Hunter's assumptions about Aryans and Santals and about the arboreal manifestations of their supposed differences—forests are noble, Aryan, and part of history; jungles primitive, Santali, and historyless—answer Bankim's similar perspective in *Anandamath*. This typically colonialist plotting of the march of history from primitive "unrest" to civilized "repose"[68] is also, of course, the template for modernity. This is likely a prime reason for Bankim's choice of Birbhum for the story's setting. The region's history of rebellions makes it "contested ground" in need of "a legitimate ruler"—exactly what the fictional *santans* can help supply, as Lipner notes.[69] In previous chapters we saw that the classical forest, whether depicted in the *Mahabharata* or in Kalidasa's *Shakuntala*, supplies a necessary realm for the moral education of kings. Bankim largely retains this arboreal quality, even if kings have been superseded by a class of spiritual warriors. Conversely, the absence of such moral leadership and its necessary arboreal home leads to despotism, a charge Bankim levels against the historical, and by this period (1770) merely nominal, Muslim king of Bengal, Mir Jafar. The still-commonly told story is that Jafar's opium addiction resulted in mismanagement of food distribution, which resulted in famine, making Jafar a byword for dissolute rule. Yet Bankim, as we will see, characterizes Jafar in such a way as to indirectly critique British governance and the resulting environmental transformations of Bengal's landscape. Bankim's use of colonial history is therefore partial, since he recognizes that Hunter's history of the famine depends on naturalizing rural and forested parts of Bengal and placing them outside of history[70]—a view Bankim rebuts, just as he draws only partly on European narrative strategies to tell his story.

To see how Bengal's forests function in *Anandamath*, we can, to begin with, see the clear contrast of Hunter's "gorgeous" yet malicious jungle creepers with Bankim's depictions of creepers as consolatory reminders of the life force, in keeping with their classical Sanskrit assignation. For example, when Mahendra and his wife have fled their famine-riven village, they at one point "rested in the deep shade of a dark-leafed tree with fragrant blossoms and encircling creepers" (133). The fraternal virtue of the forest is also apparent when thousands of *santans* gather in "a great recess of [the] immense forest" in which they have been residing to hear what their leader Satyananda has to say to them on the eve of a great battle against British forces. This is a forest "enlivened by the mango and the jackfruit, by palmyras, tamarinds, and peepuls, by the wood-apple, banyan, silk-cotton and other trees" (203). The naming of trees here is significant. Lipner, in general commentary on the novel's forest symbolism, rightly observes that the *santans* enter the forest as "individual householders or men of the world" and "are transmuted into a higher order of celibates." This status, he notes (quoting from Thomas Parkhill), "reinforces the liminal *persona* or thresholder" by rejecting the former "structure" of conjugal life in favor of "new forms unknown to that structured world."[71] This is enabled, Lipner says, by "the amorphous setting of the forest."[72] While it is true that Bankim frequently paints the forest in this manner, the specific trees he lists in the scene described here are far from nebulous. They can hardly be so if they are to fill the *santans* with the fighting spirit needed to face British cannons, in which endeavor they must be willing to sacrifice themselves for their homeland. The naming of the trees particularizes this forested homeland, conveying to Bankim's readers a situational authenticity that a generalized description would lose. The particularity on view here is not an isolated instance in the novel, but a recurring narrative strategy, in which named trees supply the indexical resonance that iconicity, though vital in other contexts, cannot alone do.

More frequently, Bankim combines such realist particularity with motifs of classical romance as a means of sustaining the setting's historical quality along with the forest's liminal potentiality. We can see this when, for example, the narrator instructs the reader as follows:

> Picture the scene: the clamorous voices of ten thousand men [the *santans*], the rustle of the foliage swept by a gentle breeze, the soft lapping of the waves against the riverbank, moon, stars and a white cloud-mass in an indigo sky, the verdant forest on the dark earth, the clear river and its white bank, and clusters of flowers in bloom. And every now and then that cry dear to all: *Bande Mataram*! (203)

Particular trees represent more than literary realism, for they also emblematize the superior qualities of arboreal India as compared to Europe's. As Bankim puts it elsewhere, the sheer scale and richness of India's epics, the *Mahabharata* and *Ramayana*, far outweigh European epics, which is like comparing a "terrier … to an elephant, [a] willow or cypress … to a banyan tree or a mountain stream … to the Ganges."[73] The banyan, as previously mentioned, is the greatest of trees in Hindu traditions, and India's national tree, its descending epiphytic roots—the technical term for aerial roots that germinate from a seed lodged in a host plant—representing the never-ending, regenerative life cycle. In this way, it resembles the forest itself.[74] It is underneath the banyan that people repose in serious meditation to acquire the mental and physical discipline which, in Bankim's view, characterizes a mature civilization and which the Vedas espouse—a virtue that, once again, Europeans' relatively recent forebears did not learn despite residing in forests.[75]

How, then, did Europeans emerge from a "barbarian" hunter-gatherer existence to acquire the scientific rationality that, in the view of Bankim and his peers, allowed them to supersede Indian society in recent times? Bankim, again accepting the colonialist yarn, believed he knew the reason: Indians had become fatalistic and passive subjects, rather than the active agents of change that the rebels in *Anandamath* embody.[76] Asceticism by itself would stultify; ascetic warriors, on the other hand, possess the martial spirit needed to defeat alien conquerors.[77] The forest is therefore an essential stage for national rebellion because it enables the necessary revision of conventional views, and offers a fresh start. This generative capability is emphasized in several ways, beginning with the novel's opening lines that describe a "vast forest" that is a "boundless ocean of leaves" (129). Lipner importantly observes that this is a frequent "uterine" metaphor in Hindu philosophical works to represent the primeval ocean that creates life.[78] The sanctified forest here is similarly womb-like, a "pregnant darkness" that promises the "passage from an old, worn-out state to the threshold of a new."[79] The naturally generative verdure, like the banyan, presages a new, authentically rooted nation as envisioned by the *santans*.

Bankim's Debts to Mughal Stories and Popular Tales

Bankim's accent on Vedic-Indian authenticity as exemplified by the forest returns us to the problem of national inclusion and exclusion in his novel—a problem because of the aforementioned (mis)representation of Muslim Indians. On the one hand, Bankim and his peers accepted the colonialist view of Muslim rulers as ruthless marauders who had overrun the presumptively indigenous Aryans. On the other hand, Lipner observes, "Bankim included the Bengali Muslims among [the Mother's] children," who under a restored Hindu sovereignty would be "assimilated"—that is, reconverted—into a restored "Aryan" societal order.[80] There are additional, ironic complications in the novel's depictions of Indian Muslims. For one thing, the iconic *Bande Mataram* song, in both its manifest and implicit meanings, and especially as conveyed by the Goddess Durga's representation of motherland, counters the very notion of Aryanism that Bankim wants his forest to support, a point to which I will shortly return. Bankim's denigration of Muslims is also ironic in light of his literary debts to the immensely productive, centuries-long interactions between the Mughal Persianate and Sufi literary cultures and local literary traditions, as I noted in the book's Introduction, a period when "Bengali started to flourish as a vibrant language of the common people."[81] For instance, the eighteenth-century Sufi poet Bullhe Shah famously "interweaves," says Shankar Nair, "Qur'anic, Sufi, Hindu devotional (*bhakti*), and local Punjabi literary forms into his *kāfī* lyrics."[82] Shah "overlays the Sufi trope of the reed flute's (ney) mournful sound—most famously depicted in the opening of Rumi's Masnavi, where the reed laments at being separated from its Beloved/place of origin—with the intoxicating flute play of Krishna," whose tunes "lure" Vrindavan's *gopis* "into the forest for nighttime romantic trysts. Both of these literary motifs are additionally juxtaposed with the flute-playing folk hero of local Punjabi legend, Ranjha."[83] Two centuries before Shah, numerous works appeared, including popular genres like *mangalkavya*, of which Mukundaram Chakravarti's immensely influential, "nonsectarian" *Chandimangal* (late 1500s) and Bharatchandra Ray's *Anandamangal* (1753) are perhaps the most famous.[84] Nair importantly adds that to describe this literary intermixing as simply "hybrid" or "syncretistic" is to imagine a combination of unchanging forms designated "Hindu" and "Muslim," ignoring the diverse faith and regional communities that contributed to these compositions.[85]

Bankim would have been familiar with these sources, and his use of everyday Bengali in his fiction attests to their stylistic influence.[86] As Supriya Chaudhuri observes, "the novel in Bengal is deeply indebted to indigenous narrative," including "oral storytelling," as well as to the "affective and tonal registers of classical poetics." Bankim bemoaned the "decline" of this tradition by the nineteenth century.[87] It seems clear that in writing *Anandamath*, he borrowed themes, plots, and contexts from these popular texts, including the *Chandimangal* and *Anandamangal*. (In what may be literary homage, Bankim uses, respectively, author and character names from these works for two of his characters in *Anandamath*, Mukunda and Bhabananda.) It may also be that Bankim was enamored of the performative features of *mangalkavya*, which in the case of the *Chandimangal* are actually part of the poem's composition, as its "rhyming verse, repetitions, and … instructions for the use of particular rhythms (*taal*), modes (*raga*), and dance" make clear.[88] We might say that the *santans* stage rebellions as performances that are improvisational, informed equally (with respect to national consciousness) by past example and unrealized potential. But actions like these need spaces that are away from the confines of city life, and the *Chandimangal* may have given Bankim an idea of how a forest could provide the appropriately evocative setting for his novel. By "appropriately" I mean a range of emotive associations that would particularly resonate with his modern readers and their commingled European and Indian sensibilities. The *mangalkavya* narratives would have been especially fitting given that they are part of a tradition that, as Kumkum Chatterjee points out, celebrated "the particular association of the goddess"—that is, the forest goddess in different forms—"with the establishment of forest kingdoms by political adventurers, who were almost always of low-caste or adivasi [*sic*] origin." These stories show that Durga herself, especially in the form of Chandi, originated "as a forest deity or *vanadevi* who was worshipped by communities of low-caste, low-status people." A prevailing storyline has the goddess helping a low-caste man defeat his foes to found a just kingdom.[89] In one of its three tales, the "Book of the Hunter," Mukunda's *Chandimangal* tells of Kalketu, "an untouchable hunter dwelling on the agrarian frontier between the Bengal delta and the Chota Nagpur plateau," who with Chandi's help "cleared the forest and established … a kingdom."[90]

A leitmotif in Mukunda's version of Kalketu's remarkable story is the traditional gifting of *paan*, which, as described in my Introduction, is a practice that signifies social propriety, with the betel leaf-and-areca nut *paan* itself a metonym for society's agrarian basis. Modern history in Mukunda's narrative serves as both a reference point for his contemporary, late-fifteenth-century readers as well as a foil for the story's mythic layering. Mukunda's *Chandimangal* mixes a variety of narrative genres in a way that is typical of the *mangalkavya* tradition. Mukunda's text is notable, for instance, for "probably [making] the first mention in Bengali literature of the Portuguese *haramada* (armada), … which infested the waters of India's east coast" at the time.[91] David L. Curley observes that in establishing his kingdom, Kalketu offered *paan* "to all subjects who came to settle" there.[92] What is significant here is Kalketu's inclusiveness, for he breaks with normative practice by distributing *paan* to *all* his subjects, "both Muslim and Hindu, and both high-born and low," illustrating how these "gifts" of *paan* "were socially and religiously neutral symbols of inclusion in a kingdom which contained very different kinds of subjects."[93] This was, in other words, a contractual exchange. The social code of the time permitted a person to refuse such an offering if he declined the implied agreement to the ruler's conditions. The success of Kalketu's offering—he becomes, after all, a rare low-caste king—was aided, it seems plausible to conclude, by his intimate knowledge of the forest. Not only does this connection enhance his association with the Goddess Chandi, it also intimates a closer connection to the *paan*'s pepper leaves and areca nuts. For this reason, it seems to me, Curley's conclusion about royal *paan* giving in Mughal Bengal especially applies to Kalketu. For if his offering "leav[es] a trace of the ruler's body in [his] subjects' bodies" and thereby "changes" them,[94] then Kalketu has effectively transferred to them not only a part of his "untouchable" self, but also the arboreal investiture of that self. His forest realm is transubstantiated in the corpus of his subjects.

This forest realm, and Kalketu's intimate and enabling knowledge of it, likely influenced Bankim's choice of setting for *Anandamath*. The novel's monastery is, as one scholar says of Bengal's Birbhum area during both Bankim's time and after, "situated in a forest clearing and more or less self-contained (primarily because of the plant food resources available in the forests)."[95] While Kalketu's knowledge of the forest's "plant" resources adds weight to his *paan* offering, as I have said, his transformation from a property-less, low-caste forest hunter to significant ruler is also suggestive of the forest as a liminal setting that stages unusual rites of passage. *Anandamath* is filled with similar transformations, which are signaled by changes in the forest's qualities according to the types of characters who inhabit it and whose varying conditions set the mood of the moment.[96] These adaptations by Bankim of Bengali literature and folk traditions, imperial history (Hunter's *Annals*), and social symbols as ingredients in his innovative novel give equal weight to symbolic, supernatural, and historical accounts of forests. While this mixture, as we have seen, served very well to convey the range of national aspirations and emotions Bankim felt were vital to the creation of a modern Indian sensibility, the "problem" of Hindu-Indian "essence" and Muslim exclusion remained.

Ironically, however, the Mughal past that became a bugbear for Hindu intellectuals like Bankim was part of the historical idiom he favored, even as he sought to typify—to de-historicize—Mughal rule. This is analogous to his treatment of the forest as being both timeless and existing within modern time. This regard for forests, as we have seen, is widespread within human societies. In the case of *Anandamath*, which fascinatingly presents us with a great variety of significations for the forest, we have an opportunity to probe how its manner of "project[ing] certitudes about the lives of others," to borrow from Mrinalini Chakravorty's examination of the stereotype in fiction, tells us just as much about who is making these assertions.[97] It seems to me that Bankim's novel, while advocating practical action, also seeks an idealized plenitude in the forest of the monastery that the colonial city cannot provide, given the inherent fracturing of colonized life. But the forest, ultimately resistant to the modern gaze, can never provide this plenitude.[98]

The Forest of *Anandamath*: Inclusivity and Exclusivity

In Bankim's hands, Jafar's habit seems to be a sign, on one level, of his irresponsibility. The historical Jafar is easily vilified because, as a (Muslim) Bengali general, he betrayed his leader, the Nawab of Bengal Siraj ud-Daulah. Bankim, in a single sentence, appears to make Jafar's habit precipitate the cataclysmic effects on eighteenth-century Bengal that occasion the rebellion at the heart of the novel: "Mir Jafar took opium and slept, the British took in the money and issued receipts, and the Bengali wept and went to ruin" (140). But as Tapan Raychaudhuri argues, the investment of full responsibility for this ruin in the nawab—more specifically, Jafar's purported mismanagement of food distribution during a draught and the resulting famine—was obvious hyperbole to Bankim's readers. Sudipta Kaviraj reads Bankim's move as intentionally suggestive of "folk tales," an authorial device to signal to the reader "the onset of narrative irony."[99] The historical Jafar had, after all, been dead five years by the time of the famine, a fact Bengali readers knew well.[100] Opium taking, moreover, was not entirely proscribed at the time, being used by certain religious devotees, for instance. More revealingly, a character in another of Bankim's works sees, in an opium vision, Durga, goddess of strength (*shakti*) and war, who is frequently associated with Shiva: "Was this my Mother?" the narrator, an upper-caste Hindu, asks himself in awe. "Yes, it was she! I knew her for my mother, the land of my birth (*janmabhiimi*), made of earth, in the form of clay, adorned with endless gems, now hidden in the womb of time ... Slayer of the enemy! Ten-armed One! ... Give your children [*santan*] power ... We sixty million bodies will die for you."[101] Being Muslim, Jafar's opium taking cannot, in Bankim's theology, invite such visions; but the mere indulgence of the drug, as this example shows, is not of itself incriminating and further undercuts the typology of Jafar as an agent of the British and their destructive acts. Yet Jafar's name was, and is still, a synonym for traitorous conduct. The nuance in Bankim's depiction of the man mirrors the author's complicated regard for Muslims.

More revealing of Bankim's wink to his Bengali readers is that the pejorative statement about Jafar appears in the middle of a paragraph that is framed in conventional historical language. It begins by baldly stating that "in 1770 Bengal had not yet fallen under British sway. The British at the time were Bengal's tax collectors." It concludes with a like tone of authoritative historicity: "So while Bengal's revenue belonged to the British, the burden of government fell on the nawab." To heighten the contrast between the "fabular" depiction of Jafar and the surrounding text, Bankim then declares: "Wherever the British collected their own dues, they would appoint a collector ... People could die of starvation, but the collection of revenue didn't stop" (140). As Raychaudhuri observes, these words "leave ... little doubt" that Bankim's real target is the British, not Jafar.[102] Kaviraj agrees, but goes further in arguing that the effect of this strategy is "exactly the opposite of" that of "the European historical novel." For rather than "give a concrete sense of a historical period," Bankim instead wishes "to "falsify history" (as with Jafar's dissolute culpability) in order to "explore the peculiar terrain of history's nonactualized possibilities."[103] This depiction of a fabular nawab also, I suggest, served Bankim's larger interest in assuaging the guilt that, as Tanika Sarkar has persuasively argued, Bankim shared with his *bhadralok* class for their "refusal" to join other Indians in rising up against the East India Company in 1857. To achieve this "redemptive mission" (as Sarkar characterizes the novel's fictional rebellion) in a censorious climate, Bankim had to find an antagonist whom his *bhadralok* readers would find worthy, and this was the Muslim.[104]

These points Bankim's contemporary readers would have detected. It is also possible, I think, that the exaggerated image of Jafar taking opium would have reminded readers of an additional, equally painful reality: Britain's enforced cultivation of poppy for opium production across northern India, which led to a concomitant increase in opium addiction. In the mid-1800s, the "export of opium from British India to China" made up about "15% of total colonial revenue in India and 31% of India's exports," which "was arguably the largest and most enduring drug operation in history." This resulted in lower literacy rates and quality of life in the regions of Bihar and Bengal, where opium was produced.[105] Bankim's readers would have shared his resentment of Britain's agricultural and economic exploitation, even while many were, like him, employed by the colonial bureaucracy. By 1882, when *Anandamath* appeared, the British had mastered the art of statistical surveys of land, extending their disciplinary reach. Bankim had also laid the groundwork in his previous works for *Anandamath*'s oblique criticism of British policy, such as in the 1875 novel *Chandrasekhar*, in which "the arch villain is … an English factor," while the "avenging hero … dies fighting for Mir Qasim, 'the last king [nawab] of Bengal.'"[106] Jafar's opium, then, is in Bankim's hands a layered index of the British-engineered environmental degradation that has beset Bengal and that the land's true children must rehabilitate.[107] An East India Company edict of 1799, periodically updated over the next century, compelled peasants in Bengal and Bihar to "cultivate a specified amount and plot of land and to deliver its entire production, unadulterated, at the fixed government price to the agent."[108] The company's thirst for new taxable agricultural lands, among which poppy cultivation was a prime revenue maker, meant the removal of more and more forests and the displacement of their inhabitants.[109] The nomadic lifestyles of foresters and herders that had prevailed in large parts of the country began to come to an end. C. A. Bayly notably observes that "India as it is commonly conceived, a land of settled arable farming, of caste Hindus and of specialist agricultural produce, was very much a creation of [the early nineteenth century] period."[110] To enforce these changes, the East India Company enlarged and exploited the preexisting system of landowners, or *zamindars*, in tandem with "pacification" raids against indigenous groups, such as the Bhils, who were then, in the words of one contemporary administrator, "allotted [waste lands]" and told to farm them.[111] Poorer farmers seeking to escape the company's punishing taxes "moved up into the hills or on to poorer soils and cleared forest as they went," contributing to the overall denudation of many regions.[112] The future Duke of Wellington, Arthur Wellesley, who made his name fighting in India, participated in this forced coercion while campaigning against southern India when, as the nineteenth century dawned, he "drove roads through the forests of Malabar and cleared trees to a mile on either side."[113] (Wellesley's tactic was, not coincidentally, part of a six-year war against poligar chiefs who refused to give up their productive lands for company profits and attacked British spice plantations.[114] Bayly notes that "most of the Deccan was … completely treeless by 1840."[115])

In addition to opium, cotton and indigo also featured as favorite revenue-generating crops for the company to plant in deforested lands. The resulting impoverishment of Indian peasant farmers was exacerbated when European "planters," seeing these crops' profitability, began to take over large tracts of land in the early 1800s, as they did with indigo fields—an injustice that was deeply felt by, among others, Bankim and his professional colleagues.[116] One friend, Dinabandhu Mitra, anonymously penned the famous 1860 play *Nil Darpan* (*Mirror of Indigo*), which attacked English planters and championed the Indian peasant farmer, or *ryot*, who had recently rebelled

(1857–9) in Bengal.[117] This social and political context illustrates the extent to which British colonialism's profound environmental changes and their effects had stirred the emotions of the Bengali intelligentsia. Not surprisingly, Bankim, who had lauded *Nil Darpan*, dedicated *Anandamath* to its author.[118] "This land," laments a character in Michael Madhusudan Dutt's 1861 translation, "was as the Kingdom of Rama before Indigo was established; but the ignorant fool is become a beggar, and famine has come upon the land." Another cries out, "Oh Indigo! You came to this land for our utter ruin."[119] The play itself should not be seen as reflective of a monolithic Indian reaction to colonial rule; rebellions of indigenous peoples against kings of settled societies, of peasants against landowners, and of Hindu chieftains against Mughal rulers had long featured in India's history.[120] What is noteworthy, however, is that the play's rhetorical flair (illustrated above) elicited powerful feelings in Bengali audiences about not only economic and racial injustices, but also territorial injustices: an acute sense of colonialism's theft of lands from a wide range of Indian social groups. The emotive power of language is especially strong in this case because, as Lakoff and Johnson observe, "There are few human instincts more basic than territoriality."[121] *Nil Darpan*'s appeal to a homeland besieged by outsiders was, I suggest, due not just to the appropriation of Indian-owned indigo plantations, but also, more broadly, to a landscape suffering from the accelerating "destruction and degradation of forest[s]."[122]

How, then, does Bankim's subtle, partial absolution of the historical Muslim ruler Jafar mesh with the novel's targeting of Muslims? And what does this move indicate about his forest setting? These are questions whose answers can provide guidance for our readings of later forest fictions and their relationship to national ideals. A short answer is that the forest in *Anandamath* signifies several different qualities, depending on the particular scene it serves: a liminality characteristic of epic forests; feminine purity derived from goddesses like Durga—especially in her form as Lakshmi, goddess of wealth and beauty—who are embodied in certain female characters; a hideout for starving, opportunistic bandits; and, of course, a place for the holy rebels' (the *santans*') spiritual-patriotic retreat. In order to answer these questions more substantially, though, we must consider the novel's historical, ideological, and literary contexts. The novel is most famous for the song, "*Bande Mataram*," or "Hail to thee, Mother," which Lipner describes as "an intensely passionate devotional hymn to the mother figure of India and to goddesses like Durga and Lakshmi."[123] It is first sung by Bhabananda as he leads Mahendra to his wife and daughter. Mahendra is amazed to see the rebel leader transform as he enters the forest:

> No longer was he the grave, calm renouncer, the skilled, valiant figure of the battlefield, the man who had cut off the head of a commanding officer! No longer the man who had just rebuked Mahendra so haughtily. It was as if seeing the radiance of plain and forest, mountain and river of a peaceful, moonlit world had invigorated his mind in a special way, like the ocean gladdened by the rising moon. He was now light-hearted, talkative, friendly, keen to make a conversation. (144)

To understand the scene's context, and so the full implications of the song, we need to look more closely at the lyrics. These would, within a few years, be set to music and go on to become a patriotic anthem, as it is today—though with strenuous and understandable objections from Muslim Indians, as I discuss below. More pertinent to my point is that the song was soon "detached from its narrative [context]" and "given a life of its own."¹²⁴ Lipner's rich discussion of this paratextual life of the song touches on a number of important factors, such as its role in the Gandhian movement; how it was viewed by other nationalist leaders, particularly Tagore and Aurobindo; its mix of Sanskrit and colloquial Bengali (which translations cannot replicate); and the criticisms of Muslim nationalists.¹²⁵ Equally important in my reading of the song is its removal, almost immediately after publication, from its forest environs, which, as we will see, are a crucial feature of the maternal iconicity that is continually identified with the pure national spirit of Bharat Mata (Mother India), both within and beyond the novel.¹²⁶

Before turning to that influential image, however, it is necessary to foreground the song's evocation of the associative imagery of the Mother, which also sets the reverential mood. The Mother—the embodiment of Bengal, and, by extension, India—is, to cite from the opening stanza, "rich in waters, rich in fruit," and "cooled by southern airs."¹²⁷ The Bengali original, according to Lipner's gloss, more specifically speaks of southern India's Western Ghats. I would add that Bankim uses the word "Malaya" for "south," rather than the more common "*dakshina*," because in ancient *puranas* and epics, Malaya refers to the southern Western Ghats. The word connotes, as Lipner observes, the fragrance of sandalwood, which grows in these hills (ghats). Bankim's use of classical terms in this way adds to the song's poetic effect, which heightens its contrast with the prosaic world Bhabananda and Mahendra have just left behind. Bankim will use classical imagery to a much different effect when, a few pages later (and, appropriately, in conversation), Bhabananda asks Mahendra rhetorically if he isn't "fed up with" the effects of the famine, which is causing people to "[eat] creepers from the forest" (147). As we saw in the discussion of Kalidasa's *Shakuntala* in the previous chapter, the drama's trope of creeper vines enhances the eponymous heroine's natural beauty and purity, attributes that are embodied by her forest home. Bhabananda's words are meant to shock Mahendra (with the aim of making him renounce his worldly life) by reminding him of the degradation of Bengal's beauty. The creeper would likely have also reminded readers of Shakuntala's own beauty, and of her long-suffering, but ultimately successful, effort to have King Dushyanta (after a curse has been lifted) recognize her, thereby uniting forest and court. In other words, the famine is degrading not only Bengal's flora, it is also corrupting its feminine beauty.

The invocation of the Mother India image is "innovative," Sumathi Ramasamy argues, in that it projects onto the subcontinent's geography, which the British had assiduously mapped, an "anthropomorphic-sacred" conception "of land and country" that drew on a repertoire of goddesses.¹²⁸ As he does with history and myth, and with contemporary Bengali and Sanskrit, Bankim combines familiar goddess worship with reverence for a "geo-body" that has been "rendered visible at one glance to the citizen-devotee's eye through … cartographic practices."¹²⁹ This innovative image would be incomplete, however, without noticing the "*Bande Mataram*" song's leitmotif, the floral attributes of the goddess, who is a version of Durga. Durga has the virtue of being a warrior goddess, who is typically depicted riding a lion, with her many hands grasping weapons. She represents the elemental feminine power of *shakti*, or divine energy, which expresses itself as *prakriti* (nature), as her association with trees indicates.[130] In an essay written in the same year as the novel's full publication, Bankim wrote, "As destructive energy, force is *Kali*, hideous and terrible, because destruction is hideous and terrible. As constructive energy, force is the bright and resplendent Durga." He adds, "The passionate yearnings of the heart for the Ideal in beauty, in power, and in purity, must find an expression in the world of the Real"—"Real" meaning divine truth.[131] In light of these and other comments, Lipner points out that "*Bande Mataram*" clearly describes "the fusion of the Mother as the land of Bengal, and by implication, the whole of India, and the Goddess as protective, spiritually real power."[132] These qualities help explain the song's life as a patriotic anthem. When we first hear it sung by Bhabananda, it instantly transforms him, as we saw, from a ruthless outlaw into a "light-hearted" person who soaks up nature's "radiance." The second time, however, it is sung by villagers and ascetics, all devotees of Vishnu, preparing for war. In this instance, as Sarkar observes, the song "mobilizes the spirit of war and violence which are simultaneously introduced as aspects of ritual sacrifice, compulsory in the worship of the [mother] goddess."[133]

The immediate catalyst for Bhabananda's metamorphosis, as the lyrics reveal, is "the peaceful moonlit world," a world—the landscape of Birbhum—whose natural bounty "invigorated his mind in a special way." The Mother-as-land is "rich in fruit" and "verdant with the harvest." When an astonished Mahendra asks who this mother is, Bhabananda responds by singing about a motherland "radiant with foliage and flowers in bloom, … Giving joy and gifts in plenty." Yet this is not a mother content to bask in her pure beauty, for, as Bhabananda sings in the next stanza, as Durga, she instils in her "seventy millions" of children the will to hold up "sharpened swords." She is "spotless," "darkly green and also true," and "ever-plenteous land of grace." Bankim uses Sanskrit in this instance to describe the Mother's divine pedigree, which includes Kamala (hence "lotusflower," an icon of the goddess Lakshmi[134]) as well as Banu, also variously called Banai or Bani, who comes from a forest-dwelling people called the Dhangars.[135] Banu is a consort of Khandoba, a form of Shiva, whose combined attributes constitute the "beauty, graciousness and protective nature" of the mother Goddess.[136] (Another of the many manifestations of Shiva, the Bhairavas, is the Adivasi god Mailar, who also has two wives, one from a Brahmin family and thus representing settled society, the other an expression of "wild nature."[137]) The author chooses Bengali for the lines calling for "immediate, concerted action on her behalf and under her patronage." The Bengali parts of the song "tend to strike a short, sharp, yet stirring rhythm, pulsating with emotional impact that turns on two words used as familiar forms of address for 'you' and 'mother', *tumi* and *ma*, respectively." The two languages and their associative resonances are, Lipner argues, "able to grip the whole persona of the responsive individual."[138]

There is another feature of the goddess Banu, so far unremarked by critics in relation to the novel, which connects her to the forest in subtle yet significant ways: her fondness for betel nut. She is the second wife of Lord Khandoba, a form of Shiva popular in Maharashtra, and she belongs, unusually for a king (whether divine or not), to a pastoral people, the Dhangars, many of whom live in forests and are often called "ruffians."¹³⁹ Banu's name itself derives from *ban* (also *van*), for forest. She is thus from "outside" the polis, as Günther D. Sontheimer explains, as opposed to the city-bred wife named Mhalsa.¹⁴⁰ This background makes her "headstrong and resolute," and "invariably beautiful and erotic," as described in Marathi folk songs.¹⁴¹ The songs describe how the "royal god" Khandoba encounters her in the forest one day while hunting, an erotic tale similar to that of Shakuntala and King Dushyanta, who, as mentioned previously, appear in both the *Mahabharata* and Kalidasa's classic drama.¹⁴² However, Banu is not the cultivated product of an ashramic education as Shakuntala is. As a product of nature, Banu stands in contrast to the other important wife of Khandoba, Mhalsa, who represents "culture," with the divine king a presence "between them."¹⁴³ Banu's headstrong nature is in evidence when, for instance, she "pushes the king away" and exclaims, *"Hands off my sari, let me go home"* (original emphasis).¹⁴⁴ Incensed by Khandoba's marriage to Banu, Mhalsa complains to him that the new bride has "polluted" the palace, and curses Banu directly for being better suited to "the wilderness," for her body "stink[s]" of sheep.¹⁴⁵ "My mansion," Mhalsa exclaims bitterly to Khandoba, "is worth lakhs," and bemoans the "spell" Banu has cast on him. She tells him to go and "set up a house with her (Banu) in the forest."¹⁴⁶ Ultimately, the two wives make peace, which almost certainly symbolizes the necessary balance of forest (or nature) and city.¹⁴⁷

Yet the main substance of the songs, and their playful, structuring frisson, is the two wives' constant quarreling rather than a concern for Khandoba's reactions. Images that distinguish Banu, in contrast to Mhalsa (and the other wives), significantly include her love of adorning herself with bright red turmeric and *paan*. One song describes her "put[ing] turmeric dust in the part of her hair," in the traditional Hindu ritual called *sindoor*, whereas in another song, Khandoba "stealthily throws some turmeric dust on Banu"¹⁴⁸—stealthily because Banu has resisted his wish to marry her. In the collection of songs presented by Sontheimer, Banu is the agent of her fate, playing out Khandoba's desire, as compared to Mhalsa's more traditional (and arranged) marriage. (In legend, he has gone so far as to live among the Dhangars for twelve years disguised as a shepherd until he can persuade Banu to relent.) Newly wed, and admiring herself in a mirror, Banu "quickly chewed a betel leaf roll to redden her mouth" in order to heighten her beauty, which makes her even more irresistible to Khandoba.¹⁴⁹ She can maximize the cosmetic effects of *paan* because, although also prized by urbanites, its forest origin lends a special aura to this forest-bred woman. (In another folk song, for example, the famous sixteenth-century woman poet Mirabai speaks of welcoming Hari—the dark-skinned, forest-bred god Krishna—who "is coming … to play the game of Spring," by laying out "betel-leaf."¹⁵⁰) When the two wives eventually make peace, the festival of Diwali, as described in a series of songs, offers an occasion for their joint appearance with Khandoba as he bestows *darshan* on his myriad followers. Both wives now "chew scented betel-leaf rolls" to make "their lips flash like rubies." To further accentuate the wives' truce, and the coming together of forest and polis, the song describes Mhalsa, too, in vegetal terms, for she "looks fresh like the core of a banana plant, or the petal of a flower."¹⁵¹ In Mhalsa and Banu, we can see the attributes of the Durga-like goddess embodying the motherland whose praises Bankim's Bhabananda sings: the household skills of Mhalsa, akin to a "lotusflower," combine with the strength and forest know-how of Banu to produce a goddess who can properly represent the nation's different landscapes.

These associations of Durga and her affiliations with forests illustrate that removing "*Bande Mataram*" from its narrative context diminishes its variegated dimensions and meanings. By "diminishes," I mean overlooking both the song's rich arboreal associations and its place in the symbolic connection to the novel's denigration of Muslims—associations that are at cross-purposes. Durga's attributes as Banu speak to the "shadows of the forest" in which Khandoba "hunts and plays" in the way kings do, for it is amid these shadows that Khandoba, under the guise of a royal hunt, will find true love. True, it is a love in which he momentarily "loses his mind"; but for this very reason, Khandoba's love makes him alive to a world he had hitherto ignored, the pastoral world of ordinary sheepherders.[152] Bankim's *santans* similarly take momentary leave of their senses in the service of the Mother (though the narrator feels obliged to reprove their violence). Most importantly, of course, the *santans* reside in the forest, in an "abbey of bliss," as the novel's title has sometimes been translated.[153] It is significant, too, that of Khandoba's other three wives, one is Muslim, so that the god is also worshipped by certain Muslims[154]—a sign of the legend's folk origins, whose more syncretic tendencies resist the Sanskritization[155] that has become characteristic of caste affiliations in modern times, beginning with British categorization. Does the *santans'* devotion to Mother India, particularly in the form of Bengal's forests, mean that the rebel monks have come to appreciate the marginalized world of pastoralists and indigenous forest dwellers? This appears to be part of the novel's implication. But the further implication, that these groups' syncretic practices encompass Muslim devotees, as in the case of Khandoba's Muslim wife, is at odds with the novel's denigration of Muslims.

The context for the Banu attributes of Durga illuminates another feature of the novel's setting—that is, its particular blend of Vishnu and Shiva worship. As Lipner observes, Bankim's aim to speak for all Indians led him to create a new form of spiritual devotion, a "Hindu Eternal Code" that "transcend[s] the confines" of "sectarianism," and therefore has the *santans* blend the practices and outlooks of "Vaishnava, Saiva and Sakta" (goddess worship) persuasions.[156] Khandoba as Shiva therefore has a counterpart in Krishna, as when the character Kalyani on different occasions hears a heavenly voice chant (implicitly expressing her own desperate plea) the many names of Krishna: "O Gopal, Govinda, Mukunda, Krishna!" (136) By itself, the mixing of sects was not new: Durga and Radha, Krishna's consort, were (and are) equally popular forms within the same communities. What is new, as noted previously, is Bankim's effort in the novel to enlist this fusion in the service of the nation or rather, the nation-in-making. In this cause, the *santans* "stand for all Hindus" and "are ready to embrace all non-Hindus who are prepared to accept their vision for the future—but on their terms."[157] In order to offer readers a vision of an as-yet unformed community, as the novel does, Bankim must allow this community to be "fuzzily drawn," as Kaviraj puts it, accentuating the necessary "indeterminacy" of a nation composed of such diverse elements.[158] We can see more clearly now that this vision correlates with the forest's liminality, its shadows, and variety of personae, which are represented in classical, folk, or modern terms, permitting a range of possible actions and outcomes. This quality of liminality clearly clashes with Bankim's parallel aim of identifying the forest with an ostensibly authentic "Aryan" indigeneity.

The Vaishnava dimension of this new religious code is especially significant because it was this that Bankim recrafted in his own image, which reflected in the *santans*. For centuries also up to and including in Bankim's time, Vishnu worship had centered on popular stories of Krishna as a loving and playful figure who is bred in the forest, enchants women, and lives joyously. Devotional, or *bhakti*, movements had for centuries centered on Krishna, and their inclusiveness enlisted members of all castes and women, including the celebrated sixteenth-century poet Mirabai, in northern India, as well as the Tamil poet Andal.[159] *Bhakti* may be defined as "a type of Hindu … worship characterized by an intense personal devotion to a deity often expressed in love-songs."[160] *Bhakti* has had many women saints, and *bhakti* devotion famously transcends most boundaries—caste, class, profession, and sometimes even gender, to the point that some male *bhaktas* (devotees) have "wished to become women" and assumed "a kind of third gender," as Ramanujan tells us.[161] *Bhakti* songs often use the metaphor of erotic desire to express the intensity of the devotee's love for Krishna and are, for this reason, like their singers, sometimes considered transgressive.

Broadly speaking, a Vaishnava is a person belonging to a Vishnu-worshipping sect, most commonly focused on Vishnu's greatest avatar, Krishna. Vaishnavas therefore emphasize Krishna's fondness for forests. As previously noted, Krishna's home, Vrindavan, is a kind of forest-garden, where he loves to play with the *gopis*. His playfulness in this arboreal space is one of his distinctive features. As a trickster figure, the young Krishna's antics and words frequently expose societal conventions that stop people from asking questions that can empower them and lead to change. Krishna is adept at questioning the "sets of opposites" that structure our everyday "webs of signification," as Lewis Hyde puts it.[162] The famous episode of Krishna stealing butter from his mother Yashoda's pots illustrates this point well. (Hence the popular Hindi epithet for Krishna, *Makhan Chor* [Butter Thief].) When Yashoda confronts her son, his characteristically blue face streaked with butter, he replies with several shrewd alibis, such as, "How could I steal it? Doesn't everything in the house belong to us?" Krishna's response reveals, observes Hyde, how conventional "Ideas about property and theft depend on a set of assumptions about how the world is divided up."[163] Krishna acts not out of hunger, but out of desire,[164] just as he does when dallying with the *gopis* and, more significantly, with the beautiful and eternally youthful Radha. Importantly, they, too, seek him, but not within the city: they find him in the forest, which in the stories represents abundance. Radha is forever searching for her love among the trees, a key metaphor in Vaishnava worship of the struggle to find the divine. Bankim's adaptation of the Krishna–Radha relationship is a key feature of *Anandamath*, as is the spirit of *bhakti* worship,[165] the passionate and devotional intensity of which invest the novel's rebel saints. *Anandamath* is also filled with motifs of disguise and deception that are a characteristic tendency of Krishna, and which the forest invites.

Bankim, however, emphasizes the "heroic aspect" of Krishna that *bhakti* poems downplay.[166] This aspect of Krishna undergirds the *santans*' combination of warrior mindset and joyous devotion. The active warrior side is essential in order to achieve political goals in the hurly-burly of the everyday world, but must be balanced by the more long-lasting devotion to divine will. In a sense, Bankim's novel updates Krishna's lesson to Arjuna on the eve of battle in the *Mahabharata*, related in the section called the *Bhagavad Gita*, in which Arjuna, one of the five Pandava brothers, must make the painful decision to battle his family—his present foes, the Kaurava cousin-brothers—while keeping in mind the greater ethical demands of divine duty and truthful living. This is why in *Anandamath* we see, along with Mahendra, Bhabananda instantly transform from fierce warrior to joyous devotee as he enters the ashramic forest. As Lipner observes, Bankim in this way enlists *bhakti* not just in the service of the divine, but also of one's country.[167] Service to one's country when it is under a foreign yoke requires the skills that Krishna embodies: stealth, craftiness, a willingness to transgress, and utter devotion. Krishna also represents fecundity, a quality which the forest's natural abundance complements.

But the forest's abundance—which can generally be understood as both "spiritual plenitude" and the human world's bounty[168]—is available only when conventional structures are removed. This abundance also becomes more pronounced after the mid-1700s, when the Braj region's forests were in decline, with poets and painters enacting a compensatory, exaggerated verdure. This also happened to be a time in which botanical gardens and sciences were being established, which led to the formation of an increasing number of extractive plantations.[169] Krishna and Radha enjoy an increasingly verdant landscape in eighteenth-century Braj poetry and art, whose practitioners freely mixed Hindu Rajput and Mughal styles with folk motifs to create a fresh iconography of spiritual devotion.[170] This befits the *bhakti* form of Krishna worship promoted by Chaitanya, whom Bengali Vaishnavas favored, and implies a willingness to transgress boundaries and to capture a semblance of his rebellious nature so as to unlock the potentiality for change. The forest reflects this potentiality because its flora and fauna, as well as its play of light and shadow, are in constant flux and can never be fully confined. The *Bhagavata Purana*, "so central to modern Krishna devotion and familiar terrain to Bankim," tells of Krishna's birth in forest darkness.[171] This chiaroscuro effect is spiritual, as well, suggesting not only the Hindu concept of a dark age, or Kali Yuga, but also, and for Bankim more importantly, a counterpart to the light of spiritual–national awakening. Together, the "womb-like" quality and gloom of the forest in *Anandamath*, which includes "the womb-house of the monastery," provide the necessary context for crafting a new and radiant national future.[172] Fear is, as discussed previously, a constituent quality of forests when they are seen to be dangerously wild—the "wilderness" with which Mhalsa associates Banu in the Khandoba story, wilderness thus being, inferentially, allied with Shiva and Durga worship. In thus combining the outlooks of Vishnu, Shiva, and Satva worshippers, in offering the play of light and darkness, and in thus making the forest "a uterine symbol," Bankim's liminal forest enables the rites of passage toward the new nation.

The contextual background explains why the "*Bande Mataram*" is first sung (by Bhabananda in Mahendra's presence) at the threshold of the forest and in between a fierce battle and the monastery's peace. Bhabananda's change of persona from grim warrior to joyful monk as he and others enter the forest may reflect the Vaishnava trope of the *nikunja*, the archetypal sacred grove in which Radha and Krishna meet secretly in their sacred lovemaking.[173] By the sixteenth century, notes Molly Emma

Aitken, the *nikunja* (or *kunja*) came to be depicted in Vaishanava literature as a stylized, "shrine-like" web of groves or bowers that made up "a secret, magical world removed from the everyday."[174] Bankim preserves some of this archetypal quality while also invoking the aforementioned vegetal particularity of Bengal's Birbhum. This natural and literary background shows why the song's removal from the forest context changes its meanings. The song is, in effect, Bhabananda's explanation to Mahendra about why "we recognize no other mother" than this landscape. Although the *santans* are the Mother's "Children" at this moment, when the battles for national integrity are being waged, the clear implication—of the song as well as of the many discussions about national formation in the novel—is that every Bengali is the Mother's prospective child, so long as they are willing to sacrifice on her behalf. Sacrifice in this case is not only physical suffering, which the famine has already produced; it also entails celibacy (the sacrifice of desire) and patience (since national emancipation will not be achieved in one's lifetime). The dominant theme of fighting for national freedom explains the novel's "dramatic," even "theatrical" style.[175]

As a number of commentators have argued, this strategy of using character types rather than protagonists rendered "too realistically as individuals" provides the necessary space in which readers can insert themselves imaginatively in order to enter "a possible future in which" to fulfill the national project.[176] This strategy is different, however, from that of the historical novel in Europe, because, as Kaviraj argues, rather than try to convey "a concrete sense of a historical period" as such novels did, Bankim instead aims "to 'falsify' history" by inserting fictional events into the frame of historical ones, such as the 1769–70 Bengal famine.[177] A primary device for this, Kaviraj observes, is "the creation of [a] double-valued time, a mixture of the past and the future," the historical and the mythic. The *santans* perceive time both as a mythic, "endless expanse" into which their actions enter (and become mythic) *and* as part of an "unfinished process" that future patriots will conclude.[178] They are conscious of fighting within the (European) rubric of modern history.

The forest setting is vital to this mythicizing effect, relying especially on the typologies of goddess and king, or leader. Bankim's concept of Mother India is, to reiterate, "the fusion of the Mother as the land of Bengal, and by implication, the whole of India." More specifically, Mother India is, in the song's words, the "Goddess as protective, spiritually real power—for example, 'The Mother rich in waters, rich in fruit (v. i) ... who saves and drives away the hostile hordes (v. 4)' "[179] The identification of land with female qualities has, as Lipner reminds us, been a familiar feature of Hindu traditions for millennia.[180] Sita, whose name means "furrow," is a product of the earth, or *bhumi*; as such, she is also expressive of *prakriti* (nature as dynamic physical matter) and *shakti* (divine strength), and so an indispensable consort for Lord Rama, "enabling him to carry out his kingly duties."[181] Nature, especially in its forest form, is thus vital to kingly virtue, because the forest, like the goddess, combines the physical properties of *prakriti* and the spiritual force of *shakti*, both of which are necessities of just rule.[182] Bankim's idea of representational reality corresponds here to Tagore's understanding of *darshan* (divine sight, or "seeing beyond" the everyday) as a vital ingredient of the concept of truthful reality and of realism in art. In Bankim's conception, Mother India as goddess, like the forest, represents a reality that cannot be translated according to

European dichotomies. His forest is for this reason at once physical and immaterial, realistic and figurative.

As a characteristic example of the forest's different registers, consider the novel's opening:

> A vast forest. Most of the trees in it are *sal*, but there are many other kinds of tree. The trees, with foliage intertwined, stretch out in endless ranks. Without breaks or gaps, without even openings for light to penetrate, a boundless ocean of leaves, wave upon wave upon wave ruffled by the wind, rolls on for mile after mile. (129)

To remind us of the passage's verisimilitude, Lipner in his introduction provides a gloss on the sal tree: "The Shorea robusta, a widespread, gregarious tree with broad, ovate leaves, the sal aids the image of a dense forest."[183] Lipner rightly compares this opening to a passage in James Fenimore Cooper's 1840 novel, *The Pathfinder*, with which Bankim was likely familiar, reflecting the romantic ideals he had imbibed, to some degree, from European literature.[184] Lipner detects in Bankim's "boundless ocean of leaves"—almost identical to Cooper's "ocean of leaves"—a "classic [Hindu] symbol of the fertile womb,"[185] observing that both Sanskrit and folk myth liken the ocean to a womb from which the world arises. Bankim's frequent characterization of the sal forest's "profound darkness" similarly invokes the womb, both linguistically and visually.[186] I will return to this association of forest and womb in relation to the novel's female protagonists, but here, I want to highlight Bankim's signature mix of reality effects and mythicizing. The specificity of sal, which is indeed a tree common to northern Indian forests, sits alongside the image of an undifferentiated, almost impenetrable expanse of trees. The abrupt opening comports uneasily with the lyricism of the lines that follow, which seems to me suggestive of modernity's mixed attitudes to forests, simultaneously beautiful and functional—a semantic twin, I would argue, of the ambivalence with which settled societies have long tended to regard forests. We also see in these lines a characteristic urge among nineteenth-century nationalists, born of their efforts to reenvision traditional religious iconography in order to meet the needs of a modern present, to depict forests as simultaneously mythic and material. It was more common, however, for an author to treat these different qualities in distinct genres. The prolific writer Romesh Chander Dutt, for example, published his famous *Economic History of India* (1902), but also wrote (in English) historical romances and poetic adaptations of Sanskrit classics, in which heroic hunters chase "wild beasts" through "tangled trees" of "wild [jungles]" and on to "Arjun's wood."[187] In *Anandamath*, Bankim instead aimed to do this in a single fictional work.

The novel's description of the monastery's temple within this dense Bengal forest, which follows Bhabananda's full rendition of the "*Bande Mataram*" song, provides the vital visualization of the Mother India goddess's attributes that would inform the song in its paratextual career, as indicated in the discussion of Durga's forest associations (in her form as Banu). In order to understand the reasons for the description's power, as well as the implications of the song's arboreal context, we must consider the temple scene more closely. After Bhabananda has sung "*Bande Mataram*," he leads Mahendra further into "that deserted forest, dark and silent"—the adjectives momentarily accentuating the forest-as-wilderness trope—which now erupts in "bird-song" and "light," "flood[ing]" the darkened wilderness with musical "light." It is here, in the monastery, that they find the *santan* leader Satyananda sitting, in classic ashramic fashion, "on a deer-skin performing his early morning worship with Jibananda" (148). The syntactic contiguity of monastery and forest effectively merges the two: "And in that joyful dawn, in that joyous forest, in the monastery of the sacred brotherhood, Satyananda Thakur sat" (148).

Satyananda then takes Mahendra "into the temple," its dim recesses initially contrasting with "the crimson flush of the new dawn, when the nearby forest glittered like diamonds in the sunlight" (149). The temple, like the monastery, is contiguous with the dawning light upon the trees, suggestive of the aforementioned *nikunja*, or sacred bower, in which Radha and Krishna have their tryst, a trope which Vaishnava literature had refined in the preceding two centuries. In an early version of part II, chapter 8, which Bankim later revised, Shanti makes the forest–monastery convergence clear when she tells Jibananda, "Come on, let's go to the arbour." When Jibananda asks where this is, she declares, "in the monastery." Her use of the term "*kunja*" for "arbour" (in the original Bengali) underscores the association with the Radha–Krishna bower.[188] (That Shanti, still disguised as a man, is determined to enter the male-only preserve of the monastery amplifies the women-as-*shakti* theme.) No wonder the dim light of the temple and monastery is synonymous with the dimness of the thick forest, which is the sacrosanct space of the Mother Goddess. As his pupils adjust to the dimness, Mahendra sees

> a massive four-armed statue bearing a conch shell, discuss, mace and lotus, respectively, in each hand ... Two great, headless forms, painted as if bathed in blood, representing the demons Madhu and Kaitabha, stood in front of the image. On its left stood a terrified-looking Lakshmi, flowing hair disheveled and adorned with a garland of roses. On the right stood Sarasvati, surrounded by books, musical instruments ... and other objects. On Vishnu's lap sat an enchanting image, more beautiful and glorious than Lakshmi and Sarasvati. Gandharvas, kinnaras, gods, yakshas and sprites paid her homage. (149)

Satyananda leads Mahendra to "another chamber" to see a "beautiful image of the Goddess, as Bearer of the earth, perfectly formed," whom the monk describes as "She who subdued the wild beasts." He orders Mahendra to bow "before the motherland in the form of [this] nurturing Goddess," an image of the "Mother-as-she-was." Satyananda then leads Mahendra through a "dark tunnel, in the depths of the earth, lit somehow by a faint light," in whose glow they "see an image of Kali," whom the monk calls "the Mother-as-she-is." Mahendra is surprised, for the fearsome Kali contrasts with the beautiful goddess image they have just visited. "Yes, Kali," Satyananda says. "Blackened and shrouded in darkness. She has been robbed of everything; that is why she is naked. And because the whole land is a burning-ground, she is garlanded with skulls. And she is crushing her own gracious Lord underfoot. Alas, dear Mother!" (150)

Finally, Satyananda takes Mahendra through another tunnel to "a golden ten-armed image of the Goddess in a large marble shrine glistening and smiling in the early morning rays." "And this," says the monk, "is the Mother-as-she-will-be." The two men greet her "in unison," using three of her other names as *shakti*—"Tryambaka, Gauri, Narayani" (151)—attributes signaling, respectively, Siva's consort, the "fair-haired One," and Vishnu's consort and, thus, according to Lipner, demonstrating that the Goddess "transcends sectarian divisions."[189] "When will we be able to see the Mother in this form?" Mahendra asks, to which Satyananda replies, "when all Mother's children recognize her as the Mother" (151). It is at this point that the monk tells Mahendra that his wife and daughter, whom he has been searching for, are just outside the temple (151). Satyananda then separately "descended through another tunnel deep into a secret chamber" where he tells Jibananda and Bhabananda that Mahendra will likely join the *santans*, which would make his considerable wealth available for "the Mother's service" (151). The variety of attributes of the Mother—or rather, "motherland"—goddess in this scene echo the forest's variety of manifestations, both symbolic and biological, throughout the novel. At its root, this is an empowering folk-oriented, multifaceted, and inclusive understanding of the Mother Goddess as a representation of *shakti*, a power associated with the forest, and therefore an effective symbol for nationhood.[190] But this vision of *shakti* as a diffuse power that is centered in the indeterminate depths of the forest is usually superseded in Bankim's novel by the *santans*' code of celibate masculinity. In the years after the novel's appearance, this conjunction fed into the conservative nationalist construction of Mother India as embodying a mapped, "specifically delineated ... territory" whose borders had to be safeguarded by the Mother's "virile sons."[191]

Cross-Dressing Rebels and Other Tales of Transgression

Although Bankim's novel advocates a mostly exclusionary vision of the nation as Hindu, the creed he tailored from Chaitanya's *bhakti* philosophy would seem to have been less so, since the sixteenth-century Brahmin sage had prized individual devotion to Krishna above sectarian affiliation.[192] And indeed, Bankim's early works had expressed this form of *bhakti*. (I leave aside here the argument that Chaitanya's movement was, in fact, never interested in restructuring existing society.[193]) But by the time he wrote *Anandamath*, Bankim's view had changed dramatically to promote a caste-based society in which men and women held different, unequal roles.[194] For Bankim and most other reformers, Hindu women, being pure and "untainted" by Western ideas, were thought to embody the nation.[195] Because Hindu women had to endure the kind of domestic restrictions that ensured the maintenance of religious (and so indigenous) tenets, male reformers saw them as fitting vehicles for the sacrifices necessary for national independence.[196] This is one reason, no doubt, that a character like Kalyani is described in language that is almost identical to Kalidasa's arboreal description of Shakuntala. The latter's "arms resemble tendrils on a vine," and her "limbs" are "ready to burst into blossom."[197] Bankim's Kalyani, even when a "dense," brooding "cloud" hangs over her, is "the loveliest of women," with arms "more tender than forest vines" (195). Shanti is similarly beautiful, "like a lotus in bloom" (165).[198]

Curiously, however, despite this kind of idealization, it is women—namely, Kalyani and Shanti—in *Anandamath* who prove to be among the most fearless and active rebels. This is not the conceptual contradiction it initially appears to be, for as Tanika Sarkar observes, women for Bankim embodied the nation "in a far more activist way" than they did for his fellow nationalists.[199] In fact, many of Bankim's novels feature women who, by drawing on the same form of self-discipline he sees in Krishna—whose reputed playfulness Bankim reconceives as "heroic action"[200]—actively safeguard Hindu traditions. It is Hindu men who, in these novels, lack the "divine energy" to act in similarly heroic ways. It is they who have reneged on their duties and caused the collapse of Hindu governance[201]—perhaps implicitly leaving the door open for Muslim men to accept such a role. How, then, do the beautiful, Shakuntala-like heroines Kalyani and Shanti act in the service of the *santans*' rebellion? Kaviraj argues that Kalyani reflects "an artless simplicity," while Shanti is "the active face of the feminine" divine energy, or *shakti*.[202] In Lipner's view, Kalyani is Shanti's "foil," her experiential pain conditioning her to the kind of "domestic role" required of nationalist wives.[203]

Lipner's reading seems to make sense in light of Shanti's manly inhabitance, for which she has always had a predilection. Although Jibananda marries her "out of pity" after her widowed father's death, she was restless and "would never dress like a girl." Instead, like her beloved Hari (Lord Krishna), she would "join the local boys at play." Alarmed by this, her in-laws imprison her in the home, until she escapes into the nearby jungle, "dye[s] her clothes by selecting certain flowers from the jungle," and adopts "the guise of a child-ascetic" (172). She prefigures in this way Jibananda's own subsequent enlistment in the order of *santan* ascetics. But before this, he persuades her to return to their conjugal roles, and in this interlude, they come to love each other. She is described in classical terms: "Like a flower bud drenched with the first drops from a rain cloud, Shanti blossomed" (174). But when Jibananda falls under the spell of Satyananda, Shanti's frustration and restlessness return, as does her masculine inclination. She cuts her hair and uses it to "[fashion] a beard and moustache." Finding "a large deerskin" in the house, she wraps it around her in the manner of "an ascetic" and, under cover of night, plunges into "the dense forest alone." Here, with only "the goddesses of the wood" listening, Shanti sings "a most unusual song"—unusual both because she expresses her determination to join the *santans*' "battle" and because, in my reading, the adoration she expresses can be interpreted as addressed simultaneously to Krishna and to her husband.

> Hari, Hari, Hari, Hari—eager for the fight I say,
> O my love, don't you see, I'll rush into the fray today,
> Now apart we must be—stay away, O stay away! (175–6)

Shanti's song, although in the tradition of *bhakti* devotionals, is itself ambiguous in its address, mirroring her own ambiguous persona. This is not a song in the manner of, say, sixteenth-century poet-saint Mirabai's plaint that "life without Hari is no life, friend,"[204] in which amatory expressions clearly allegorize love for the divine. Shanti's is a song that is at once sacred and profane—and all the more transgressive for yearning for an ascetic husband. The solicitation of the "goddesses of the wood" underscores

Shanti's transgressive words, for the goddesses recall the attributes of folk deities who, as discussed above with regard to Durga's manifestation as Banu, cross conventional boundaries, befitting their association with arboreal imagery. Shanti indeed recalls Mirabai's songs of welcoming Hari (Krishna) with "betel-leaf," and of her readiness to "go where he lives"—that is, the Vrindavan Forest—and "color my sari red" and "let my hair grow wild."[205] This is just what Shanti does. In classic *bhakti* tradition, too, the wood goddesses appeal to everyone, regardless of creed, caste, or sex.[206]

Lipner's and Kaviraj's interpretations of Shanti's (and Kalyani's) actions as transgressive are insightful, but they leave intact a heterosexual duality that omits the many *purana* tales of ambiguous sexuality, which are frequently set in forests. Why forests? One reason, as previously mentioned, is the widespread cultural view of forests as places of penumbral activity, shape-shifting, and individual self-realization. Turner's concept of liminality fits nicely with this, as is clear from my discussion of Lipner's use of it to account for the *santans'* celibacy as a liminal, or threshold, state that is open to new ways of living in the world. Lipner follows Parkhill's argument, which adapts Victor Turner's concepts about rites of passage, that the forest in Sanskrit epic is an embodiment of oppositional tension—between beauty and ugliness, peace and violence, scarcity and bounty—and therefore a "threshold" space in which particular characters achieve proper self-awareness.[207] Thus, Bhabananda masquerades as a Muslim youth to spy in a city in search of Satyananda, Dhirananda adopts the guise of a Muslim sentry to spring Satyananda from prison, and, more significantly, Shanti disguises herself first as a young male *santan* and then as a religious singer to help her husband Jibananda develop into a full-fledged *santan*. These impersonations, Lipner reminds us, all have the aim of helping everyday Indians imagine "a regenerated national collective."[208]

Yet the forest is amorphous not simply because it enables shifts between one substantive role to another, including androgynous performance, but also because, as in *puranic* tales, it allows for ambiguous identities and states. Shanti's cross-dressing performances, in my reading, produce a semblance of the "third" sex that, in India, *hijras* have customarily embodied and that "questions binary thinking and introduces crisis," as Marjorie B. Garber puts it in her study of transvestism in Western literature.[209] Although Shanti, unlike a *hijra*, nominally retains the option of reverting to her femininity and her prescribed domestic role as soon as she removes her disguise, her lifelong sense of being out of sync with her prescribed sexuality—prompting her aforementioned restlessness—finds that the penumbral ambiguity of the forest is a space in which she can avoid such a reversion and inhabit her real self. Shanti thereby represents what Garber means by "third," which is "a mode of articulation, a way of describing a space of possibility. Three puts in question the idea of one," whether this oneness concerns "identity, self-sufficiency, [or] self-knowledge."[210] Shanti also hints at the common characterization of *hijras* as a third sex, but in a way that reflects their lived intersectionality rather than their conventionalized roles.[211]

Shanti's impersonation in effect undercuts the novel's plug for a singular and exclusionary Hindu basis for the nation.[212] Shanti-as-*santan* youth, quite unlike her initial association with classical floral tropes, is a trickster in the tradition of Krishna himself, and it is the forest that provides the arena for her actions. These are analogous to a young Krishna stealing his beloved butter, not because it is scarce but precisely because its actual abundance has been sealed off.[213] Like the British-manufactured famines that ravaged Bengal, the natural and seemingly disordered profusion of the Bengal forest—or at least part of it—is safeguarded from colonialism's notion of order. The forest as embodiment of arboreal excess is allowed to stand. In narrative terms, Shanti articulates a queer persona whose latent significations similarly exceed the novel's plot line. Although Shanti as male warrior preserves a dualistic, heterosexual paradigm, her persona is nevertheless radical at a time of growing conservatism and rebuffs the story's religious and gender codes[214] —not unlike the (considerably briefer) Muslim impersonations of Bhabananda and Dhirananda.

As the many traditional tales about ambiguous sexuality make clear, Shanti's behavior is not so very unusual. What is unusual, perhaps, is her centrality in a novel produced in the 1880s, a time in which the (male) Bengali *bhadralok* reimagined a "'traditional' order" of "respectability"[215] that sacralized the "conjugal order that bound" this society "together."[216] While Bankim famously satirized his urban milieu, such as by targeting the slavish *babu* of colonial bureaucracy, and while he advocated a fearsome, Durga-like goddess of the nation, his earnest entreaties for a more muscular Hinduism in the form of a martial Krishna, shorn of erotic baggage, trumped these. This is why Bankim's *santans* endorse celibacy: a specific kind of bodily detachment so as to channel energy into what is, for now, the worthier goal of nationhood. But societal conventions can also be an obstacle to this goal, so one must be prepared to transgress them in the manner of Krishna, and of women, who, as "objects … of [male] desire" in Bankim's novels, "create or induce transgression," just as they, too, act transgressively.[217] As a popular (and divine) trickster, Krishna answered this call. But Bankim sought to reclaim what he believed was the historical Krishna by emphasizing his "heroic" and "rational" qualities, which befit a modern, mature nation.[218] In Bankim's view, this move simultaneously shifts the male gaze from women to the proper Hindu familial province of the nation. Krishna's reconstructed liminality, like that of Bankim's women figures, is more appropriate to national consciousness precisely because it precludes settling into clearly defined articles of faith that leave no room for intellectual activity.[219] This activity is alive to possibilities and does not shut down imaginative conversation. Surprisingly, however, Kaviraj neglects to highlight that most liminal of spaces—and a favorite of Bankim's—the forest.

But warriors, those traditional leaders and protectors of national autonomy, must be willing to face death, the least known, most liminal of existential passages.[220] *Santans* die not only because they engage in mortal combat against their enemies, but also in order to emphasize the motif "of death and spiritual rebirth in … the forest setting," one that the novel frequently depicts.[221] It is Shanti and Kalyani, however, who are most dramatically reborn and whose experiences frame the novel. When Kalyani is on the verge of death after collapsing from exhaustion "under a huge tree," she is revived by a heavenly "[voice] echoing through the forest," which reminds her of the *Purana* stories she heard as a girl. She awakens in a room in the *santan* monastery, to which (as she learns) the monk Bhabananda has brought her and her child after discovering them in the forest. Here, she turns to a meditative reading of the *Gita*. Since both she and Bhabananda believe that her husband Mahendra has died in battle, he—giving in to temptation—begs her to be his wife, "a support in virtue." When she asks, "Why did you give me back my [worthless] life?" he replies, "Perhaps what I gave to you now belongs to me! Kalyani! Can you not give to me the life I have given you?" (196). Kalyani eventually relents, so long as she can remain chaste. Shanti, too, in renouncing her conventional wifely role to join the final battle at her husband Jibananda's side, is figuratively reborn a *santan*[222]—though one whose disguise, as mentioned, recalls the impersonations of a trickster, not unlike Krishna.

The depictions of Kalyani and Shanti bring to crisis not only the moral economy within the novel, but also its paratextual moral economy, in light of the book's— especially the *"Bande Mataram"* song's—subsequent role in feeding anti-Muslim sentiment. These women characters do so, as I have argued, because they inhabit ambiguous modes of sexuality and gender despite the novel's male-centered ethos. But although the latter is repeatedly expressed through tropes of masculinity, femininity, and domesticity, it is in fact the author's own predilection for the transgressive milieu of the *Mahabharata*[223] and of other story traditions that seems to be at cross-purposes with the novel's expressed paternalism. Both women's rebirth within the womb-like forest, as well as Shanti's disguises, recall stories about sexual slippage in the *Mahabharata*, such as when Vishnu at one point takes the illusory form of a woman to trick demons.[224] The *Bhagavata Purana* tells the story (as do other *puranas*) of how on one occasion Shiva and Parvati are coupling in their "enchanted" forest when they are interrupted by the forest's *sadhus*, who had come to speak to Shiva. Parvati is "ashamed," and the angry Shiva declares, "Whoever enters this place will become a female."[225] The *Ramayana* similarly tells of how King Ila is transformed into a woman by stumbling upon the same forest scene.[226] There is, then, ample precedence in ancient, venerated stories for Shanti's actions. Yet Shanti and Kalyani nonetheless trouble the image of a geographically determined Mother India that Satyananda shows Mahendra in the forest temple. Although the Brahmin Mahendra, like the other "initiated" upper-caste *santans*, represents the appropriate kind of Hindu national rebel in contrast to the often overly violent "uninitiated" *santans*, it is Shanti and Kalyani who open and close the novel. Why so, and what does this imply? A reading of the novel's forest setting would be incomplete without suggesting an answer.

Mahendra's high caste entitles him to practice, if he so chooses, the four *ashramas*, or way stations, of Hindu (primarily male) life: *Brahmacharya* (bachelor student), *Grihastha* (householder), *Vanaprastha* (forest dweller, retired), and *Sannyasi* (renunciate). Mahendra, in committing himself to the rebellion while renouncing the violent excesses of the uninitiated *santans*, proves himself worthy of the conduct that alone, the novel suggests, can lead to national consciousness. When he first encounters the *santans*, Mahendra has been searching desperately for his wife and child, whose kidnapping by starving bandits who flee into a forest serves as the novel's opening (more on which below). Mahendra comes upon an East India Company "revenue cart" heading for the Calcutta treasury. Bankim here makes one of his frequent nods to historical context, telling us that "since the fear of bandits was so great at present, fifty armed Indian sepoys (soldiers) with fixed bayonets marched in ranks before and behind the carts. The commanding officer was a white man who rode on horseback at the rear." Mahendra steps aside to stand "by the edge of the jungle adjoining the road" (140). Spotting him, the British officer's sepoys grab and bind him, along with a man named Bhabananda. As they "travel along the same high road near the jungle," Bhabananda quietly tells Mahendra to follow his lead, and then, suddenly, two hundred *santans* emerge from the jungle and attack the sepoys. Mahendra picks up a sword to join his liberators, who decapitate their English commander and "captured the money chests." Mahendra throws down his sword in disgust, believing the "bandits" are, in fact, nothing more than thieves.

This passage is an important prelude to the "*Bande Mataram*" song for a number of reasons. To begin with, the action is staged at the "edge" of a jungle, a word that connotes, as discussed previously, wildness and amorphous entanglement. The jungle's wildness gives a certain license to the *santans*' bloodletting. It is also on the edge of a road, a material effort—a doomed one, the scene suggests—to separate civilization (one distorted by colonial rule) from wildness. Mahendra has already traversed this line by leaving an inn and then standing at the jungle's edge as a cartload of money, squeezed by the British from starving peasants in the guise of legal taxation, works its way to the metropolis. In this sense, the road as well as the jungle represent a liminal, in-between space of the kind that, as Lipner observes of the forest, stages a number of transitions: Mahendra's maturation as a patriotic ascetic, the *santans*' "collective" evolution into "an egalitarian brotherhood," and everyone's awakening to national consciousness.[227] Kaviraj, while overlooking forest imagery, echoes Lipner's point in saying that Bankim's fictions are frequently concerned with "a liminality of morals, constructing … situations which pose large, often unanswerable, questions to constituted moral theory." Bankim's characters therefore inhabit "regions of intersection, where oppositions come … [into] play with each other."[228]

This interpretation is, however, made difficult by Bankim's interchangeable uses of "jungle" and "forest" to characterize the surrounding woodland. For instance, in the scene leading up to the battle between the company and the rebels, a mysterious monk is crossing "a vast plain whose edges the [moon's] light could not penetrate," making it "impossible" to discern anyone. The plain "seemed endless and deserted, a dwelling place for fear" (138–9). Noticing "a small hill" covered in "many mango and other trees," which "cast black, trembling shadows on the dark rocks below," the monk climbs the hill to "listen" and survey the landscape. Seeing "a dense jungle," the monk "set off" for it, and, "going deep into the jungle" comes upon "about two hundred" armed rebels "sitting in the forest gloom," their "weapons gleam[ing] in the dappled moonlight" (139). The monk clearly does not find it "impossible" to find the men, indicating that he has special, almost occult knowledge of this forest—the kind of forest in which mango and other fruit trees grow, and whose "thickets of trees" hide the ancient "Buddhist" monastery (described in the scene before this) from which the monk has set out (137). Yet the fruit trees are couched in gothic language, setting a mood that the prevailing gloom accentuates (both in this scene and many others). It seems significant that the monk encounters the "tall, dark" rebels in woodland that is simultaneously "forest" and "jungle" (139). As previously noted, the jungle would seem to lend its "wildness" to the men, while also preserving their association with sacred forest. Like the "deep, impenetrable forest" in which "human beings now" reside in the secretive monastery (137), informing it with the light of truth, the thick "rows of trees" in which the two hundred rebels are waiting are illuminated by both their "polished" and shining weapons and by the arrival of a monk—who turns out to be Satyananda himself, with his previously described "shining white [robes]" (136). Bhabananda, too, whom Satyananda finds among the hiding rebels, boasts a "body luminous with sandal paste (139). Here and throughout the novel, true devotion to Krishna and the Mother Goddess generates a radiance that figuratively, but also at times literally, illuminates the forest, endowing even those parts that seem to be jungle—possessing the kind of *jungli* attributes associated, for instance, with indigenous forest dwellers—with a sacred, illuminating aura.²²⁹

Here we come to a narrative crux that exposes the novel's conflicted vision of nationhood, one that is at once inclusive and exclusive. For if the Mother Goddess embodies all of Bengal's woodlands, she presumably encompasses the region's wilder jungles as well as its forests, with their "noble" trees. She incorporates, in the fullest sense of the word, attributes that are both pure and impure, disciplined and undisciplined, classically restrained (the Kalidasa inheritance) and immoderately improvisational (the *bhakti* legacy). The forest accommodates all of these. Its multidimensionality also accommodates the requirements of kingly education, as described in Chapter 1, for a proper king must be familiar with all facets of forest life, from its dangers to its resplendence. As Lipner reminds us, "It was an accepted criterion of proper kingly sway in Hindu tradition that the ruler was obliged to establish … order in his territory as allowed all his subjects to flourish according to their established ways of life so long as the stability of the kingdom was not imperiled."²³⁰ As Bhabananda says to Mahendra in justifying the theft of the East India Company's treasury, "A king who doesn't look after his kingdom is no king" (146)—for the famine clearly demonstrates the company's irresponsible rule. In this regard, Bankim separately wrote, Muslim kings had often performed "better than Hindus."²³¹ Yet as we have seen, *Anandamath* repeatedly endorses a Hindu code of governance, with Satyananda declaring the "authentic Vaishnava practice," uncontaminated by "the atheist Buddhist code" of "nonviolence," rests on "subduing the evildoer and rescuing the world" (179). This accounts for the *santans* taking over a derelict Buddhist monastery as their own. At the same time, however, it is Shanti and Kalyani who, in their actions in the forest, embody leadership qualities that exceed the Hindu code represented by the titular monastery. The two women's behavior is at odds with the text's advocacy of what Satyananda says is the exclusive, "true Vaishnava code" of a militant form of worship. Ironically, Shanti and Kalyani exemplify the ecstatic expression of Vaishnava devotion preached by the sixteenth-century sage Chaitanya, a practice Satyananda deems incomplete and therefore "false" (179).

Shanti drives the plot with her actions in the forest on behalf of the rebellion, exhibiting the qualities of a traditional king, though as a woman she is not precluded from that role. At another point in the narrative, she pretends to be a wandering singer in the tradition of Vaishnavi *bhakti*. It is significant that before embarking on her stealthy forest activities, Shanti sings parts of Jayadeva's great twelfth-century Vaishnava poem about Krishna and Radha, the *Gita Govinda*, "allowing it to break the endless silence of that boundless forest." Her singing is answered by Satyananda (201–2). Although the poem beseeches "Hari [Krishna]" to "conquer," the absence of an object for this verb leaves it open to interpretation (202). Satyananda naturally sings of, and values, the Krishna who "wield[s]" a "dreadful sword [to destroy the barbarian hordes]," whereas Shanti celebrates the Krishna who, in the form of Buddha, denounces "the slaying of animals" (201–2). As Kaviraj observes, Jayadeva transforms Krishna "from the greatest warrior to the greatest lover," with Radha his "powerful" consort.[232] This is anything but a celibate lord, making Satyananda's invocation ironic, given his resolute asceticism. (It is also ironic that Jayadeva helps make Bankim's novel possible, for he composed the *Gita Govinda* in a "democratized Sanskrit" to reach a wide audience.[233])

Kaviraj's otherwise illuminating discussion of Bankim's national–philosophical adaptation of Vaishnavism concludes that in Bankim's cosmography, Radha is turned into a non-corporeal ideal in order to be the necessary counterpart to the more material Krishna.[234] This argument, however, is obliged to ignore not only Radha's physicality in the guise of other female figures, but also how the forest setting conditions both the historical and mythic dimensions of the story. For Kaviraj, the "flowering resplendent" forest remains, like Radha, at a symbolic level.[235] But in fact, a more material form of Radha, including her erotic charge, does animate the pages of *Anandamath*, and there is a precedent in Bankim's own writings. As Tanika Sarkar informs us, Bankim's famous satirical essay "Kamalakanter Daptar" figures a widow's self-immolation, or sati, in erotic terms, with the funeral flames symbolizing her "desire," which "moves from one part of the body to another and … finally annihilates her at the moment of a longed-for, ultimate climax which is both death and love."[236] In *Anandamath*, the *santans*' very celibacy inverts, and so preserves, the erotic potentiality of Krishna's time with the *gopis*. The figure of Radha, who represents a portion of this potentiality, is Kalyani, both through her beauty and her stalwart behavior. For instance, although she tells her husband Mahendra that her dream of a nature-filled realm of divinity is not worth relating—"But what good will it do to tell you?" (153)—she goes on to do just that. In the "silence" following her account, the forest comes alive for both of them: "palm leaves murmured in a gentle wind," "wild flowers" waft "soft scents," and birds make "sweet calls." Mahendra is irresolute, wondering if he should join the *santans*, but Kalyani does not hesitate: "You should go where god wants you to go" (154).

Even more revealing of the novel's cross-purposes is Shanti, for in orchestrating the reunion of Kalyani and Mahendra, she usurps a customarily male privilege. For example, toward the end of the novel, Kalyani is again obliged to evade bandits, as she had at the start, but this time fearlessly in search of her husband. Seeing "a group of fierce, crazed rebels," Kalyani "ran with all her might into the jungle." Just as one of this group "grabbed the end-piece of her sari," "someone suddenly appeared and struck [the] attacker with a stick," laying him low. This someone is none other than Shanti in her male disguise, who, "placing both hands on Kalyani's shoulders … peered into her face in the darkness." Kalyani recoils from this, but then recognizes and embraces her friend. The scene arguably conveys a hint of homoerotic attraction, especially as it mirrors Shanti's earlier encounter with Captain Thomas, head of the British force. On a forest hunt one day, Thomas "see[s], seated there under a great tree, swathed in creepers and shrubs with flowers in full bloom … [a] young ascetic, brightening the forest with his beauty! The fragrance of the blooms seemed to increase through contact with that heavenly form." Although he soon finds that the "man" is a woman—Shanti—"of wondrous beauty," his initial "amazement" at the sight of the "young ascetic" under a tree festooned with motifs of classical feminine beauty—creepers and blooms—signifies his attraction (191).[237] (The trope of a man happening upon a forest beauty comes straight from classical and medieval narratives and continued to animate literature and film of the twentieth century, as it indeed still frequently does.) The companionship displayed by Kalyani and Shanti here will prove to be a significant feature of the novel's conclusion.

Accepting Shanti's exhortation to follow her into the forest to avoid the many *santans* and sepoys who "are up to no good on the roads," Kalyani says, "I'll follow wherever you lead" (215–16). Soon Kalyani, "with Shanti's help," reunites with Mahendra in "the silent forest, amid the dark shadows of dense rows of *sal* trees" (216). In her cross-dressed actions, Shanti exhibits the "third" space of possibility, which, as described earlier, has ample precedence in ancient literary and oral traditions. Shanti also exhibits sisterly companionship with Kalyani as the pair make their way in a male-ordered and often rapacious world. It matters that the women, along with Mahendra, congregrate under sal trees, which are associated with Vishnu. In this case, the trees' "dark shadows," far from being ominous, as the forest frequently is in the novel, are limned with the promise of "dawn." We are far from the novel's prologue, which opens by describing a "vast forest" of mainly sal trees, whose "endless ranks" and "boundless ocean of leaves" present us with a "profound darkness"—an image whose insistent repetition in a few short paragraphs establishes a leitmotif that will only infrequently be countered with images of light. The novel also, as noted, tends to match imagery with mood, so that a forest, as the less-dangerous *vana*, can become jungle (*jangala*) according to the needs of a scene and a character.[238]

Significantly, it is Kalyani and Shanti who are present at the start and the end of the novel, the inaugural darkness of the forest ultimately dispersed by the "radiance" of rational (European), "outward knowledge" that is nevertheless sacralized by the Hindu "Eternal Code." As Satyananda, Shanti, Kalyani, and the "Healer," or "Great One," gaze upon the image of the Mother "mounted on high" in the forest sanctuary, the Healer instructs them in the path forward. Now that Muslim rule "has been destroyed," he says, they must accept the mentorship of English rule until they learn "about external things." It is a curious description, as Bankim evidently strives to express something ineffable:

> The Great One took Satyananda's hand, and a wondrous radiance shone forth. There, in the dim light before the massive four-armed image, in the solemnity of the Vishnu temple, those two human forms filled with a great wisdom shone out, one clasping the hand of the other. Who had clasped hands there? Knowledge had come and taken hold of dedication … Kalyani had come and taken hold of Shanti. Satyananda was Shanti, and the Great One was Kalyani. Satyananda was honour, and the Great One was sacrifice. (232)

The ambiguity of who is "clasping" whom is apparently meant to convey their united devotion to both the Mother Goddess and national purpose. But this unity involves, unusually so, two women and a single man. It is unusual given the novel's emphasis on the (male) *santans*' celibacy as a disciplining of the body and a rechanneling of psychosomatic energy for loftier goals.[239] But just before this scene, in the preceding chapter, Shanti has told her husband Jibananda that they both "must remain just as we are, renouncers, forever following the path of celibacy." She proposes they retreat to "a hut in the Himalayas" to "worship God" in true ashramic fashion (227). Here again, Shanti usurps the defining role of a *santan* (much as Vishnu has sometimes taken the form of a woman) and of married life. In the closing tableau, Kalyani firmly clasps Shanti, and the three tried and tested worshippers' identities merge in the liminal space of the forest.

Bankim's novel continues to reverberate formally and thematically. Its "*Bande Mataram*" song is an unabashed anthem for a Hindu-centric nationalism that alienates Muslim Indians. Renditions of the Mother India Goddess image superimposed on a map of India that became common in the early 1900s continue to be reproduced, sometimes with "Bande Mataram" imprinted on them, expressive of what Ramaswamy calls geo-piety.[240] In fictional narrative terms, *Anandamath*'s innovative use of historicity, syncretic language registers, and folk traditions influenced writers across India in the decades after the novel's publication. More notably, its representation of the forest as a source of national–maternal idealism and identity maintains an uneven, and sometimes unsettling, relationship with the many other imagined forests discussed in this study.

3

Premchand's Forest, Bibhutibhushan's *Aranyak*, and the Progressive Era

Authors publishing in the first half of the twentieth century, including Premchand (in Urdu and Hindi) and Bibhutibhushan Bandhyopadhyay (in Bengali), whose works this chapter discusses, frequently turned to realism to expose social inequities in rural India as a means of exhorting their readers to conceive of a more ethical, inclusive nation-in-making. For these progressive, generally secular, sometimes Marxist writers, the forest tends to represent utopic potentiality and dystopic exploitation at the same time. This may be why villages appear in many of these novels, for as noted previously, the village was never far from portrayals of the forest, each one lending the other an aura of organic holism. Gandhi famously urged writers who truly "love the motherland" to spend time in villages, which have "not [yet] been polluted by the railways."[1] The village was therefore deemed to be more "real" than urban India and, as Toral Jatin Gajarawala observes, to return to it was thought to be like "going back in time."[2]

This utopic view is obviously ridden with perilous proclivities, as we find in the political, mostly urban right's habit of fetishizing the village as the nation's ostensible essence. No wonder Dalits (long ago rejecting the label "untouchables") want "to embrace modernity by advocating a clear cultural break with the past rather than a reification of it."[3] Dalit writers therefore see the forest not through rose-tinted glasses, but with a clear sense of its current exploitation. Not having the privilege of making connections to a past that can inform an integrated, national present, Dalit writers today favor a more avowedly aspirational outlook than we find in earlier, more privileged writers like Bankim. The novels by Premchand and Bibhutibhushan discussed here—*Godaan* (for which I concentrate on a single forest episode) and *Aranyak*, both published a half century after *Anandamath*—occupy a literary landscape roughly midway between Bankim's hybrid genre of romance, history, and epic and notable realist and magic-realist novels of the second half of the twentieth century. Although *Godaan* and *Aranyak* contain both romantic and aspirational perspectives, and are in equal measure utopic and critical of modern "development," these narratives are nonetheless more literarily assured than those of Bankim and his peers. This is not surprising, since this nineteenth-century cohort, having imbibed colonialist versions of history that depicted Europe as advanced (and advancing) and India as stuck in a traditionalist morass, endured what Sudipta Kaviraj describes as the "melancholy of living in an alien and intractable history."[4] This inevitably induced the ambivalence this cohort felt regarding English and Bengali, though this was also a spur for Bankim's influential experimentation in *Anandamath*. Although writers like Premchand and Bibhutibhushan experienced their own forms of ambivalence, by the 1920s and 1930s, the nationalist movement had matured and spread enough—and gained global credibility, in tune with revolutionary changes in Ireland and Russia—to allow them to assert their politically inflected voices.[5] These inflections, as I show here, are dramatized through forest settings and scenes whose effectiveness owes as much to their invocation of classical tropes as to their implicit dialogue with Bankim's iconic forest.

The Forest Maiden's Moral Vision in Premchand's *Godaan*

Premchand, born Dhanpat Rai into an upper-caste family, was perhaps the most influential of those writers who trained a realist eye on village India in order to expose the state's—and its landowning agents'—exploitation of the farming communities. Although he began by writing in Urdu, he turned to Hindi early in his career.[6] Among his most famous works is the 1936 Hindi novel *Godaan* ("Gift of a Cow"), which focuses in roughly equal measure on an impoverished farming family in a village in what is today Uttar Pradesh and on the land's wealthy owners living in the city of Lucknow. The novel is rich in detail and in its variety of speech patterns,[7] but I focus here on a single scene in this capacious narrative to illustrate the prominence of the Shakuntala-like "forest nymph," as we might name this idealized and popular character type. The trope enters religious lore as well: the Buddha's mother Mayadevi is famously said to have birthed him among trees, an account that Miranda Eberle Shaw says likely "evok[ed] a longstanding association between fecund women and flowering trees."[8] Such a character may seem out of place in a social–realist work like *Godaan*. But as Gajarawala observes, this brand of "social realism" is "overlaid by Gandhian romance,"[9] a mode that characterizes numerous literary works and films in the twentieth century, such as Rao's *Kanthapura* or Narayan's *Waiting for the Mahatma*. Although the forest nymph trope is not present in all these works, it is part of the same romanticization of rural lives by urban writers. If Gandhian idealism reflects a moral universe with the idealized village at its heart, it is the village's association with the forest that activates this universe's associational power. For example, as I previously discussed with regard to both classical and nineteenth-century tropes, this idealized forest is chiefly depicted as maternal, like Bankim's, though with some additions, such as infusing the forest with potentially dangerous elements: the erotic forest maiden (who can threaten traditional matrimony), the dacoit (bandit), and natural calamities. We can detect the lasting influence of this trope in twentieth-century literature, song, and film, though with noteworthy changes. Consider, for instance, director–producer Raj Kapoor's 1978 Hindi film *Satyam Shivam Sundaram* ("Truth God Beauty"), a version of the Shakuntala story set in a present-day village. Roopa (played by Zeenat Aman) is the daughter of a local Hindu priest, and her natural allure (she likes to bathe under a waterfall, and her songs enchant the sylvan setting) enchants Rajeev (Shashi Kapoor), a handsome engineer working on a nearby dam. Only after they marry does he see the burn scars on one side of her face, which she had kept hidden. Feeling cheated, he banishes her—until a storm destroys the dam and triggers a flood during which Rajeev saves Roopa, sees his fault, and recognizes the meaning of beauty (which his modern learning had obscured). Embodying the values in the film's title, Roopa is Raj Kapoor's combinative metonym for village India. The film assures us that she will be a devoted domestic partner to Rajeev, preserving a patriarchal structure in which maternity and beauty merge.

Like Kapoor, other writers and filmmakers throughout the twentieth century experimented with popular ways of mediating Indian and Western values by turning to the city–country duality. Premchand's forest scene illustrates a secularized version of this feminized duality as a way to comment on the immorality of modern commercialism and traditional feudalism. Although the scene and its personae may seem contrived, it was in fact recognizably so to Premchand's contemporary Hindi readers, who understood and even expected, as Rosie Thomas has said of twentieth-century popular Hindi film, the idealized components of this trope.[10] *Godaan*'s forest nymph scene unifies and condenses the several parts of the prevailing "discourse on traditionalism and nationalism," particularly its emphasis on ideals of family and sexuality. This discourse is, broadly speaking, composed of the good mother and the villain and first appeared on screen in the iconic 1957 film *Mother India*.[11] As Thomas puts it, "The Hindi film can be regarded as a moral fable that involves its audience largely through the puzzle of resolving some (apparently irresolvable) disorder in the ideal moral universe."[12] While this partly explains Premchand's inclusion of the fabular forest interlude in a narrative of otherwise unremitting social realism, we should also bear in mind Premchand's activist dictum, expressed elsewhere, that "it would be good for the realist not to forget idealism."[13] More surprising, perhaps, is that the firm conceptual boundaries of this moral matrix may seem to contradict treatments of good and evil in Sanskrit epics and scriptures, where the two poles sometimes overlap.[14] For Premchand, this figure, like Kapoor's Roopa or Kalidasa's Shakuntala, embodies the kind of guileless purity that India's future citizens must strive to emulate, one that is unrefined by city standards and exudes natural vigor.

Despite this idealization, *Godaan* is rare in describing "the vast web of connections … between [the village of] Belari and Lucknow."[15] These locales are represented most prominently by the peasant paterfamilias, Hori, and by the *zamindar* Rai Sahib, who pays lip service to the Gandhian reform movement. The novel exposes the uncomfortable truth to readers that, as Sudhir Chandra puts it, "The course of nationalist politics is determined by monied interests."[16] After all, Hori and his family don't have the luxury of "returning" to a timeless village: they have never left. The cycle of debt that brings down Hori and his fellow farmers reflects the "near total breakdown of moral economy," one that is instigated not by villagers but by city dwellers.[17] But while the narrative explicitly directs readers' sympathies at Hori and his family, sympathy *within* characters as a catalyst for reform is expressed by upper-caste characters like Dr. Malti and her fiancé, Professor Mehta, whose activism supposedly demands greater sacrifice of them than of those with less to lose.[18] (Ambedkar, the influential Dalit leader, in fact accused Gandhi of defending caste, a view Dalits continue to hold.[19])

The scene describes the activist–philosopher Mehta's hunting expedition in a forest with his fiancée. They are engaged in a discussion of romantic relationships—indirectly, their own—and Malti has just said teasingly, "I think it's preposterous that you claim to understand the feelings of women" (101). Mehta interrupts the conversation by shooting a bird, which "fluttered some distance and then fell into [a] stream, where it began floating with the current" (103). Determined to retrieve it, Mehta jumps into the water, but is unable to catch up with it. Exhausted, he watches as the bird, "though dead … still seemed to be flying away from him. All at once he saw a young woman emerge from a hut on the bank" and "jump into the water." She retrieves the bird "in a flash," and Mehta, "charmed by her ability and courage," swims to the bank to join her. We view the young woman through Mehta's eyes:

> The girl was dark—very dark, in fact. Her clothes were extremely dirty and coarse, her hair was tangled, and her only ornaments were the two thick bangles on each arm. None of her features could have been called beautiful; but the fresh and pure surroundings had given her dark complexion such lustre, and being raised in the lap of nature had made her body so trim and shapely, that an artist seeking a model of ideal youth could have found no greater beauty. Her robust health seemed to radiate strength and energy to Mehta. (103)

"If you want to kill a leopard," she tells him, "I'll show you where one is." About her "soaked" clothing, she remarks, "We're jungle people. We go around all day in the sun and the rain—but you're not used to it" (104). She insists on going to fetch "Miss Malti" on the forest path, telling him to rest because "City people aren't used to the jungle. We belong here" (104). Mehta, accepting this, sits in the "shade" of a *pipal* tree, where his musing adds to the clichéd contrast between city and "jungle" folk. "Love for this free land welled up inside him. In front of him a range of mountains" that "seemed to be proclaiming the wisdom of the ages … On a high peak in the distance was a small temple, as lofty and yet as lost in this vastness as his thoughts—like a bird which had perched there but was still looking for a resting place" (104). The narrative further confirms the forest–city distinction when the young woman returns with Mehta's fiancée and seems to be "blooming in the sunshine like a wild flower." Malti, by comparison, is "drooping and faded like a potted plant" (104). Aware how much Mehta admires the young woman, Malti expresses her jealous annoyance in the pages that follow.

The scene self-evidently eulogizes the young woman's unrefined, and therefore uncorrupted, wildness—a "wild flower" to Malti's "potted" variety of womanhood, a sense also conveyed by Premchand's use of *jangal* in the original Hindi.[20] Her "very dark" complexion and rough clothing mark her as Adivasi. The young jungle woman lives off the land and is almost naively trusting of the interloping Mehta. Of course, she recognizes his urban middle-class demeanor, which elicits an almost instinctive submissiveness; and yet being "raised in the lap of nature" (*prakriti ki god main*), she has none of the self-conscious—and in Premchand's treatment, potentially inauthentic—propriety of a woman like Malti. There is no indication of dramatic or authorial irony, as today's more-skeptical reader would expect of such typology in an otherwise realist work. Premchand defended the inclusion of such characters as representing the "idealistic aspirations" of nation-making that he believed were necessary in fiction[21]—a variation on the use of character types by Bankim to help render "possible futures," as discussed in Chapter 2.

There is more to the role of the young jungle woman, however. We learn that Malti's cosmopolitan outlook (she has been educated in England) clearly benefits from this forest excursion, for it initiates, much to Mehta's satisfaction, a gradual peeling away of layers of upper-class politesse to reveal her core qualities. The process initiated by the forest continues, later in the novel, with Malti's and Mehta's "tour" of impoverished villages to evaluate their health needs. The villagers, beaten into submission by feudalism and unable to rouse any political passion, but still closer to earth's beneficence than city dwellers, welcome Malti. With Mehta looking on approvingly, she is "as involved with the village women as though she were one of them," even "holding a baby in her lap" (378). When they take an evening walk beside the nearby river, the "carpet of moonlight" makes the "jewel-studded river" seem to "dance before the branches" of low-hanging trees. Like the forest nymph, this "natural splendor" radiates well-being, nearly "intoxicat[ing]" Mehta (378–9). Seeing a "forest of tamarisk trees," he is inspired to build a raft to reach the other side of the river, which he playfully describes to Malti as "a deserted place where dreams hold sway" (379). Later, in her role of doctor, Malti cares for a sick village child with such "tenderness" and "motherly devotion" that Mehta cannot help but admire her. He becomes aware that his modern fiancée is "not just a beauty, but a mother too," and thus "a woman in the truest sense—a giver of life, who could consider another's child her own" (408).

Malti's movement from city to forest to village is presented, then, as a progressive realization of what matters most—namely, natural innocence and health, motherhood, and caring for the poor. Though villages are impoverished, and though (as the novel elsewhere describes) they harbor unscrupulous characters, these conditions are shown to be caused by the cruel, urban-based *zamindari* system. If Premchand's village is, as Vasudha Dalmia observes, not the changeless "agricultural idyll … conjured up by colonial officials,"[22] neither is it inherently corrupt. The point, as the novel makes clear, is to change the system. The villagers' innate goodness, which Hori exemplifies (despite lapses that include beating his wife, ostensibly due to economic pressures), reflects what Shashi Bhushan Upadhyay, drawing on E. P. Thompson and James Scott, calls the "moral economy of the peasant," in which "the roles of individuals and groups in society" are "legitimized by tradition."[23] Like the forest woman, villagers—at least when not exploited—live off the land, which Premchand portrays in conventionally maternal ways. The peasant "became the preeminent potential citizen."[24] It is this moral economy, with its traditional roles, that is under severe threat in the novel. It is also a clearly idealized morality, much like the good mother/villain trope in Hindi films. This paradigm, as Dipesh Chakrabarty has observed, "generates a tension between the two aspects of the … peasant as citizen. One is the peasant who has to be educated into the citizen and who therefore belongs to the time of historicism; the other is the peasant who, despite his or her lack of formal education, is already a citizen." It seems to me that Premchand's "pedagogic mode"[25] incorporates both of these peasant types, and while he does not attempt to offer a resolution of this tension in his novel, the forest scene seeks to mediate it.

The forest scene, then, far from placing either Malti or the reader in a potentially disorienting "jungle," throws into relief the moral perspicacity that the novel as a whole seeks to impart. Malti, in short, enters this moral economy to learn something of the natural, unselfconscious maternity whose chaste counterpart she encountered in the forest. She unites the jungle woman's natural health with village morality to set up her imminent marriage and subsequent motherhood. Here, however, we come to a crux in the text, for if the forest and village are morally analogous in their ideal states, the women of these realms are not.[26] Premchand's jungle woman differs from both classical, religiously oriented female tropes and many of the women in the novel in the remarkable degree of agency she displays. She differs, too—more revealingly, in my view—in possessing acutely sharp vision, enabling her to immediately "spot" the bird Mehta has shot. If the fable-like[27] quality of the scene is due to its function as a secular "idealistic aspiration," as in the description from the novel quoted above, her retrieval of the bird is recounted perfunctorily. The one is couched in modal verbs— "could have been," "seemed"—while the other is all action. Even Mehta's view of the dead bird floating downstream makes it "seem ... to be flying away." The fabular style also explains, I believe, Mehta's inability to pin the jungle woman's "beauty" to any visibly identifiable feature, except to say that she "radiat[es] strength and energy." (She is not, as in Bankim's works, a version of either Radha or Durga.) Broadly stated, fables privilege imaginative vision, and realism, ocular vision. The woman's visual acuity and forthrightness would seem to resist her idealization. Yet the latter, as I have said, has very real effects on Malti's subsequent development toward a new kind of motherhood, illustrating Premchand's mixing, not unlike Bankim's, of realism and the mythic. Malti is clearly not the idealized Hindu wife who, for early (male) nationalists, sustains the spiritual sanctum of the home in opposition to a corrupting material public sphere.[28] Nor is she like Bimala in Tagore's 1916 Bengali novel *The Home and the World* (*Ghare Baire*), whose worldly, emancipating education is encouraged by her land-owning husband Nikhil, but who, as Indrani Mitra observes, "can be free only by disciplining ... her sensual nature."[29] It is important to note, at the same time, the influence of Tagore's novel on other twentieth-century Indian writers in raising, as Ulka Anjaria points out, "persistent questions" about "what realism is," presenting it as "a site of both promise and disillusion."[30]

The "very dark"-complexioned, apparently virginal indigenous woman in *Godaan* can help foster the upper-caste Malti's maternal instincts because, in the first place, her complexion implicitly recalls Krishna's own dark (often called blue) skin, and also because her forest home is redolent of the Sanskrit figuring of forest as womb, a trope which, as we saw in Chapter 2, Bankim's novel explicitly avows. Premchand's Hindi term for forest is revealing, for he uses *jangal* to mean both jungle and forest, neglecting the equally familiar terms *van* or *aranya*, even for the apparently statelier "forest of tamarisk trees": Premchand uses *jangal* here, whereas his translator Roadarmel rightly chose "forest" to be faithful to the setting's context. This usage makes sense given Premchand's emphasis throughout the text on rusticity, which *jangal* tends to evoke. It also seems likely that he wished to avoid the other terms' religious associations. While one could argue, precisely for this reason, that a word like *aranya*, with its Vedic pedigree, would have suited Premchand's stated aim of exposing the class divides of an unjust social system, using *jangal* in fact aids his goal. This rhetorical strategy is not a solely semantic one; it is equally, as the tamarisk "forest" illustrates, situational.

My point is that in order for the novel to sharpen readers' and certain characters' perceptions of rural India's social reality, it cannot rely on typologies of nature, the predictability of which would render them invisible. Nor, conversely, can the novel rely solely on realist detail, which, taken to its conventional limits, would result only in utter bleakness and demolish the work's trust in a just future.[31] Premchand must balance his visual detail, such as Hori's tragic denouement, with elements of the fabular, like the jungle woman. Her acute ocular vision complements the rhetorical vision of the novel as a whole, just as her vigor and harmonious relationship with the jungle, though impossible to delineate (from Mehta's viewpoint), bear the imprint of moral vision. Like Deeti in Ghosh's *Sea of Poppies* (as we will see), *Godaan*'s young woman enacts two kinds of perception; and as in Ghosh, this double—we might say, as described in the Introduction, *darshanic*—vision is one of several varieties, no single one of which can bear the burden of representational authority. Premchand confirms this in having Mehta, as indicated above, catch sight of the "small temple" atop a distant hill. The temple seems to him "as lofty and yet as lost in this vastness as his thoughts," its apparent material and symbolic permanence diminished both by its inconsequential remoteness and by its resemblance to a restless bird. The temple holds no primacy over the natural environment, just as its material reality does not precede its figurative reality. The jungle "hut" is comparatively more substantial. What matters, the novel seems to say, is what we do with our realities.

Romancing the Forest: Bibhutibhushan's *Aranyak*

The *zamindar* system of India's landowning elites that figures heavily in the novels of Premchand and his progressive-era peers, and whose encouragement by the British colonial system leads to the immiseration of peasants like Deeti and Hori, is the backdrop of Bibhutibhushan Bandyopadhyay's episodic and elegiac 1930s Bengali novel *Aranyak: Of the Forest*,[32] virtually all of which is set in forests in the early 1900s. Bibhutibhushan[33] is most famous today for his first novel, *Pather Panchali* ("Song of the Little Road"), published in 1929 and adapted in 1955 by Satyajit Ray for his great film of the same title. Ray adapted the author's second (1932) novel, *Aparajito* ("The Unvanquished"), in 1956, extending it into a third film, *The World of Apu* (1959).[34] *Aranyak* is the title, transliterated thus, which the translator Rimli Bhattacharya has chosen to preserve, but with the added subtitle "Of the Forest," a translation of the Bangla word *aranyak*. These choices are productively conflicted and directly pertinent to the novel's thematic concerns. Preserving the original (transliterated) title makes sense since, as previously discussed, the *Aranyakas* (Forest Books) of the *Mahabharata* and the *Ramayana*, as well as forest episodes in innumerable *puranas* and regional folktales, constitute a familiar genre across the subcontinent, regardless of language and religious avocation. But the elective subtitle implies, to the contrary, that the term is not familiar to everyone, especially English readers, and that it requires a gloss to adequately convey its meaning. Although "of the forest" reflects the word "*aranyak*" grammatically, the phrase is superfluous for Indian readers.

These choices do, however, productively underscore the narrative's "linguistic layering,"[35] a point Bhattacharya herself makes in her "note on translation." This layering is inescapable, given that Bhibhutibhushan's narrator describes "a land … outside the usual topos of Bengali literature," where inhabitants speak dialects of Hindi as well as indigenous languages like Gondi and Santali. This means that the narrator, like the author, has effectively had to translate the region's linguistic registers into Bangla. (The narrator tells us, for instance, that it took him some time to "understand well the speech of the local people" [10].) This layering "is compounded," Bhattacharya observes, "by intricacies of land and labour relations inflected by caste, gender and region," which the novel records. Embedded in the terms for land management, for example, are both English words (owing to British control) and Persian and Arabic words (which preceded British usage, though some were retained into the 1900s).[36] This linguistic context reflects the region's geopolitical turmoil: the British had divided Bengal in 1905, ostensibly to facilitate governance, though it produced a mostly Muslim eastern segment and a mostly Hindu western one. Vehement protests by the latter led to the region's reunification, though this parallels the creation of the new state of Bihar, in which parts of the forestland featured in *Aranyak* are today located. This backdrop explains why transplantations, migrations, and blurred boundaries feature so prominently in the novel. This context also suits Bibhutibhushan's interest in familiarizing for his urban readership large regions of their state that they had hitherto viewed through a prism of sometimes arcane textual topoi.

Paradoxically, then, this is also a defamiliarizing text, the author working to strip away readers' enculturated expectations of Bengali forestland—although to do this, he occasionally resorts to far-flung allusions: forests "so close to Bengal" and yet feeling entirely "unreal" and "in no way inferior to the rocky deserts of Arizona or the veldts of Rhodesia" (60). In fact, he declares that the "forest world" boasts a "civilization" greater than the modern world's (178). Bibhutibhushan's title cues us to the uncanniness of the setting, for in echoing the *Aranyakas*, the title would seem to promise a similarly conservative, ritually laden ethos of Aryan conquest and consolidation. For instance, in the novel's focus on the lives of displaced indigenous groups like the Gonds as well as other migrants to the forest, Bibhutibhushan's narrator superficially echoes the *Aranyakas*, which are populated with a broad cast of characters. But in describing the cruelties of the colonial state's mantra of "progress," which depends to a large degree on deforestation, the narrator is haunted by his certainty that these forests he loves will "not stand for long" (192). Civilization is the enemy.

The novel is for this reason a confessional and concludes with the narrator lamenting his role in "destroy[ing]" forests, the memories of which still "haunt" him (247). The text's affective appeal depends, therefore, on pressing home this contrast between forests still standing in the fictive present (but historical past), in which a young Santal man can still boast "a body like a young sal tree" (152), and a future bereft of both Santals and forests—a future that in the narrator's time of writing, fifteen years after he departed the forest, has become the present. At root, this is, like many other literary works in the years preceding independence, a meditation on what it means to be Indian, with the attendant concerns about authenticity, difference, and territoriality. The disjunctive tragedy of the forest's past and present condition is an index of this meditation, which, I will argue, the novel seeks to convey by invoking, and reflecting on, a form of *darshanic* vision—or rather, visions. The representations of vision, I suggest, are the narrator's attempts to understand the connections among ordinary sight, enculturated perception, and visionary awareness. The novel does so in at least two specific ways: by distinguishing between its fictive (diegetic) past and present, and between the historicizing gaze and "immediacy of ... presence"[37]; and by avowing a tension between material reality and the extent to which language—the author's, the narrator's, the local people's—creates that reality, thereby calling attention to different ways of seeing the worlds one inhabits.

Our narrator is Satyacharan, or simply Satya (which, tellingly, means "truth"), who after college finds work as the revenue official of a vast, forested estate belonging to a friend's landowning family. He establishes his mournful tone right away, telling us in the prologue that the memories of his years in Bhagalpur, where he relished the "dense splendour of green forestland," "are filled with sorrow" (3-4). "By my hands," he laments, "was destroyed an unfettered playground of nature," a "crime" he now, fifteen years later, wants "to confess" (4). He describes his initial "loneliness" and his "homesickness" for Calcutta and of "find[ing] the jungle suffocating" at first (11, 14, 86). But within a few days, Satya tells us, "I became increasingly ensnared by my fascination for the forest"; also, he realizes that he does not at all miss "the hurly burly of Calcutta" (20). One day in particular opened his eyes to the forest's enchantment. Late that night, after the estate's "guards" and a few others had finished their musical celebration of the Dol-Purnima festival, he looked out of his house window and felt "overwhelmed by the indescribable light of a full moon night." Going outside, he discovered "there was no one to be seen" and that the "unblemished moonlight ... glinting on ... the forest of *kash*" (tall grasses) had "creat[ed] an otherworldly beauty that was frightening even to look at. I felt within myself a sense of liberation, of being supremely detached, untrammeled ... I felt that I had chanced upon an unknown fairy kingdom" into which "no mortal" should "enter without permission" (21). These "vast tracts of forestland, uninterrupted and open, so exquisitely beautiful, comprised a national treasure" (113). Satya speaks of "Arjun and *piyal*" trees, "creepers and orchids" (favored tropes for arboreal beauty, as in Kalidasa), the "medley of fragrances" from "strange flowers"— these and other sights and scents saturate his senses to the point of intoxication (80), not unlike a forest in Kalidasa. The forest is "a land of dreams" that can seem "unreal" (61). He is occasionally filled with a "strange joy" that he can only express as "*udaas*," a term familiar to *rasa* theory that can mean sad or, as here, wistful (20, 80). (The word is left untranslated and unglossed in Bhattacharya's English version, but in the final pages of the novel, the narrator contrasts his specified use of the term with the diffuse local usage [246].) The forest, which takes on a life of its own, is many things at once: a dangerous realm, in which tigers sometimes prey on vulnerable and solitary villagers (130), as do "spirit[s]" (37) and "ghosts" (147); a bewildering, dark, and largely "unpeopled" maze, with "branches from huge trees" that appear to be "pressing down upon" the narrator (36, 53, 80, 91); an ashram-like abode in which to "meditate" (31, 85); and a "no man's land" in need of "survey[s]" (65, 84). Satya is also appalled—and in this he resembles Premchand—by the region's feudalism, where a few ruthless and "virtual king[s]" hold sway (86) and by the impoverishment of the many, who struggle "to survive" (91) while being exploited by "rich moneylender[s]" (42).

We can glimpse in these lines how Satya's response to this forest environment combines romantic, social realist, and modernist tendencies. He alludes at times to European and American texts, frequently voices his moral conscience, and infrequently invokes traditional epics and traditions. The narrator seems eager to locate his forest chronicle in a global literature and history, invoking, for instance, late-nineteenth-century Swedish explorer Sven Hedin and Columbus (30, 164), as well as "Marco Polo, Hudson and Shackleton" (95), as compeers who have, like himself, "heard the call of the wild" and "abandon[ed] their homes" (95). He compares people he meets to characters in Bengali literature, including Bankim's eponymous forest heroine Kapalkundala, whose likeness he sees in a poor young woman of Bengali Brahmin heritage whom he once encountered in a remote village (201). The narrator occasionally strains at allegory, too, as when he describes an "old woman" in a village near "the jungle" who is to him "a symbol of civilization of the forest: for generations, her ancestors have been living" here (81–2). Most often, however, the imagery and language elicit a keen environmentalism. As Vidya Sarveswaran observes, following Scott Slovic's usage, the novel is "both" rhapsodic in its eulogizing of nature and jeremiadic in its warning of impending doom, features that reflect the narrator's "self-realization" in the vein of a deep ecologist.[38] The forest—or jungle, for Satya uses the words as synonyms[39]—is primeval and lush, but also on its way to extinction.

Yet for all his expressed love for the forest, which suggests something of the Vedic *vanaprastha* (forest retirement) phase of an ideal upper-caste Hindu man's life,[40] Satya does not enter into a "seamless" identification with his surroundings, as has been suggested.[41] Satya's stance, as his intertextual references indicate, is a self-conscious reflection of the forest as object that effectively keeps it at arm's length. Although he "discovers new worlds" in those he meets in the forest, these are people who, as Satya says of a man named Raju, "had no idea of world outside the jungle," and to whom cities—which is the "world" Satya has in mind—are "vague and unreal" places where "evil" reigns (159). To the Adivasi communities, the neighboring counties in which they are obliged to "roam" for seasonal work amount to "foreign lands" (133). Satya finds the man's tales risible, such as his declaration of having "seen ... with my own eyes" how rainbows stem from "termite heaps" (160). As if aware of his patronizing tone, Satya backtracks, saying of another story, this one of Raju's courtship and marriage, "had I heard it amidst the din of city life, [I might have laughed [it] off as a rustic idyll] .... But in these surroundings, I was captivated by the singular charm" (160). There is never a question of his class status: he is "Sahib" and "Huzoor" (162), a man for whom an "unmarried Bengali [Brahmin] woman" equates to "wasted youth" (202). Satya's disclaimer notwithstanding, his male-oriented perspective frequently calls up versions of Premchand's and Bankim's forest nymph tropes. Satya frequently expresses his enchantment with Santal women like Bhanmati, "this innocent forest maid" to whom he cannot voice his "love" for her (240). Bankim's *Kapalkundala* (which might be taken as a trial run for *Anandamath*) similarly has a male character, lost in a "pathless forest," be "transfixed" by the "extraordinary apparition" of "an exquisite female figure" (the eponymous heroine), whose natural "beauty" makes him wonder if she is "a goddess, a human being, or merely an illusion."[42]

The forest-world has, nonetheless, made him acutely aware of the comparatively boorish behavior of his urban peers. When he encounters a *bhadralok* family picnicking in some "jungles," they appear, in his "eyes," "completely out of place," indifferent to their "beautiful" surroundings. They are "completely devoid of imagination," so that "nothing held any attraction for them" (185). In both situations, Satya commands the more accurate sight or insight. His wink at the reader about Raju having "seen" the rainbow's source contrasts with his own authorizing account of the conversation, just as he provides us with his customarily detailed observation: "We were drinking our tea sitting beneath a big *ashan* tree that was next to Raju's *khupri* [hut]. Wherever you looked, you could only see the dense jungle and kend, amoki, clumps of bahera creepers in flower" (160). These details similarly leave us in no doubt that Satya appreciates the beautiful lushness in a way that escapes the picnicking urbanites.

Here and throughout his narrative, Satya resorts to a presumptively transparent account of his surroundings in order to elicit in his readers a like regard for the region. Yet many other times, as indicated by his aforementioned dubbing of forests as "unreal," Satya is hard put to describe what he sees. He frequently draws on a literary romantic archive of imagery to articulate what he sees: "The setting sun splashed the tops of trees and bushes," he declares early in the novel, resplendence that induces the Wordsworthian insight that he is "the sole human being" here, with "no one to come and break my quietude under the peaceful evening sky" (14). These make the forest seem to him "an unknown fairyland" (60). These idylls, however, are interspersed with (though in no way displace) reminders of everyday life, as when Satya is "startled to hear a woman wailing frantically"—which turns out to be an expression of joy characteristic of "local custom" (57). At times he sounds like Thoreau, relishing "nothing but birdsong, and the rustling and snapping of twigs" (105). The narrator seems to advertise, even gently mock, his own bookish outlook by listing Hindi books "on sale" at the local fair, such as romantic tales of *Laila-Majnun* and *Premsagar*, Lallulal's early-1800s retelling of the Krishna legends, and the first printed Hindi (Khari-boli dialect) work (57).[43] Satya more noticeably comments on the role his own words play in constructing the forest region of Bhagalpur when, for example, he comments that in attempting to reach the fair, he traverses the "hilly [jungle] terrain" in which "there was no path to speak of" (52). Having nonetheless "gone on absentmindedly," he soon finds that he is "lost" and beyond "the limits of our jungleland"—and that besides the absence of a path, "every feature of the landscape looked exactly the same" (53). In contrast to the itemized differentiation of the numerous trees, shrubs, and animals he elsewhere provides, in this case, such description eludes him. The "scenario" he had "imagined" before embarking on this trek, of one day "enraptur[ing]" children with "tales" of his adventures (52), has evaporated in the face of its inexpressibility. In a sense, the oft-mentioned unreality of the forest has overwhelmed its own materiality. As on several other occasions, Satya has reached the limits of language. "When I try and write about this store of precious experience," he writes in a later chapter, "I only write page after page, without ever being able to express all I wish to" (94).

These optical shifts resonate with Satya's references to "the gods" as "mysterious apparitions," to "ghosts," terrifying "creatures from strange lands" (71), and to "*peris*," beautiful winged spirits (147). These intimations of both the powers and limits of perception—empirical and lyrical, supernatural and linguistic—coalesce in the closing pages of the novel and center on the figure of Bhanmati, a young Santal woman. She is the daughter of a once "royal" now impoverished Santal family, and thus a "princess" (153). The decline of the family and their "lands" are now, according to Satya, "threatened with extinction" due to "the advent of a new ethos, a different civilization." "Whenever I saw her," he says, "this tragic chapter from the unwritten annals of Indian history flashed before my eyes" (239). To Satya, Bhanmati is "innocent and free in how she conducted herself," her name rooted in the locally pronounced word for forest, *bhan*. She also embodies the virtues of another young woman Satya knew, Manchi, who "was like the goddess of plenty in these forests—brimming with youthful vitality, spirited and vibrant, yet … unspoilt like a little girl" (176). Manchi has since "disappeared" with a young man "playing on her desire to see Calcutta" (189), but Bhanmati steps into the narrative void, exuding the same arboreal "vitality" (238). More importantly, Bhanmati prompts the "vision" that Satya feels has "blessed" him as he makes his final farewell to the forest and its people. Seeing Bhanmati "in the midst of the thick forest of wild chhatim flowers" (239) and intoxicated by the "scent of sheuli" (jasmine) (240), Satya declares, "I felt as though I had been blessed with a vision of the presiding deity of the forest herself, a goddess as dark as Krishna!" Yet this divine vision of the forest and the beautiful Bhanmati, which induces another of Satya's "unreal," "dream"-like sensations, is clouded by the aforementioned knowledge of their imminent demise, so that for a moment "Bhanmati appeared … like any other Santal girl" (239).

This scene is a crucial point in the narrative, and fittingly appears in its concluding pages, for it presents an unresolved tension between the narrator's historicizing perception of the country's changing reality and his romanticized vision of an "untrammeled" (as Satya likes to say) future. "A beautiful vision!" he says of Bhanmati (244), and, alarmed at the thought of "a time when men would no longer be able to see the forest," entreats an unnamed benefactor (the reader or gods, or simply a collective conscience): "For those people, yet to come, let the forest stay pristine, undisturbed" (241). But this vision, he knows, cannot be realized in the face of "progress"—a word he contrasts with "happiness" (244). Modern progress means "mining the place for copper ore," "chimneys of … factories, trolley lines," "heaps of ash spewed from engines, clusters of shops, tea joints, cheap films," and "coaldust" (237). Satya nonetheless persists in saying, as if his words will create the reality, that "no one would destroy this forest of Bhanmati's homeland" (237). People may come and go, but the Santal "forestland [remained]"—forests of "mahua," *chhatim*, "kelikadamba," and "chinar" trees (236, 238, 240), all of which have a variety of uses for indigenous communities.[44] As throughout his account, Satya here details forest trees on which the Santals and Gonds rely for their livelihood, distinguishing them from trees like the kadamba, which is sacred, as we have seen, to Krishna (238). (Satya earlier comments on "the wonderful shade" of a "banyan tree" under which "Krishna himself might have played his flute" [46].) The "flowers" of the *kelikadamba* are "not [those] of the kadamba" but of an "altogether" different "species" of tree (238). Satya, in other words, eulogizes an indigenous cultural outlook by, in part, differentiating it from that of mainstream traditions common to his own class and caste, in which Krishna—or more accurately, a certain version of Krishna—is a presiding deity.

This ostensibly indigenous outlook is, of course, filtered through the narrator's romantic eyes, and it is not proffered as the only option for nationhood. The narrator keeps his three possible perspectives in play—romantic-pastoral (his rendering of indigeneity along with classical literary tropes), modern-managerial (which his job calls for, and which is reflected in his empirical detail), and mainstream-traditional. Yet the novel offers an alternative imagining of nationhood that is not restricted to the Aryan purview of *bharatvarsha* (or *aryavarta*), but instead includes "many jati," as Partha Chatterjee has called such an alternative—a country that is not defined by center–periphery, "'national' and 'regional,'" but decentered.[45] When Satya sees Bhanmati for the last time, he asks, "Have you heard the name, Bharatvarsha?" She "had not" (242). Satya claims that his question reflects his larger wish to understand "how little was Bhanmati's world" (242). Yet it is clear by this point that his time in the forest has soured him on his own mainstream, upper-caste Hindu views, including the concept of Bharatvarsha. Midway through the novel, just after meeting Bhanmati and her people for the first time, he visits their "burial ground" and experiences another of his visions. "I could glimpse quite another world, in comparison to which the Puranic and Vedic age seemed like time present" (156). The sense of this presence infuses his visionary sight: "I saw the nomadic Aryans … come down like a torrent into an ancient India ruled by primitive non-Aryan tribes." He feels painfully that he is among the "representatives of that victorious race," which "had never been anxious to decipher [the Santals'] script," which is "written only in … caves" and "forests," and instead "enacted the great tragedy of history" by leaving the Santals "wretched" (156). The Aryans refuse to learn such indigenous sign systems as the knotted grass tips that serve as local markers for forest trails, which enable Satya to immediately "decipher the way" (97). The Santals' burial ground figuratively evokes the same impression, for Satya finds that a "banyan," sacred to Vedism, "had grown to immense proportions killing off all the other trees in the process." It was now "so old that the original tree was long since gone" (155).

The novel drives home this sense of Vedism being comparatively recent (part of "time present") by having Satya on rare occasions remind us that he is writing this retrospectively, years after his visionary experiences. In one such moment of retrospection, he sets the stage for us: "One afternoon, many years later: I have left behind my life of freedom and have become a householder. I sit in my room in a narrow little lane in Calcutta and listen to my wife at her sewing machine" (99). Present-tense usage and modern domesticity abruptly intrude in these narrative breaks to enact the sense of disjunctive temporalities Satya once felt—and that, given that he is recollecting those past visions so intensely, he clearly still feels. If his forest sojourn resembles the *vanaprastha* stage of the Vedic ashram paradigm, he has chronologically reversed the sequence by now living as a *grihastha*, or householder, which traditionally precedes *vanaprastha*. Narratively, Satya is perpetuating the latter stage both for himself and for his reader, so that his cautionary tale of environmental and cultural destruction has a certain immediacy that can disturb the dominant discourse of a historicism, "the metanarrative of progress."[46] This perpetuation in narrative allows him to tolerate the householder stage, which, as he says earlier in the novel, is "impossible" for anyone "who has heard the call of the wild" (95).

On the one hand, these occasional interruptions signal the narration of the past from a fictive present, as if to expose and take apart the inner workings of narrative mechanisms, among which are assumptions about national–historical time and their attendant verbal tenses. This exposure invites us to see the Bhagalpur forests in the way that the Santals see them, not as objects but, like humans themselves, agential entities that are "constantly changing" and "continuous with [their] past and potential future instantiations."[47] On the other hand, the narrator's very invocation of "householder," like his overriding tone of lamentation for lost worlds and references to "unreality," clearly stems from an outlook anchored in modern temporality. Santals and Gonds remain "primitive tribes" for him (151). Yet it seems to me that in Bibhutibhushan's novel, the *darshanic* perspective of "godly time" qualifies the book's anchoring historical perspective. In both novels, the forest as setting and as metaphor, with its "amazing variety" of life (104) (as opposed to modern life's "uniform[ity]" [244]), accommodates these divergent temporalities, whose representations are at once familiar and unfamiliar. Satya's visions, not unlike those of Deeti that we will encounter in Ghosh's *Sea of Poppies*, produce new archives of the nation that chip away at history's perceptual "homogeneity."[48] Bhanmati, we might say, meets the sewing machine.

4

History, Nation, and Forest in Salman Rushdie and Amitav Ghosh

"Historyless" Mangroves: The Sundarbans in *Midnight's Children*

W. W. Hunter, the British historian whose 1875 essay on the Sundarbans I alluded to in Chapter 2, described this vast area of dense mangrove forests on the Bengal coast as "a sort of drowned land, covered with jungle, smitten by malaria, and infested by wild beasts."[1] "So great is the evil fertility of [its] soil," Hunter concludes, "that reclaimed land neglected for a single year will present to next year's cultivator a forest of reeds (*nal*). He may cut it and burn it down, but it will spring up again [as jungle] almost as thick [and bad] as ever." As Paul Greenough observes, for Hunter and his British-Indian peers, the forbidding Sundarbans region (Figure 4.1), which seemed to be bereft of human settlement, defied analysis and was therefore judged to be "wasteland."[2] Hunter seeks to invest the region with meanings that agree with his symbolic axes of purity and danger, but finding that he is unable to do this, he concludes that the area is utterly abject, a "place where meaning collapses."[3] It eludes his controlling gaze and so unsettles him.

Yet the Sundarbans region following India's independence from Britain has for various reasons come to seem more, not less, unsettling to outside entities—the Indian Government, of course, but also industrial and tourist interests—who wish to manage it. The Sundarbans area is today divided between India and Bangladesh and has seen both governments subject it to systems of control that directly descend from British colonial practices.[4] The region's inhabitants, who largely depend on fishing, honey harvesting, wood harvesting, and, in recent times, tourism, have had little say in these developments. Despite state incursions, however, the area's international borders have remained porous enough to make it a site of frequent crossings by Bangladeshi refugees—many of whom have, indeed, settled there. It is a demanding environment for its growing population of humans, who share it with abundant nonhuman animals, including tigers, crocodiles, river dolphins, pythons, and macaques. The tiger's endangered status in the area instigated another layer of external governance when, in the early 1970s, much of the Sundarbans was designated a tiger reserve, resulting in further limits on human activity. As elsewhere in India, tigers sometimes prey on vulnerable residents, whose fellow villagers then direct their frustrations at the cats,

Figure 4.1 Sundarbans mangrove trees in tide
Source: Photo by author.

occasionally killing them, a circumstance Ghosh describes in *The Hungry Tide* in graphic detail. This human presence belies the ostensibly "historyless" Sundarbans in *Midnight's Children*. Yet as we will see, Rushdie's characterizations of the mangroves are not denotative; they are instead connotative and at times surreal admixtures of material and imagined forests.

A century after Bankim produced his novelistic imagining of future nationhood, Salman Rushdie's magic realist novel *Midnight's Children*, published a generation after India's independence and in the immediate wake of Prime Minister Indira Gandhi's 1975–7 Emergency powers declaration (which his novel rebukes so strenuously that it was banned by her), is already looking back to a time when the Nehruvian idea of a unified, secular, and democratic nation held sway. Rushdie's novel, like those of many other writers of his generation, in effect eulogizes that apparently vanished ethos.[5] I place Rushdie's novel in line with Bankim's because each work has been seen as inaugurating particular phases in India's literary mythopoesis, and also because their representations of forest are significant to their fictional projects as well as to subsequent interpretations of those projects. Although *Midnight's Children* does not foreground the forest in the way that *Anandamath* does, appearing relatively late in the book, the Sundarbans encompasses Rushdie's key themes in a mode that is at once allegorical and realist, the style itself a representation of the entanglements and indeterminacies that forests typically connote. The question is, Does Rushdie's arboreal venture critique such conventions, reinforce them, or offer an altogether different treatment of the forest? This begs the further question, in the context of the novel, about what role the forest plays in Rushdie's rendering of independent India's birthing pains.

Midnight's Children[6] is narrated by Saleem Sinai, one of the eponymous "children" of India born on August 15, 1947, when the British Raj officially relinquished their hold on the subcontinent. Saleem recounts his, and his family's, entanglements in events leading up to and following India's independence at "the stroke of the midnight hour," as Nehru famously said in his radio announcement at the time (129). More specifically, the novel is, as Priyamvada Gopal puts it, "at once a family saga, a national history, a fable, an epic, a coming-of-age story, and a political *Bildungsroman*."[7] Many of the novel's events occur in Bombay and Delhi, but a sprinkling of references to forests throughout the narrative foreshadow the late Sundarbans episode, amplifying its thematic significance to the book as a whole. Saleem, recounting his life's story to Padma, his housekeeper-turned-fiancée, tells of how his adoptive mother, Amina (also called Mumtaz), has "an enigmatic dream" of "stumbl[ing] through [an] impenetrable papery forest" of "flypaper," the latter a metaphor for the intertwined history of nation and family (Amina "dreamed of being glued to brown paper like a fly," Saleem feels "saddled now with flypaper-dreams and imaginary ancestors") (122–3). Among the 420 children of midnight is "a sharp-tongued girl whose words had the power of inflicting wounds," inciting some "adults" to "lock her in a bamboo cage and float her down the Ganges to the Sundarbans jungles (which are the rightful home of monsters and phantasms); but nobody dared approach her" (227). Two of the children are from "the Gir Forest" of Gujarat, home to the last Asiatic lions: "a witch-girl with the power of healing" (228) and a "boy ... whose face was absolutely blank and featureless ... and could take any features he chose" (260). Saleem, being adept at storytelling, continually hints to Padma of adventures to come, protesting her interruptions by exclaiming, for example, "I'm not finished yet! There is to be electrocution and a rain-forest; a pyramid of heads on a field ... narrow escapes are coming" (398).

The ominous "papery forest," the two occult progeny of the Gir Forest, and Saleem's promise of a "rain-forest" adventure later in his story together inform, and amplify the thematic concerns of, the chapter titled "In the Sundarbans." The year is 1971, during the Indo-Pakistan war that produced Bangladesh (the former East Pakistan). The adult Saleem, we learn in the previous chapter, titled "The Buddha," having been "brained ... by my mother's silver spittoon" in a bomb blast (fulfilling the prophesy of the seer Ramram [96, 393]), loses his memory. The narrative's numerous previous allusions to partial sight, fragmentation (the subcontinent's division, Saleem being switched at birth with another child, his sense of leaking "history" [37]), and ambiguity ("Nothing was real; nothing certain" [389]) are figured in the mangrove forests. The chapter is a crescendo of the symphonic notes Saleem has been striking in the foregoing chapters to highlight the enabling as well as disabling fictiveness of national histories. The spittoon, it should be said, which Saleem has carefully safeguarded since inheriting it, symbolizes, among other things, a container for the memories he is recounting to Padma as well as the emptying of those memories. It also signifies impotence—"I cannot hit her spittoon," he says of Padma (38)—and, with double and triple entendre, a vanishing era when men enjoyed "playing the ancient game of hit-the-spittoon" with their gobs of "betel-juice" (36, 44).

Saleem's skill at expectorating betel-juice in a long arc "to hit, with commendable accuracy," his "beautifully-wrought silver spittoon" connects the past—that of his family and of India's—with the fresh, perishable, "soul-chewing" present (401, 414). Just before entering the Sundarbans, we see the amnesiac Saleem demonstrating his spitting skill while sitting "cross-legged ... beneath a tree." Nicknamed the "buddha" by his three fellow (and teen-aged) Pakistani soldiers, Ayooba, Farooq, and Shaheed, because he is a comparatively "old man" (which is what *buddha* means in Hindi and Urdu), Saleem enacts a profane version of his historical-religious namesake (although, as he rightly points out, the pronunciations for "old man" and "enlightened one" differ, and cannot be transliterated [402]). The *chinar* tree, he says, must stand in for the historical Buddha's iconic Bodhi (peepul). Owing to his uncanny ability to track the stealthy East Pakistani (soon to be Bangladeshi) rebels fighting the Pakistan Army, Saleem leads the three young soldiers into Dacca, unmindful of the atrocities and devastated refugees. But then, no longer able to see "their unseen prey," "a foe who endlessly eludes them," and weary of this "meaningless chase" in a "drowned" landscape, Saleem leads them into the Sundarbans, "the jungle which is so thick that history has hardly ever found the way in." And "it swallows them up" (412–13). They disappear "into the historyless anonymity of rain-forests" (414).

Here Rushdie, through Saleem, makes plain once again his metafictional reflections on the important role stories play in producing archives of personal and national history. The narrator's generalized use of "rain-forests" here is self-evidently, and self-consciously, contradicted by the "thick [history]" of the Sundarbans. Saleem tells us that he has hitherto "hope[d] to immortalize in pickles as well as words" the concentrated memories that animate individual and national lives, his condiment factory's jars representing the stimulation of both physical and imaginative palates by means of "an overdose of reality" (414). This narrative self-reflection demands a variation on the question I posed about *Anandamath*'s setting, and which I will try to answer: Why devote a chapter to this mangrove forest, and, more importantly, why does it prompt metafictional considerations that seem almost too obvious? It is as if "the sepulchral greenness of the forest," with its "labyrinthine salt-water channels overtowered by cathedral-arching trees" (415), press up against the limits of verbal representation, as these baroque descriptions themselves suggest. Saleem's self-referential pronouns, too, slip from "I" to "he," exhibiting his dissociation of self in this episode, which resonates with his overriding effort to make sense of his own and India's (as he sees it) fragmentation.

There is more than a little of Joseph Conrad's impressionistic and surreal account of the Belgian Congo Forest in Rushdie's chapter. The Sundarbans figure as an infernal Eden whose "sundri[8] leaves and ... branches and nipa fronds" capture life-giving water, but that, once imbibed, plunges them "deeper and deeper into the thralldom of that livid green world where the birds had voices like creaking wood and all the snakes were blind" (417). But "finally," after weeks of misery during which they have all "forgotten the purpose of their journey" (417), Saleem begins to remember. "The forest found a way through to him" following the bite of a "serpent" whose venom causes him to sit for "two days ... as rigid as a tree" under a "sundri-tree," but that then affords him, if not enlightenment, at least "nostalgia" (419). Marlow-like, the buddha regales his companions with stories, and in doing so is "rejoined to the past," "all of it, all lost histories" (419). This, in turn, "restore[s] in him the sense of responsibility," so that "it seems that the magical jungle, having tormented them with their misdeeds, was leading them by the hand towards a new adulthood" (419).

The four travelers' phantasmagoric journey invites us to read it allegorically, as a rite of passage through a liminal realm of illusion, a forest which seems to have continually "changed its nature," into a new self-awareness—in effect, a new birth, for "having passed through the childish regressions and childlike sorrows of their earliest jungle days," they find that they are "leaving infancy behind for ever" [sic] (420–1). In this sense, Rushdie's Sundarbans resembles not Conrad's terrain but Bankim's womblike forests of Birbhum, whose amniotic darkness nurtures young men by teaching them, in an update of the classic epic trope, to be responsibly dedicated to the national cause. Rushdie further resembles Bankim in having his characters stumble upon a "monumental" Kali temple in the "centre" of a "glade filled with the gentle melodies of song-birds," "a sight so lovely that it brought lumps to their throats." We can almost hear the "sweet calls" of birds and "murmur[ing] palm leaves" that enchant Mahendra and Kalyani early in *Anandamath*—though Mahendra has the presence of mind to resist mere "dreams" that "arise in the mind and then vanish in it."[9] In Rushdie's forest glade, the four soldiers see that the temple had been "carved in forgotten centuries out of a single immense crag of rock," and "its walls danced with friezes of men and women, who were depicted coupling." Entering "this miracle," the men discover the figure of the goddess, "fecund and awful"; then, exhausted, they fall asleep "at her feet" (421). Although such allusions to eroticism are not explicit in Bankim's novel, we have seen how the presence of young women like Shanti trouble the *santans*' avowed asceticism. A further resemblance to Bankim is Rushdie's echo of Hunter's 1875 account of the Sundarbans, which, as I noted in the discussion of *Anandamath*, Bankim likely knew and whose colonialist tropes have been naturalized: the mangrove world is a "drowned" land, its soil "fertile" but dangerous and occult, according to both Hunter and Rushdie (Hunter's forest is "evil," Rushdie's possesses "time-shifting sorcery" [423]). Curiously, however, the ruined temple is naturalized, and the forests do not seem to have a history at all; it is as if the four interlopers are the first humans to have entered an area that is not unlike the forests in *Anandamath*.

Rushdie's forest, however, soon loses its maternal associations when, in a dream-like state, his four characters encounter "four houris" (422), beautiful virgins who proverbially await the Muslim faithful in paradise. These nymphs are clearly beyond the pale of Bankim's view of femininity, which is, I suggest, part of Rushdie's point: the indefinability of the forest and its residents can serve no definable nation. Broadly speaking, the houris belong to a long-standing, seemingly global trope of beautiful forest women, usually spirits, who tempt male heroes. These figures include, to name a few, the demoness Surpanakha in the *Ramayana*, who shapeshifts to try to lure Rama; forest nymphs seducing male heroes in Western folktales; the beautiful women-spirits conjured by Mara to try to tempt the Buddha sitting under the Bodhi tree; and forest versions of the mythic Lamia, a beautiful child-eating daemon.[10] But although "the houris looked real enough, and their saris ... were torn and stained by the jungle," these "daughters of the forest" eventually prove to be "the last and worst of the jungle's tricks." Emerging from these hallucinations after having lost track of time ("in the Sundarban [sic] time followed unknown laws" [422]), the men now "looked at the temple with new eyes," noticing with alarm its "gaping cracks" and the remains "of uncrushed bones" (423). As they flee this "forest of illusions," it seems to bear down upon them, as if "ejecting them ... from its territory" along with "fallen branches" and other debris, depositing them "back ... in the world of armies and dates" (423). The jungle that had swallowed them and digested their dreams regurgitates—or births?—their altered selves.

These passages illustrate the eclectic conjoining of conventional literary tropes, national history, surrealism, and mythic suggestion that is a hallmark of Rushdie's novel as a whole. We could illustrate the mythic component of *Midnight's Children* further, for instance, by comparing its Sundarbans episode to the Mayasabha, or hall of illusions, described in the *Mahabharata*. Built for the five Pandava brothers on Krishna's orders, an envious Duryodhana, the eldest of the Kaurava brothers (cousins to the Pandavas), comes to see it for himself but becomes disoriented in its corridors, stirring the embers of resentment that will precipitate the great war. But mixed in among the mythic, surreal, and colonial-tropic features of Rushdie's forest, we must add the mundane: "rain-heavy jungle mud," "three-inch-long leeches" that "covered" the men's bodies, "falling nipa-fruits smash[ing] on the jungle floor," "flies" (416, 421). The physicality of their day-to-day survival weighs on them as much as the psychic toll, and at times the two dimensions converge, as when Saleem says that to stop the hallucinatory "singsong accusations of the forest," the "three boy-soldiers" should plug their ears with the aforementioned "jungle mud," with its mix of "jungle-insects" and "bird-droppings." Although the maddening, "unpalatable secrets which the sundri-leaves had whispered" to them cease, the mud "infected [their] ears," leaving them stone deaf (421). Here, the "mud of the dream-forest" is at once an occult and terrestrial substance, just as, on a narrative level, this phrase points to the novel's overlapping of realism and allegory, or "allegorical realism," to employ Hamish Dalley's useful term.[11] This allows Rushdie to shuttle back and forth between, and at times intermix, the material and imaginative worlds his characters inhabit. In fact, Rushdie metafictionally demonstrates, as mentioned, that even materiality as we conventionally understand it is made so partly by our imaginations.

Rushdie's Sundarbans episode therefore invites several interpretations at the same time, just as the forest itself seems to continuously "change its nature" to the human eye. The forest may be a symptom of the characters' PTSD (post-traumatic stress disorder), a manifestation of repressed trauma (the narrator later wondering if Ayooba is affected by "his ... breakdown in the Sundarbans" [426]); a delirium induced by their physical deterioration; an allegory of the subcontinent's 1947 Partition; an uncanny tale produced by a dissociative narrator; or, as it appears on the page, the account of survival in an unfamiliar forestland that does not match anything in the characters' cultural storehouse of arboreal images. The men, missing their families (Ayooba imagines he "saw his mother," for instance [418]) and wracked by guilt for "their victims" in the war, imagine that the "ghostly monkeys gathered in the trees" at night are singing Tagore's lyrics, "Our Golden Bengal" ("*Amar Sonar Bangla*"), which had already become the anthem of the new Bangladesh (as it still is). Rushdie provides a few pertinent words from the song: "Our Mother, I am poor, but what little I have, I lay at thy feet. And it maddens my heart with delight." Also in the song, but not quoted by Rushdie, are, for example, "the aroma of the mango orchard," "fields of paddy," and "banyan trees," which together form the motherland.[12] It is the sense of "shame" this song induces in the three "boy-soldiers" that compels them to put jungle mud in their ears. Whereas Bankim's arboreal–maternal hymn "*Bande Mataram*" inspires patriotism in its listeners, in the Sundarbans a like hymn stirs emotions of a very different, and deeply ironic, kind. In both cases, the powerful effect on the senses of the listeners has as much to do with their forest surroundings as with the words being sung. The fact that "jungle mud" does double duty as natural matter and as metaphor in Rushdie's novel reminds us of this. The mangrove forest in these ways reflects the novel's representation of Indian history as multiply told, multiply imagined, and phantasmagorical, as befits the region's cultural intermixing.

The Changing Forest of *The Hungry Tide*

Amitav Ghosh's *The Hungry Tide*, set in the Sundarbans, is among the most scrutinized novels in the field of ecocriticism, both because it is clearly an ecocritique and because it is part of the far-ranging oeuvre of a major writer who insistently decenters dominant worldviews and who compels readers to see that these worldviews cannot be understood without recognizing their interconnection with the natural environment. Ghosh himself identifies this overarching theme in his 2016 study of how climate change has shaped literature, *The Great Derangement: Climate Change and the Unthinkable*. It was while visiting the Sundarbans as he worked on *The Hungry Tide*, he writes, that he "became aware of the urgent proximity of nonhuman presences."[13] This was partly because, he says, the "landscape" of the Sundarbans is "so dynamic that its very changeability leads to innumerable moments of recognition," such as the fact that it "is demonstrably alive," and not an inert "stage for the enactment of human history."[14] He also noticed "portents" that the forests were enduring "irreversible change" due to global warming. The Sundarbans, he saw, is "itself a protagonist" in the story of environmental changes and human relationships to them. But Ghosh observes that he would not have perceived these truths unless "some prior awareness of what I was witnessing had not already been implanted in me" in "childhood."[15] The root of "recognition," he notes, means—as the word's prefix indicates—that a moment of real insight "occurs when a prior awareness flashes before us," an awareness borne of previous experiences and stories, such as the family lore that his nineteenth-century "ancestors" had been forced to migrate from Bengal to Bihar after the river on which they depended changed course drastically. The story enabled him to recognize that his ancestors "were ecological refugees long before the term was invented."[16] As he writes in *The Hungry Tide*, in the voice of a character named Nilima, boats are finding it increasingly hard to traverse the Sundarbans waterways because "there isn't much water in the rivers nowadays" (22).

In his depiction of the Sundarbans in *The Hungry Tide*, therefore, Ghosh adds a crucial element missing in other writers' descriptions of the region, including Rushdie's, which is the reality of drastic anthropogenic changes in its environment. To demonstrate this, Ghosh gives us a sense of how the Sundarbans region has been administered by both colonial and nation-state authorities, who share a view of the region's inhabitants as intruders into a generically wild environment rather than—as the novel shows—as people who live within what is called an "ecology of selves."[17] Ghosh does not romanticize these inhabitants, whose forebears in fact mostly arrived in the nineteenth century.[18] (As early as 1200, groups of Sufis, cleared several areas of forest for settlement, but "brutal piracy" in the 1500s by the Portuguese, and to some extent by the Arakan Burmese, displaced most of these settlers.[19]) Ghosh instead illustrates, through characters whose livelihood depends upon this watery world, how comparatively detached most people (including his readers) have become from the natural world. It is they—we—who preserve the "wild/civilized" duality. The Sundarbans inhabitants, as Annu Jalais concludes in her close study of the region, have a deep understanding of their "relatedness" to an environment that is especially taxing on humans.[20] They rely on two main activities, fishing and gathering wild honey and beeswax, both of which expose them to attacks by the region's Royal Bengal tiger, which has learned to eat human flesh (and fish) in the forbidding environment. To help readers gain some understanding of this mutually respectful human-environment relationship, Ghosh flourishes a number of narrative devices, including folk songs, staged dramas, animal calls, a character's diary, and the motif of translation. It will be important to keep Ghosh's emphasis on recognition—on seeing anew—in mind when I presently turn to *Sea of Poppies*, the novel that appeared immediately after *The Hungry Tide*. Here, however, I focus on three intertwined features of Ghosh's representation of the Sundarbans in *The Hungry Tide* that offer significant insights into current environmental paradoxes: first, the prominence of visual as well as emotional vision as a means of making the reader aware of "nonhuman presences"; second, the manner in which narratives stage history; and finally, the stylistic and thematic interfusion of materiality and immateriality, of real and imagined forests, somewhat as Rushdie does, but with more far-reaching commentary on how this interfusion has shaped commercial and other intrusive human activities.

At the heart of Ghosh's Sundarbans, the "hungry tide" of the title, is the syncretic folktale of Bon Bibi (Figure 4.2). One of the novel's protagonists is Piya, an Indian-American cetologist visiting the mangrove delta to research the endangered Gangetic and Irrawaddy rivers dolphin, and it is partly through her outsider eyes that we learn about the region. The other "eyes" we share belong to Kanai, a professional translator from Calcutta, and Fokir, a local fisherman intimately familiar with the land who lends his knowledge to Piya. Kanai's widowed aunt, Nilima, has headed a health-care trust here for decades and has asked Kanai to translate her late husband Nirmal's diary recounting the notorious Morichjhapi massacre of 1979, of which Fokir is a child survivor. Ghosh does not invent this event. Morichjhapi was, as we learn from Nirmal's contemporary diary, a forest reserve island on which several thousand low-caste Hindu refugees from Bangladesh settle.[21] They appeared to have established a fairly harmonious settlement but were ordered by the West Bengal government to vacate the island in the name of preserving it as a tiger refuge. A "siege" ensued, leading to near famine and several deaths. Despite successfully petitioning a judge to declare the siege illegal, the police eventually opened fire, killing many—with precise numbers having become a point of contention between factual and amnesiac histories, as Ghosh shows.

The massacre parallels a "killing" in the present: the death of a tiger at the hands of frightened villagers, including Fokir, which angers the idealistic Piya. The novel teases

Figure 4.2 Bon Bibi figure
Source: Photo by author.

out the ethical complexities of the act, most notably mainstream society's privileging of ostensibly people-less land (and its selectively prized mammals) over poor human inhabitants. As Upamanyu Pablo Mukherjee observes, the government's violent act was premised on "a fundamental difference between human and non-human communities," unmindful of their "complex but palpable continuities" in the practices of local fisherfolk and villagers. This dangerous ignorance is precisely what the legend of Bon Bibi, the jungle goddess who is believed to preside over the Sundarbans and its creatures, including tigers and dolphins, warns against. The legend, we learn, is composed of Arab-Islamic, Hindu, and folk narratives, and its ultimate message is that "the rich and greedy would be punished while the poor and righteous were rewarded" (88).

The three entwined features of the Sundarbans I cited above are perhaps best illustrated by Kanai's attendance of a local staging of a play, "The Glory of Bon Bibi." The story is the regional inhabitants' origin myth of sorts, explaining how they came to settle here and how they regard the forest and its tigers. Kanai is "surprise[d]" to see that the "opening scene [is] set in a city in Arabia," Medina, where "a Sufi *faqir*" has twin children, the goddess Bon Bibi and Shah Jongoli, who move to the Sundarbans. There, they contend with the fearsome demon Dokkhin Rai, ruler of "every animal as well as every … malevolent spirit," and agree to share the forests with him, "one half … remain[ing] a wilderness" for the demon-king, the other half for Bon Bibi and the humans she invites into the land. But then "human greed," in the form of a person named Dhona, "upset[s] this order" when he and his ships enter Dokkhin Rai's realm to horde honey and wax. The latter demands tribute in the form of a boy named Dukhey (meaning "sorrow"), but when the demon-king, in the form of a tiger, is about to attack Dukhey, the boy calls out to Bon Bibi, who instantly appears and saves him. She returns him safely to his mother, along with "a treasure trove of honey and wax." This "show[s] the world the law of the forest, which was that the rich and greedy would be punished while the poor and righteous were rewarded" (85–8).

What interests me in Ghosh's presentation of this richly suggestive folk myth is that Kanai, to his great surprise, is pulled into the story world being staged before him despite its schematic melodrama and rudimentary costumes. Kanai feels Dukhey's "terror" as "real and immediate" and weeps with "joy and gratitude" when Bon Bibi saves the boy (88). Though actors stray from verisimilitude—the woman playing Bon Bibi taking a moment "to lean over the side of the stage in order to clear her mouth of a wad of paan" (88)—the story's evocative power is undiminished. One reason the play overcomes Kanai so unexpectedly is precisely that: it is an unexpected, unfamiliar story, staged in an unfamiliar environment. Yet its emotional truth is somehow greater than that of the sophisticated dramas Kanai has seen in Calcutta. His emotional investment is due in part to the lack of culturally encrusted—in his case, *bhadralok*—pre-expectations about both the landscape and its peoples, so that the staging of the Bon Bibi tale is not filtered through an anticipatory feedback loop. (His uncle reflects this outsider view by calling the Bon Bibi belief "false consciousness" [84].)

This does not mean, however, that Kanai's emotional investment has no antecedent catalysts or that viewing the Bon Bibi story in this context is to somehow glimpse a traditionally pure, unadulterated artifact in the way that "primitive" art was said to have been offered to moderns.[22] Kanai has, after all, previously "heard mention of this story" (84). An equally strong stimulant for his investment in the play is his fondness for Kusum, who had "gasped as if in shock" when he told her he did not know the story's "particulars." "Then whom do you call on when you're afraid?" she asks. "The question nagged at [Kanai's] mind," which leads him to ask his uncle for the details (84). He is affected by Kusum's question in the first place because ever since hearing about her when she was fifteen, impoverished, and in the care of the "Women's Union" his aunt assists, Kanai has been intrigued by her and had "look[ed] forward to [meeting]" her (26). Soon after their meeting, and leading up to the Bon Bibi drama scene, Kusum "became Kanai's guide and mentor" in Lusibari, and "told him about its people and their children and about everything around it—cockfights and pujas, births and deaths." She, in turn, "would listen" to his stories of Calcutta "with rapt attention" (84). Their companionship prompts the sharing of meaningful elements of their lives, activating a mutual sympathy. When Kanai learns that he is ignorant of Bon Bibi's great significance to Kusum and her community, it is his investment in Kusum's affective world that prompts his determination to find out more. The viewing of the play, in turn, sets the stage for Kanai's growing recognition of the local community's investment in the natural environment, as the narrator describes, and that the fisherman Fokir exemplifies.

The audience of this traveling theater in Bengal, called *jatra*, is part of an "emotional community," as Upamanyu Mukherjee has observed, in which actors and viewers participate.[23] Mukherjee rightly notes that this dialogic, participatory experience resembles that of *bhakti*, which, as mentioned previously, is a form of worship characterized by "intense personal devotion to a deity often expressed in poem-songs" and was especially strong in the fifteenth through eighteenth centuries (though it was not, as Mukherjee implies, confined to Bengal).[24] As Mukherjee observes, this "anti-realist, musical, melodramatic and stylistically uneven folk theatre," with its "anachronistic representation of time," is well-suited to "expressing popular political perceptions and sentiments."[25] *Bhakti* incorporates features of *darshan*, the aforementioned practice of "divine sight" common throughout India, with audience members (the devotees need not be conventionally religious) "seeing" as much with their emotions and ears as with their eyes. *Bhakti* as a form of worship likely originated in southern India at least 1,500 years ago—a millennium before the fifteenth-century movement in the north— in the Tamil Sangam collection titled *Paripatal*.[26] Sangam love poems, as we recall, rely for their affective power partly on poetic tropes composed of five *tinai* landscapes, each one associated with particular emotions. Thus, *mullai*, "jasmine," bespeaks forests of pastureland that convey a lover's "painful separation from her lover."[27] Expressions of love evoked by whichever of these affective landscapes the poet chooses to use, therefore, enable the listener to see the material landscape as well as feel its emotional power. This power, in other words, is evoked by a rich repertoire of topographically inflected moods.[28] In much the same way, though without any written aid, the Bon Bibi *jatra*, informed by *bhakti*, elicits in its audience the emotions associated with the goddess's (and their) jungle home. The text implies that to perform the play in a city like Calcutta would diminish its power: Kanai had, for instance, earlier discouraged Kusum from visiting it, "cring[ing]" at the thought (84).

The correspondence between language and landscape in the novel encompasses the three significant features I listed above (which might be called the narrative's visionary apparatus), which help the reader understand the paradoxes inherent in today's environmental challenges—in this case, the fact that people and protected animals often occupy the same lands. Reading a fact-based report about the Morichjhapi massacre is an important consciousness-raising exercise, certainly, but one that, by placing it on a historical time line, cuts it off from the interwoven strands of ecology, storytelling, and "unseen presences" that together open a window onto the deeper implications of environmental justice. In closing my discussion of the novel, I therefore want to probe this language–landscape connection a bit more, particularly in light of Ghosh's comment from *The Great Derangement*, cited above, that real recognition, such as his understanding of the anthropogenic threats to the Sundarbans, occurs when one's "surroundings" stir up "a prior awareness" to suddenly make clear its true implications.[29]

When Nilima, soon after she and her husband arrive in Lusibari, has her "epiphany" about how to help the "startlingly large proportion of the island's women" who are "dressed as widows," she discovers that there is no Bengali word for them as a group. This is because they are not all widows in the conventional sense, but instead adopt the clothing and behavior of widowhood each time their husbands go fishing as "a way of preparing themselves" emotionally for the always-real possibility that some fishermen may die at sea. Although the women "were not condemned to lifelong bereavement" in the way their urban counterparts might be, Nilima finds that they nevertheless endure "years of abuse and exploitation." Searching for an appropriate collective noun, Nilima discovers that "reality ran afoul of her vocabulary" (68). Nirmal, more in tune with words than action, recommends the word "*badabon*," Bengali for forest. He likes the word because, as he tells Nilima, it derives from the Arabic word "*badiya*," meaning "desert," as well as the Sanskrit *bon*. He feels "it is as though the word itself were an island, born of the meeting of two great rivers of language—just as the tide country is begotten of the Ganga's union with the Brahmaputra" (69). The reader sees the irony, though Nirmal is unaware of it, that the word's fusion of local and Arabic roots mirrors the syncretism of the Bon Bibi myth. Both Nilima and Nirmal experience moments of recognition, however imperfect, that are borne of some previous knowledge: etymology, in his case, the convention of Hindu widowhood in hers—even if the convention has here, "on the margins of the Hindu world," been transformed. Whereas Nilima herself recognizes (in Ghosh's sense of the word) the women's plight and need, Nirmal's recognition is on the level of narrative, for it is the reader who gains insight from his logophilia.

Nirmal, to be sure, is a transplant from Calcutta who believes that the mangroves "do not merely recolonize land; they erase time." For Nirmal, time is history and modernity—though he, too, as we know from his diary, learned to see the world anew during and after the Morichjhapi massacre. Nirmal's diary provides much of the raw ecological detail about the Sundarbans. "When the tides create new land," he writes, "overnight mangroves begin to gestate." This is why a "mangrove forest is a universe unto itself, utterly unlike other woodlands or jungles" (7). We also learn that although the name Sundarbans "means 'the beautiful forest,'" "there are some who believe [it] to be derived from the name of a common species of mangrove—the sundari tree, Heritiera minor" (7). These topological properties make it hard to sustain human-made borders, which words are hard put to describe. As Nirmal observes, the "origin" of the name Sundarbans "is no easier to account for than its present prevalence," since different people have used different names (7). The landscape's changeability as depicted by Nirmal suggests the kind of surreal representation we saw in Rushdie's novel. What is different about Ghosh's rendering of the Sundarbans is that he affords us many different perceptions of it, which the novel's interleaved narratives enable and emblematize in a formal way. Nor is any one character's perception held up as definitive: they are mutually dependent, as are each character's successive moments of recognition.

The reader's participation in this process of recognition is as important as any single epiphany in the novel, for we, of course, can see parallels and echoes the characters cannot: correspondences between characters' inner thoughts, between history and the present, between otherwise outwardly distinct events, and between Ghosh's text and his literary interlocutors. The parts are greater than the whole. For example, when the Indian-American Piya is on Fokir's boat in search of dolphins, she takes her turn at bathing and sees that the towel provided for her is a piece of "checkered cloth" that she recalls, first vaguely and then clearly, her father using in America. He had never parted with it, even when "old and tattered," because it reminded him of home. "What was it he had called" the towel? Piya wonders, searching for a word that "she had known ... once, but [which] time had erased from her memory" (73). Later, after an intervening chapter titled "Kusum" that further describes Kusum's friendship with Kanai, Piya learns through "signs and gestures" with Fokir that the word for towel which she had forgotten is "*gamchha*," one "she had known ... all along." "How do you lose a word?" is Piya's question, delivered as free indirect discourse. "Does it ... lie hidden in cobwebs and dust, waiting to be cleaned out and rediscovered?" (78) The setting is crucial to Piya's emotional remembrance. Her struggle to recall the word at this time, in this place—on a boat in a Sundarbans channel, after surviving an involuntary dunk in its "muddy brown water"—has led her to a greater appreciation of why her father was so attached to his towel. She has recognized its affective component by inflecting the present with the past.

It is at this point that readers are able to understand, along with Piya, that her insight is induced by an interdependent mix of language, memory, and physical environment, which I will call visionary sight, as we will also see in the following chapter. Ghosh's readers understand Piya's visionary sight because the "Kusum" chapter, appearing between Piya's fall into the river and her later encounter with the towel, has allowed us, through Kanai's similar moment of recognition, to move through the process of her gradual sharpening of vision. This intervening chapter opens in the present:

> From the far side of the Guest House roof Kanai could see all the way across the island ... to the spot where Nirmal's house had once stood. It was gone now but the image of it that flickered in his memory was no less real to him than the newly constructed student hostel that had taken its place. (73)

His memory is "no less real" today because, as the chapter goes on to tell us through a flashback, of his first face-to-face encounter with Kusum in the Lusibari Women's Union, when they had "held each other's gaze" and he "saw in her eyes ... an awakened curiosity he knew to be a reflection of his own" (76). When she later comes upon him reading a book, she is the one "who spoke to him first." And here "the gap that separated them"—the anglicized, bookish young urbanite and the illiterate young village woman who had fled domestic violence—closes a little, adding to the accretion of bits of understanding that have the potential to bloom into deeper insight. After Kanai has "dismissed her request" to show her his book (because "It won't make any sense to you"), she responds by opening her hand to reveal a grasshopper and asking, "Do you know what this is?" Kanai, his "lip curl[ing] in contempt," says, "Those are everywhere. Who's not seen one of those?" She then "put the insect in her mouth and closed her lips," which, of course, "caught Kanai's attention and he finally deigned to lower his book. 'Did you swallow it?'" he asks, at which Kusum opens her mouth "and the grasshopper jumped straight into Kanai's face. He let out a shout and fell over backward while she watched, laughing." She says, 'It's just an insect ... Don't be afraid'" (77). This light-hearted exchange suggests that Kusum's easy access to the natural environment is a form of perceptual power equal to Kanai's book-focused knowledge. We also see how this episode, coming before Kanai's viewing of the Bon Bibi play, foregrounds that moment of recognition. For the reader, it makes sense that these episodes appear in contiguous chapters: our recognitions gather accretive power, as do the palimpsest of memories. Widening our purview even more, we might also notice that Kusum's rapport with insects is a far cry from Saleem's and the three soldiers' disgust at the insect-laden jungle mud in Rushdie's depiction of the Sundarbans. Just as Piya comes to see the emotive threads interconnecting words, things, and memories, so do Kanai and Ghosh's readers increasingly perceive that in the Sundarbans, people and jungle do not remain apart. Kusum and (as we learn) her son Fokir, who rescues Piya from the muddy river after an angry forest guard has pushed her in, reveal to their urban companions that an environmentally sensitive understanding of the Sundarbans depends on lessons borne of everyday inhabitance: an intimacy with jungle, river, and mud as living entities. It is mud, in fact, that exerts on both Piya and Kanai a physical, semiotic, and imaginative force that paradoxically, though in different ways, clears their vision.

A pivotal illustration of this, and of the cumulative enlarging of vision, begins with a song that Piya hears Fokir sing, whose words she does not understand but whose music has an effect on her "right then, in that place," which is inexpressible and eye-opening. Piya "began to ask herself whether it was she who was naïve" rather than Fokir, as she initially thought (83). This revelation is the start of a cascading, though not straightforward,[30] series of other recognitions that culminate in Piya's deep awareness, in the novel's conclusion, that her home is in the Sundarbans because this "is where the Oracella [dolphins] are," as she tells Nilima (329). The dolphins, as Piya knows, see their surroundings through the conal "prism" of sunlight just below the water's surface. But the "curtain of silt" in the rivers feeding the Sundarbans, the Ganga, and Brahmaputra, "shroud" that prism of light, "confus[ing]" ordinary spatial orientation and causing the Gangetic dolphin to "swim on its side … with one of its lateral fins trailing the bottom" as a referential aid (46). (It is worth noting that the first Mughal emperor Babur saw Gangetic dolphins in the early 1500s, when they were comparatively plentiful.[31]) When Piya falls into the river (the chapter is actually called "The Fall"), she experiences something of its "disorientation," which causes her to "panic" and nearly drown, until Fokir dives in, hoists her into his boat, and "suck[s] the water from her throat" (48).

The river episode looks ahead to a far more disorienting event, the powerful cyclone that arrives near the end of the book and during which Fokir once again saves Piya's life. On Fokir's boat and far out from any settlement, they are caught in a "tidal surge." Fokir, knowing the impending surge will be life-threatening, ties himself to Piya, and both of them to a tree by knotting "an old sari" stored in the boat. He also "upturned the boat and ran a line through its timbers and around the trunks of the surrounding trees" (311). People, boat timber, and tree thus linked together express a semiotics of the forest that does not need human words to make meaning. As elsewhere in the novel, this section is animated by a motif of sight represented in a variety of ways— ocular, inner, and visionary for humans, as well as nonhuman animal perceptions— to resonate with the book's insistence on epistemologies, ontologies, and languages that depart from the conventions of modern recognition. As the cyclone's eye reaches them, for example, Piya "opened her eyes and was amazed by what she saw": "as far as [her] eye could reach, was a heaving carpet of leaves," under whose "green" mantle "the water's surface … had disappeared," as has "the island itself," whose "shape could be deduced only from the few thickets of trees whose uppermost reaches were still visible above water." When the storm hits them, with Piya "facing the tree," Fokir shields her body from its powerful wind. "Where she had had the tree trunk to shelter her before, now there was only Fokir's body." His body is effectively tree-like, and because Piya feels she and Fokir are "so close" as to have "merged," she can "sense the blows raining down on his back ... it was as if the storm had given them what life could not; it had fused them together and made them one" (321). Taken out of context, the scene can seem overwrought, with a subaltern's body sacrificed for the life of someone comparatively privileged. But as I have said, it must be read in conversation with the several other moments of recognition in the novel. (We can also read it in conversation with other texts, including Bibhutibhushan's *Aranyak*, in which, as I note in the following chapter, the narrator compares a young Adivasi man to a sal tree.) Piya's culminating desire to remain in Lusibari has much to do with her relationship with Fokir and his sacrifice, but it also derives from her fall into the muddy river, her learning of Bengali and the local dialect, and even her presence at the villagers' tiger killing. Shortly before the storm arrives, Piya has once again asked Fokir to sing—"and suddenly the language and the music were all around her, flowing like a river, and all of it made sense" (298). It matters that Fokir's song, at her request, is the story of the forest goddess Bon Bibi, indicating that the forests that are "all around" Piya and Fokir elicit in their inhabitants (for Piya has now become one) an acute recognition of environmental interconnectedness and heterogeneity.

    I close by reemphasizing the role of mud and sight in the context of this arboreal interconnectedness, which is especially visible in Kanai's struggle to understand it. He is finally able to discern the forest in something like the intersubjective reality[32] in which Fokir perceives it, an insight precipitated by an intensely sensory and psychological experience. This, in turn, triggers his momentary dissolution of self in what we might call a *darshanic* epiphany, recalling Chakrabarty's characterization of *darshan* as "both a subject-centered and subjectless" mode of ocular and spiritual-affective perception.[33] When Fokir, having dared Kanai to show that he is unafraid of the jungle, takes Kanai on his boat to one of the area's many remote islands, the first crack in Kanai's bravado happens when he "step[s] into the mud" on the shore. His condescending words are cut off when it "suddenly" seems "as though the earth had come alive and was reaching for his ankle. Looking down, he discovered that a rope-like tendril [of a mangrove] had wrapped itself around his ankles." Because "the consistency of the mud was such as to create a suction effect ... he could not break free." Lashing out at Fokir, Kanai catches "a glimpse of [his] eyes" and abruptly understands why Fokir "had brought him here." It is "not because he wanted him to die, but because he wanted him to be judged." Kanai's work as a professional translator has, he now believes, primed him for this recognition, because looking into Fokir's eyes is "exactly" like those "few instances in which the act of interpretation had given him the ... sensation of being transported out of his body and into another." At these moments, it seems as though "a prism"—an echo of the dolphin's conical prism—is "allow[ing] him to look through another set of eyes." And now, too, on shifting soil in between water and jungle, "it was as though his own vision were being refracted through those opaque, unreadable eyes and he were seeing" the truth: that just like "the outside world," he viewed Fokir as "a man [who] counted for nothing" (270). As he "wipe[s] the mud from his eyes," Kanai sees Fokir, who "has stepped out of his field of vision," leaving in his boat. Alone on the island, Kanai is overcome with such fear that he cannot "recall the word[s] ... Fokir had used" for tiger, words which seem to have "been replaced by the thing itself." Kanai is certain that he sees a tiger appear, that the mangrove "branches" are "clos[ing] around him," and that the tiger, "caked with mud," is about to attack. But "when next he open[s] his eyes," it is Piya he sees, who, along with the older fisherman and guide Horen, confirms that there is no trace of a tiger (270). When Piya later asks Kanai if Fokir had intentionally left him on the island, Kanai "firmly" says "No," adding, "I happened to fall in the mud and lost my temper" (275).

Once again, the mud is simultaneously tactile and symbolic, signifying a fusion of material and imaginative worlds in the way that Bon Bibi does, a fusion Kanai now begins to perceive. He understands that the point is not whether or not he saw a living tiger, but that emotion proved to be an equally powerful kind of sight. The reader sees, too, that Kanai's response to the Bon Bibi play has prepared him for the island experience. For among the truths Kanai learned from his affective participation in the play is that ocular sight does not necessarily equate to apprehension and that his presumptions about knowledge have been wrong, such as that humans are always in charge of creating meaning. He also learns that knowledge is not static and that one has to continuously open one's eyes, as he learns subsequently to do with the mangrove forests. This is why "even before the performance [of the play] had ended Kanai knew he wanted to see it again" (88). Kanai's revelation parallels the narrator's descriptions of the "tide country," as it is called, which in the words of Nirmal, his uncle, "resembles a desert [in] that it can trick the eye with mirages" (42). *The Hungry Tide* invites the reader to see that Nirmal's essentially urban eye chooses to define the region's "tricks" as illusion only because his standard of reference is confined to mainstream understandings of reality, which are still in thrall to colonial treatments of forest. Ghosh's novel provides a corrective to this not only by calling attention to these mainstream treatments, but also by offering some alternative ways of seeing and describing—representing—the forest.

Indexical Forests, Subaltern Lives, and Global Maritime Commerce in *Sea of Poppies*

The instances of *darshanic* epiphany depicted in *The Hungry Tide* echo the *darshanic* perspective I noted in Bibhutibhushan's novel *Aranyak* in the previous chapter. Ghosh's 2008 novel *Sea of Poppies*[34] repurposes this visionary aptitude for double-sightedness— that is, the combination of spiritual and ocular forms of perception—to amplify a supranational sensibility, and does so by ironizing the classical forest trope in light of this theme. In this sense, *Sea of Poppies* departs from both Bankim's *Anandamath* and Bibhutibhushan's novel, in which the forest is a form of allegorical realism (to recall Dalley's term) that anchors the two texts' aim of eliciting in their readers an emotional response to forestland as a "national treasure," to repeat Bibhutibhushan's phrase. The forest, in other words, is at once a material and spiritual wellspring of national authenticity, in which characters always already belong to, and are products of, the land—though a land in desperate need of proper stewardship. Ghosh's *The Hungry Tide*, as we have seen, does not share this essentialist view of nationhood, instead describing the effects of displacement and migration, both forced and voluntary, on the

Sundarbans' inhabitants. The novel emphasizes the blurring of boundaries (which also, as we saw, characterizes classical works) as a feature of the planetary consciousness that is necessary for comprehending today's climate calamity. Far more than *The Hungry Tide*, however, *Sea of Poppies* figures its characters' abilities to alternately enlarge and narrow their fields of vision as a primary means of acknowledging the loss of forestlands and of then imagining those forests anew. This double-sighted, *darshanic* vision, like that of Fokir in the Sundarbans, manifests in the later novel's subaltern characters and is a perspicuity enabled by the environmental sensibilities of these characters.

In the discussion that follows, I focus on the character Deeti to show how her visions are indispensable to a more integrative idea of social affiliation than is afforded by Bankim's exclusionary narrative. Deeti's visions are integrative because they reveal connections among seemingly unrelated arboreal objects and images. These forest indices characterize the colonial-era sea trade of the 1830s that backlights the lives of Deeti and everyone else. Such visionary moments in the context of a work of historical realism echo Bankim's fusion of mythic and historical structures, but to entirely different ends. Unlike Bankim's religiously inflexible sal forest, whose womb-like features and male ascetics represent a conservative familial narrative, Ghosh's passengers experience a "rebirth in [their] ship's womb" (420) that effectively inverts that influential national narrative. The ship at the center of Ghosh's novel, the *Ibis*, facilitates this inversion, with its "forest of masts" (271) and "weeping" timbers (12) recalling both its forest provenance and its arboreal purpose, for the ship is a veritable floating arbor. The irony is that the *Ibis* is to be used to transport Indian laborers to work on the distant plantations, whose products—timber, sugar, fruit, and spices—sustain the British empire. Unlike in novels previously discussed, the forest in *Sea of Poppies* is not so much a topographical place in which people, nonhuman animals, and supernatural figures interact than it is an assemblage of forest materials and motifs. A ship's mast, a neem tree, and allusions to Krishna's Vrindavan forest all inflect integrative, *darshanic* forms of perception enacted by Ghosh's characters, whose lives and ways of seeing help to provincialize Europe.

Deeti's Visions

Sea of Poppies is the first of a trilogy dubbed the Ibis Trilogy, a tag appropriate to the ship's literal and figurative centrality in the three novels.[35] The ship's journey reminds us that oceans rather than terra firma were "central" to people's everyday worlds and imaginations until the early twentieth century.[36] For centuries, sailing ships built of forest wood transported enormous amounts of yet more wood from Malabar to Mauritius, and to points in between, linking up interior and littoral woodlands with riverine and nautical traffic in both material and cultural ways. Ship-building enterprises dotted the lengthy coastlines of India, with forests of Burmese and Malabar teak and northern Indian shisham, or sissoo (rosewood), being among the favored trees for this timber. Such forests, a British official observed in 1802, seemed to be "inexhaustible."[37] It is this historical context—more specifically the lead-up to the first Opium or Anglo-Chinese War of 1839–42—in which the novel is set. With the official end of the British slave trade, the East India Company turned to Indian indentured labor and opium production to fill its coffers.

Sea of Poppies opens with a description of Deeti's "vision of a tall-masted ship, at sail on the ocean," an "apparition" that, though she lives "four hundred miles from the coast," "she knew instantly … was a sign of destiny" (3). So powerful is this vision that Deeti, who is illiterate, is compelled to draw it. Only much later will she see the actual ship, whose form matches the prefiguring apparition. Deeti's double-sightedness, as I have argued, is a form of *darshanic* vision, which, to recall the Introduction, is rooted in the traditional term *darshan*—the dual sense of both seeing and being in the presence of a sacred person or manifestation[38]—and is a phrase I use to indicate that Deeti's visions, both here and at other times, register both ocular and semidivine sight. In an otherwise assiduously realist narrative, this description conveys to us a sense of the mesmerizing effect that Deeti's observation has on her, the moment when "[her] eyes suddenly conjured up a picture of an immense ship with two tall masts. The prow of the ship tapered into a figurehead with a long" (7)—a form that is and is not (yet) real. Deeti impulsively sketches what she has envisioned by applying "bright red sindoor" (a traditional cosmetic made of vermillion and turmeric) to "a green mango leaf."[39] Her swift rendering produces "two wing-like triangles hanging suspended above a long, curved shape that ended in a hooked bill." Deeti places these sketches in her "puja [worship] room," in which she has put up her schematic drawings of both "forebears" and "living relatives" and set up *murti*, or figurines, of familiar gods like Shiva, Ganesh, Durga, and Krishna (8). When Deeti tells her daughter Kabutri, "I saw a jahaj—a ship," she can only describe it, and draw it, in the likeness of "a great bird." Seeing her mother's drawing, Kabutri "recognized it at once for what it was—an image of a two-masted vessel with unfurled sails," and is "amazed that her mother had drawn an image as though she were representing a living being" (9). Kabutri in this way glimpses a strange (because hitherto unseen) yet somehow familiar shape and experiences a vicarious form of *darshanic* vision. The reader participates in this uncanny sight by having to hold in view the ship's material as well as figurative qualities, much as its avian name elicits both biotic and metaphorical meanings.[40]

Deeti's vision is also in dialogue with what other characters, including her daughter Kabutri, perceive. It is in fact Kabutri's question to her mother about the destination of a small, "one-masted pateli barge" on the Ganga River near their home "that triggered Deeti's vision" (8). ("Pateli" likely derives from Parsi shipbuilders who had long before taken the common Gujarati surname "Patel," or roughly "lord." They operated in several port cities, including Calcutta, and usually used teak for construction.[41]) At Kabutri's query, Deeti's "eyes suddenly conjured up a picture of an immense ship with two tall masts … The prow of the ship tapered into a figurehead with a long bill, like a stork or a heron." (The word "conjure" recurs in some other scenes to convey a character's sense of wonder at a strange experience, further accentuating the motif of perception.) Deeti sees the ship's "dazzling [white]" sails and the "distinctive yet unfamiliar presence" of "a man … near the bow" (8)—a man who, as we learn, is Zachary Reid, the ship's second mate.[42] When Kabutri wonders why her mother would place this sketch in her worship room, she voices the question of those, including the reader, who cannot yet see in the way that Deeti does, but a sight that Ghosh's narrative enables. Deeti responds simply,

"I don't know. I just know it must be there; and not just the ship, but also many of those who are on it" (9). Deeti's placement of the *Ibis* sketch alongside her other *murti* makes it contiguous with them and transforms the ship into a manifestation of divine destiny.[43]

Deeti's visions are important features of the novel because they accommodate the dialogism intrinsic to human perception, as opposed to the one-to-one correspondence between an object and its description that we often assume to be what distinguishes realism. Ghosh's presentation of Deeti's vision is in this sense a commentary on the fictional-yet-truthful history he renders on the page, for it highlights the contiguity (though not identity) between a material object—in this case, the wooden ship—and the web of events and meanings in which the object is enmeshed. This recalls Charles Sanders Peirce's concept of the index, discussed in the Introduction, whereby we interpret an object as reflective of its particular characteristics at a given moment while also treating it as a sign of possible future events involving similar objects. As Kohn puts it, indices "encourage us to make a connection between what is happening and what might potentially happen."[44] Deeti reverses this process by first envisioning the ship and then, at a later date, seeing and touching it—which is not unlike what a novelist does. What remains crucial to the indexical process is the dialogism on which it—and all meaning—depends. In the historical context of *Sea of Poppies*, Deeti's visions are indexical in that they interconnect global maritime trade, the forested resources on which that trade depends, and the ordinary lives that toil in this environment, notably indentured laborers like Deeti and Kalua. Her visions also constitute, as several commentators have shown, a counterweight to the predominantly male and upper-class perspective of conventional historical narratives.[45]

Deeti's drawings of what she envisions are no less important to the novel's emphasis on the virtues of the dialogic imagination, for they prompt us to question those visions of the future—including future nationhood—that are too often predicated on difference and exclusion. The *murti* of family members that Deeti collects and enshrines in her village home, and her later assemblage of etchings on board the *Ibis*, speak to the critical role of aesthetic perspective in this dialogism. The correspondence of aesthetic and divine sight is, indeed, a characteristic of *darshan*, which is inseparable from worshipful art.[46] But as Dipesh Chakrabarty observes, approaches to the aesthetic dimension of *darshan* are somewhat different for the print cultures of city dwellers as compared to the oral cultures of villagers like Deeti. Arguably, her *darshan* of the ship is comparatively less mediated, and more "performative," than the experience a "formally educated" person would have to such a vision. Print-based urban cultures will tend to interpret such a "sighting" as something—a dream, for instance—that facilitates a modern political stance, which by definition requires an individual subject.[47] These differences are not qualitative, such as would be implied by treating Deeti's experience as "more authentic" simply because it goes through fewer pedagogical filters. The two modes of *darshan* are, rather, two alternatives to perceiving a changing world. Ghosh's decision to open his modern historical narrative with a village woman's vision effectively (to use Chakrabarty's words) "brings gods and spirits into the domain of the political."[48] Ghosh does so not to proffer a supposedly primitive or originary experience, which a conventional "historicist framework" demands, but instead to show that the ostensible disenchantment of the modern world is misguided and that Deeti, as her subsequent adventures attest, engages with the political as much as any romantic–realist character, such as in a Walter Scott novel, would do.[49] Deeti's vision sets the stage for the novel's refiguring of India's global history—or rather, histories, which encompass India's migrant populations—as inherently polyvocal and heterodox. The novel thus exhibits, through Ghosh's art, the polyvocal propensity we see in Tagore's work as well as, to some extent, in Bankim's (in his linguistic and narrative innovations), a multiplicity that is articulated especially through forest metaphors and metonyms. But unlike in *Anandamath*, this propensity in Ghosh's novel, dramatized as ocular and *darshanic* visions, is inclusive and multifarious. Ghosh, by having the pages that follow confirm the reality of Deeti's vision of the *Ibis*—that is, her insight that the ship is "a sign of destiny"—refutes our assumptions about how national-historical fiction ought to approach its subject. What the narrative does call into question, ironically, are the empirically visible features of colonial life—clothing, language, pigmentation, colonial legal documents, the ship itself—by showing them to be less than they seem to be at first sight.

For all their perspectival benefits, however, Deeti's visions can be only partial. As indices of the broad historical canvas the novel conjures up for us, her visions function like forest depictions in classical texts, where forests hide as much as they reveal. At times, the mention of a single tree branch can amplify a text's arboreal and cultural registers, such as when *The Cilappatikaram* describes the royal scepter made of kadamba wood.[50] At other times, however (staying with this analogy), the forest is ideal cover for a man wishing to spy on women, which is a familiar classical trope.[51] But whether or not the forest hides or reveals, it is clear we are meant to read it situationally in each case, as an index rather than as a representation of the whole. Similarly, Deeti may be able to sketch her vision of the ship, but she does not know what to put inside those lines. It is left to the unfolding story to provide the contents; and it is left to Ghosh's readers to discern and make sense of the many storylines that bring the contents to life.

What is clear, however, is that *Sea of Poppies*, unlike *Midnight's Children*, depends on historical particularity as both a mechanism of plot and a thematic concern. Without the contours of history—the maritime timber trade, the opium war, indentured labor, and so on—the motivations and actions of Ghosh's characters would make no sense, nor would we be able to understand Deeti's (and other characters') arboreal imaginations. Ghosh's novel is far from Rushdie's allegorization of history, a difference most noticeable in the two authors' treatments of the Sundarbans. In *Midnight's Children*, the mangrove forest is empty of other humans, much as Hunter viewed it in the 1870s, the forest an allegory of both history writing and the novel in which it appears—the "enigmatic dream" Amina has of "stumbl[ing] through [an] impenetrable papery forest." The surreal tangle of Rushdie's Sundarbans can also be read as the nightmare of political corruption, as opposed to the kind of positive "dream" (a word Rushdie favors in his essays on nations and affiliative identities.[52]) In Ghosh's *The Hungry Tide*, the Sundarbans Forest is notably inhabited by people whose inner lives and particular material conditions resist allegorization. In *Sea of Poppies*, too, the material particularities of characters inform the promise of a true commons, a vision of which the novel elicits in the reader through the *darshanic* visions of characters like Deeti. Although, as we learn at the outset, Deeti's village occupies "a featureless stretch of mud and mangrove, on the edge of the Sundarbans" (60), it is her ability to perceive the connections between this marginal inhabitance and the maritime timber trade that coercively displaces her that ultimately underwrites Ghosh's refashioned history.

5

Indigeneity, Forestry, and the State in C. K. Janu, Mahasweta Devi, and Easterine Kire

The deciduous *mahua* tree[1] has rightly been described as "one of the most important forest trees of India," a source of cooking and lighting oil, soap, timber, and edible flowers, which are also used to make liquor, an important part of tribal festivals. Producing an abundance of these valuable products each year, *mahua* forests were a vital food source for Adivasis in Central India during the 1897 and 1900 famines.[2] But as more and more outsiders developed a taste for *mahua* liquor starting in the late 1800s, its indigenous guardians (for that is how they see their role) had less and less access to the trees, especially when the British "centralized distilleries and leased them out to ... others," which "extinguished famous indigenous brands of" the liquor.[3] The fate of the *mahua* is thus entwined with that of forest-dwelling communities, whose livelihood and culture have suffered as outsiders have exploited the tree on an industrial scale. The consequent marginalization and displacement of forest-dwelling Adivasis is then judged by these outside urban interests, with predictable circular reasoning, to be the result of the Adivasis' intrinsic laziness and degeneracy.[4] Seen as ignorant of the forest's productive (read: lucrative) potential, forest dwellers are thought to be undeserving of the land they inhabit, providing an alibi for outsiders to occupy it.

The plight of the *mahua* tree in many ways parallels the plight of indigenous communities in India today. However, as the works I examine in this chapter illustrate, the diminishing access that Adivasis have to this and other traditionally managed trees does not mean that these practices, or related Adivasi traditions, have entirely disappeared. The works by Adivasi activist in Kerala, C. K. Janu, the late Bengali activist-writer Mahasweta Devi, and the Naga novelist Easterine Kire serve two vital needs: they attest to the painful predicaments of indigenous communities in today's India, and they depict, and so help preserve, a number of forest practices that face a very uncertain future. These works exemplify a command of both oral and literate narrative structures, interweaving them in powerfully poetic and inventive ways. Even when a story is set far from actual forests, the narrative communicates the significance of those far-off trees—of the memory-laden trees' emotional pull—for the inner lives of the indigenous characters. Many of these works delineate, in fact, two kinds of mobility experienced by their characters: traditional nomadism, whether in the form of wide-ranging forest hunts or seasonal migration, and involuntary migration to towns and cities to earn a living now that outsiders have ended traditional livelihoods.

Such nomadic lifestyles did not fit with the colonial state's assumptions about the ownership and taxation of land, nor do they mesh with those of the postcolonial state.[5] A historical irony worth noting is that the "shifting cultivation" that forest dwellers continue, to some degree, to practice had in fact been productively tied to a "market exchange" with precolonial urban entrepôts—meaning that it would have been in British interests to allow this practice to continue.[6] But ideology has a way of discounting fact and rigidifying policy, and it led, in the early twentieth century, to the repression of peasants' grazing and logging rights, which in turn triggered the famous "forest satyagraha" protests against this repression.[7] The great irony, of course, is that modern polities have been far more wasteful managers of forestland. In contrast, even when indigenous communities cleared a section of forest to grow crops, as they had done for millennia, they "carefully preserved" select *mahua* trees to ensure that they would rebound, a strategy that also prevented the overuse of soil.[8] Colonial officials dispensed with this practice and thereby greatly taxed the health of the tree and its ecosystem.[9] The colonial government's perception that indigenous groups were misusing forestland put tremendous pressure on forest settlements, with many of them ultimately forced to become farmers on lands that the British could document and tax.[10] The advent of railways, telegraph, and other technologies facilitated the effectiveness of colonial exploitation, even in thickly forested areas (in contrast to their predecessors, the Mughals, for whom such terrain was a formidable obstacle).[11] Equally exploitative were the Europeans hired to manage India's forests and to plant and sell marketable products, from tea to timber. These planters and foresters immediately "became competitors with villagers for access to the land," with the result that forests disappeared at alarming rates.[12]

Indian writers in the late nineteenth century, as we have seen, were well aware of the baleful effects of colonialism's ecological transformation on the lives of everyday Indians, such as the many famines in Bengal attest, even as they held grudging admiration for the purported benefits of the European technologies that aided this transformation. We have also seen how later generations of writers, such as Ghosh, have largely shed this ambivalent regard to describe in powerful ways the detrimental consequences of modern metropolitan assumptions about forest ecologies. The writers I examine in this chapter seek to convey these developments through the eyes of those who have borne the brunt of their effects. But these authors' compelling depictions are noteworthy, as well, for avoiding the tendency, evident in much mainstream fiction as well as in certain scholarship, of idealizing indigenous communities. The danger is that this tendency effectively universalizes Adivasis as unassailably selfless and benign, which makes them more, not less, open to appropriation by dominant histories.[13] For example, Vandana Shiva's[14] pioneering efforts to raise public awareness of industrialism's environmental lethality, not to mention her early celebration of the remarkable Chipko Andolan (Movement) of the early 1970s, has not prevented her from arguing that marginalized groups like the Bhotia, whose women spearheaded Chipko, should be viewed as part of a pan-Indian collectivity whose practices exemplify "indigenous" forms of Hindu "Shakti."[15] Shiva's view illustrates today's dilemma of having to advocate for Adivasi participation in mainstream political cultures as a means of shoring up their rights, while recognizing, at the same time, their uniqueness.

This dilemma resembles the one Bankim and his peers faced, if on a comparatively more privileged level—since this is the quintessentially modern dilemma of feeling obligated to represent one's constituency in politics while also feeling the urgency of representing it on the page.

Regardless of how one deals with the dilemma, writers, activists, and scholars broadly agree that commercialized forestry inevitably fractures local communities' long-standing "social bonds which had regulated the customary use of forests," as Ramachandra Guha puts it, creating a sense of "alienation."[16] While Gayatri Chakravorty Spivak and others have refuted the notion that outsiders can know and represent subaltern communities without mediation, they acknowledge that literary treatments are among the most effective ways of conveying to an urban readership something of the ethos of these groups and the challenges they face in a rapidly changing world. The works discussed below do this by portraying very human personae whose challenges and successes are alternately cautionary and inspiring.

C. K. Janu's *Mother Forest*, Roy's Paternal Forest, and the Filter of Modernity

The Malayali tribal activist Janu, also known as C. K. Janu, has been a well-known advocate for her community since 2001, when she organized a sit-in for forty-eight days outside the state Secretariat in the city of Thiruvananthapuram to protest the increasing deforestation in Kerala that was destroying her people's livelihood and homeland, rendering them landless. Her story, titled *Mother Forest: The Unfinished Story of C. K. Janu*,[17] is multiply mediated: transcribed in Malayalam by Bhaskaran and translated into English in 2004 by N. Ravi Shanker for the publisher Kali for Women. Like Central and South American *testimonio*, Janu describes the erosion of a close-knit community at the hands of exploitative government officials and the harsh responses of mainstream governance to the protests she led. In 2003, to cite one example, Janu led members of her community into a Wayanad District reserve forest—that is, one requiring an entrance permit—to occupy land that was rightfully theirs. Police arrived and fired on the group, killing at least two (possibly more) and injuring dozens. Janu and others were imprisoned. Arundhati Roy, in a letter sent to Kerala's Chief Minister shortly afterward, likened the event to Jallianwala Bagh, the infamous 1919 machine-gunning of peacefully protesting men, women, and children in Amritsar on the orders of British General Dyer, which left hundreds dead. Roy meant by this comparison to ascribe the same significance to the deaths of indigenous peoples that the Jallianwala Bagh incident immediately acquired in India's national history.[18] Janu's published life story is an attempt to do the same by showing an urban readership that the subject's motivations are no different from any other unjustly besieged group yearning for freedom.

Mother Forest distills many of the themes we see in Mahasweta's Adivasi and forest-centered narratives: the revision of maternal–nationalist ideals; the commercial exploitation of forestland by outside interests (noted in *Aranyak* as well[19]); the challenges that women in particular face, both within and outside of their communities; and the cynical behavior of state representatives. It also enacts in its English presentation, whose peculiar form and style translator Shanker describes with refreshing candor, the problematic dualistic view that authenticity is domestic, while political engagement is public.[20] He notes that one challenge, for instance, was deciding how to translate the Malayalam word meaning both "I" and "We," which Janu typically uses when "describ[ing] herself or her community," leading him to dispense with many pronouns altogether in the book's first half. Shanker also tried to preserve "the flavour of Janu's intonation and the sing-song nature of her speech," such as by dispensing with some punctuation. This last tactic prompted his most visible editorial decision, which was to render the first half of the text in a format "closer to Janu's inner world," which he indicates with a more conversational style, and to present the second half, which concerns Janu's adult, activist life, in formal English. As Ellen Turner observes, this choice is also a political one based on presumptions about Adivasis and their relationship to educated urban readers. Turner notes, for instance, that the first half's diction "roughly follows a stream of consciousness narrative style" in which the "senses are privileged … and nothing is done alone," which "distances" the narrative of Janu's upbringing and suggests a timeless, "pre-rational" worldview.[21]

The translation's published edition, with the English translator's editorial choices—like those of Janu's interlocutor and amanuensis, Bhaskaran, the appended letter by Roy, and simple spot illustrations throughout—all serve as filters for Janu's story, and need to be kept in mind by English readers and critics. I mention this both to illustrate the challenges of transcribing, as it were, subaltern lives for public consumption and to preface my reading of Mahasweta, who writes about tribal communities in Bengali and is then translated into English. We must similarly keep in mind Janu's decision to make her story available in translation. To reiterate a point in my "note on translation" in the opening chapter, India's polyglot cultures mean that any attempt, such as mine, to compare texts across the country's cultures and languages requires the use of translated editions. As Janu's memoir illustrates, even transcribing her words into Malayalam incurs difficulties and decisions. These facts also remind us that although a work of nonfiction, and despite Kali for Women's admirable and vital endeavor, *Mother Forest's* appearance in print places it within the orbit of a "republic of letters" (to adapt Casanova's phrase) that is beholden to the marketplace and its packaging demands. The back cover of my paperback edition exemplifies this by applying a narrative arc to Janu's life: "Janu speaks of her childhood and her life in the forest, her political awakening as a party worker in the CPM [Communist Party of India (Marxist)], her growing disillusionment with it, and her break from it after she felt it had betrayed the tribals." When, therefore, we encounter Mahasweta's renditions of Oraon or Santal women, we are obligated to keep these points in mind. This is not to say, however, that unmediated access to the imaginative and political worlds of indigenous communities is possible, only that linguistic, cultural, and imaginative translations like these compel us to critique conventional assumptions about authenticity and regional and national self-perceptions. More significantly, as I have been arguing, such critique must engage with representations of forests in these texts.

A brief consideration of forest images in *Mother Forest* illustrates my prefatory remarks. Janu recalls her childhood in the Wayanad forests as challenging—with "howling wind" and "frightening" creatures (4)—but, because the forests had not yet seen the degree of exploitation that the 1980s would bring, a time of deep connection with these forests. She recalls "listening to what the [unending] forests mumbled" (3), "see[ing]" both "herds of elephant" and many other animals, such as deer and "pigs" (4), catching the "scent" of the "earth" in its "different seasons" (13), and harvesting forest food like "tender bamboo reeds" (20). She describes a ritual for girls entering puberty as being held "when trees were shedding their leaves and new buds were emerging. a time when the red ... flowers of the coral tree were blossoming, and a very dry wind blowing" (20). Janu also tells us (as presented in Shanker's unpunctuated style): "it was when i was sixteen or seventeen that the Literacy people came to Chekkote [village]. i used to work as a wage labourer at that time" (20). (Note that Shanker capitalizes words associated with modernity, in this case formal education and larger settlements. This stylistic choice, as we will see, resembles Mahasweta's transcription of English words into Bengali—indicated in Spivak's translation by the use of italics—that derive from modern institutions and technologies.) Janu fondly remembers the stories and songs of her childhood told by the women of her community, who "preferred to learn from observing the forest" (22). She describes a number of foods, tools, and forest products: areca nuts, but not "Coffee" or "Pepper," which had not yet been introduced to the area (3, 14).

Amid this verdure, however, are clear markers of modernity: "as we walked [in the fields] we could hear the chug chug of a Motor Pump from the fields. and get the sharp smell of a Chemical sprayed on the paddy" (7); "an old Radio" in her "Teacher's" "house" (9); and the "dark inside" of the "*Talkies*" [*sic*] in the town where she attended school. Watching films in this "Cinima" house was "very unlike being inside the forest" (11). She describes attending her first CPM "rally" and feeling "nice to hear" the "slogans" and songs affirming her people, and the "Stage" on which people gave "Speeches" (26–8). Janu concludes the book's first half by describing the "Migrants" who begin to move into the area to plant "Coffee," bringing their own food and drink habits, including liquor—that is, "*toddy*" and "*arrack*" (28). The abrupt transition from the party rally to the new migrants presages the book's second half, which, as mentioned, concerns Janu's adulthood and activism. The opening of this section, presented now in standard English, is ominous: "Our people had turned into mere wage labourers. Mother Forest had turned into the Departmental Forest. It has barbed wire fences and guards. Our children had begun to be frightened of a forest that could no longer accommodate them. All the land belonged to the migrants" (30).

The shift to more formal diction signals these drastic social and ecological changes, suggesting that Janu's education in the ways of mainstream Kerala culture cuts two ways: it is a symptom of cataclysmic change, but also gives her the tools to fight the injustices that attend that change. But the political party (the CPM), being a modern political machine, soon disillusions her, a point she captures in a powerful image: "We started hanging [the party's] calendar pictures on the same walls where we used to hang seeds of *thina* [millet] and *thuvara* [dal]." She continues with a litany of dispiriting changes—logging, displacement, the growing power of boorish outsider—that reflect "the Party's mute support" of them and "its greed for power," saying that "we could no more collect even fallen twigs from the forest" or "thatch our fallen roofs" (38). She bemoans how the men of her community now drink, grow "lazy," and "spend a lot of time" aimlessly "wandering about in the forest" (46). It is up to the women, she says, to work for change, for after all, "[our] women always take up more responsibilities than men" (46). Here she movingly invokes the book's title, speaking of her community's closeness to the forest and the "earth," and the trauma of a "civil society" seeking to "transplant us to where there is no space even to stand up straight" (47). This society, says Janu, has begun to lure younger members of her community to cities where they "have lost their balance" and "their minds" (48, 51).

The title of the book, taken from Janu's own characterization of her people's forest as "Mother," implicitly calls for a comparative comment on previously published uses of the term, notably in Bankim's *Anandamath* but also in mainstream iconography, as previously noted. There is no indication, as far as I can see, that Janu intentionally maternalizes the forest as a way to counter mainstream figurations, such as Mother India. But when we place her memoir alongside Roy's 2016 novel *The Ministry of Utmost Happiness*, whose maternal forest image explicitly contrasts that of dominant society, Janu's fearless fight for her "Mother Forest's" survival shows her designation to be similarly contrastive. Roy's image occurs in a letter by a tribal, Telugu-speaking woman from what is now the south-central state of Telangana who, having joined a group of tribal Maoist guerillas in the dense Bastar forests, has left her infant girl in New Delhi. The infant is discovered by a mostly impoverished group of women, *hijras*, and men whose stories form a key strand of the narrative, and it is the letter's addressee, one of the few literate friends of the group, who reads it to them. The guerilla fighter, named Revathy, has written it in English since neither the recipient nor any other likely reader knows Telugu. Revathy explains why she could not keep her child and that she had named her Udaya, "sunrise" in Telugu, "because she was born in the Dandakaranya forest during sunrise" (423). The forest's name immediately tells us that Revathy's story subverts dominant narratives, for this is the forest in which Lord Rama, as related in the *Ramayana*, has to dispatch resident demons, the Dandaka, who give the forest its name: Dandaka plus *aranya* (forest). As previously noted, demons in Sanskrit epics likely represent indigenous forest dwellers whom Aryan settlers displaced. Equally subversive is Revathy's designation of her child's parentage: "Forest is her Father" (note the capitalization), while "River is her mother" (423). Revathy recounts her own abandonment in infancy as a result of being too "black" (424), her warrior name "Comrade Maase," meaning "Black Girl" (427), and her rape at the hands of the police, one of whom "is Udaya's father" (428). She escapes back to her comrades in the forest, but the male leaders of the People's Liberation Guerilla Army (PLGA) are unsympathetic and say that female members are "banned" from "hav[ing] children" (430). Ordered to a village "outside" the forest for the birth, Revathy's intention to kill the infant cannot overcome her maternal instinct (430). Because she is educated and a good speaker, she is asked to visit Delhi to address the "National Media," which is where she deposits the baby (430). Despite her party's male bias, she declares her loyalty to it—"My Party is my Mother and Father"—and says she "cannot live outside" the forest or the group (431). "In the forest," she writes in her closing lines, "every day police is burning killing raping poor people. Outside there is you people to fight and take up issues. But inside there is us only. So I am returned to Dandakaranya to live and die by my gun" (431).

Revathy's upbringing, including the hatred she expresses for her father, as well as the circumstances of her child's birth clearly inflect her letter, as its many references to parentage indicate. The most salient feature of this reconfiguration of the family unit, however, is the refrain that she can no longer live "outside" the forest and that she figures the forest as the "Father" of her child—an effort to erase the girl's human father, but also, as I have suggested, to evade dominant society's maternal assignation of the forest, and, by extension, of the nation. In *Walking With Comrades*, Roy's 2012 nonfiction account of her surreptitious, weeks-long visit with the People's War Group (PWG), one of the PLGA's earlier forms, she details the political and military contexts of the tribal-rights Naxalite movement, as it has been broadly called since its origin in the late 1960s, and notes that in Bastar, "the villages are empty, and the forest is full of people."[22] This fact not only disturbs the Village India conceit I have previously examined, it also, inverts the conventional "inside/outside" notion of forests. Not only have many tribal villagers in the region chosen to join or live among their guerilla brethren, but also "though the theatre of war is in the jungles of Central India, it will have serious consequences for us all," Roy writes.[23] She observes, too, that as harsh as the Forest Department has been in displacing tribal villages in these forests, such as by "burning new villages," the department has now been displaced by the police, whose tactics are far deadlier.[24]

Roy's nonfiction account echoes her later novel by noting that, just as Revathy understands clearly that the state, regardless of which arm it uses, "want[s] adivasi [*sic*] people to vacate forest so they can make a steel township and mining" (427), so have numerous companies been issued carte blanche licenses to mine lucrative forest minerals, many of which are in Bastar, on which a modern state depends. Mining encroachments not only incite forest dwellers to battle for their basic rights, but they also leave in their wake "polluted rivers" and "wrecked ecosystems."[25] In this light, Revathy's refiguring of the forest as her daughter's paternal right indicts the violent polluting of both her parents, forest and river. It is notable that Roy concludes her novel on a hopeful note, with the arrival of Revathy's daughter Udaya giving the small community of *Hijras* (the so-called Third Sex, and a name Roy capitalizes) and others the shared responsibility of raising the child, whose survival on the edge of Delhi—in the mortuary that has served as the marginalized community's home—and on the edge of history means that "things would turn out all right in the end" (444). Among the text's many references to forests and trees, which prefigure both Revathy's letter and the book's conclusion, perhaps the most noteworthy, given Udaya's birth in the Dandakaranya forest, is a point made earlier in the novel by one of their own: When Lord Rama and his brother and wife were leaving the city of Ayodhya to begin their fourteen-year forest exile, this character (named Gudiya) says, the divine king stopped where city ended and "the forest began" to instruct his people to return to the city. "The men and women" did so, says Gudiya, and "Only the Hijras waited faithfully for him at the edge of the forest for the whole fourteen years, because he had forgotten to mention them" (56). Gudiya's tale does not invalidate the mythic belief system of which Ram is a part; rather, it indicts the society that has produced him. The novel suggests that Udaya's human guardians will ensure that she is not forgotten in spite of inhabiting a liminal space that can reconfigure the normative places on either side of it.

C. K. Janu's "unfinished" memoir concludes with a number of images that complement Revathy's voice in Roy, particularly when Janu emphasizes that the forest is not just a physical reality for her people, but also vital to their cultural imaginary. Although this translated, published presentation of Janu's account ironically frames her voice in conventions of the very modernity she opposes, the text nonetheless stands as a significant record of the oppression of indigenous forest communities in contemporary India.

Sacred Forest, Maternal Forest, and Indigenous Inhabitance in Mahasweta Devi's Fiction

In a poignant scene near the end of Mahasweta Devi's story "Douloti the Bountiful," the eponymous tribal protagonist, having been forced from her home village into a life of bonded urban prostitution, chances upon her Uncle Bono in town. Overcome with nostalgia, Douloti recalls the old banyan tree in the village and begs her uncle to "speak of it." "I swung myself on its branches when I went to graze the goats," she continues before he can say anything. In her rush of memories, of the days when her uncle "beat on *cans*, made a great uproar to chase away tigers," Douloti feels her loss all the more painfully (87). Nevertheless, she takes on the aspect of "a mother" as she urges her uncle, upset by her plight, "not to cry" (88). The reader, too, remembers a similar arboreal image from earlier in the story, when a 14-year-old Douloti "sits under a tree and rests a bit" as she accompanies her supposed husband, Paramananda, to her urban fate. Mahasweta[26] thus shows Douloti to be a child of the forested land on which her people live and whose resources "god"-like outsiders are now greedily consuming in the form of timber (47). The motif of the stalwart banyan and other such benign trees contrasts sharply with the "sacred wood apple tree" growing in front of an office belonging to the village's exploitative "owner," its suggestively "hollow" roots causing it to fall during a storm (33).

These images, together with Douloti's moment of nostalgia, encompass both the emotional and physical registers that make Mahasweta's narrative so remarkably "scandalous," to use her translator Gayatri Chakravorty Spivak's characterization of the story (127). Spivak argues that Douloti's (and her people's) indigenous "space" has been ignored, and thus "displaced," by the national zeal for "capitalist development" that helps sustain the bonded-labor system plaguing low-caste and Adivasi peoples and that the story describes (106–7). The answer to this national silencing, as Mahasweta has asserted through both her writings and activism, must be a complete revamping of such predatory practices and the system that encourages them. Spivak concludes that in the absence of such change, Douloti's longing for home is problematic, since the normative concept of home necessarily depends "on a conservative coding of the sexual division of labor" that props up the system of exploitation (125), such as when Douloti acts "like a mother" to Bono (88). For real change to happen, this familiar domesticity will have to be relinquished. One reason Mahasweta chooses to present this dilemma in fiction (rather than essays, which she also published), suggests Spivak, is because it allows her to imagine alternatives to the pressures of forced labor and domesticity. On this count, Mahasweta shares with her predecessors in Bengali literature a conviction that fiction can articulate possible futures in support of real social change. Mahasweta contrasts with many of her predecessors, however (including those discussed in previous chapters), in choosing to write about Adivasi communities who live far—both geographically and culturally—from centers of modern power. This is a critical point since both past and current conservative nationalists claim that Adivasis belong to the Vedic belief system and that those who have sought to leave the fold, whether by adhering to Buddhist or Marxist practices, must be reclaimed.

Mahasweta conveys these possible alternatives through, for example, the poetic description of Douloti's "transformed" vision as, while "stumbling home at night," her senses are suffused with the "smell of catkins" and "chiming" of cowbells (93). Douloti, her 27-year-old body ravaged by venereal disease and emotional torture, lies down on the chalk map that the schoolmaster has "carefully drawn" in the schoolyard. The story ends with the visually arresting image of her "filling the entire Indian peninsula from the oceans to the Himalayas," announcing in effect that "here lies bonded labor spread-eagled" in the form of "kamiya- [laborer] whore Douloti Nagesia's tormented corpse." She is thus "all over India" (93). Spivak notes that here, Mahasweta's "sweeping elegance of high Sanskritic Bengali" is an ironic contrast to the language, including vernacular style, the author uses in the rest of the story (127). Mahasweta echoes her Bengali predecessors in this intermixing of styles, but, because her subject is a marginalized Adivasi woman, avoids tropes that Bankim, Bibhutibhushan, Gangopadhyay, and other (mostly male) writers use to characterize indigenous peoples.

Mahasweta's fictional works have generated insightful commentary about their feminist, political, and linguistic features.[27] Here, however, I restrict my attention to the story's arboreal imagery—such as the banyan tree—to expand on Spivak's suggestive comment that Douloti's final act is an embodiment of the "decolonized space of difference" (117). This imagery illuminates Douloti's ties to her environment, but not by relying on the problematic trope of effeminized landscape, such as Mother India. Mahasweta revises this trope by accentuating Douloti's and her people's emplacement in their land. I use the word "emplacement" because it conveys three interrelated meanings that characterize the situation of Adivasis in India: the act of constantly trying to find a place for their cultural expressions in a changing and often predatory world; the safeguarding of these cultures, sometimes by force, more often by wit; and the ecological fluctuations that shape their physical environment. More importantly, I suggest, Mahasweta shows this natural environment to be different from that of India's urban and agricultural centers in terms of both its natural and supernatural features, a linkage seldom developed in assessments of her work.[28] Her stories, as we will see, accomplish this in both substantive and formal terms, their unorthodox mix of rhetorical strategies manifesting a version of the emplacement described above. The discussion that follows illustrates how some notable stories exemplify her characters' arboreal emplacement in the context of their supernatural beliefs and the pressures of modernity. The stories also, for these reasons, revise conventional understandings of national narrative.

Mahasweta simultaneously uses a range of narrative modes, including "the documentary impulse of her activist journalism,"[29] allegory, the romance plot, religious epic, and folk legend. She chooses this strategy for a number of reasons. To begin with, it enables her to more effectively counter mainstream assumptions about indigenous women, ecology, and the very categories that govern these assumptions. At the same time, and in order to avoid the liberal tendency to romanticize indigenous subjects and render the forest a pastoral wonderland, Mahasweta does not ignore prejudices, especially related to gender, within Adivasi communities. Her aim is neither to attempt a mimetically realistic rendering of nature nor to conspicuously avoid this by slipping into allegory alone—although both veins are evident in her work. Mahasweta's stories instead overlay a "geological sense of deep time" with an unashamedly "mythic" palimpsest, as Parama Roy observes.[30] Mythic here would seem to invoke an indigenous religious–historical worldview that is morally antecedent, and therefore superior, to either Aryan latecomers or colonial modernity. Yet Mahasweta balances such allegorical implications, Roy notes, with a documentary realism that exposes the everyday oppression of Adivasis at the hands of the state.[31] Allegory and realism, as in the hands of other writers I have examined in previous chapters, work in tandem to produce a narrative of moral and political weight. The resulting tension between form and substance enables, on one level, a pointed irony that drives home to her urban readers their own complicity in the undoing of indigenous traditions. The strategy simultaneously preserves a poetics of religious belief that expresses the "times of gods" that undercuts the colonially inherited rational historicism of the state.[32] Inextricably linked to this narrative strategy of emplacement are women who are subjected to the same violence visited on the proverbially virgin land, but who nonetheless seek ways of controlling their own destinies, not least by themselves knowingly combining mythic and allegorical beliefs with their everyday practices.

Two motifs that reappear in Indian narratives (including C. K. Janu's memoir) as touchstones for the expression of mainstream national, cultural, and social ideals, and which Mahasweta therefore wishes to reimagine, are, as we have seen, the forest and the mother. In Sanskrit epics, to briefly reiterate previous points, the long-standing distinction between forestland and human settlement serves to express both the potentiality and limitations of so-called civilization. It is in the forest that a hero faces his greatest fears on the way to greater self-awareness, though always with the aid of enlightened sages who choose to live there, far from the corrupting cities.[33] India's forest thus possesses something of the same ambivalence we find in Western cultural treatments of forestland.[34] For European-American nature writers like Henry David Thoreau, the forest was a space in which to "uncover the hiding places of the self, leaving it exposed to the facts of life, whatever they be."[35] As I have argued in previous chapters, however, narratives from across India, and across many centuries, have expressed a wide variety of attitudes toward forests that very often register not the mapped borders familiar to us, but liminality and blurred boundaries.[36]

Mahasweta's characters directly challenge mainstream depictions of Mother India whose powerful "patriotic pastoral" imagery infuses the modern mapping of India with a poetics of pan-Indian belonging, the most iconic version of which we encountered in Bankim's *Anandamath*.[37] Ironically, as we have seen, Bankim and other nineteenth-century nationalist writers sought to combine a modern sensibility with traditional, mostly upper-caste value systems in the face of the immense challenge of crafting a distinctly Indian national identity. This tended to result in increasingly hardening positions about caste and domesticity, which were grafted onto the colonial state's own social categorizations. The upshot was that Adivasis bore the brunt on both counts, seen as people who had strayed from their original Hindu affiliation (and who had been civilized by later settlers) and as representatives of "wildness" who needed disciplining.[38]

But to counter these typologies by romanticizing Adivasis would, as mentioned, be a mistake, a prospect Mahasweta avoids by instead humanizing her subjects. Like their urban counterparts, she shows Adivasis to be just as susceptible to mystifying forests by characterizing them as alternately "enchanting" and "ghoulish."[39] Her story "The Witch-Hunt," for example, describes an "illicit" love affair that defies caste boundaries and becomes part of a larger tale about a witch who haunts the forest and the villagers who hunt her down.[40] The two lovers "seek out ways to have their paths cross, one returning from the market, the other from the forest carrying wood (250). "Drive[n] … into one another's arms," the couple escapes into the woods for privacy—only to confront "an ugly dark young woman, naked," who, seeing them, "bares her teeth and howls ferociously" (252). The lovers alert the village, and the "hunt" ensues, transforming villagers into a reflection of the ferocity exhibited by the witch. In their "ferocious intensity," the "killer crowd" pursues its prey, and their mob frenzy infects even the "rational" schoolteacher and aspiring writer (266, 269). When they finally corner the witch in a cave, they are confused to hear the cry of, first, a woman "in terrible pain"—and then the "cry of a newborn" (269). The "witch" turns out to be the "mute and dumb daughter" of one of the village headmen. She was, another village elder reports, raped by a high-caste townsman whose father, attempting to stamp out the inconvenience, declares her a witch who must be driven away (270).

What Mahasweta's stories convey, however, are the long list of injustices indigenous communities have suffered at the hands of the modern state, a point C. K. Janu, as we saw, also makes plain. To work against the trope of wildness means having to undo a potent discourse that, as we have said, modern society sustains in order to justify itself. By labeling jungles and their inhabitants "anachronistic, we fix them in place and place them outside of history."[41] Familiar European colonial rendering of jungles as having a "thousand eyes" that watch your every move[42] and "freeze a man's blood"[43] do such rhetorical work, which functions in much the way Bakhtin describes classical romance, as effecting limitless "adventure-time" predicated on "empty space."[44] In thus supporting a dominant culture's ideas about individual human agency, the jungle is a threshold, or liminal space, between civility and wildness, as discussed in my opening chapter. To depict indigenous characters as agents of their own lives, with all of their human foibles, as Mahasweta does in her fiction, is to re-historicize them.

Mahasweta's "Draupadi"

Mahasweta begins her 1978 story "Draupadi,"[45] set in Jharkhand in the context of a tribal revolt, in the telegraphic language of a police report sprinkled with the perspective of local functionaries:

> Name Dopdi Mejhen, age twenty-seven, husband Dulna Majhi (deceased), domicile Cherakhan, Bankrajharh, information whether dead or alive and/or assistance in arrest, one hundred rupees ...
> An exchange between two liveried *uniforms*.
>
> **First Livery:** What's this, a tribal called Dopdi? The list of names I brought has nothing like it! How can anyone have an unlisted name?
> **Second:** Draupadi Mejhen. Born the year her mother threshed rice at Surja Sahu (killed)'s at Bakuli. Surja Sahu's wife gave her the name.
> **First:** These officers like nothing better than to write as much as they can in English. What's all this stuff about her?
> **Second:** *Most notorious* female. *Long wanted in many* (392; original emphasis)

The disjointed phrasing and strained use of official English words (in italics in the original), lack of reference points, and particularly Draupadi's name together signify an uneasy convergence of state government language, local policing practices, and, for the officials, unfamiliar tribal names and dialect. The protagonist, Draupadi, is a "black-skinned" tribal rebel whose "Austro-Asiatic" features, as the sympathetic narrator wryly describes them, make the non-tribal policeman nervous. She is named for the famous Draupadi of *Mahabharata* fame, whose five Pandava husbands lose her in a dice game wager to their jealous cousins, the Kauravas. The original Draupadi shames her husbands by appealing to traditional honor, an argument that nearly persuades some of the onlooking Kaurava men. This prompts an order to strip her and thereby subjugate her now profligate body to the victorious Kauravas. Draupadi, in this original epic tale, pleads with her husbands to save her, but they only look down. Lord Krishna, however, hears her plea and works a miracle: as the Kauravas unwrap the sari from her body, the cloth uncoils endlessly, safeguarding her honor. The effect of Mahasweta's use of this name for her indigenous, noncaste heroine is two-fold. She has been given a classical name that already transgresses orthodoxy; and yet she has retained its local elision, Dopdi. Mahasweta registers defiance here as a willful crossing of nominative boundaries before Dopdi has even taken up arms. The narrator signals her respect and sympathy for Dopdi by abruptly shifting at times from officialese, or from the mindset of Senanayak and the policemen, into a journalistic voice that declares unequivocally (to cite one example), "All around the ill-famed forest of Jharkhani, which is under the jurisdiction of the police station at Bakrajharh (in this India of ours, even a worm is under a certain police station) ... one comes across hair-raising details in the eyewitness records" (393).

The most visible transgression, however, is Mahasweta's upending of the iconography of Mother India. Bankim's "deep forest" in *Anandamath*[46] is, as discussed previously, the feminized and ostensibly originary space of Vedic purity (as it was conceived by Bankim), with the "ocean of leaves" on the forest floor also translatable as "womb." The jungle is quite explicitly the incubating space of incipient nationalism. Just as Bankim's British forces, led by a Captain Thomas, stalwartly but ignorantly "penetrate" a "dense jungle" "infested" with wild animals in their effort to crush the rebellion of ascetic warriors, so do Senanayak's men (the gender is important) scour the jungle in search of Dopdi. Bankim's forest is conspicuously absent of indigenous inhabitants like Dopdi and her community, whose presence Mahasweta wishes to make plain. Dopdi, like Douloti, is also very far from being the kind of feminine figure whom mainstream society chooses to represent the motherland. Nor can she be viewed as part of a lineage of India's famous warrior queens, since Dopdi is battling not a conventional invader, but rather the nominative defender of an ostensibly unified state. Mahasweta grants Dopdi, and by extension her arboreal homeland, the agency and purpose denied to her by these normative narratives.

Dopdi's husband Dulna has been killed in a police "*encounter,*" and his body left as bait for his "*most notorious*" wife. The ploy does not work. Dopdi flees into "the forest *belt* of Jharkhani [i.e., of Jharkhand]" and "the *Operation* continues—will continue," for "it is a carbuncle on the government's backside" (395; original emphasis). When Dopdi is finally, and inevitably (given her namesake as well as the known history of the particular events), captured, the exultant policemen drag Dopdi away to torture and rape her in a frenzy of resentment disguised as information gathering. An elderly Bengali "specialist in combat and extreme-Left politics" named Senanayak is brought in to sift through Dopdi's information more methodically, but his real ambition is to gather raw material so he can write about tribals like Dopdi and on "all this in the future" (394). Ironically, this specialist in the Indian civil service of the early 1970s, just one generation after the British have departed, continues to think like his colonial tutors, much as the commissioner at the end of Chinua Achebe's *Things Fall Apart* surveys the tragedy of a Nigerian Igbo village and can think only about a possible title for his future book, *The Pacification of the Primitive Tribes of the Lower Niger*.[47] The story ends with Dopdi, her body torn and bleeding, tearing off her own cloth covering to stand defiantly before Senanayak and his flunkies:

> There isn't a man here that I should be ashamed. I will not let you put my cloth on me. What more can you do? Come on, *counter* me—come on, *counter* me—?
>
> Draupadi pushes Senanayak with her two mangled breasts, and for the first time Senanayak is afraid to stand before an unarmed *target*, terribly afraid. (402; original emphasis)

Only in this final third section of the story does Mahasweta give Dopdi back, as it were, her full name, Draupadi Mejhen. It would be possible to interpret this as meaning that the tribal rebel has fused with her Vedic namesake as a measure of the respect and honor she has earned amid an otherwise violent, cruel shaming. But the forest setting is crucial to Mahasweta's different aim, as is the long history of jungle warfare in the region. As Arundhati Roy puts it in describing her visit to a neighboring tribal hotspot, "the villages are empty, but the forest is full of people." This displacement underscores

Roy's previously quoted words that the war in these forests affects "us all." The Indian government's tactics, in other words, reflect those of British colonialists, who endeavored to "civilize" the "wild tribes" by laying claim to their jungle homelands. (The nearby Jungle Warfare College Roy cites boasts a motto directly inherited from the Senanayak school of counterterrorism: "Fight a guerrilla like a guerrilla.")[48] The paramilitary troops have replaced the police, who replaced the Forest Department, enacting a string of collusion that the story unflinchingly records.

For example, the voice of officialdom in Mahasweta's narrative responds to a reasonable, and presumably public, question—"Is it justifiable to maintain a large battalion in that wild area at the taxpayer's expense?"—with the answer: "*Objection.* 'Wild area' is incorrect. The battalion is provided with supervised nutrition, arrangements to worship ... opportunity to listen to 'Bibidha Bharati' [All-India Radio] and to see Sanjeev Kumar and the Lord Krishna face-to-face in the movie *This Is Life*. No. The area is not wild" (396). The ironies are obvious: Because they listen to national radio and watch a famous actor portray Krishna, the policemen are civilized. More significant is the policemen's ignorance of Dulna and Dopdi's language: they puzzle in vain over his last words, "Ma-ho." Stymied, they fly in "two tribal-specialist types ... from Calcutta," who unsuccessfully "sweat over the dictionaries put together by worthies such as Hoffmann-Jeffer and Golden-Palmer." It is left to Senanayak to ask the local water carrier, who utters his interpretation: "It's a battle cry." And thus the "problem is ... solved" (395). The inability to interpret, to make sense of, the tribals at all levels, including their jungle habitat, is at the heart of Mahasweta's indictment of state policy. As she observes in an interview with Spivak that prefaces the latter's translation of the story, this home is disappearing: "The tribals and the mainstream have always been parallel. There has never been a meeting point ... As long as the forests were there, the hunting tribes did not suffer so much ... But now that the forests are gone, the tribals are in dire distress." They have, she says, "paid the price" for decolonization.[49]

We readers, like Senanayak, must work to make sense of Mahasweta's mixture of dialect, English, and voice, making us to some degree complicit in the need to plumb the depths of unaccustomed practices. Indeed, Senanayak is, at root, a writer, one who likens himself to Prospero in his urge to "represent the particular world" and deliver it "into youth's hands" (394). We might say that Senanayak's presentation of himself in everyday life depends upon his decipherment of the liminal jungle and its people. Like Senanayak, we must rely on Spivak's translation of the story, which in turn relies upon her conversations with the author about a Bengali whose mix of vernacular and formal is said to be difficult. As Spivak writes in her prefatory notes to the story, "In the matter of 'translation' between Bengali and English, it is again Dopdi who occupies a curious middle space. She is the only one who uses the word 'counter' ... an abbreviation for 'killed by police in an encounter,' the code description for death by police torture" (391). When, therefore, Dopdi challenges Senanayak to "*counter*" her at the conclusion of the story, he is as terrified by her uncompromising challenge as by her savvy use of the English word he had believed to be part of his own special knowledge. Caliban-like, Dopdi has learned the master's tongue, and the exchange is one-way. The police, despite "embrac[ing] the leafy boughs" of the forest "like so many great god Pans" in order to ambush the rebels, fail to enter that alien space—as Senanayak, like Bankim's Captain Thomas, himself dreams of doing (395).[50] Far from understanding the tribals' habitus of the forest, Senanayak recoils at the shock—not unlike Burke's repulsion of the banyan tree image—and is himself metaphorically stripped of language. Dopdi, by contrast, "*counters*" him with her "mangled" body and ironic English (401). And it is in the final pages of the story that Mahasweta offers her readers a glimpse of Dopdi at the moment of her capture: "Now Dopdi spreads her arms, raises her face to the sky, turns toward the forest, and ululates with the force of her entire being. Once, twice, three times. At the third burst the birds in the trees at the outskirts of the forest awake and flap their wings. The echo of the call travels far" (401). Whereas earlier we may have shared Senanayak's ultimately futile wish to "decipher … Dopdi's song" (395), here we come to recognize that although Mahasweta herself can provide only its "echo," it is at least a sound rooted in its environment.

Shadows of Enchantment in Fiction

Linda Hogan reminds us that there are indigenous modes of being, which she describes as a "dusky space between us [moderns] and others," and a "time between times,"[51] that elude the historicizing gaze of reason. Modernity prefers to treat such worldviews as excessively irrational or innocent, grounded in myths that derive their force from nature. This section focuses on two works of fiction about tribal groups in northern India to argue that the authors' fictional characters, and to some degree their readers, dwell in environments that have always been enchanted and that therefore demand profound existential choices. This is not to say that the relationship between an Adivasi woman and her environment in northern India is identical to that of a metropolitan reader. This is far from the case, as we have seen; indeed, writers of both forest fiction, like Mahasweta and Hansda Sowvendra Shekhar (a discussion of whose work I do not have space for here),[52] and memoir document the erosion of particular indigenous environments and cultures at the hands of modern industry. But just as an Adivasi woman today must confront the entanglement of her mythopoetic worldview with that of modernity, so is a reader compelled to see how such a worldview challenges the common sense of late modernity, including first-person fictional narration itself.

I take as my premise Dipesh Chakrabarty's point that modern narrative, including the two texts I examine here, is unavoidably part of a "mode of being in the world which is aligned with the principle of 'disenchantment of the universe' that underlies knowledge in the social sciences."[53] It is revealing that writers like Hogan and Chakrabarty, who eloquently articulate other ways of knowing, frequently reach for the word "shadow" to characterize these alternatives to the post-enlightenment worldview and that these shadowy worlds are grounded in nature. Robert Pogue Harrison, as noted, describes forest symbolism as "the shadow of civilization"; Hogan speaks of our usually ignored and therefore "shady" connection to the earth[54]; and Chakrabarty describes the "penumbra of shadow" that haunts history as such.[55] We are therefore obliged to read and reflect on narratives that, although still reliant on modern discourse (especially its inescapable sense of historical irony), can nonetheless reveal other times and spaces. Rather than romanticize their subjects, the fictional works on which I focus present us with characters, especially tribal women, who break down the false dichotomy of enchantment and disenchantment.

Mahasweta's Bengali short story "The Hunt," written in 1974 and translated into English in 1990, focuses on forest dwellers in what is now (since 2000) the northern state of Jharkhand. These narratives dramatize the interconnections between human and nonhuman environments, and they do so by demonstrating that despite the dominant narrative of global disenchantment, there are in fact countless enchantments (or re-enchantments) of more localized worlds, whether distinctively "modern" or not.[56] This is because enchantment is not a singular, transhistorical ideal or outlook separable from everyday life but is instead made up of innumerable "moments" in our "contemporary world,"[57] somewhat like that of Clarissa Dalloway in Virginia Woolf's eponymous modernist classic of the same name (1925). More specifically, these texts present us with what Chakrabarty describes as "subject positions and configurations of memory that challenge *and undermine* the subject that speaks in the name of history" (emphasis added).[58] By "history," Chakrabarty means a hyperreal "Europe" that shadows all other modern narratives as well as our severance from nature. The attitude to nature—especially, as I have been arguing, trees and forests—is crucial to an understanding of modernity, and so of disenchantment, precisely because these have been made to seem "natural." In modern[59] literature, to reiterate a point I made in my introduction, this regard for nature, such as in the English romantic poets, is unavoidably ironic because it is the acute awareness of natural depletion at the hands of humans that prompts this kind of "nostalgic" writing.[60]

While this ironic, disenchanted outlook also infuses modern postcolonial fictions, I believe that the fictions about indigenous lives considered in this chapter are notable for turning the ironic gaze back upon the reader. They do so in two ways: first, by self-critically accenting the gap between the attempt to bring the lives of dispossessed individuals into the light of reason and the limits of their own reasonable rhetoric and, second, by embracing that very gap by leaving in place—leaving untranslated—certain features of their characters' worldviews, whether these untranslated words are transliterations of the local vernacular or modern English terms incorporated into that vernacular. As we will see, the irony in these texts is not (or not only) the self-reflexive kind we typically associate with a modern narrator;[61] the latter form of irony depends, after all, on some combination of knowing subject, or interpreter, and her target.[62] Instead, these works display an ironic edge that points to the reader as well as to mainstream histories and social expectations. An example of this is when Mahasweta ironizes her narratives by juxtaposing the modern English-language terms of policing, law, and industry, especially commercial forestry, that have been incorporated into local vernaculars. This estranges the reader in a way that is comparable to the estrangement Mahasweta's Adivasi characters experience each day.

Linguistic and cultural translations are important considerations in our reading of these stories, including the nonhuman and supernatural environments they describe, which the texts do not question.[63] If modern subjectivity depends on a self-consciousness that regards nature as distinct from itself, "set aside from the rest of creation,"[64] then the counterclaim of recent material ecocriticism that we must "re-enchant" nature by acknowledging its own subjectivity and its relatedness to humans would appear to undermine the claim to modern consciousness.[65] As Wendy Wheeler observes, the positivist, ostensibly tolerant, and disinterested scientific worldview whose dominance we need to resist itself relies on a dogmatic resistance to any narrative that does not accord with its presuppositions.[66] But rather than try to "undermine" entirely the "subject that speaks in the name of history," as Chakrabarty has it,[67] these works of fiction represent on an affective level the kind of aforementioned ecological "*active zone of tension between society and nature*" (original emphasis) that Michael R. Dove ascribes to the historical construction of the jungle in South Asia.[68] I mean that the forest-world is still, for indigenous characters, a partially enchanted realm and that this sensibility to environment and affect is in constant tension with a world that is ostensibly disenchanted. The supernatural in these texts—that is, the treating of "gods and spirits" as if they are "existentially coeval with the human"[69]—is part of the non-positivist semiotic that science decries, and it coexists in tension with the unavoidably modern sensibility of the author and the genre.

Such features invite us to treat such works as examples of magic realism. On one level, they certainly are, inasmuch as they naturalize the supernatural in the context of realist, often historicized narrative. However, in expressing their tribal characters' predicament of having to contend with the incursive power of the postcolonial state, these texts do not simply speak for so-called non-Western modes of being. They also call into question the very conventions that figure world regions in terms of an East/West, or traditional/modern, dichotomy, and highlight the impossibility of speaking of a monolithic "postcolonial world."[70] They remind us that the state's discourse of modernity, like that of the British before India's 1947 independence, casts what is effectively a magical spell over its agents and its citizens. For Euro-style modernity has assumed a powerfully mythologized mode of being that straddles the globe.

Historical Time, Mythic Time, and Psychic Disorder

The "tension between society and nature" that Dove describes belongs to a long tradition in both European and non-European texts of infusing forests with contradictory elements of dreamlike mystery and danger, magic and awe. Harrison recalls that Dante begins his epic poem "lost" in "a dark forest"; the Brothers Grimm, as previously noted, render forests as the site of a "lost" German unity; and the outlaw Robin Hood hides in Sherwood Forest not in order to break away from society but, on the contrary, to redeem it.[71] These European tales, as Harrison observes, reflect the broader story of humans' interactions with the natural environment, ranging from Gilgamesh's epic urge to control it (by killing the forest's guardian and then cutting it down) in an effort to transcend mortality, to the post-Cartesian "mastery" of it, reflected in Descartes' ironic use of Dante's trope to insist on the "straight" path out of the "forest" of tradition by means of rational "method."[72]

But if modernity's "demystification" and "[scientific] control of nature" usher in the disenchantment of the world, modernity also creates its own enchantments, including violence.⁷³ As Saurabh Dube, Jane Bennett, and others have noted, and as this essay argues, the Weberian version of modernity thus sets up the false dichotomy of a modern, rational, disenchanted world cut off from natural life rhythms. I follow Dube's and Bennett's lead in arguing that we should instead be thinking of modern*ies* and be mindful, as Bruno Latour has argued, that the idea of nature as sacred and set apart from us is an equally enchanted view.⁷⁴ Indeed, the reified terms themselves perpetuate certain enchantments. A corollary of this notion, I suggest, is that to say that modern disenchantments are purely Western products and experiences ironically risks precisely the kind of privileging that ecocritical practice aims to dispel.

The works of fiction and memoir I examine here illustrate these points in several ways. On the one hand, they show that despite India's frenzied race to achieve a vaguely imagined postindustrial society, some groups have maintained a respect for the natural world that derives from both mainstream religious epics, such as the *Ramayana*, and local folk traditions. Indeed, Annu Jalais, in her anthropological study of the Sundarbans in West Bengal, reports that for indigenous peoples there, "the forest [is] a kind of commons to which all have equal access."⁷⁵ On the other hand, these works make it clear that these peoples and their environments do not exist in an innocent world cut off from India's various modernities. They show that indigenous cultures, however nonnormative their views may be, harbor their own blind spots and that these intersect with modern sensibilities to produce unexpected outcomes. Rather than presume to "speak for" the subjects whose cultures they depict, writers like Mahasweta highlight, through both narrative style and paratextual commentary (such as interviews, essays, and acknowledgments), their roles as imperfect mediums between metropolitan and indigenous societies.⁷⁶ They recognize, in short, that writing is never an unmediated representation of a subject; after all, as Hogan observes, writing is "all about enchantment."⁷⁷ One especially valuable insight I take from this is that regardless of where we live, we must, as Greg Garrard says about ecopoetics, "reflect ... upon what it might mean to dwell with"—that is, to be involved with, rather than remain apart from—"the earth."⁷⁸ The concept of dwelling speaks to these authors' understanding of a healthy Earth as one that is intimately involved with human presence, not bereft of it, as some environmental policies make it seem. As Naomi Klein reminds us, "green" policies that do not account for indigenous inhabitance can amount to a neocolonial "ranking [of] the relative value of humans."⁷⁹

These texts do not presume to offer solutions to the dilemmas facing tribal communities. But they offer alternative frames for how we make sense of contradictions on the ground, by focusing on marginalized communities and landscapes that enable us to see both environmental and representational crises anew. Without romanticizing their subjects, these fictions show us that what Timothy Clark calls the Anthropocene's "psychic disorder" is not new;⁸⁰ it has been long familiar to indigenous peoples, whose natural dwelling places have been colonized. They are painfully aware that their traditional perceptions of, and relations to, time and space are often incompatible with a modernizing world, one that, ironically, offers them the very tools, especially education, needed to counter it.

Forests of Enchantment and Violence in Mahasweta's "The Hunt"

Sudipta Kaviraj has described how nationalists, many of them novelists and poets, in nineteenth-century Bengal not surprisingly succumbed to the European scientism that instigated a "disenchantment" with the natural world.[81] While these earlier writers' focus on historicizing Indian culture in the interests of a nascent Indian state is understandable, later narratives, as Alex Tickell reminds us, have critiqued this tendency by turning, for example, to the traditions of *purana* (traditional local lore) and *itihas* (history) that Raja Rao famously espoused in his 1938 novel *Kanthapura*.[82] Yet even these non-European narrative traditions often overlook the marginalized lives and worldviews of tribals and other disenfranchised peoples. Rumina Sethi's discussion of Rao's use of the *puranic* tradition to evoke a localized oral culture and its natural environment is instructive here. Despite Rao's brilliant evocation of narrative voice in the person of an elderly woman from the titular village, he presupposes a "universalism" and nationalist "oneness between 'indians' " [*sic*], thereby "creating the impression of joint resistance" to colonial rule and "common suffering."[83] This universalist presumption, Sethi observes, is understandable given both the Gandhian-nationalist context in which Rao wrote and the determinants of the novel form.[84] The mainstream nationalist logic of Rao's novel, in other words, frames and detracts from its otherwise powerfully localized voice. We can thus detect in Rao's novel the kind of universalist logic Chakrabarty cautions us about (and which Sethi, following other historians, calls a "synthesiz[ing]" logic[85]). To cite one salient example, the use of the phrase "Once upon a time" by *Kanthapura*'s illiterate protagonist and narrator may "situate events in a hoary past," but they are ultimately subsumed into the "linear time-consciousness" of an "eventful" national history.[86] The narrator's storytelling phrase in the service of nation differs, as we will see, from Mahasweta's use of it to differentiate indigenous cultures from the national project.

The considerable challenge, then, is to depict these worlds within the historical frame of the nation-state. This is why Mahasweta, who famously fought the state's appropriation of forestland and its "dispossessed" inhabitants, nevertheless wished to see a "general" tribal identity that "belong[s] to the rest of India."[87] Like her Adivasi protagonists, she does not wish for the state's demise (since that is effectively impossible) but, instead, its transformation. Her stories describe the state in its current form as one that finds Adivasis to be "easy [target]" for its own ends. The "system hunts them" as uncivilized "prey,"[88] a designation that undergirds the state's master–slave rationale and self-styled superiority.

Mahaweta's story "The Hunt," translated by Gayatri Chakravorty Spivak, illustrates many of the points I have been making, not least in its ironic, double-entendre title. The protagonist is Mary Oraon, the half-tribal, half-white product of a white Australian whose father had been a colonial planter. Her ethnicity makes her doubly marginalized: from mainstream society, because a tribal, and from her own Oraon people due to her ethnic heritage. At the same time, she "has countless admirers" among men of all communities because of her exotic beauty (3). The world she and her people inhabit is a disenchanted one, in the sense that outsiders have long exploited the Oraons and their forestland. Modernity is signaled, in part, by transliterated English words, which in Spivak's translation appear in italics: words like *train*, *station*, *coal halt*, and *junction*. These words signify the Oraons' exploitation, of which they're well aware but which they feel powerless to halt. Thus, "sal [tree] logs" from the forest "are split in sawmills and sent in every direction." While "silence" reigns over Mary's village of Kuruda, the nearby junction town is "bustl[ing]" with trains, trucks, and buses (2). Once modern industry has transformed a local landscape and economy, this bustle, ironically, though not surprisingly, promises jobs for those whose land it takes.[89]

Mary's marginal ethnic status, which I take to be, on one level, a representation of Indians' perception of tribals as a whole, has the advantage of instilling within her a rare defiance toward outsiders, all of whom are men. Variously seen as alluring and fearsome, Mary plays this to her advantage. "Everyone is afraid of Mary," we are told (5). She daringly "picks the fruit of the … mahua trees on the … property" of her employers, the higher-caste Prasads (4), and presides at her market stall "like a queen" (3). All of these tags and associations—arboreal, royal, exotic—highlight their thematic interconnection. Thus, in a rare moment of ironic levity that reveals both Mary's physical difference and the contrast between tribal and state worldviews, Singh, the government representative, tries to compliment Mary for her beauty by comparing her to a famous Hindi film actress. "You look like Hema Malini," he says. To which Mary responds with a "What?" (10), for the name means nothing to her.[90] Mary's association with trees is equally revealing of her intimacy with the Oraons' forested environment and the dynamics of a predator–prey world ushered in by outside business interests, which are the "real beneficiaries" (2) of the modern logging industry. Singh, the local Tehsildar, or government revenue collector, tellingly equates "the [profitable] business of felling trees in the forest" with sexually "profitable" liaisons with tribal women (9). Mary's defiant attitude, exoticism, and Oraon identity provide the potent mix that, as we see by the story's conclusion, both catalyzes her deadly act and encapsulates the story's themes.

When, therefore, we are told that "the felling goes on" throughout the year, the double meaning is clear, both to us and to Mary (12). When the Tehsildar "caught Mary's hand one day," she immediately sees that "the timing was good. No hunt for the men this year" (13). She sees, in other words, that the once-in-twelve-years hunt for women that is about to begin is her chance to re-enchant her world through a violence learned from these outside antagonists. But "enchant" in what way? One possible reading is that Mary wishes to maintain, or shore up, the natural enchantment that outside forces have been eroding. Mahasweta does, after all, make clear that the Oraon world is both ecological and cultural, since for them there can be no division between the two. However, the narrative also makes clear that Mary reflects on this conflation in a way that appropriates her assailant's modus operandi, which is predicated on exploitative capitalism, as his use of English business terms illustrates: *investment*, *virgin area*, *felling monopoly*, and so on (7). In other words, Mary's social motivation to participate in the ritual hunt coexists with her individual, self-conscious motivation to harm this representative of modern violence, whose target is her physical person as well as her culture. Re-enchantment in this case does not, therefore, mean a return to a pristine natural past, but rather the uneven combination of individual and social motivations by using the conceptual tools—in Mary's case, the conflation of individual and ritual violence—at hand.

Mary, wielding her machete to join in the ritual Oraon hunt, lures the Tehsildar into the forest—and, once there, sees him as species of animal prey. "A-ni-mal," she tells herself—and "smile[s]" (13). The story builds to a climax with the Tehsildar panting after Mary, as we listen in on her thoughts. "Today," she feels, "a small thing cannot please her. She wants to hunt the big beast!" (16) As you might guess, the Tehsildar does not come to a good end. I find the language Mahasweta uses to describe the scene revealing: the man's face "begin[s] to look like a hunted animal's," and she "caresses" it (16). He, of course, thinks this is foreplay; for Mary, it's a prelude to his death, but one that's done ritualistically, as her machete "lowers … lifts, lowers" (16), ironically echoing the sexualized rhythm[91] of the tribal women's trance-like refrain at the onset of the hunt (15).

By ritualistic I mean that her killing of the man is of a piece with the hunt's killing of animals, implying not a singular event but its repetition, as well as a recognition of their (human and animal) shared corporeality. A few lines before this, Mary spots a hedgehog, and we are told that "if it hadn't been today Mary would have killed it, eaten its flesh" (16). The description of her plan contextualizes its spontaneity, for it is framed by the natural world: the gitginda vines, its yellow flower, and the seemingly "bottomless" ravine, in which she later "throws" the man's body (16–17). This natural frame is figuratively homologous with the narrative frame, which accords her real-time, present-tense act a measure of planning and prediction by virtue of appearing in a printed, rereadable format.[92] The act becomes, in effect, an historical artifact, which arguably allows Mahasweta to preserve the simultaneity of Mary's individual as well as social motivations along with the act's spontaneity. Her act is simultaneously spontaneous and planned, individually self-conscious and socially linked with the ritual hunting of other Oraon women that night—much as Mary herself is simultaneously non-Oraon (by virtue of her half-English blood) and very much Oraon.

We can therefore say, by one reading, that Mary reclaims a sense of enchantment by redressing a wrong, a move the story plainly endorses. Her murderous act can be said to be violent (or just or wrong) only in the context of a rigid juridical generality. For here, the violence shades unexpectedly into erotic pleasure. This pleasure appears, too, to derive from her exultant feeling of being free of the evil Tehsildar and to then shade into an almost spiritual awakening. The finite time of justice that we recognize in Mary's act thus coexists, to the modern, secularist reader's discomfort, with a mythic timelessness. When, after Mary has "bath[ed] naked in the cut," it's "as if she has been infinitely satisfied in a sexual embrace." This infinitude has been presaged by her sense, just after the murder, that a "few million moons [have] pass[ed]" (17). This timelessness is nothing like the proverbial modern-colonialist view of indigenous peoples as lacking history, but instead an enchanted time–space in which Mary is fully alive and "fears no animal" (17). As the author says in an interview with Spivak, the real-life model for Mary "resurrected the real meaning of the animal hunting festival day by dealing out justice for a crime committed against the entire tribal society."[93] Mary Oraon does this not by pretending that the modern world does not exist, but by incorporating it into her own. This is signaled, in part, by her use of English words (appearing in italics) at the end of the story. She decides she will "walk seven *miles* tonight" to be with her lover, Jalim, and then take one of the "*buses*" or "*trucks*" to go with him "somewhere." The final paragraph finds her walking at night by "watching the *railway line*" (17).

The motif of ritual sacrifice also, then, recasts the more familiar structure of mythic narrative, in which "magical flight" plays the key role.[94] Walter Burkert summarizes the basic format:

> [A]s the heroine or hero or both flee from the dominion of a witch ... or other unpleasant company, the powerful and swift adversary realizes they have escaped and takes up pursuit. There is just one way to stop him: the fleeing person must throw things behind that will grow into barriers to halt the pursuer at least for a while, until a decisive point is passed and safety is regained. Throw a comb, and it will grow into a forest or into a mountain range.[95]

Burkert reads this as a version of "that biological trick for survival to distract the attention of the pursuer by abandoning, by throwing," which among animals (including us, it seems) is the abandonment of "young or feeble quarry."[96] Mary Oraon revises this by leaving behind not just her predator's body, but also his "*wallet, cigarettes*, his *handkerchief*" (17; original emphasis).

Given that Mary's pursuer is dead, these talismans of his modernity are ironic counterparts to the magical obstacles that characters encounter in mythic narrative. A possible reading of this is that Mahasweta has Mary enact a conventional trope only to mock it, thereby signaling a refusal to play by the usual narrative rules. However, rather than stop at Burkert's insightful but somewhat reductive notion of the magical, I believe it is important to notice that Mahasweta does not mock this or any other storytelling tropes. She makes Mary credible to us not by a rational explanation of her motivations and actions, which would presume the kind of secular historicity that Dipesh Chakrabarty rightly views as one-sided, but by presenting Mary's (and other tribals') mythic outlook as simultaneously, if not fully, modern. Her act is simultaneously a claim to justice in real time, for both social and individual wrongs, and one that cannot be subsumed within the grand narrative, or the "generalizing impulse," of secular historical time.[97] This denouement is an ironic counterpoint to the phrase "Once upon a time" that appears twice at the start of the story, implying that what ensues will be mere fairy tale, one that modern readers associate with quaint tribal beliefs. The upending of this trope by the conclusion of the story allows us to retrospectively perceive the terrible, very real cost of what's identified in the rest of the sentence: "Once upon a time, whites had *timber plantations*" in the area (2; original emphasis). Having read the story's conclusion, we are better able to understand the contextual irony of the italicized English phrase. This is not, in my reading, the irony of historical disenchantment, which is predicated on the supposed "rupture" between traditional and modern worldviews,[98] but rather an irony that critiques the very notion of rupture. This suggests that Mary's elation at the end of the story does not mean she has learned to balance mythic and modern times, as I used to think. She instead suspends, for the time being at least, the colonial and postcolonial timescapes (the plantation capital) of which she is a product.[99] Her (and the author's) celebration of a particular non-modern time and space cannot be relegated to a linear timeline in which it is generally styled as "primordial" or "pre-modern" and therefore irrational. It's the story's modern representatives, such as the Tehsildar, who view her through this generalizing, disenchanted template.

Thus, while it is true, as Kavita Daiya observes, that Mahasweta's stories of Adivasis, especially women, expose how their "bodies are snared in circuits of … capitalist modernity,"[100] it is also true that her stories show us that modernity is not merely an "external force," for it is no longer separable from her protagonists' forest homes. In "Douloti the Bountiful," as we saw, Mahasweta depicts a tribal woman, ravaged by disease caused by sexual servitude, falling upon a map of India drawn in chalk, in a schoolyard, to celebrate Independence Day. The image subverts the nationalist Mother India iconography described previously and that the women in Raja Rao's *Kanthapura* exemplify.[101] Mother India is unsurprisingly linked directly to the natural environment, both local and national (especially visible, as noted, in the oft-reproduced image of the Mother India goddess superimposed over a map of India).[102] Mahasweta's depiction of Douloti on the Indian map thus disenchants customary symbolic and territorial boundaries and re-enchants her protagonists' worlds. Another way to gloss her stories is to say that they belie the supposed break between enchanted pasts and a disenchanted, modern present by demonstrating that these terms have never been fixed, but are instead remnants of a rhetorical move fashioned in Europe and inherited, for better or worse, by modern India. The consequences are stark, for in staking a purely utilitarian claim to forestland, modern states displace the land's inhabitants and their cultures. The paradox, of course, is that states mystify their origins by locating them in precisely these forested (or once-forested) spaces. It should not be surprising, then, to see tribal activists, obligated to enter the discourse of modern politics, reach for the very same Mother-as-nature image in their multimedia advocacy of indigenous motherland.[103]

Were-Tigers, Predation, and Naga Forests: Easterine Kire's *When the River Sleeps*

Easterine Kire, a novelist and folklorist from India's Northeastern state of Nagaland, writes fiction in English about her region and culture. This region, composed of many groups and languages that are distinct from the rest of India, is experiencing an explosion of writing, often in English, with Nagas, Mizos, Apatanis, Assamese, and others tapping into rich veins of orality to describe cultures and landscapes that are typically unfamiliar to "mainland" Indians.[104] Many of these works are conditioned by the authors' forested homelands, which, like the indexical *mahua* tree, frequently signify both past practices and present predicaments, including the conflicted inner lives of many of the region's inhabitants. This inner conflict is not surprising, given their sense of being doubly subjugated: by Europeans from the late 1800s to 1947, and then by the Indian state. Northeastern groups have therefore sought a measure of political autonomy in a variety of ways.

Kire's 2014 novel *When the River Sleeps*,[105] set entirely in a forest, follows the journey of a middle-aged Naga man named Vilie, who works for India's Forest Department. We are never told exactly when the story takes place, except that it is in the modern period and after the advent of Christianity to the region in the nineteenth century (54). (Of Nagaland's current population of two million, about 88% are Christian according to the last census.[106]) The topographical details, on the other hand, are richly described: teak trees, riverine ferns (97), plantain trees (97), and herbs like bitter wormwood and amaranth (32).

Vilie's fellow Angamis, a clan within the larger Naga tribal group, think he is odd for preferring to live year-round in the forest rather than in the village. He does miss "the ordinary things of village life," but, after twenty-five years at his job, concludes: "The forest is my wife, and perhaps this is what marriage is like; with periods when a chasm of loneliness separates the partners" (9). More than anything, he wants to find a "sleeping river" he first heard about as a boy and that he's been dreaming of ever since. The story "was more than a story to him." He has always wanted to "'catch' [the river] when it went to sleep" so that he can "wrest a stone from the heart [it] and take it home," where the stone "will grant you whatever it is empowered to grant you. It could be cattle, women, prowess in war, or success in the hunt." One can, in short, make the "magic" of this "heart-stone [yours]" (3). "Is it possible," he asks himself, "that only forest dwellers can understand such things exist in the places not frequented by man? Will the magic of the river work only for a believer? Would it work in spite of lack of faith?" (11).

To get to the river, Vilie will have to trek through different forests, some familiar and some dangerously unfamiliar. And so he packs his essentials—hunting knife, tobacco, tea, salt, gun, and salted venison—and, after a four-hour hike to a settlement of itinerant Nepali woodcutters who are his closest "neighbors," Vilie is "swallowed up by the trees" of the forest (20). He spends the night in an empty shed belonging to another Naga clan. This is still somewhat familiar territory. But in the middle of the night, his hunter ear picks up "the softest fall of padded feet." He "woke with a start, the hair on his arms standing on end at the knowledge that he was not alone." And then "a great paw" smashes through the shed's "old tin and weak wood," and, as Vilie runs to the door, a "tiger came at him fearlessly, throwing itself at the outline of the man." Vilie "sidestepped" the beast, which "crashed into the door, breaking it, and leaving torn fragments of wood hanging on the hinges. Vilie shot off a bullet," and in the flash, "he saw that the tiger was much bigger than any he had ever seen" (24).

But the tiger returns, and Vilie now understands that this is likely a "weretiger," since "ordinary tigers kept their distance from man." "This one," moreover, "was coming back for more," unafraid of the gun. Vilie "rapidly thinks of the names of those men … in this region" who knew the "art" of "transforming their spirits into tigers" and yells their names at the approaching were-tiger. "Why are you treating me as a stranger?" he cries. "'I come in peace. You owe me your hospitality, I am your guest!' He shouted these words out with absolute faith that they were being listened to and heeded. Sure enough the animal retreated for the second time, but not before it had made a call like a warrior's ululating cry" (25–6). Vilie recalls the words of his village seer, who had told him years ago that to find the sleeping river he would "sometimes" have to "struggle … against spiritual powers" that no gun could stop (31).

The next day, Vilie's hike takes him into the "Nettle Forest," an area avoided by his clan but frequented by another. As he reached it, "he saw three figures ahead" and "became tense" wondering "if this seemingly real sight" would "[metamorphose] into something else" (33). Vilie is relieved to find that they are women from a friendly "border village" of the Zeliang clan who are "harvesting nettle" to make "yarn." He finds it "refreshing to meet real people and have a normal conversation" (34). He and the older woman of the group reminisce about past times when their two clans bartered with each other and knew one another's tongues. "Sad that the younger ones haven't learned other languages," Vilie says (35). Trying his hand at pulling out the nettles, Vilie is immediately stung. "Damn!" he exclaims. "That was more painful than the nettle we have in our village." "It's stronger than the species found in your area," the woman says. "It yields better yarn but it stings harder too" (37). She applies some "rock bee honey" to the sting to stave off the possibility of Vilie getting "a nasty little fever" (39).

Kire's novel highlights several interrelated topics discussed previously. In this Naga forest-world that is far removed from modern life, it makes sense that Vilie's worry about what is "real" is not the same as our conventional notions of the reality–unreality divide or the distinction between dreams and wakefulness. For Vilie, as we have seen, a spirit animal like the were-tiger is as "real" as anything else. The phenomenon of humans taking nonhuman form is not new, of course; therianthropy, as anthropologists term it, is a familiar feature of scholarship on so-called animist cultures. My interest here is in the Northeast Indian setting of this phenomenon, where forests are rapidly disappearing. And as we know, when a people's forests disappear, their belief systems tend to crumble. Indigenous groups like the Naga do not simply live within a forest, they "think" it, as Eduardo Kohn puts it.[107] To lose the forest would be to lose one's habits of thought and therefore, ultimately, one's sense of habitus. Kire's focus on a solitary resident of the forest, Vilie, reminds us that habitus is as much individual as it is communitarian. The novel is not, in other words, an ethnographic record, in the way that dominant societies all too often treat postcolonial fiction. Although the text is directed at a mainstream readership, it demands to be taken at face value—that is, as a story about arboreal and intersubjective enchantments that asks its urban interlocutors to unthink customary ways of reading about unfamiliar, non-modern subjects. It asks not to be taken as a singular, representative Naga story, but as one of many diverse stories about Naga individuals, such as Vilie, who inhabit forests in their own way.

The novel's particular narrative mode reconnects us, as well, to questions about language. Presented in an orthographic and material medium—an English-language novel—that many Nagas do not have access to, we may wonder how the novel reshapes folk stories expressing the overlap between biological and spirit worlds. Does this presentation, in other words, package regional identities in ways that make them more amenable to an urban, largely non-Naga readership? How does its forest-inflected regionalism either echo or contrast with expressions of national identity in other works I have examined? For instance, Kire's novel about forest spirits intersects in certain ways not only with Mahasweta's fiction, but also with Ghosh's *The Hungry Tide*. For one thing, readers will immediately note the conspicuous absence of history as such in Kire's novel. There are no references to the larger entity called India and very few to non-Naga actors, except the Forest Department Vilie works for and the brief mention of Christianity. Vilie's gun and other modern artifacts attest to interaction with outsiders, but none are mentioned except the Nepali couple—a feature of the novel that non-Naga readers may find surprising given the region's mostly one-dimensional representation in mainstream media as a site of separatist and political tensions.

Predation is a key motif in this episodic novel, as it is in other forest fictions, but not in the conventional senses of either the hunting of animals or the predatory exploitation of forest and people by outsiders. The narrative could be characterized as expressing what Kohn calls an ecology of selves, or a "relational" system of being, in which the question of "who is predator and who is prey is contextually dependent."[108] Not only is Vilie preyed upon by other men, and not only does he hunt animals for food, but he is also attacked by were-tigers and other spirit beings. But if the relationships in these cases are "contextually dependent," is it accurate to describe them as "predatory"? Unlike, say, Mary Oraon in Mahasweta's "The Hunt," Vilie's understanding of human–animal spirits is part of his accepted social imaginary rather than a representation of outside intrusion.

How we make sense of such features depends to some degree on where we place Kire's novel in terms of genre and literary history. To read it in the same way as mainstream fiction invites us to do is to bring to it a certain skepticism, or hermeneutics of suspicion, about human systems of belief, natural reality, and the supernatural. Such a reading also asks that we compare the novel to other accounts, whether familiar or unfamiliar, of indigenous lives, in order to evaluate its generic features. We might, for instance, contextualize Kire's implied realism with village belief systems in other parts of India as well as with the aforementioned typology of "village" or "tribal" India as timeless, natural, and naturally moral. Yet Kire's novel resists alignment with allegory or fable, or even with the mix of allegory and realism that Mahasweta's works so rewardingly exhibit. Kire's novel, I suggest, resists such interpretations because it disconnects its realist tropes from their expected signifiers and presents scenes that read as subtle critiques of these interpretations. One example is when Vilie happens to witness a man's murder by two Nagas who are not part of his clan village and then becomes their prey. Captured and accused of being a threat to the men's clan, Vilie is brought before their village elder. He is saved by coincidence: the elder remembers meeting him long before and is favorably inclined. The man points to the burn mark of a bullet that grazed Vilie's skin as proof that he, not the other two men, is the hunted rather than the hunter. Vilie is deemed innocent and freed, and carries on with his episodic, dream-infused quest for the river stone.

This highly contingent circumstance, together with Vilie's encounters with were-tigers, presented in the absence of any other familiar pattern of justice or fate, unsettles our expectations. Whereas novelists like Rao or Ghosh can rely to some degree on their Indian readers' familiarity with village tropes, Indo-Islamic traditions, and literary patterning, Kire's readers are thrust into a region that usually appears in mainstream media as a space of either natural wildness or insurgency—typologies that reinforce each other. To counter the latter, Kire at times throws us the bone of visual "proof"—such as when a character sees a tree or some other observable entity—but at other times proffers equally visual "proof" of a were-tiger or other spirit's presence. None of these circumstances, we might say, can be treated as entirely credible outside its context: each perception makes sense only in the time and place in which it occurs. Vilie is an independent-minded individual who thinks on his own, such as when he chooses to enter a dense rainforest deemed "unclean" by his clan because it is "spirit-infested" (47). One possible interpretation is that the break between past and present on which modern history depends is shown to be just as contingent, or uncertain, as the existence of spirit worlds. Kire's narrative attempts to place the reader in a semblance of the continuum, rather than the break, between spirit and human worlds. This outlook differs, for example, from notions of "nomadic" and "becoming-animal" that Gilles Deleuze and Felix Guattari advocate,[109] or from Donna Haraway's theorization of "becoming with animal,"[110] both of which ultimately depend on conceptual (though no less productive) categories rather than on the interactive presence of material entities. Vilie, in other words, engages with not only the nonhuman animal world, but also with spirit–animal–human selves.

Consider, by way of illustration, that in the forest deemed "unclean" by his clan, Vilie awakes from a terrifying dream of "being chased by angry spirits" and finds himself set upon by a "dark, indistinguishable shape sitting on top of him" (82). He thinks the shape is "part of his dream. But the weight was real enough" (82). Remembering the command of his village seer to "let your spirit be the bigger one," Vilie casts off the thing—and discovers that "it had no human shape." It shrivels to the size of a beetle, and Vilie now feels that "the forest was his as much as it was theirs" (83–4). This is not the act of interpreting a bounded dream but instead a situational moment of coexistence with normally terrifying forest spirits. By "situational" I mean that although Vilie's particular frame of mind during this brief stay in the unclean rainforest has convinced him of his right to it, he nonetheless flees at dawn, glad to return to a more-familiar spirit world (86), rather than (as a conventional protagonist might do) remain to stake his claim to the physical forest. He thus acts not according to what we may imagine to be fight-or-flight instinct, but according to his village seer's counsel and the rules of his clan. In fact, his behavior answers a different order of "instinct" than the average reader of the novel can fully comprehend.

Vilie's journey concludes with his murder, making the irony clear: he has survived attacks by were-tigers and spirits, but cannot escape human violence. In the closing chapter, a young woman whom Vilie saved from a were-tiger attack with the help of the river stone returns to his ruined forest hut and asks her new husband to repair it. In what I read as a flawed concession to conventional closure in an otherwise unconventional novel, the conjugal ending and the woman's desire for a physical reminder of the man who saved her from "spirits of darkness" (194) returns us to the world of everyday human existence. Or perhaps the author is indicating that a novel set entirely in a Naga forest will be deemed credible to its English readership only if it offers an ending that redeems its human protagonist in an expected manner. Meanwhile, the forest as protagonist remains, cognizant and singular.

Conclusion: The City in the Forest

In this book, I have argued that forests in India, both real and imagined, are key sites for expressing both regional and national belonging, sometimes in a transnational context. I have also argued that modern writers have used certain literary features, including *darshanic* vision, forest indices, and the combination of demotic and formal rhetoric, to represent forests as spaces that can accommodate a diversity of ideas, personae, and cultures. Some of these features characterize ancient and medieval literary works, but I have argued that it was in the modern period that, because of dramatic industrial and bureaucratic changes associated with European colonialism in the nineteenth century, writers in India sought ways to articulate the challenge of balancing older, often religious, traditions of belonging with new forms of affiliation and sustenance that a modern nation seemed to demand, such as the sciences, historiography, and related forms of record keeping. These first-generation nationalist writers also, however, saw the destructive effects on India's landscapes due to ostensibly efficient British colonial practices. For these reasons, writers variously turned to idealized forest images, historical records of forest-associated events (especially justified rebellions), and allusions to arboreal flora and products in order to find ways to express the often conflicting ideals related to modern national formation.

Within a generation of India's independence in 1947, writers and filmmakers were reevaluating their predecessors' efforts with varying measures of praise and criticism, or both. Some, like Bengali writer-filmmaker Satyajit Ray, Malayalam novelist Thakazhi Sivasankara Pillai, Kannada writer U. R. Ananthamurthy, and Bengali writer Mahasweta Devi, had come of age during the independence movement or soon after. Others, including Assamese writer Indira Goswami and Amitav Ghosh, were born in the decade leading up to or following independence. The first generation had inevitably imbibed colonial-era ideas, but by the 1960s and 1970s were at a sufficient distance from both colonial rule and early nationalist promises to gain some perspective on this past. In this period, small towns across the country gained economic prowess with the growth of agricultural output and, in turn, political clout, challenging the influence of urban India's young and aspiring educated classes.[1] Political agitation in towns and cities on numerous fronts, from anti-Hindi Tamil movements and anti-immigrant Marathi regionalists to communist movements in West Bengal and Kerala, further induced a feeling of insecurity among young urbanites, who clung to idealizations of village India—a motif represented in numerous Hindi films at the time[2]—despite evidence to the contrary.

It is context that Sunil Gangopadhyay examines in his 1968 Bengali novel *Days and Nights in the Forest* (*Aranyer Din Ratri*),[3] which Satyajit Ray made into an admired film[4] of the same name in 1970. A well-known work that exposes the paradoxes and facades of the Calcutta[5] *bhadralok*, Gangopadhyay notably chooses to set the novel in a forest, and for these reasons serves as a particularly illuminating coda to my study. Gangopadhyay tells the story of four young, male friends from Calcutta—Shekhar, Robi, Ashim, and Sanjoy—who one day decide to take a trip into the Palamau Forest of Bihar (now part of Jharkhand State). Infused with idealizations of "tribal" men and, especially, women whom they identify with the "wilds" of the jungle, each of the friends is forced to confront his own racial, cultural, and sexual prejudices. Gangopadhyay's forest—or jungle, since he uses both terms—is associated with the full range of images and tropes we have previously encountered: It is "a veritable garden" (19), an "enchanting" (39) chiaroscuro (invoking the book's title) of "daylight … fad[ing] slowly" and "darkness descending" (20), and where "everything has become easy" (148), including the availability of sex. "One doesn't have to affect modesty in the jungle," Robi exults. The forest is also a "wilderness" in which "there is nothing to see or do" (39), where the local Santals (Adivasis) "behaved rather peculiarly, even mysteriously" and "lived according to a different set of rules" (72). It is a "jungle" that "alter[s] the appearance of things" (123). These are tropes the young city men (and the two young Calcutta women they meet there) bring with them and project onto the forest. What surprises the young men, however, is that money has found a purchase in this forest-world: it is not the untouched retreat they had imagined it to be. To the contrary, as the author shows, this is a world that still, a generation after independence, perpetuates colonial practices.

Gangopadhyay portrays a forest that is nothing like the idyll of ashramic detachment from materiality that Hindu traditions celebrate, nor the site of a journey of self-transformation. It is decidedly not a kind of *tapovana*, or forest school, that Tagore emulated. The forest instead stages the rape of a Santal woman, Duli, at the hands of one of the four men, Robi; the men's superficial dalliances with the two genteel Calcutta women; and the city dwellers' condescending attitudes toward the Santals and the workers of the Government bungalow the men occupy. By the end of the novel, Robi has been beaten by a group of Santal men for the rape, the four men have had their friendships tested, and each one has had to confront the prejudices hiding behind his bourgeois self, especially when interacting with the Santals.

In these and other ways, Gangopadhyay's novel, much like Ray's film version, indicts the modern middle classes for having made a mockery of the epic warrior-hero's forest journey and of the Vedic ideal of meditative retreat in the woods, which continue (in the 1960s as well as today) to undergird the traditional urban regard for forests. This regard is most clearly exhibited by the two Calcutta women whom the men meet in the Palamau Forest, Aparna and Jaya, who are visiting their land-owning family's ancestral bungalow. The novel is also for this reason a lament for the loss of the Tagorean ideal, which the author's (and Ray's) generation felt acutely, of a forest retreat that can instill genuine love of nature and, in turn, love of learning.[6] The four male characters, as the first generation to come of age in an independent India, are shown to be unworthy of leading it.

The novel would seem, then, to be an indictment of both religious hypocrisy and class pretension as well as of the romantic tradition of pastoralism. It can certainly be read as such, echoing in some ways Bibhutibhushan's *Aranyak*. The trouble is that this interpretation presumes that the forest is a lapsed world that can, with the right vision and administration, reassume a lost wholeness—that it can regain its ashramic values and ecological balance and pastoral aesthetic. Such a reading assumes that the "young sal trees planted by the government" (19) simply need more time and sustenance, just as the Santals need meaningful employment to steer clear of the "sal-leaf bowls" they now fill with alcoholic Mahua brew and "gulp ... down" (67). It is also possible to fruitfully read the novel—as Suranjan Ganguly does with Ray's faithful film version— as showing that those ideals cannot be recuperated, partly because of irrevocable change and partly because these ideals are, at root, the constructs of urban elites, with no place for forest inhabitants like the Santals. These interpretations are accurate as far as they go, but overlook the polyglossic, multivocal, and polysemous features of many ancient literary treatments of the forest that I described in Chapter 1. Although it is true that the four Calcutta men's family backgrounds make them aware of Vedic treatments of the forest as well as of English romanticism, these outlooks are no more (and perhaps less) consequential to their behavior than their bourgeois points of view. While their return to the city at the end of the novel after their excursion could be read as an ironic reflection of the classical return-from-exile motif, such a reading must still keep the Vedic *ashrama* concept—in this case, the *vanaprastha*, or "way of the forest," stage of a Brahmin man's retreat—as its central focus.

It makes better sense, I believe, to see the final line of the novel—Robi "turned his face towards the bare wall" (178)—as pointing not to an ironic take on that tradition, but rather to the young men's recognition that city and forest are not the distinct spheres they had imagined them to be. The two spaces constitute each other, although power still clearly lies with the city. This is a horrific recognition for them since it breaks down their carefully nurtured egos and the societal ethos undergirding them. Robi turns away from Aparna in shame, knowing that what he has done to Duli mocks Aparna's praise that he is "a saint" (178). He had viewed Duli and other Santal women as "belonging to nature itself" (137), and so no different from consumable forest materials. Now, following his beating by Santal men and his return to the city, he has begun to see through the pretensions of his class, a recognition inseparable from his shock at seeing the Santals actively defend their community. This closing scene encapsulates the novel's key motif of illusion: the deceptiveness of fantasies we all create, and on which we often act. The Calcuttan characters' romantic images of the forest—images that had helped prop up their urban gentility—have crumbled, a conclusion whose denouement the author sets in motion in the novel's first pages.

The mutuality of city and forest is also illustrated, however, by the irony that the Santals, who have been exploited by outside interests economically as well as culturally, feel the pull of the city, enticed by news of employment and modern goods. As Duli asks an inebriated Robi shortly before he assaults her, "Why would you want to stay on in the jungle when you can work in Calcutta?" (138). This is among the most revealing lines of the novel, for it highlights the paradoxes ushered in by modernity and that the new nation faces. The four men are surprised to learn that the Santals' desperate circumstances have made them "come from unknown fields and forests, from the edges of rocky uplands to conduct cold-blooded transactions—all engaged in the utmost impossible task of staying alive" (97). This prompts Shekhar to express a painful recognition to his friends: "Do you realize we are aliens here? We are so different from these people in the way we walk, talk and behave. Who would say we belonged to the same country? How can there be a social revolution if they don't think of us as one of them, if they don't do as we say?" (98). Their forest excursion, far from offering a respite from the anxieties of their city lives, has in fact magnified those anxieties by hollowing out cherished beliefs.

The forest in Gangopadhyay's novel, in these ways, affords its central characters a new, painful understanding of the modern nation's paradoxical composition. The metaphor of nation-as-family and related notions of maternal and arboreal purity dissolve, illustrating Partha Chatterjee's observation that the Indian middle-class home was "the original site on which the hegemonic project of nationalism was launched" and Ajay Skaria's point that modernity needs "wildness."[7] We can see these needs exhibited, for example, in the nation's championing of "authentic" folk, or "ethnic," traditions, such as handicrafts sold by the Government's Cottage Industries initiative.[8] While such initiatives provide a livelihood for indigenous craftspeople, their products, sold to city dwellers as authentic artifacts of "tribal" groups, in effect naturalize these communities. (Some items in the Cottage Industries emporia now bear a "Geographical Indication" [GI] label that identifies its specific provenance, a governmental strategy to both market and unify its constituent regions.[9]) Those handicrafts that are made of wood, from carved figures to items of furniture, are sourced from teak, sheesham, sandalwood, and other forest plantation trees overseen by the Indian Forest Service, representatives of which, as we saw in Mahasweta's stories, are viewed by Adivasis as usurpers. This is why Forest Service officials appear in forest fictions across India as menacing agents, Government ciphers, or cynical and aloof administrators.

This last specimen of Government administrator is brought to life in the form of Upamanyu Chatterjee's Indian Administrative Service character Agastya Sen, a disaffected, anglicized young man who is assigned far from his home city of Calcutta to the provincial region of Madna to administer, in part, the region's forest plantation–related bureaucracy. Chatterjee's 1988 novel, *English, August: An Indian Story*,[10] told from Agastya's perspective, describes an area active with Naxalites, the indigenous Maoist rebels who have taken up arms to fight the Government over rights to their forests (124). Although much can be said about Chatterjee's often sardonically humorous accounts of Agastya's marijuana-stoked ennui, I will restrict this concluding discussion to the young man's encounter with these forests and his already jaded take on the Government's—and his office's—presence there. On one of his many excursions, this one for pleasure in the company of friends (one of whom is named, with no doubt ironic intent, Sita—just as the narrator's namesake is Vedic India's revered Vedic *rishi*, or sage), Agastya sees "isolated teak trees, like a disorderly vanguard" and immediately understands that "this was no virgin forest." For he notices that "everywhere there were symptoms of desecration, tree stumps, clumps of decaying bamboo, gaps in the trees … too many new saplings planted by an assiduous Forest Department." To Agastya, "the road itself, new and black," is "an interminable cicatrice on the flesh of the forest"

(199). He frequently alludes to classic texts—the now-distant visions of Tagore (277), the *Bhagavad Gita* (195)—with either intentional or unintended irony and above all sees the baneful presence of governmental controls. The Government's Rest House, despite being "new," mirrors the Forest Service bungalow Gangopadhyay's young characters occupy: a latter-day avatar of the British Dak Bungalow whose welcoming caretakers crowd together "to see," ironically, "an Englishman"—that is, Agastya, whose speech and mannerisms appear to everyone to make him such (201). The Rest House, like the others in the region, serves government officials with titles inherited from the British, like District Inspector of Land Records and Collector. The bureaucratese is an uncanny presence in the forest, alien as well as familiar, and it is this uncanniness that Agastya tries, with only partial success, to resolve within himself. He comes to sympathize with the "tribals," but cannot, like his older friend, the cartoonist Sathe, come to feel "at home" there (285). Here, in the novel's conclusion, Chatterjee has Sathe echo the title and themes of Gangopadhyay's novel (and, given Agastya's Calcutta sensibility, no doubt Ray's film). Explaining to Agastya why he loves this forest region, Sathe recalls his father's need "to work" in "an inhuman way" for the reward of "a lot of money": "Days and nights in the forest, bribing the Forest officials, underpaying the tribals, beating others like him to a timber contract" (284). That kind of life appalls Sathe, driving him from the city (Bombay, in his case). The echo of Gangopadhyay's novel title accentuates Sathe's disaffection.

Chatterjee, a generation younger than Gangopadhyay, describes an India that has in some ways fulfilled the early nationalist dream of tying together its astonishingly diverse regions by amplifying modern methods of administration, mobility, and manufacturing. Chatterjee's Agastya nevertheless sees his assigned region as one that has been "bypassed by ... history ... impervious to the Mughals and 1857 and [Bankim's] Bande Mataram [*sic*] and the mid-century travails of megalopolitan India" (45–6). Although we are already at some distance here from Gangopadhyay's sociopolitical context of the late 1960s, and obviously very distant from Tagore's and Bankim's, many of the same tropes and images apply. Chatterjee leaves us with a sense of stasis that characterizes both Agastya's outlook and the country's. As Agastya prepares to return to Calcutta, Sathe tells him, with a laugh, that "no one, but no one, is remotely interested in your generation, August" (286). The reader knows by this point, however, not to take any statements, including Sathe's somewhat grim view of the nation's future, at face value. Importantly, Sathe has also just told Agastya that Madna "is home for me" because "my best years, my past, is here" (285). This intimation of the need for individuals and collectives to create a useable past through their inclusive inhabitance of place encapsulates a key aim of this study, which has probed the many ways in which literary forests inflect different ways of being and of imagining possible futures.

In 1991, however, just three years after Chatterjee's *English, August* appeared, the Indian government enacted monetary reforms that enlarged the role of urban centers in the national economy and in the media. Cities have asserted themselves as never before, attracting rural migrants on a huge scale and playing key roles in today's accelerating processes of globalization.[11] According to one recent report, urban centers are "economic powerhouses," generating "70% of the country's GDP."[12] Along with greater opportunities for employment, a sharp rise in entrepreneurship, and the expansion of the middle classes have come the challenges endemic to rapid urban growth worldwide, from air pollution and housing shortages to crime and wealth gaps. It is not coincidental, therefore, that many of the novels published in the post-1991 period focus on dissecting the cultural sensibilities, uncertainties, and ideologies that such changes have produced and, often, magnified. Among the significant motifs expressive of these changes is not so much the forest as such, but, as we saw in several of the works discussed in this book, indexical referents of the forest, particularly trees.

We have seen, for instance, how, to speak broadly, human cultures turn to arboreal images to express the loss of forestlands, a loss that is figured as indicative of, and prefatory to, the recuperation of wholeness—the Edenic national wholeness that Camões imagines in *The Lusiads*, the natural-political unity of Ayodhya in the *Ramayana*, the maternal forest in *Anandamath*, and the indigenous forest of *Aranyak*. Voicing self-evidently anthropomorphic outlooks, these works are grounded in what Donna Haraway has summarized as the "troubling dualisms" of, for example, "self/other … culture/nature, male/female, civilized/primitive, reality/appearance, whole/part, agent/resource … truth/illusion," and "God/man." This dualistic logic derives from a "founding myth of original wholeness," most often figured as primeval garden forest.[13]

A number of noteworthy novels appearing in recent years strive to resist these dualisms, sometimes through irony, and in part by allowing their characters to "live on the boundaries." This is not the same as a liminal stage one passes through in order to achieve a transformative self-awareness (a view dependent on dualism) but is instead an insistence on remaining within the liminal and the contingent.[14] To question dreams of wholeness and to invoke the potentialities of boundaries, these novels must somehow displace the forest-as-whole trope that urbanism continues to cherish. This is one reason the main characters in Indra Sinha's *Animal's People* (2007) and Aravind Adiga's *The White Tiger* (2008), for example, see themselves or others as "animal" and why, in Karan Mahajan's 2016 novel *The Association of Small Bombs*,[15] arboreal referents elicit a sense of personal disintegration that mirrors the exploding bomb at the center of the story. Vestigial forests in these novels remind us not simply that cities have displaced forestland, but more significantly that the notional forms of city, village, and forest are composed of other forms, including their supposed oppositions. Cities, in other words, contain and are conditioned by arboreal features, just as forest environments are conditioned by urban interests. In this sense, city and forest are not unlike the forest referents in Ghosh's *Sea of Poppies*, which are discrete parts as well as parts of a whole (the *Ibis*).[16]

Narrative resistance to tropes of wholeness does not mean, however, that Adiga, Sinha, and Mahajan reject the possibility that their individual characters will find ways of reintegrating their sense of self. They reject, rather, those tropes of presumptive wholeness that, as Haraway indicates, have actually depended on subjugation of one kind or another—the subjugation of particular communities, of nature, and of narratives deemed to be inauthentic. In the hands of these recent writers, the vestiges of past forests in the space of the city—a forlorn tree, say, or a copse marooned in a cement sea—may well be indexical of ecological crisis, but they are not for this reason indexical of a mythic past whose reputed plenitude must be recuperated. More significantly, arboreal allusions in these urban fictions are not simply evocative of biotic loss, but also of cultural and affective loss. Memories rooted in particular sites may transport a person beyond the present, but without the person or the narrative losing sight of the multiple pasts that inform the present. The recollection of a beloved but now-transformed place may elicit mourning, but the very act of remembering refashions that remembered place, such as by recalling the accretions of cultural meaning over time that enfold the living. In post-1991 novels, arboreal indices register myriad, as opposed to singular (or singularly authorized), ways of articulating and coming to terms with cultural–ecological accretions like these.

In *The White Tiger*, for example, an upper-class school inspector in "a blue safari suit" visits a village and decides that the young Balram's intelligence deserves a more fitting moniker: "White Tiger." This is because, the inspector declares, "In any jungle," a white tiger is "the rarest of animals." "That's what you are," the inspector says, "in *this* jungle," by which he means a low-caste village "of thugs and idiots" (30; original emphasis). Balram goes on to prove the inspector right, but also to resist the ethos that produces this outlook. Throughout the book, the jungle's different designations evoke often conflicting outlooks that Adiga refracts through trees. A young Balram admires chandeliers, those talismans of wealth, that have been strung up on a banyan to be sold. The sacred tree aligns with—perhaps even justifies—his deep veneration for the ornate light fixtures, a reverence he thinks is both unique and common. The reader's perception of the arboreal image's associative resonance with Balram's inner conflict is a form of *darshanic* vision, in this case a vision that will, in turn, attune the reader to the disjunctive effects of the city on its inhabitants.

Mahajan's *The Association of Small Bombs* opens with a mise-en-scène of urban disjunction: a bomb blast has destroyed a Delhi market "square" but left intact its "massive trees" (4, 241). Though the trees had "[firmly] rooted" Lajpat Nagar square for many years, "their shadows dingy with commerce, their branches" weighted with "wares, their droppings of mulberry collected and sold," they "had gone all but unnoticed." They suffer as much as the human victims, for the blast has "loosened the [trees'] green gums ... and sent down a shower of leaves" upon the body-strewn ground. The leaves are like "shards" to an inconsolably sorrowful parent who has lost both his sons, and a tree's roots seem to him to be "trying desperately to hold on to sinking soil" (147). Mahajan's references to trees and leaves, jungles and forests, register different ways of seeing that readers must actively and continuously reassemble to consider their implications, just as the characters must do. These shards include ocular vision (the trees), emotional projection (Mr. Khurana's grieving outlook), individually self-conscious but mysteriously shared metaphor (Mansoor's and Mr. Khurana's independent fears of becoming a bomb), and otherwise unexplainable correspondences (the omniscient narrator and Mr. Khurana independently likening leaves to shards). Some of these fragments serve as metaphors of psychological trauma and introspection.[17] Equally, they call attention to the characters' desires to author, and authorize, their fates in a capricious world, much as writers and readers do. Yet these instances of *darshanic* vision refracted through forest imagery do the heavier lifting, I believe, of expanding our perspectival compass, particularly by troubling restrictive models of national affiliation reliant on tropes of marriage and family.

Indra Sinha's *Animal's People* similarly troubles such prescriptive affiliations through arboreal images. The novel describes a community of survivors of the 1984 Bhopal tragedy in which the American-owned Union Carbide pesticide factory leaked toxic gas that killed some 3,000 and injured tens of thousands. The self-named Animal, a young survivor who narrates his story some two decades after the disaster, invites us along on his surreptitious visits to the locked-up site, "the Kampani's factory." "Look inside," he says in his idiolect, "you see something strange, a forest is growing, tall grasses, bushes, trees, creepers that shoot sprays of flowers like fireworks" (29). Born just before the event, the gas having killed his mother and disfigured his spine, Animal walks on all fours. Here, in the abandoned factory site that he calls "my kingdom," he is able to climb the rusting edifice for lofty views of a compound in which "Mother Nature's trying to take back the land" (31). Shunned by everyone else for being "haunted by those who died"—and by some for its still-toxic chemicals—Animal relishes how "wild sandalwood trees," "herbs," and creepers are overtaking the plant's "rotting guts," pushing "up through the pipework" to reclaim the land (31). Despite feeling a spine-tingling "terror" whenever he visits, Animal returns frequently to this "enchanted forest" (32, 42). Where family is a corrosive agent in *The White Tiger* and a besieged, isolating presence in *The Association of Small Bombs*, Animal's adoptive family expands to encompass not only his human community, but also the still-toxic "jungle" of the Kampani (29). Animal's surprising perspective inverts the typically grim prognostications of toxic discourse.

Sinha, like Ghosh, Adiga, Roy, and Mahajan, blurs the boundaries that, under the sign of modernity, are meant to distinguish spheres of agency: human animal and nonhuman animal, natural and supernatural worlds, reality and illusion. This last ostensible division is, as I discussed in my introduction, a symptom of European modernity's insistence on referential meaning, of one-to-one correspondences between object and symbol, such as when colonial authorities believed the chapati circulating in northern India on the eve of the 1857 war was purely a signal to rebel and could not understand its multiple implications or polysemy. The British could not, in short, imagine alternative, coexisting ways of perceiving the world. Sinha wryly plays on this supposed reality-illusion divide by describing, for example, the effect on Animal following his ingestion of hallucinogens: He believes he is among "trees, thorns, dry grasses"—that is, a jungle (342). In a surreal, ironic take on the classical forest exile trope, Animal encounters a "strange … forest floor" in which the trash he was accustomed to in the Kampani grounds—"beedi wrappers," "plastic"—is replaced with "bent grasses" and "twigs" (343). He eventually perches himself on a "tree" from which he can "survey the moonlit jungles of my kingdom" (350), until finally, searching these "endless jungles" for "the city of god," he thinks he has entered "paradise" (353–4). The paradisal city he encounters is, in fact, his old community, which welcomes him "home." Concurrent with Animal's forest exile dream is, as he learns, a fire (which he may or may not have started) on the old factory grounds, which, like the Khandava Forest conflagration in the *Mahabharata*, seems to have spared nothing in its path—not even Animal's surrogate mother, who dies trying to save others. But the "charred jungle" that remains on the factory grounds "is pushing out green shoots" (365). The conventional figuring of the forest as maternal and pure is transformed through Animal's (and the reader's) unverifiable vision.

Pristine forests in these ways figure, in post-1991 works, as scattered, ironic indices of the desires of urban inhabitants and of the environments they inhabit. Trees signal local ecologies, but also point us to both narratorial double-sightedness—the authorial privilege of simultaneously seeing past, present, and future—and the limits of individual perception. We see this in Arundhati Roy's *The God of Small Things*, which she opens by describing Kerala's lush vegetation, its "immodest green," as characteristic of "boundaries" that "blur."[18] Trees in the novel, which are typically those found in plantation forests—rubber, mango, jackfruit—for this reason blur the lines between the living and the dead. The character Vellya Paapen, "hunting for a nutmeg tree to make a [healing] paste" for his sick wife, is startled by what he believes is the ghost of a "pedophile" Englishman haunting a forested house. Vellya "hurled his sickle" at the apparition and "pinned [it] to the trunk of a rubber tree." The irony of Vellya's proud story is that, as the narrator tells us here (and as the novel will go on to show), this very house, "the History House" in the shadow of the area's "old rubber trees," is the site of an event that will lead to Vellya Paapen's role in a tragedy governed by social and spatial hierarchies (35, 189–90). The ghost pinned to the rubber tree haunts both the novel's protagonists and the narrative by implicating the colonial past in the unfolding present. History is measured by the growth of "old" trees,[19] but also by the often violent uses to which they are put. Yet this violence, Roy emphasizes throughout her novel, is usually as invisible as a ghost, requiring nonempirical forms of detection.

Anuradha Roy, in her 2008 novel *An Atlas of Impossible Longing*,[20] riffs on this arboreal motif of intersecting human and supernatural temporalities by having a character explain, in 1954, his transition from the "timber trade" to "mica mining" (261). The man's story, which he recounts to the narrator, Mukunda, is notable for both its historical and forest settings and for its unintentionally ironic characterization of visionary and ocular perceptivity. He explains how he moved from working in an industry (logging) that is still, seven years after Britain's withdrawal, tinged with colonial exploitation to the appropriately modern, post-independence trade in mica. (The man contrasts Nehru's industrial "care" for the country with Britain's lack of care: echoing Nehru's own words, the man says that "Panditji ... is nation-building" with "temples to modern India, mines, dams" [261].) The event that he claims reconfirmed his change of profession is the arrival of a "spaceship" while he is "camping in the middle of wild land" to mine the mica. He and his "adivasi labour" do not know what this "strange" object is "flying in the sky." "Was it a problem of vision?" he asks himself. Or "a chariot from heaven"? The spaceship illuminates "everything ... in white light," while "all around us the forest had gone quiet" (262–3). "Nobody" else witnessed the phenomenon, he tells Mukunda, who declines to offer his opinion of it, either to the man or to the reader—which is somewhat surprising, given Mukunda's work as an appraiser of houses working on behalf of a city investor, with eyes that detect the smallest material details, from "ornate frames" on family "portraits" to "mould" on old "curtains" (211). But some days later, Mukunda begins to wonder if "the flaming trail of light" he and his childhood love, Bakul, "had seen in the sky years ago" was in fact "a spaceship" (273).

The entry of a spaceship into a forest encapsulates, in an exaggeratedly emblematic way, the intrusion of modern technology into "wild" forestland. The account needs no authorial comment for us to see its irony, for this is a novel in which trees and forests appear elsewhere in familiar ways, from "mango trees" and "grove[s]" uprooted from the grounds of a dilapidated house to please its new owners, to "sturdy little peepul trees" emerging from "cracks and crevices" in another home (97, 201). But the spaceship's unexpected arrival—unexpected both as a material object appearing before the mica merchant's eyes and as a motif in an otherwise historicist narrative—is shown to be no more "strange" or unaccountable than the technologies and habits that, as Roy describes, perpetuate environmental damage. This is one reason why Mukunda reflects that he and Bakul may have seen the spaceship years ago: although clearly expressive of his wish to redo his life and reunite with Bakul—"What if ... space-people had touched her and me with their magic that evening?"—the reflection is symptomatic of Mukunda's growing unease at preying on cash-strapped owners of "ruin[ed]" homes (211). The adult Mukunda begins to question his "predatory" "trade" (205, 293), a change of view that is ironically initiated by the story of the spaceship. Just as Mukunda's memories inform his changing adult vision, so do Roy's depictions of dead and dying trees, and of decaying wooden objects in ruined bungalows, condition our reading of Mukunda's story. He wishes to return to a time when, as a boy, he happily frequented the neighbor's garden, which seemed to him "more a wild forest," and in whose "large pond" he "stared" at a half-naked Bakul (130–1). The novel closes with the adult Mukunda reuniting with Bakul on the riverbank beside the family's old "ruined house," with "all kinds of rubbish—bits of wood, dead fish, a dented enamel bowl—strewn around the grounds" (301).

It turns out that "the problem of vision" that was voiced by the man telling the spaceship story is a phrase that sums up Mukunda's—and the reader's—predicament in an acquisitive and increasingly fractured world. Mukunda's struggle to reconcile his different motivations and environments reflects the commonly shared challenge (and often unwillingness) in our times to perceive the connections between seemingly unrelated objects and phenomena. The ability to perceive such interconnections distinguishes, as I have been arguing, the kind of *darshanic*, socially integrative vision practiced by Ghosh's Deeti and narratively reproduced by authors like Ghosh and Roy. The disjunctions that characterize late-twentieth and early twenty-first century globalization are, however, arguably more resistant to such integrative capabilities. This may be why the "shards" of trees blasted by a bomb in Mahajan's novel, or the pieces of "plastic" intermixed with "twigs" on a surreal "forest floor" in Sinha's, resemble the detritus of outdated, decaying houses in Roy's. At the same time, however, these disjunctive indices are visibly entwined in each writer's poetic rendering of inclusive double-sightedness.

Notes

Introduction: Imagining India's Forests

1. Gajendra Singh and G. S. Rawat, "Depletion of Oak (*Quercus spp.*) Forests in the Western Himalaya: Grazing, Fuelwood and Fodder Collection," in *Global Perspectives on Sustainable Forest Management*, edited by Clement Okia (InTech, 2012), 29–42, 30.
2. A. K. Ramanujan, "Afterword," in *The Interior Landscape: Classical Tamil Love Poems*, translated and edited by A. K. Ramanujan (NYRB Poets, 2014), 79–102, 89–90; Meera Baindur, *Nature in Indian Philosophy and Cultural Traditions* (Springer India, 2015), 111–12; David Shulman, *Tamil: A Biography* (Harvard University Press, 2016), 50–4.
3. Jennifer Wenzel, "Epic Struggles over India's Forests in Mahasweta Devi's Short Fiction," *Alif: Journal of Comparative Poetics*, no. 18 (1994), 127–58, 130.
4. Paul Robbins, "Policing and Erasing the Global/Local Border: Rajasthani Foresters and the Narrative Ecology of Modernization," in *Regional Modernities: The Cultural Politics of Development in India*, edited by K. Sivaramakrishnan and Arun Agrawal (Stanford University Press, 2003), 377–403, 378.
5. Ashis Nandy, *The Intimate Enemy: Loss and Recovery of Self under Colonialism* (Oxford University Press, 1983), xv.
6. Ibid., xii.
7. Elias Canetti, *Crowds and Power* (Farrar, Straus and Giroux, 1984), 84.
8. Peter Wohlleben, *The Hidden Life of Trees: What They Feel, How They Communicate—Discoveries from a Secret World*, translated by Jane Billinghurst (Penguin India, 2016), xxii–xxiii.
9. Mary Douglas quoted in Canetti, *Crowds and Power*, 129.
10. Canetti, *Crowds and Power*, 84.
11. Douglas, quoted in Canetti, *Crowds and Power*, 129–30.
12. Robert Pogue Harrison, *Forests: The Shadow of Civilization* (University of Chicago Press, 1993), 1.
13. Ibid., 8.
14. Ibid., x.
15. Ibid., 7.
16. Ibid., xi, 1.
17. Keith Thomas, *Man and the Natural World: Changing Attitudes in England, 1500-1800*, new ed. (Penguin, 1991), 193.
18. Fredrik Albritton Jonsson, "Chapter 4: Adam Smith in the Forest," in *The Social Lives of the Forests: The Past, Present, and Future of Woodland Resurgence*, edited by Susanna Hecht, Kathleen Morrison, and Christine Padoch (University of Chicago Press, 2014), 45–54, 47–8.
19. Harrison, *Forests*, 169.
20. Ibid., x.
21. Ibid., 246.
22. Ibid., 49.

23. See Thomas, *Man and the Natural World*, 194; Harrison, *Forests*, 169; and Online Etymology Dictionary, "Forest," accessed May 12, 2021, https://www.etymonline.com/search?q=forest.
24. Thomas, *Man and the Natural World*, 194.
25. Harrison, *Forests*, 28.
26. George Lakoff and Mark Johnson, *Metaphors We Live By* (University of Chicago Press, 2003), 40. Also see Michelle Balaev, *The Nature of Trauma in American Novels* (Northwestern University Press, 2012), 39.
27. Kalidasa, *Abhijnanashakuntalam: The Recognition of Shakuntala*, translated and edited by Vinay Dharwadker (Penguin India, 2016), 291.
28. This is noted, for example, on one of many websites selling this and other traditional oils: Ananda Apothecary, accessed May 31, 2022, https://milled.com/ananda-apothecary/what-really-is-a-pure-essential-oil-74qJEQzSHY2uei9x.
29. Kalidasa, *Shakuntala*, 291.
30. Lakoff and Johnson, *Metaphors We Live By*, 146.
31. Ibid., 29.
32. See Ranajit Guha, *Elementary Aspects of Peasant Insurgency in Colonial India* (Oxford University Press, 1992).
33. Nicholas Blomley, "Making Private Property: Enclosure, Common Right and the Work of Hedges," *Rural History* 18, 1 (2007), 1–21, 2.
34. Ibid., 4.
35. Siraj Ahmed, *Archaeology of Babel: The Colonial Foundation of the Humanities* (Stanford University Press, 2017), 7.
36. See, for example, Romila Thapar, "Perceiving the Forest: Early India," in *Environmental History of India Vol. 1: From Ancient Times to the Colonial Period: A Reader*, edited by Mahesh Rangarajan and K. Sivaramakrishnan (Permanent Black, 2012), 105–25; Philip Lutgendorf, "City, Forest, and Cosmos: Ecological Perspectives from the Sanskrit Epics," in *Hinduism and Ecology: The Intersection of Earth, Sky and Water*, edited by Christopher Key Chapple and Mary Evelyn Tucker (Oxford University Press, 2000), 245–68; and Thomas Parkhill, *The Forest Setting in Hindu Epics: Princes, Sages, Demons* (Edwin Mellen Press, 1995); David Arnold, *The Problem of Nature: Environment, Culture and European Expansion* (Blackwell Publishers, 1996).
37. Sheldon Pollock, "Introduction," in Valmiki, *Ramayana Book Three: The Forest*, vol. 15, translated by Sheldon Pollock (Clay Sanskrit Library, 2006), 13–34, 17–18.
38. R. Parthasarathy, "Postscript," in *The Cilappatikaram: The Tale of an Anklet* (Penguin India, [1993] 2004), 279–369, 297.
39. Philip D. Curtin, *Cross-Cultural Trade in World History* (Cambridge University Press, 1984), 149.
40. Ibid., 154.
41. T. B. Macaulay, "'Minute' on Indian Education," February 2, 1835, accessed April 28, 2021, http://www.columbia.edu/itc/mealac/pritchett/00generallinks/macaulay/txt_minute_education_1835.html.
42. Ibid.
43. Bankim Chandra Chattopadhyay's most authoritative (and most recent) translator, Julius J. Lipner, whose translation I rely on, explains his choice of the anglicized Chatterji spelling, which is the one the author used in his lifetime when writing in English. See Lipner's introduction to his edited translation of Bankimcandra Chatterji: Julius J. Lipner, "Introduction," *Anandamath, or The Sacred Brotherhood* (Oxford University Press, [1882] 2005), 5, note 8.

44. Dipesh Chakrabarty, *Provincializing Europe: Postcolonial Thought and Historical Difference* (Princeton University Press, 2000), 32.
45. Sudipta Kaviraj, *The Imaginary Institution of India* (School of African and Oriental Studies, 1991), 41–64, 50.
46. Ibid., 245.
47. Both quoted in Anne Norton, *Bloodrites of the Post-Structuralists: Word, Flesh, and Revolution* (Routledge, 2002), 140.
48. Both quoted in Siraj Ahmed, *The Stillbirth of Capital: Enlightenment Writing and Colonial India* (Stanford University Press, 2012), 8–9.
49. See, for example, Meera Nanda, *Prophets Facing Backwards: Postmodern Critiques of Science and Hindu Nationalism in India* (Rutgers University Press, 2003); Subir Sinha, Shubhra Gururani, and Brian Greenberg, "The 'New Traditionalist' Discourse of Indian Environmentalism," *Journal of Peasant Studies* 24, 3 (1997), 65–99; and Emma Mawdsley, "Hindu Nationalism, Neo-Traditionalism and Environmental Discourses in India," *Geoforum* 37 (2006), 380–90.
50. Chakrabarty, *Provincializing Europe*, 83.
51. Ibid.
52. Hamish Dalley, *The Postcolonial Historical Novel: Realism, Allegory, and the Representation of Contested Pasts* (Palgrave Macmillan, 2014), 28.
53. Walter Benjamin, "Thesis XVII, Theses on the Philosophy of History," in *Illuminations*, translated by Hannah Arendt (Harcourt, Brace & World, 1968), 264.
54. Albert Atken, "Peirce's Theory of Signs," *Stanford Encyclopedia of Philosophy*, November 15, 2010, accessed July 30, 2020, https://plato.stanford.edu/entries/peirce-semiotics/#SigVeh; A. K. Ramanujan, "Three Hundred *Ramayanas*: Five Examples and Three Thoughts on Translation," in *Many Ramayanas: The Diversity of a Narrative Tradition in South Asia*, edited by Paula Richman (University of California Press, 1991), 45; and Eduardo Kohn, *How Forests Think: Toward an Anthropology Beyond the Human* (University of California Press, 2013), 8, 31, 59.
55. Ramanujan, "Three Hundred *Ramayanas*," 45.
56. Ranajit Guha, *Elementary Aspects of Peasant Insurgency in Colonial India*, 240.
57. Chakrabarty, *Provincializing Europe*, 14.
58. Dalley, *The Postcolonial Historical Novel*, 28.
59. Chakrabarty, *Provincializing Europe*, 90.
60. Ranajit Guha, *Elementary Aspects of Peasant Insurgency in Colonial India*, 245.
61. For a nuanced discussion of what the modern European worldview entails, see Chakrabarty, introduction to *Provincializing Europe*, 3–23.
62. Gayatri Chakravorty Spivak, *A Critique of Postcolonial Reason: Toward a History of the Vanishing Present* (Harvard University Press, 1999), 382, 384.
63. Chakrabarty, *Provincializing Europe*
64. Diana L. Eck, *Darśan: Seeing the Divine Image in India*, 3rd ed. (Columbia University Press, 1998), 9.
65. John Berger, *Ways of Seeing* (Penguin, 1990).
66. Chakrabarty, *Provincializing Europe*, 178.
67. Ibid.
68. AmitavGhosh, *Sea of Poppies* (Penguin, 2008), 3.
69. Ibid., 5.
70. Ibid., 3.
71. Frantz Fanon, *The Wretched of the Earth*, translated by Richard Philcox (Grove Press, [1961] 2004), 123–4.

72. Ngũgĩ wa Thiong'o, *Petals of Blood* (Heinemann, 1977), 11.
73. Gabriel García Márquez, *One Hundred Years of Solitude*, translated by Gregory Rabassa (Harper Perennial, [1970] 2006), 11.
74. Tayeb Salih, *Season of Migration to the North*, translated by Denys Johnson-Davies (New York Review of Books, [1969] 2009), 32. Also see 78 and 120.
75. Harrison, *Forests*, 55.
76. Bankimcandra Chatterji, *Anandamath, or The Sacred Brotherhood*, translated and edited by Julius J. Lipner (Oxford University Press, [1882] 2005), 229; and see Sudipta Kaviraj, *The Unhappy Consciousness: Bankimchandra Chattopadhyay and the Formation of Nationalist Discourse in India* (Oxford University Press, 1995), 102–3.
77. See, for example, Tapan Raychaudhuri, *Europe Reconsidered: Perceptions of the West in Nineteenth-Century Bengal* (Oxford University Press, 1988); and Priya Joshi, *In Another Country: Colonialism, Culture, and the English Novel in India* (Columbia University Press, 2002).
78. Charles Mann, *1491: New Revelations of the Americas Before Columbus* (Vintage, 2006), 304; Beth Fowkes Tobin, *Colonizing Nature: The Tropics in British Arts and Letters, 1760–1820* (University of Pennsylvania Press, 2004), xv, 6.
79. See Katie Trumpener, *Bardic Nationalism: The Romantic Novel and the British Empire* (Princeton University Press, 1997); Ian Duncan, *Scott's Shadow: The Novel in Romantic Edinburgh* (Princeton University Press, 2007); and Tobin, Colonizing Nature.
80. Gustave Flaubert, quoted in Raymond Schwab, *The Oriental Renaissance: Europe's Rediscovery of India and the East, 1680–1880*, translated by Gene Patterson-Black and Victor Reinking (Columbia University Press, 1984), 417.
81. Bankim's "acceptance" of the British contention that "free trade … had increased India's wealth," despite all evidence to the contrary, is a case in point, as Raychaudhuri observes in *Europe Reconsidered*, 142–3.
82. See for example Chakrabarty, *Provincializing Europe*, 155, 156; and Tanika Sarkar, *Hindu Wife, Hindu Nation: Community, Religion, and Cultural Nationalism* (Indiana University Press, 2002), 141.
83. Harrison, *Forests*, 201.
84. Ibid., 175, 231.
85. Diana Donald, *Picturing Animals in Britain, 1750–1850* (The Paul Mellon Center for Studies in British Art and Yale University Press, 2007), 11.
86. Bernard Picart, *Cérémonies et coutumes religieuses de tous les peuples du monde*, 9 volumes (1723–43), translated anonymously as *Ceremonies and Religious Customs of the Various Nations of the Known World* (Claude du Bosc, 1786). Archive.org: accessed May 22, 2021, https://archive.org/details/ceremoniesreligi05pica/page/n5/mode/2up.
87. Srinivas Aravamudan, *Tropicopolitans: Colonialism and Agency, 1688–1804* (Duke University Press, 1999), 200.
88. Ibid.; also see Sara Suleri Goodyear, *The Rhetoric of English India* (University of Chicago Press, 1992), 24–49.
89. Romita Ray, *Under the Banyan Tree: Relocating the Picturesque in British India* (Paul Mellon Centre for Studies in British Art, 2003), 186.
90. Robert Southey, *The Curse of Kehama*, in *The Poets and Poetry of the Nineteenth Century: Robert Southey to Percy Bysshe Shelley*, edited by Alfred H. Myles (George Routledge & Sons, 1905), 25–34, 30–1.
91. George Henry Noehden, "Account of the Banyan-Tree, or Ficus Indica, as Found in the Ancient Greek and Roman Authors," *Transactions of the Royal Asiatic Society of Great Britain and Ireland* 1, no. 1 (1824), 119–32, 121.

92. David L. Haberman, *People Trees: Worship of Trees in Northern India* (Oxford University Press, 2013), 165.
93. Ray, *Under the Banyan*, 185.
94. Ibid., 194.
95. Ibid., 99; also see David Arnold, *The Tropics and the Traveling Gaze: India, Landscape, and Science, 1800–1856* (University of Washington Press, 2014), 136.
96. Romita Ray, "Inscribing Asymmetry: Johann Zoffany's Banyan and 'The Extension of Knowledge,'" *South Asian Studies* 27, no. 2 (2011), 185–98, 185.
97. Priya Satia, *Empire of Guns: The Violent Making of the Industrial Revolution* (Penguin, 2018), 10, 12, 166; Ahmed, *Stillbirth of Capital*, 6, 26.
98. Harrison, *Forests*, 164–5.
99. Ibid., 165.
100. Ibid., 211.
101. Partha Chatterjee, *Nationalist Thought and the Colonial World: A Derivative Discourse?* (University of Minnesota Press, 1986), 16 and passim.
102. Harrison speaks generally of "civilization" in much of his study, but at times qualifies this as "Western" (*Forests*, 133). It is important to recall, however, that "Western" and "Eastern" were colonial coinages used to reinforce Europe's self-superiority. See Donald Moore, "Beyond Blackmail: Multivalent Modernities and the Cultural Politics of Development in India," in *Regional Modernities: The Cultural Politics of Development in India*, edited by K. Sivaramakrishnan and Arun Agrawal (Stanford University Press, 2003), 165–214, 176.
103. Bruce Robbins, "The Politics of Theory," *Social Text* 6 (Winter, 1987–88): 3–18, 15.
104. Jack Zipes, *The Brothers Grimm: From Enchanted Forests to the Modern World*, 2nd ed., reprint (Palgrave Macmillan, [1988] 2022), 68.
105. Ibid.
106. Ibid.
107. Johann Gottfried Herder, quoted in Richard H. Grove, *Green Imperialism: Colonial Expansion, Tropical Island Edens and the Origins of Environmentalism, 1600–1860* (Cambridge University Press, 1996), 370.
108. Willhelm Halbfass, *India and Europe: An Essay in Philosophical Understanding* (SUNY Press, 1988), 72.
109. Jon Stewart, *Hegel's Interpretation of the Religions of the World: The Logic of the Gods* (Oxford University Press, 2018), 115.
110. Gauri Viswanathan, *Masks of Conquest: Literary Study and British Rule in India* (Columbia University Press, 1989), 5–6.
111. Rosinka Chaudhuri, "'Young India: A Bengal Eclogue': Or Meat-Eating, Race, and Reform in a Colonial Poem," *Interventions: International Journal of Postcolonial Studies* 2, no. 3 (2000), 424–41, 433.
112. See, for example, Chen Tzoref-Ashkenazi, "India and the Identity of Europe: The Case of Friedrich Schlegel," *Journal of the History of Ideas* 67, no. 4 (October 2006), 713–34.
113. Ibid., 724. Vestiges of this cultured harmony were, they thought, alive in the Volk, offering a reminder of national origins tied to a vague notion of primordial Indo-Aryans. We know all too well that the results of this idealism would lead to the tragedy of post-Weimar German racism. In the 1850s, Wilhelm Heinrich Riehl, whose ideas would seed ethnocentric myth, trumpeted that in Europe, Germany alone preserved "real" forests and "ancient Germanic sylvan liberty." Though a folklorist who celebrated the Volk, Riehl treated them as innocent

naïfs who needed supervision of the "civilized" aristocracy. Declaring that forests alone provided the "soil" for raising an "aristocratic [race]" sufficient to "vigorous nationalism," Riehl advocated, in effect, a form of colonial rule for his homeland. Kaiser Wilhelm would use these ideas to underwrite his policy of Ober Ost, effectively a colonial takeover of Eastern Europe in 1914, at the outset of the First World War. (Ironically, German occupying forces were startled to find that Eastern Europe had the truly "primeval forests," in contrast to Germany's "managed woods.") See Wilhelm Heinrich Riehl, "Field and Forest" (1853), translated by Frances H. King, in *The German Classics of the Nineteenth and Twentieth Centuries: Masterpieces of German Literature, Vol. VIII* (Project Gutenberg, [1914] 2004), accessed April 19, 2022. http://www.gutenberg.org/cache/epub/12573/pg12573.html; and Vejas G. Liulevicius, *War Land on the Eastern Front: Culture, National Identity, and German Occupation in World War I* (Cambridge University Press, 2000), 27, 45, 59.

114. Ajay Skaria, "Gandhi's Politics: Liberalism and the Question of the Ashram," *South Atlantic Quarterly* 101, no. 4 (Fall 2002), 955–86, 961.
115. See, for example, Brian K. Smith, "Classifying Animals and Humans in Ancient India," *Man* (New Series) 26, no. 3 (September 1991), 527–48.
116. Rabindranath Tagore, *Glimpses of Bengal* (Macmillan & Co., 1921), 145.
117. Lipner, "Introduction," 98.
118. Don Handelman and David Shulman, *Śiva in the Forest of Pines: An Essay on Sorcery and Self-Knowledge* (Oxford University Press, 2004), 2.
119. Ibid.
120. A. K. Ramanujan, "Afterword," in *The Oxford India Ramanujan*, edited by Molly Daniels-Ramanujan (Oxford University Press, 2004), 231–97, 249.
121. Ibid., 249–50.
122. See Sumathi Ramaswamy, *Passions of the Tongue: Language Devotion in Tamil India, 1891–1970* (University of California Press, 1997), 90; also see Thapar, "Perceiving the Forest," 9, on the forest's role in such sacred geography.
123. Ibid.
124. Lutgendorf, "City, Forest and Cosmos," passim; Parkhill, *The Forest Setting in Hindu Epics*, vii–viii.
125. Ashok K. Banker, *Prince of Ayodhya: Book One of the Ramayana* (Penguin, 2005), 19.
126. Brett M. Bennett, "The El Dorado of Forestry: The Eucalyptus in India, South Africa, and Thailand, 1850–2000," *IRSH* 55 (2010 Supplement), 27–50, 41–5.
127. Ibid., 40.
128. Ibid., 41.
129. Vandana Shiva, "Reductionist Science as Epistemological Violence," in *Science, Hegemony and Violence: A Requiem for Modernity*, edited by Ashis Nandy (Oxford University Press, 1988), 232–56, 245.
130. Bennett, "The El-Dorado of Forestry," 41–2; and see Ramachandra Guha, *The Unquiet Woods: Ecological Change and Peasant Resistance in the Himalaya*, expanded ed. (University of California Press, 2000), 56.
131. Ibid., 29, 33.
132. Grove, *Green Imperialism*, 6.
133. Mahesh Rangarajan, "Forest as Faunal Enclave: Endangerment, Ecology, and Exclusion in India," in *The Social Lives of Forests: Past, Present, and Future of Woodland Resurgence*, edited by S. B. Hecht, K. D. Morrison, and C. Padoch (University of Chicago Press, 2014), 192–8, 192.

134. Jawaharlal Nehru, *The Discovery of India* (Oxford University Press, [1946] 1989), 59, 189, 270.
135. V. D. Savarkar, quoted in Diana M. Eck, *India: A Sacred Geography* (Three Rivers Press, 2012), 98.
136. Rajah Rammohun Roy, *Exposition of the Practical Operation of the Judicial and Revenue Systems of India, and of the General Character and Condition of Its Native Inhabitants, as Submitted in Evidence to the Authorities in England* (Smith, Elder & Co., 1832), v.
137. Sumathi Ramaswamy *The Goddess and the Nation: Mapping Mother India* (Duke University Press, 2010), 142.
138. Quoted in Ramaswamy, *The Goddess and the Nation*, 118.
139. David Hewitt calls Scott's "encounter with German Romanticism" a "transformative experience." David Hewitt, "Scott, Sir Walter (1771–1832)," in *Dictionary of National Biography* (n.p., [2004] 2008), accessed February 4, 2022, https://doi-org.libpublic3.library.isu.edu/10.1093/ref:odnb/24928.
140. See Dalley, *The Postcolonial Historical Novel*, 26.
141. Ibid., 22–33.
142. Ibid., 25.
143. Ibid., 26.
144. Ibid.
145. Sir Walter Scott, *Waverley; or, 'Tis Sixty Years Since* (Adam and Charles Black, 1897), 105.
146. Georg Lukács, quoted in Joshi, *In Another Country*, 158.
147. Joshi, *In Another Country*, 159, 165.
148. Dalley, *The Postcolonial Historical Novel*, 28–9, 37.
149. Joshi, *In Another Country*, 162. Like Dalley, Joshi argues that both colonial and postcolonial Indian novels have often reconceived the past to effect "dislocation to the discourse of historiography itself, defamiliarizing it and its authority upon the referential illusion" (261).
150. Ian Ferris, "'Before Our Eyes': Romantic Historical Fiction and the Apparitions of Reading," *Representations* 121, no. 1 (Winter 2013), 60–84, 76–7.
151. Ibid.
152. Pollock, *Ramayana, Book Three*, 83.
153. S. Mahdihassan, "Three Important Vedic Grasses," *Indian Journal of History of Science* 22, no. 4 (1987), 286–91, 286.
154. David Lee, "The Natural History of the *Ramayana*," in *Hinduism and Ecology: The Intersection of Earth and Sky*, edited by Chapple and Tucker (Harvard University Press, 2000), 245–68, 250.
155. Ibid., 249–51.
156. Ibid., 251.
157. Ibid.
158. Ibid.
159. Ibid., 252.
160. Michael R. Dove, "The Dialectical History of 'Jungle' in Pakistan: An Examination of the Relationship between Nature and Culture," *Journal of Anthropological Research* 48, no. 3 (Autumn 1992), 231–53.
161. Dieter Demske et al., "Record of Vegetation, Climate Change, Human Impact and Retting of Hemp in Garhwal Himalaya (India) During the Past 4600 Years," *The Holocene* 26, no. 10 (2016), 1661–75, 1667.

162. Ibid.
163. Ibid., 1667, 1670.
164. Raymond Williams, *The Country and the City* (Oxford University Press, 1975), passim; Thomas, *Man and the Natural World*, 250–2.
165. Homer, *The Odyssey*, translated by Emily Wilson (W. W. Norton, 2018), 182.
166. Classifying India's literary heritage in English is challenging, in part because English and Sanskrit (like English and Tamil) terms do not mesh well and also because classical genres, so-called by modern scholars, are more expansive. Some commonly used generic descriptors to which I will sometimes refer include the following: *kavyas*, elaborate works in Sanskrit, Tamil, and other languages, written by court poets from ancient to medieval times; *puranas*, legendary tales evoking locales across India that date from ancient to modern times; epic, or *mahakavya* (literally, great poem), well-known epic stories that include the *Ramayana* and *Mahabharata*; and classical Sanskrit drama, encompassing Kalidasa's medieval era, starting in about the fifth century CE and lasting several centuries. Also see, to name only a few among many, Shulman, *Tamil: A Biography*; Ramanujan, "Three Hundred *Ramayanas*"; and Philip Lutgendorf, "The Secret Life of Ramchandra of Ayodhya," in *Many Ramayanas: The Diversity of a Narrative Tradition in South Asia*, edited by Paula Richman (University of California Press, 1991), 217–34.
167. A. R. Venkatachalapathy, *The Province of the Book: Scholars, Scribes, and Scribblers in Colonial Tamilnadu* (Permanent Black, 2012), 140–1, 147.
168. Ibid., 141, 159.
169. Ibid., 159–60.
170. See Vasudha Dalmia, *Hindu Pasts: Women, Religion, Histories* (SUNY Press, 2017), 110–38.
171. Partha Chatterjee, *The Nation and Its Fragments: Colonial and Postcolonial Histories* (Princeton University Press, 1994), 95.
172. Peter Morey and Alex Tickell, "Introduction," in *Alternative Indias: Writing, Nation and Communalism*, edited by Morey and Tickell (Rodopi, 2005), ix–xxxviii, xii–xiii; and Dalmia, *Hindu Pasts*, 125.
173. Dalmia, *Hindu Pasts*, 110.
174. Chatterjee, *The Nation and Its Fragments*, 147.
175. See Christian Lee Novetzke, *The Quotidian Revolution: Vernacularization, Religion, and the Premodern Public Sphere in India* (Columbia University Press, 2016), 6–7.
176. Phillip B. Zarrilli, *Kathakali Dance-Drama: Where Gods and Demons Come to Play* (Routledge, 1999), 106.
177. D. Appukuttam Nair and K. Ayappa Paniker, quoted in Zarrilli, *Kathakali Dance-Drama*, 53.
178. Zarrilli, *Kathakali Dance-Drama*, 195.
179. Brigid Lowe, quoted in James Wood, *How Fiction Works* (Picador, 2008), 237.
180. Ursula K. Heise, "The Hitchhiker's Guide to Ecocriticism," *PMLA* 121, no. 2 (March 2006), 503–16, 511–12.
181. Kohn, *How Forests Think*, 9.
182. Ibid., 9, 59.
183. Pierre Bourdieu, *Outline of a Theory of Practice* (Cambridge, 1977), 38, 79, 89.
184. C. A. Bayly, *Indian Society and the Making of the British Empire (The New Cambridge History of India)*, rev. ed. (Cambridge University Press, 1990), 138–9, 148.

185. Pallavi V. Das, "Railway Fuel and Its Impact on the Forests in Colonial India: The Case of the Punjab, 1860–1884," *Modern Asian Studies* 47, no. 4 (July 2013), 1283–309, 1286, 1307–8.
186. Quoted in Gregory Allen Barton, *Empire Forestry and the Origins of Environmentalism* (Cambridge University Press, 2002), 55.
187. Tagore, Rabindranath, "Santiniketan Song," Tagoreweb.in, accessed November 27, 2020, https://www.tagoreweb.in/Verses/collected-poems-and-plays-197/she-is-our-own-2609.
188. John Stratton Hawley, *At Play with Krishna: Pilgrimage Dramas from Brindavan* (Princeton University Press, 2014), 8.
189. Ibid., 50.
190. Ibid.
191. Hemant Kumar Das, "The Origin of Oriya Jatra," *Indian Literature* 50, no. 1 (231) (January–February 2006), 166–71, 169.
192. Jayadeva, *Gita Govinda*, translated by Colin John Holcombe (Ocaso Press, 2008), 3, 9.
193. Eck, *India: A Sacred Geography*, 372–3.
194. Quoted in Bruce M. Sullivan, "Chapter 10: Theology and Ecology at the Birthplace of Krishna," in *Purifying the Earthly Mother of God: Religion and Ecology in Hindu India*, edited by Lance E. Nelson (SUNY Press, 1998), 247–68, 248.
195. See Parkhill, *The Forest Setting in Hindu Epics*, passim; and Ray, "Inscribing Asymmetry."
196. Thapar, "Perceiving the Forest," 106 and passim.
197. Sugata Ray, *Climate Change and the Art of Devotion: Geoaesthetics in the Land of Krishna, 1550–1850* (University of Washington Press, 2019), 99–100.
198. Benedict Anderson, *Imagined Communities: Reflections on the Origin and Spread of Nationalism* (Verso, [1983] 2006), 12.
199. Baindur, *Nature in Indian Philosophy and Cultural Traditions*, 111.
200. *Simsapa* is likely another name for *shisham*, or Indian rosewood (*Dalbergia sissoo*), while the grove itself is said to have been on the fringe of the forest. See, for example, "*Dalbergia sissoo*, Shisham Tree Uses, Research, Side Effects," accessed March 20, 2021, https://www.easyayurveda.com/2015/10/15/dalbergia-sissoo-sisham-shimshapa/.
201. Chakrabarty, *Provincializing Europe*, 142.
202. See Ajay Skaria, *Hybrid Histories: Forests, Frontiers and Wildness in Western India* (Oxford University Press, 1999), vii.
203. Anand Vaidya, "*Woh Jungle Hamara Hai*," *Seminar* 690 (February 2017), 68–71, 70.
204. Ibid.
205. Sudipta Kaviraj, "The Imaginary Institution of India," in *Subaltern Studies VII: Writings on South Asian History and Society*, edited by Partha Chatterjee and Gyanendra Pandey (Oxford University Press, 1993), 1–39, passim.
206. Vaidya, "*Woh Jungle Hamara Hai*," 69.
207. For a discussion of British labeling and the nationalist response in colonial India, see Gyanendra Pandey, *The Construction of Communalism in Colonial North India* (Oxford University Press, 1992), 110–15. Also see Partha Chatterjee on urbanites' disdain for the "peasantry": Chatterjee, *The Nation and Its Fragments*, 158.
208. Ramaswamy, *The Goddess and the Nation*, 123, 304 n16.
209. Ibid., 52; and see 9.
210. Kathleen D. Morrison, and Mark T. Lycett, "Constructing Nature: Socionatural Histories of an Indian Forest," in *The Social Lives of Forests: Past, Present, and Future*

of Woodland Resurgence, edited by Susanna B. Hecht, Kathleen D. Morrison, and Christine Padoch (University of Chicago Press, 2014), 148–60, 151.
211. Describing the literary genre called *Mahatmya*, which describes local myths eulogizing a deity and place, Anne Feldhaus informs us that even the *Mahatmyas* of the Deccan that ostensibly address the region's holy rivers actually have more to say about the forests through which the rivers flow. The Brahmin authors also express "a grudging admiration" of the inhabitants of these forests. Anne Feldhaus, "The Image of the Forest in the *Mahatmyas* of the Rivers of the Deccan," in *The History of Sacred Places in India as Reflected in Traditional Literature: Papers on Pilgrimage in South Asia*, edited by Hans Bakker (E. J. Brill, 1990), 90–102, 99.
212. Matthew Edney, *Mapping and Empire: The Geographical Construction of British India, 1765–1843* (University of Chicago Press, 1997), 25.
213. Mahatma Jyotirao Phule, *Slavery (In the Civilised British Government Under the Cloak of Brahmanism)*, translated by P. G. Patil (Government of Maharashtra, [1885] 1991), 17.
214. See Ramaswamy, *The Goddess and the Nation*, 140.
215. Vandana Shiva is among the notable environmental activists who have found both personal and pedagogical inspiration in Tagore's essay, as she says in her 2013 essay, "Everything I Need to Know I Learned in the Forest," *The NAMTA [North American Montessori Teachers' Association] Journal* 38, no. 1 (Winter 2013), 273–6, 276.
216. Rabindranath Tagore, quoted in Ramaswamy, *The Goddess and the Nation*. A poem by Tagore about Bengal, "Amar Sonar Bangla" (My Bengal of gold), became another national anthem, that of Bangladesh, in 1972. Addressing Bengal as "Mother," he lyricizes the landscape as, for example, a "sari's border … spread round roots of banyan trees, on the bank of rivers." Quoted in Ramaswamy, *The Goddess and the Nation*, 137–8.
217. Rabindranath Tagore, "The Religion of the Forest," in *Creative Unity* (Macmillan & Co., 1922), 45–68. Note that the Sanskrit word "tapovan" translates roughly to "Forest of Spiritual Retreat."
218. Tagore, "A Vision of History" (1903), reprinted in *Journal of Studies in History & Culture*, accessed June 30, 2020, http://jshc.org/a-vision-of-indias-history/.
219. Ibid.
220. Tagore, "The Religion of the Forest."
221. Rabindranath Tagore, "From *My Reminiscences*," in *Tagore: An Anthology*, edited by Krishna Dutta and Andrew Robinson (St. Martin's Press, 1997), 55–83, 58–9.
222. Hans Harder, "Nostalgia and Autobiographies: Reading Rabindranath Tagore's *Jībansmr[i]ti* (1912) and *Chelebelā* (1937)," in *HerStory: Historical Scholarship between South Asia and Europe: Festschrift in Honour of Gita Dharampal-Frick*, edited by Rafael Klöber and Manju Ludwig (XAsia Ebooks, 2018), 189–209, 200.
223. The representation of nation as feminine by male nationalists is, of course, common to many countries. Annette Kolodny commented some time ago that (white) American revolutionaries used the image of the new nation's "feminine landscape threatened by invading British" soldiers as "a rallying cry for patriotism," and that America's "pastoral impulses"—primarily farmland—promised European immigrants "a return to primal harmony within the bosom of maternal landscape"— in effect, a "rebirth." Annette Kolodny, *The Lay of the Land: Metaphor as Experience and History in American Life and Letters* (University of North Carolina Press, 1975), 26. India's numerous, long-standing regional cultures and languages meant that while Bankim and other (mostly male) Indian writers similarly conceived of

224. Tagore, "From *My Reminiscences*," 388–9.
225. Rabindranath Tagore, "Letter to Prashanta Chandra Mahalanobis," in *Tagore: An Anthology*, edited by Krishna Dutta and Andrew Robinson (St. Martin's Press, [1921] 1997), 176–7.
226. Tagore, "A Vision of History."
227. Ibid.
228. Skaria, *Hybrid Histories*, vii–viii.
229. Eck, *India: A Sacred Geography*.
230. Ibid., 8.
231. Ibid., 17.
232. Ibid., 57, 59.
233. Richard Eaton, quoted in Eck, *India: A Sacred Geography*, 89.
234. Eck, *India: A Sacred Geography*, 90.
235. Amir Khusrau, quoted in *India as Seen by Amir Khusrau*, edited by R. Nath and Faiyaz "Gwaliori" (HRD, [1933] 1981), 35, 49.
236. Francis Buchanan-Hamilton, *A Journey from Madras through the Countries of Mysore, Canara and Malabar Performed Under the Orders of the Most Noble the Marquis Wellesley, Governor General of India*, vol. 1 of 3 (W. Bulmer & Co., 1807), 201–6.
237. Hasan Nizami in his thirteenth-century *Taj al-ma'asir* (or *Taj ul-Ma'athir*), quoted in Sunil Sharma, *Amir Khusraw: The Poet of Sufis and Sultans* (Oneworld, 2005), 10.
238. Amir Khusrau, *The Book of Amir Khusrau: Selected Poems and The Tale of the Four Dervishes*, translated by Paul Smith (New Humanity Books, 2015), 116, 120–1.
239. Ibid., 308.
240. Ibid., 54.
241. Sufism and the *bhakti* movement both influenced the founding of Sikhism, whose sacred book the *Guru Granth Sahib* contains poetry from these nonhierarchical movements. For example, *bhakti* singing performances, called *kirtans*, are open to all. See Francesca Orsini and Katherine Butler Schofield, "Introduction," in *Tellings and Texts: Music, Literature and Performance in North India*, edited by F. Orsini and K. B. Schofield (Open Book Publishers, 2015), 1–27, 23.
242. Muzaffar Alam, "World Enough and Time: Religious Strategy and Historical Imagination in an Indian Sufi Tale," in *Tellings and Texts: Music, Literature and Performance in North India*, edited by Francesca Orsini and Katherine Butler Schofield (Open Book Publishers, 2015), 107–36, 108, 125.
243. Ibid., 108.
244. Allison Busch, "Listening for the Context: Tuning in to the Reception of *Riti* Poetry," in *Tellings and Texts: Music, Literature and Performance in North India*, edited by F. Orsini and K. B. Schofield (Open Book Publishers, 2015), 249–82, 259.
245. Amrit Rai, quoted in Busch, "Listening for the Context," 259–60.
246. Ibid., 260.
247. Busch remarks on the text's "performative features," "Listening for the Context," 260. Also see Pasha Khan, "What Storytellers Were Worth in Mughal India," 575; *Comparative Studies of South Asia, Africa and the Middle East* 37, no. 3 (2017), 570–87.
248. Orsini and Schofield, "Introduction," 6.
249. Ibid., 21.

250. Edward M. Yazijian, "Introduction"; in *Chandimangal*, by Kavikankan Mukundaram Chakravarti, translated by Yazijian (Penguin, 2015), vii–xvi, vii; Thibaut d'Hubert, "Patterns of Composition in the Seventeenth-Century Bengali Literature of Arakan," in *Tellings and Texts: Music, Literature and Performance in North India*, edited by F. Orsini and K. B. Schofield (Open Book Publishers, 2015), 423–43, 428, note 14; and glossary entry, 487.
251. See Supriya Chaudhuri, "Chapter 6: The Bengali Novel," in *The Cambridge Companion to Modern Indian Culture*, edited by Vasudha Dalmia and Rashmi Sadana (Cambridge University Press, 2012), 101–23, 104.
252. Amartya Sen, "The Argumentative Indian," in Amartya Sen, *The Argumentative Indian: Writings on Indian History, Culture and Identity* (Picador, 2006), 3–33.
253. O. P. Dwivedi, quoted in Mawdsley, "Hindu Nationalism," 384.
254. Nanda, *Prophets Facing Backward*, 95. An example of the Hindu revivalist application of modern science to ancient epic is the claim that the land bridge to Sri Lanka, built by Hanuman's army as recounted in the *Ramayana*, is visible in satellite images. See Murali Krishnan, "A Bridge that Lord Ram Built—Myth or Reality?" *Deutsche Welle (DW)*, accessed July 28, 2020, https://www.dw.com/en/a-bridge-that-lord-ram-built-myth-or-reality/a-41797300.
255. On anachronism in modern European culture, see Paul Oppenheimer, "Goethe and Modernism: The Dream of Anachronism in Goethe's 'Roman Elegies,'" *Arion: A Journal of Humanities and the Classics* 6, no. 1 (Spring–Summer 1998), 81–100, 81. Also see Emma Mawdsley, "Hindu Nationalism," 384–5.
256. Williams, *The Country and the City*, 96.
257. See Chakrabarty, *Provincializing Europe*, 230.
258. K. Sivaramakrishnan and Arun Agrawal, "Regional Modernities in Stories and Practices of Development," in *Regional Modernities: The Cultural Politics of Development in India*, edited by K. Sivaramakrishnan and Arun Agrawal (Stanford University Press, 2003), 1–61, 2–3.
259. Ibid., vi, 4; and see Chakrabarty, *Provincializing Europe*, 12–14.
260. Sivaramakrishnan and Agrawal, "Regional Modernities in Stories," 2–3.
261. Chakrabarty, *Provincializing Europe*, 245.
262. Ibid., 8.
263. S. Sinha et al., quoted in Emma Mawdsley, "Hindu Nationalism," 387; and see 382–3.
264. Ramaswamy, *The Goddess and the Nation*, 141.
265. Chatterji, *Anandamath*, 145–6.
266. Rens Bod, "Introduction: The Dawn of Modern Humanities," in *The Making of the Humanities, Vol. II: From Early Modern to Modern Disciplines*, edited by Rens Bod, Jaap Maat, and Thijs Weststeijn (Amsterdam University Press, 2012), 3–19, 11.
267. Harrison, *Forests*, 6–8.
268. Ibid., 8, 13.
269. Chakrabarty, *Provincializing Europe*, 40–1.
270. Edmund Burke, "Speech on Fox's India Bill," December 1, 1783, quoted in Keith Thomas, *Man and the Natural World*, 195.
271. Mahasweta Devi, "Why Eucalyptus?" *Economic and Political Weekly* 78, no. 32 (August 6, 1983), 1379–81.
272. "Centre's Nod for Mining in 170,000 Hectares of Forest in Chhattisgarh," *Hindustan Times*, March 21, 2019, accessed July 28, 2020, https://www.hindustantimes.com/india-news/centre-s-nod-for-mining-in-170khectares-of-forest/story-F60Pb7W8ybegHntaQ9YBwK.html; and "India's Ancient Tribes Battle to Save Their Forest

Home from Mining," *The Guardian*, February 10, 2020, accessed July 28, 2020, https://www.theguardian.com/environment/2020/feb/10/indias-ancient-tribes-battle-to-save-their-forest-home-from-mining.
273. Chakrabarty, *Provincializing Europe*, 7.
274. Ibid., 10.
275. Francis Zimmermann, *The Jungle and the Aroma of Meats: An Ecological Theme in Hindu Medicine* (University of California Press, 1987), viii, 6.
276. Ibid., 18.
277. Ibid., 118.
278. Ibid., 10, 12, 48.
279. Ibid., 18.
280. Ibid.; and Dove, "The Dialectical History of 'Jungle' in Pakistan."
281. Nilakanta Sastri, *History of Southern India from Prehistoric Times to the Fall of Vijayangar* (Oxford University Press, 1958), 130.
282. Ibid., 36, 120, 133. Historian K. V. Krishna Ayyar, in his pioneering study of the Calicut Zamorins, claims that the city owes its prime location to the "genius" of the Zamorins, who in the early 1200s transformed a "barren strip covered all over with thorny jungle [into a mighty sea-port where the Arabs and the Chinese met to exchange the products of the west with those of the east]." Areas of thorny, or "scrub," jungle are deemed to be inferior to more robust forests, with the implication that the jungle's inhabitants are also inferior. These semantic distinctions mirror moral ones: forests and gardens align with civilized peoples and jungles, with so-called wild tribals. Krishna Ayyar, *The Zamorins of Calicut: From the Earliest Times Down to A.D. 1806*, reprint (University of Calicut, [1938] 1999), 80.
283. Sastri, *History of Southern India*, 365.
284. Zimmermann, *The Jungle and the Aroma of Meats*, 7.
285. *Oxford Reference*. s.v. "Sādhāraṇa Dharma," accessed May 2, 2021, https://www.oxfordreference.com/view/10.1093/oi/authority.20110803100436176.
286. Parkhill, *The Forest Setting in Hindu Epics*.
287. Lipner, "Introduction," 62. Ironically, as Lipner points out, Bankim and his peers accepted the British trope of the "barbarian" Muslim invader who ostensibly destroyed India's indigenous "Aryan" culture, a myth that has had devastating consequences.
288. Lipner notes that in Bengali, the title is best transliterated as "*Bande Mataram*" to affect the Bengali pronunciation of the Sanskrit phrase, which elsewhere in India is commonly rendered "*Vande Mataram*." Lipner, *Anandamath*, 48, 70.
289. Pascale Casanova, *The World Republic of Letters*, translated by M. B. Debevoise (Harvard University Press, 2007), 103.
290. Anjali Narlekar, *Bombay Modern: Arun Kolatkar and Bilingual Literary Culture* (Northwestern University Press, 2016), 197.

1 Moral Kingship, Forest Dwellers, and Epic and Vernacular Forests

1. As Dipesh Chakrabarty observes in *Provincializing Europe* (2000: 7), the intensely historical consciousness developed by European nationalists compelled nationalists in regions occupied by Europe to apply the same temporal framework to their own visions of independence.

2. Among these influential models is the Sanskrit treatise on statecraft, the *Arthashastra*, commonly attributed to Kautilya, in particular the text's comments on the Mauryan kingdom's treatment of forests. The work illustrates a nonreligious, coolly pragmatic conception of strong and proper kingship that has long circulated in India, one that acknowledges the importance of autonomous forest communities. Kautilya, *Arthaśāstra*, translated by R. Shamasastry (Sri Raghuveer Press, 1951).
3. Parenthetical page references that follow are to Parthasarathy's edition of the epic.
4. Ilanko Atikal, *The Cilappatikaram: The Tale of an Anklet*, translated and edited by R. Parthasarathy (Penguin, [1993] 2014) Canto 20, line 105, p. 190; Canto 21, lines 52–3, 59, and 69–72, pp. 193–4; and Canto 22, line 56, p. 197.
5. R. Parthasarathy, "Introduction," in *The Cilappatikaram: The Tale of an Anklet* (Penguin India, [1993] 2004), 4–5.
6. *The Cilappatikaram*, translated by R. Parthasarathy, Canto 5, line 108, p. 49.
7. Parthasarathy, Postscript, 285–7; in his edition of *The Cilappatikaram*, 279–369.
8. The liana, a forest vine common in India, appears frequently in *The Cilappatikaram* (in Parthasarathy's translation), as in the "trembling liana" characterizing a "wood nymph" in Canto 11, lines 205 and 209, p. 116 and the Maturai "courtesans like golden lianas" in Canto 14, line 91, p. 143. Note three other of the many examples, all in this translation: "women" of Maturai are "delicate as vines" (Canto 14, line 144, p. 145); Matavi (also the name of a creeper), the male protagonist Kovalan's mistress, is "slender as a creeper" (Canto 6, line 177, p. 63); and a "girl" who "lives/In the cool seaside grove,/Wild with the goatsfoot creeper" is as alluring as a "goddess" (Canto 6, Song 13, p. 69).
9. Parthasarathy observes, for example, that even this early epic contains the seeds of "mid-twentieth century [Tamil separatism]." Postscript, 344; in his edition of *The Cilappatikaram*, 279–369. This early standpoint is, Parthasarathy argues (344), a result of "the Aryan penetration of the south," including Mauryan emperor Ashoka's invasion that concluded in present-day Odisha with his overthrow of the Kalinga kingdom in 260 BCE, so bloody that it is said to have prompted his famous conversion to Buddhism.
10. Parthasarathy, glossary, in his edition of *The Cilappatikaram*, 382.
11. Ibid., Canto 25, lines 143–4, p. 224.
12. Ibid., Canto 24, Stanza 24, p. 217.
13. Ramaswamy, *Passions of the Tongue*, 6.
14. *The Cilappatikaram*, Canto 6, line 40, p. 58.
15. Ibid., Canto 14, lines 208 and 214, p. 147, and line 252, p. 149.
16. Parthasarathy, "Postscript," 296.
17. *The Cilappatikaram*, ibid., Canto 21, lines 59, 61, 68–75, pp. 193–4.
18. Ibid., Cantos 24 and 25, pp. 211–26.
19. Ayyar, *The Zamorins of Calicut*, 285.
20. Marco Polo claimed to have visited the city, and even if not, his account clearly depended on descriptions by prior European travelers. Polo notes, among other things, the production and use of spices. A century or so after him, in the 1440s, the Timurid emperor Shah Rukh's ambassador to India, Abd-al-Razzaq Samarqandi, remarked on the same, as well as on the large numbers of Muslim residents. It was around this time, writes K. V. Krishna Ayyar, that the kingdom enjoyed "an outburst of genius in literature and philosophy similar to the Periclean age in ancient Athens and the Elizabethan age in Modern England." See Ayyar, *The Zamorins of Calicut*, 70.

21. *The Cilappatikaram*, Canto 25, line 60, in Parthasarathy's translation.
22. P. J. Cherian and Giulia Rocco, "Excavations in Kerala's Pattanam Reaffirm Its Trade Links with Rome," *Frontline Magazine*, October 9, 2020, accessed June 6, 2021, https://frontline.thehindu.com/arts-and-culture/heritage/the-roman-connection/article32588974.ece. Also see "Muziris Heritage Project," accessed July 8, 2021, https://www.muzirisheritage.org/; and Steven E. Sidebotham, *Berenike and the Ancient Maritime Spice Route* (University of California Press, 2011), 191.
23. The historical importance of the hill dwellers to Calicut is evident from the legal "distinction" its rulers made, "for taxation and other purposes," "between garden lands," or "orchards," and the forests beyond. Sastri, *History of Southern India*, 318. Also see Krishna Ayyar, *The Zamorins of Calicut*, 161, on the close ties between Cochin and the "inland [pepper country]"; and see the similar point detailed by Sebastien Prange, "'Measuring by the Bushel': Reweighing the Indian Ocean Pepper Trade," *Historical Research* 84, no. 224 (May 2011): 212–35, 215.
24. K. S. Mathew, ed. "Calicut, the International Emporium of Maritime Trade and the Portuguese During the Sixteenth Century," *Proceedings of the Indian History Congress* 67 (2006–7), 251–70, 253–4.
25. Geetha Ramaswami and Suhel Quader, "The Case of the Confusing Kanikonna Trees," *The Wire*, June 26, 2018, accessed October 27, 2020, https://thewire.in/environment/the-case-of-the-confusing-kanikonna-trees; and K. Pradip Kumar et al., "Shade Trees and Its Importance in Cardamom Plantations," *Indian Journal of Arecanut, Spices & Medicinal Plants* 14, no. 4 (October 2002), 22–6, 24.
26. A. Shrikumar, "Where Once Stood a Forest of Kadamba Trees …," *The Hindu*, December 7, 2018, accessed December 1, 2019, https://www.thehindu.com/life-and-style/homes-and-gardens/tamil-literature-refers-to-madurai-as-kadambavanam-but-today-less-than-20-kadamba-trees-are-found-in-the-city/article25689117.ece.
27. Susan J. Lewandowski, "Changing Form and Function in the Ceremonial and the Colonial Port City in India: An Historical Analysis of Madurai and Madras," *Modern Asian Studies* 11, no. 2 (1977), 183–212, 187.
28. Banabhatta and Bhushanabhatta. *The Kadambari of Bana*, translated by C. M. Ridding (Royal Asiatic Society, 1896), 39–40.
29. Parthasarathy, in commentary accompanying his authoritative translation, expresses the scholarly consensus that the reputed author, though very likely a Jain, is unlikely to have been the Chola king's "brother," as the epic's Prologue states. The actual author was more likely an unnamed scribe "who took the story … from oral tradition and put it into writing." "It is in keeping with the conventions of early Indian literature," adds Parthasarathy, "to ascribe the composition … to a prince" (p. 7). Parthasarathy, "Introduction," 1–16.
30. See, for example, P. M. Jussay, "A Jewish Settlement in Medieval Kerala," *Proceedings of the Indian History Congress* 57 (1996), 277–84, 278.
31. *The Cilappatikaram*, Canto 6, line 7, p. 57.
32. Ibid., Canto 11, lines 93–5 and 250, pp. 112, 118.
33. Holly Baker Reynolds, "Madurai: *Kōyil Nakar*," in *The City as a Sacred Center: Essays on Six Asian Contexts*, edited by Bardwell L. Smith and Holly Baker Reynolds (E. J. Brill, 1987), 12–44, 18.
34. K. S. Mathew, "Introduction," in *Imperial Rome, Indian Ocean Regions, and Muziris: New Perspectives on Maritime Trade*, edited by K. S. Mathew (Routledge, 2016), 9–30, 21.

35. For a discussion of popular interpretations of these variants by women, see Madhu Kishwar, "Yes to Sita, No to Ram!: The Continuing Popularity of Sita in India," *Manushi* 98 (January–February 1997), 20–31.
36. Writer Shankar Dayal Singh, quoted in Kishwar, "Yes to Sita," 28.
37. Coralynn V. Davis, *Maithil Women's Tales: Storytelling on the Nepal-India Border* (University of Illinois Press, 2014), 128.
38. Ibid., 127. Davis notes, as does Kishwar's article (cited above), that the Mithila region, straddling today's Bihar and Jharkhand, as well as a portion of Nepal, is noted for its many temples dedicated to Sita. Tradition holds that she was born here, and this, together with details from the many Maithil stories circulated about her, have made the region a pilgrimage site for Sita devotion.
39. *The Cilappatikaram*, Canto 25, line 195, p. 226.
40. Parthasarathy, "Introduction," 15.
41. Ibid., Canto 14, lines 152–3, p. 145.
42. Ibid., Canto 11, line 8, p. 109, and line 38, p. 111.
43. Ibid., Canto 5, line 237, p. 54; and Canto 14, line 91, p. 143.
44. Even if the tribute is read as pertaining to the royal office as much as to the person of the king, the indictment stands.
45. Parthasarathy, "Introduction," 7; postscript, 321.
46. Siraj Ahmed argues, for example, that Kalidasa's use of Prakrit is a subtle critique of the Brahmin–Kshatriya alliance's authority. Ahmed, *Archaeology of Babel*, 147–86.
47. Parthasarathy, "Introduction," 15.
48. Reynolds, "Madurai," 15.
49. Reynolds (15, 17) quotes from the *Pathupattu*, collection of Sangam poems composed between 300 BCE and 200 CE, in which we hear of how "a warrior-king would attack an enemy's city and destroy its streets and buildings, turning it back into the forest or jungle from whence it came."
50. Reynolds, 19.
51. Ibid., 13–14.
52. Ibid., 14.
53. Parthasarathy, Postscript, 348.
54. Ramaswamy, *Passions of the Tongue*, 12.
55. Ibid.
56. The poet is familiarly called Valluvar, *thiru* being an honorific prefix for a person held in the highest regard. For more on Valluvar and his beloved work, see Kamil Zvelebil, "The Book of Lofty Wisdom," in *The Smile of Murugan: On Tamil Literature of South India* (E. J. Brill, 1973), 155–71.
57. Ibid., 92.
58. Ramaswamy notes the irony that despite "the important role played by print capitalism in disseminating the assertions of Tamil devotion, there are very few visuals which show her with a printed book." *Passions of the Tongue*, 153–4.
59. See Parthasarathy, Postscript, 347.
60. Ibid., 18.
61. Ibid., 55.
62. Ramaswamy, *The Goddess and the Nation*, 310, n32.
63. Devaneyan, quoted in Ramaswamy, *The Goddess and the Nation*, 153–4.
64. Handelman and Shulman, *Śiva in the Forest of Pines*, 2–3.
65. Ramaswamy, *Passions of the Tongue*, 15.
66. Shulman, *Tamil: A Biography*, 50.

67. Ibid., 167.
68. Ibid., 26–7.
69. Cited in Shulman, *Tamil: A Biography*, 65, from the 1997 translation by David C. Buck and K. Paramisiva.
70. The translators of this poem, David C. Buck and K. Paramisiva, add yet another modern layer to this distillation of arboreal senses by choosing to use the English terms "ipecacunaha" and "baradoes pride." These refer, respectively, to a variety of ipecac introduced to India from Brazil by the British in 1866 and a variety of the flowering *Delonix regia* plant, commonly called the "peacock" or "bird of paradise," native to the West Indies. Yet different varieties of the two are also native to India, with the "peacock" tree, for instance, also more commonly called *gulmohur*. See H. H. Fisher, "Origin and Uses of Ipecac," *Economic Botany* 27, no. 2 (April–June 1973), 231–4, 233; and D. V. Cowen, *Flowering Trees and Shrubs in India*, 6th ed. (Thacker, 1950), 1–2.
71. Ramanujan, "Afterword," 91; in *The Interior Landscape*, 71–102.
72. Ramanujan, *The Interior Landscape*, 23, 47.
73. Ramanujan, "Afterword," *The Interior Landscape*, 100.
74. Ibid., 101.
75. Ibid.
76. Sumathi Ramaswamy, *The Lost Land of Lemuria: Fabulous Geographies, Catastrophic Histories* (University of California Press, 2004), 134–5.
77. Ramaswamy, *Passions of the Tongue*, 144.
78. Ibid.
79. Shulman, *Tamil: A Biography*, 236, 259. "Republic of Syllables" is a possible play on, and counter to, Pascale Casanova's celebrated idea of a "World Republic of Letters," detailed in her book of the same title, which, despite its astonishingly wide reach, neglects to consider similar "republics" outside Europe.
80. Shulman, *Tamil: A Biography*, 265.
81. Vasudha Narayanan, "Religious Vocabulary and Regional Identity: A Study of the Tamil *Cirappuranam* ('Life of the Prophet')," in *India's Islamic Traditions, 711–1750*, edited by Richard M. Eaton (Oxford University Press, 2003), 393–410, 394–5.
82. Shankar Nair, *Translating Wisdom: Hindu-Muslim Intellectual Interactions in Early Modern South Asia* (University of California Press, 2020), 6.
83. Ibid.
84. Narayanan, "Religious Vocabulary and Regional Identity," 398.
85. Kampan, quoted in Narayanan, "Religious Vocabulary and Regional Identity," 400.
86. Umaru, quoted in Narayanan, "Religious Vocabulary and Regional Identity," in "The Chapter on the Countryside," verse 12, 404, n31.
87. Narayanan, "Religious Vocabulary and Regional Identity," 406.
88. Manu Goswami, *Producing India: From Colonial Economy to National Space* (University of Chicago Press, 2004), 144.
89. Ibid., 143.
90. Zipes, *The Brothers Grimm*, xiii, 25, 53.
91. See Novetzke, *The Quotidian Revolution*, and Shulman, *Tamil: A Biography*.
92. Novetzke, *The Quotidian Revolution*, ix, 184, 274.
93. Ibid., 8.
94. See Cristina Bignami, "The Indian Huntresses: Nymphs or Goddesses?" 393; *Rivista degli Studi Orientali* 84 (December 2011): 385–404.
95. Bayly, *Indian Society and the Making of the British Empire*, 14.

96. Shaha Parpia, "Mughal Hunting Grounds: Landscape Manipulation and 'Garden' Association," *Garden History* 44, no. 2 (Winter 2016): 171–90, 171.
97. Lutgendorf, "City, Forest, and Cosmos," 274.
98. Quoted in Lutgendorf, "City, Forest, and Cosmos," 274.
99. Parpia, "Mughal Hunting Grounds," 171, 179.
100. Dove, "The Dialectical History of 'Jungle' in Pakistan," 241–2.
101. Lutgendorf, "City, Forest, and Cosmos," 282–3. Lutgendorf quotes from Dove's "Dialectical History of the 'Jungle.'"
102. Lutgendorf, "City, Forest, and Cosmos," 281, 283.
103. Amartya Sen, *The Idea of Justice* (Belknap Press, 2011), 20.
104. Angelika Malinar, "Arguments of a Queen: Draupadi's View on Kingship," in *Gender and Narrative in the* Mahabharata, edited by Simon Brodbeck and Brian Black (Routledge, 2007), 79–96, 88.
105. *Mahabharata* 3.28.34, quoted in Malinar, "Arguments of a Queen," 82–3.
106. See Paula Richman, "Introduction: The Diversity of the *Ramayana* Tradition," in *Many Ramayanas: The Diversity of a Narrative Tradition in South Asia*, edited by Paula Richman (University of California Press, 1991), 4; and Eck, *India: A Sacred Geography*, 429.
107. See Velcheru Narayana Rao, "A *Ramayana* of Their Own: Women's Oral Tradition in Telugu," in *Many Ramayanas: The Diversity of a Narrative Tradition in South Asia*, edited by Paula Richman (University of California Press, 1991), 130–2; and S. R. Thengane et al., "Micropropagation of Indian Laurel (*Calophyllum inophyllum*), a Source of Anti-HIV Compounds," *Current Science* 90, no. 10 (May 25, 2006): 1393–7, 1393.
108. Swarnalatha Rangarajan, "Ecological Dimensions of the *Ramayana*: A Conversation with Paula Richman," *The Trumpeter* 25, no. 1 (2009): 22–33, 26.
109. Meenakshi Mukherjee, "Epic and Novel in India," in *The Novel, Volume 1: History, Genre, and Culture*, edited by Franco Moretti (Princeton University Press, 2006), 596–631, 602. Sheldon Pollock, "Introduction," 22; in his translation of *Ramayana, Book III: The Forest*, 13–34. The *Ramayana*, as compared to the *Mahabharata*, falls within the parameters of the *kavya*, or "narrative in verse." The English label "epic," Mukherjee points out, brushes over these differences, as it does the many narrative subgenres about the relationship between the divine and the human, collectively called *puranas*. The *Mahabharata* is frequently described, more specifically, as *itihasa-purana*, whereas local legends are *sthala-purana*, "place legends," and pilgrimage tales are *tirtha-purana*. The *Ramayana*, being *kavya*—a term often prefixed by *maha*, meaning both "great" and "long"—has what we might call archetypal characters, such as ideal heroes battling demons. A. K. Ramanujan has observed that because the *Ramayana*'s numerous versions invite equally numerous performances, each retelling and staging is effectively a reinterpretation. See Ramanujan, "Three Hundred *Ramayanas*," 22–48.
110. Mukherjee, "Epic and Novel in India," 602.
111. Eck, *India: A Sacred Geography*, 72.
112. Wendy Doniger, *The Hindus: An Alternative History* (Penguin, 2010), 261, footnote.
113. Eck, *India: A Sacred Geography*, 72.
114. Shulman, *Tamil: A Biography*, 26; and see note 67.
115. Ibid., 142.
116. Those who have argued that the animals incinerated in the forest-burning episode of the *Mahabharata* represent indigenous forest dwellers include Irawati Karve, in

Yuganta: The End of an Epoch, translated by Norman W. Brown (n.p., 2006); and Madhav Gadgil and Ramachandra Guha, in *This Fissured Land: An Ecological History of India* (University of California Press, 1993), 79.
117. Davis, *Maithil Women's Tales*, 115, 127.
118. Lipner, Introduction to his translation of *Anandamath*, 52; and Bankim, in the same translation of his novel, 233.
119. Lutgendorf, "City, Forest, and Cosmos," 274.
120. Ibid., 277.
121. Ibid., 278.
122. See for example Sugata Ray, *Climate Change and the Art of Devotion*, 100, 102.
123. Kampan's twelfth-century Tamil *Ramavataram*, a version of the *Ramayana*, likens Krishna's dancing to the "changing boundaries" of a rushing river. Lutgendorf, "The Secret Life of Ramchandra of Ayodhya," in Richman, *Many Ramayanas*, 220. And see A. K. Ramanujan's translation of the *Ramavataram*, also in Richman, 42.
124. Amita Sinha, "The Sacred Landscape of Braj, India: Imagined, Enacted, and Reclaimed," *Landscape Journal: Design, Planning, and Management of the Land* 33, no. 1 (2014): 59–75, 63.
125. Lutgendorf, "City, Forest, and Cosmos," 280.
126. Nancy E. Falk, "Wilderness and Kingship in Ancient South Asia," *History of Religions* 13, no. 1 (August 1973): 1–15, 10–11.
127. Paul Salopek, "Millions of Indigenous People Face Eviction from Their Forest Homes," National Geographic.com, May 15, 2019, accessed June 30, 2020, https://www.nationalgeographic.com/culture/article/millions-india-indigenous-people-face-eviction-from-forests?loggedin=true.
128. Xavier Mariona Martins, "Portuguese Shipping and Shipbuilding in Goa, 1510–1780," PhD diss. (Goa University, 1994), 121.
129. Ibid., 256.
130. M. N. Pearson, *The New Cambridge History of India, Vol. I: The Portuguese in India* (Cambridge University Press, 2008), 107.
131. In the course of describing India's wealth of spices, d'Orta makes the startling admission about Portuguese behavior further south, in Malabar. For although Malabar "was a very rich place … now, in revenge for what we did in Calicut, all that business is lost." Garcia d'Orta, *Colóquios dos simples e drogas he cousas medicinais da Índia*, 1563. Translated by Sir Clements R. Markham as *Colloquies on the Simples and Drugs of India* (Henry Sotheran, 1913), 159, 219, 477. d'Orta asserts that, "It is true that the Portuguese are not very curious, nor are they good writers" (373), possibly a backhanded compliment from a Jewish scholar who had to contend with Jesuitical inquisition.
132. Markham, "Introduction," x; in his translation of Garcia d'Orta, *Colloquies on the Simples and Drugs*, vii–xvi.
133. Shankar Raman, *Renaissance Literature and Postcolonial Studies: Renaissance Literatures and Postcolonial Studies* (Edinburgh University Press, 2011), 111.
134. Buchanan-Hamilton, *A Journey from Madras Through the Countries of Mysore, Canara and Malabar* (1807), 227.
135. Contemporary British views quoted in Arnold, *The Tropics and the Traveling Gaze*, 99.
136. Fraser, quoted in Arnold, *The Tropics and the Traveling Gaze*, 100.
137. Arnold, *The Problem of Nature*, 142, 155.

138. On the colonial rhetoric of "improvement," see Arnold, *The Problem of Nature*, 74–108.
139. Young, quoted in Keith Thomas, *Man and the Natural World*, 255.
140. Barton, *Empire Forestry and the Origins of Environmentalism*, 48–9.
141. Ibid., 49.
142. Ibid., 50.
143. Barton, *Empire Forestry*, 49, 62.
144. Ibid., 62.
145. Ibid.
146. Ibid., 59.
147. See Krishnadas Rajagopal, "What Is Forest Rights Act?" *The Hindu*, March 2, 2019, accessed May 6, 2021, https://www.thehindu.com/sci-tech/energy-and-environment/what-is-forest-rights-act/article26419298.ece.
148. Barton, *Empire Forestry*, 63.
149. Ramaswamy, *The Goddess and the Nation*, n3, 305–6.
150. Ramaswamy, *The Goddess and the Nation*, 77; Gadgil and Guha, *This Fissured Land*, 133.
151. Guha, "Prehistory of Communal Forestry," *Environmental History* 6, no. 2: Special Issue: Forest History in Asia (April 2001): 213–38, 223.
152. Barton, *Empire Forestry*, 91.
153. Ibid., 78–9.
154. Gadgil and Guha, *This Fissured Land*, 134.
155. Ibid., 125.
156. Ibid., 135, 175.
157. Ibid., 175.
158. Ibid., 135.
159. Ibid., 180.
160. Ibid., 169–70.
161. Bennett, "The El Dorado of Forestry," 41.
162. For example, in 1848 the great botanist Joseph Dalton Hooker, visiting the Sundarbans ("Sunderbunds") found the mangrove forests aesthetically "disappointing." And Clements R. Markham, Secretary of the Royal Geographical Society and a critic of colonial plantations in the Western Ghats, could not resist describing indigenous groups in the southern Palani Hills, which he visited in the 1860s, as a "race of wild men of the woods" who "run … like wild goats [in the jungle]." Joseph Dalton Hooker, *Himalayan Journals* (John Murray, 1854), vol. I, 1; vol. II, 354; and *Life and Letters of Sir Joseph Dalton Hooker*, vol. I, edited and annotated by Thomas Huxley (John Murray, 1916), 240, 288, 334–5; Clements R. Markham, "On the Effects of the Destruction of the Forests in the Western Ghauts of India, on the Water Supply," 1866, Royal Geographical Society (RGS), CRM Collection, Scott Polar Research Institute Archives, University of Cambridge; and C. R. Markham, "Journal: India 18 Oct.–25 Nov, 1860 (Vol. 4)," entry for November 25, 1861; RGS CRM/67. As Marianna Torgovnick observes, the Western image of the tropical jungle was, and in many ways still is, a muddled composite of vastly different topographies, constructed as an atavistic foil to Western knowledge. Simon Gikandi similarly notes that for nineteenth-century European travelers to Africa and the Caribbean, the regions' forests variously represented "irrational" and "blank darkness"; an "enchanting and yet corrupted place," redeemable by European civility; and an ecological cornucopia that science could "decode." Marianna Torgovnick,

Gone Primitive: Savage Intellects, Modern Lives, Reprint Edition (University of Chicago Press, 1991); Simon Gikandi, *Maps of Englishness: Writing Identity in the Culture of Colonialism* (Columbia University Press, 1996), 147, 152.

2 Colonial History, Home Forests, and Mother India in Bankim's *Anandamath*

1. I refer throughout this discussion to Julius J. Lipner's edited translation of the novel, the most authoritative we have: Chatterji, *Anandamath*). Subsequent parenthetical page references are to this edition.
2. Lipner, "Introduction," 3–124, 3.
3. Besides Lipner's fine introduction, see for example Kaviraj, *The Unhappy Consciousness*; Joshi, *In Another Country*; Raychaudhuri, *Europe Reconsidered*; Sarkar, *Hindu Wife, Hindu Nation*; and Upamanyu Pablo Mukherjee, "'Yet Was It Human?' Bankim, Hunter and the Victorian Famine Ideology of *Anandamath*," in *Victorian Environments: Acclimatizing to Change in British Domestic and Colonial Culture* (Palgrave, 2018), 237–58.
4. Joshi, *In Another Country*, 162.
5. Tabish Khair, *Babu Fictions: Alienation in Contemporary Indian English Novels* (Oxford University Press, 2001), 9–15.
6. Lipner, "Introduction," 123–4. Lipner observes that the first words of the song can be translated as either "I bow to thee" or "I hail thee."
7. Ibid., 61.
8. Ibid., 52.
9. Bankim, quoted in Chatterjee, *Nationalist Thought*, 60. Chatterjee quotes from Bankim's *Kamalakanter Daptar*.
10. Raychaudhuri notes that despite Bankim's admiration for the nineteenth-century French philosopher Auguste Comte's tenets of scientific reason, Bankim retained his "belief in the supernatural." Raychaudhuri, *Europe Reconsidered*, 145.
11. Ibid., 134.
12. Ibid., 143, 150. For further discussion of the Bengali Hindu elite's advocacy of the four Vedic *ashramas*, see also Chatterjee, *Nationalist Thought*, 58–9, 66.
13. See Harrison, *Forests*, 164–77.
14. Ibid., 81. For an incisive account of the modern social bandit, also see Eric J. Hobsbawm, *Bandits* (Penguin, 1985).
15. Sir William Jones, trans. "Preface," in *Institutes of Hindu Law, or, The Ordinances of Menu, according to the Gloss of Cullúca* (n p., 1796), iii–xvi, ix.
16. Ibid., viii–ix.
17. Zipes, *The Brothers Grimm*, 11.
18. Halbfass, in *India and Europe* (339), notes Bankim's reading of romantic essayists.
19. Raman, *Renaissance Literature*, 110.
20. Ibid., 109. No wonder the German romantic Schlegel was therefore doubly entranced by Camões, for the latter's year-long stay in Goa demonstrated to Schlegel that a poet could have one foot in imaginative vision and another in the everyday, a combination that enabled the creation of a moral future.
21. Roger Bismut, quoted in Sanjay Subrahmanyam, *The Career and Legend of Vasco da Gama* (Cambridge University Press, 1998), 159.

22. Raychaudhuri, *Europe Reconsidered*, 174. The "eastern" imagery *Paradise Lost* appears to derive from Richard Fanshawe's 1653 English translation of Camões' *The Lusiads* as well as from the chronicles of da Gama's voyages and the narrative of Sir Thomas Roe's 1616–19 embassy to Mughal emperor Jehangir's court. See David Quint, *Epic and Empire: Politics and Generic Form from Virgil to Milton* (Princeton University Press, 1993), 253; James H. Sims, "Christened Classicism in *Paradise Lost* and *The Lusiads*," *Comparative Literature* 24, no. 4 (Autumn 1972), 338–56, 338; John Broadbent, *Paradise Lost: Introduction* (Cambridge University Press, 1972), 31–2; Pompa Banerjee, "Milton's India and *Paradise Lost*," *Milton Studies* 37 (1999), 142–65, passim.
23. Raychaudhuri, *Europe Reconsidered*, 175–6, 188, 203.
24. Chatterjee, *The Nation and Its Fragments*, 94.
25. Taranicharan, quoted in Chatterjee, *The Nation and Its Fragments*, 96.
26. Ibid., 110.
27. The British borrowed the word "*jungli*" and its meaning, spelling it *jungly*, from Hindi. For an example of how British-Indian writers applied the term, see my essay "'Going Jungli': Flora Annie Steel's Wild Civility," in *Flora Annie Steel: A Critical Study of an Unconventional Memsahib*, edited by Susmita Roye (University of Alberta Press, 2017), 123–60.
28. C. S. Peirce, "On the Algebra of Logic: A Contribution to the Philosophy of Notation," *American Journal of* Mathematics 7, no. 2 (January 1885), 180–96, 181.
29. Lipner, "Introduction," 96, in his translated edition of *Anandamath*. Bankim's regard for his Muslim compatriots' faith was, according to Julius Lipner, complex, mixing genuine admiration for Islamic-Indian culture with selective denigration. Yet the popularity of *Anandamath*, and especially a song included in it (more on which later), has led, as Lipner reminds us, to the view that Bankim was a religious chauvinist.
30. Ibid., 88.
31. Ibid., 137–8.
32. Ibid., 138.
33. See, for example, Meera Baindur, *Nature in Indian Philosophy*, 48–51.
34. Rashmi Bhatnagar and Rajender Kaur, "South Asian Realisms and Its Futures," *South Asian Review* 32, no. 1 (2011), 13–38, 15.
35. See Jennifer Dubrow, "Space for Debate: Fashioning the Urdu Novel in Colonial India," *Comparative Literature Studies* 53, no. 2 (2016), 289–311, 307.
36. Manju Gupta, "About This Novel" (n.p.), her note as the English translator under the title *In the Mysterious Ruins* (Star Publications, 2004).
37. Arthur Dudley, on Columbia University website introducing Hindi edition of *Chandrakanta*: "*Chandrakanta* by Devaki Nandan Khatri," accessed February 3, 2021, http://www.columbia.edu/itc/mealac/pritchett/01glossaries/busch/chandrakanta.htm.
38. Musharraf Ali Farooqi, translator's note, "*Tilism-e-Hoshruba* (excerpts translated from the Urdu)," *Words Without Borders* (December 2009), accessed February 3, 2021, https://www.wordswithoutborders.org/article/tilism-e-hoshruba; for more on *tilism*, see Katherine Butler Schofield, "Learning to Taste the Emotions: The Mughal Rasika," in *Tellings and Texts: Music, Literature and Performance in North India*, edited by Francesca Orsini and Katherine B. Schofield (Open Book Publishers, 2015), 407–22, 416; and Pasha M. Khan, "A Handbook for Storytellers: The *Ṭirāz al-akhbār* and the *Qissa* Genre," in *Tellings and Texts: Music, Literature and Performance in North India*, edited by Francesca Orsini and Katherine B. Schofield (Open Book Publishers, 2015), 185–207, 195.
39. Dubrow, "Space for Debate," 289.

40. Ghalib, quoted in Sunil Khilnani, "Gandhi and Nehru: The Uses of English," in *A History of Indian Literature in English*, edited by Arvind Krishna Mehrotra (Hurst, 2003), 135–56, 156.
41. Meenakshi Mukherjee, *Realism and Reality: The Novel and Society in India* (Oxford University Press, 1996); Rumina Sethi, *Myths of the Nation: National Identity and Literary Representations* (Clarendon Press, 1999); Venkatachalapathy, *The Province of the Book*.
42. Joshi, *In Another Country*, 151–2. As Mukherjee puts it, "One of the problems of the early [Indian] novelist was to reconcile two sets of values—one obtained by reading an alien literature and the other available in life," *Realism and Reality*, 7.
43. "The British," C. S. Bayly dryly remarks, "were not enamored of the nomad"; in Bayly, *Indian Society*, 143.
44. Mukherjee, *Realism and Reality*, 8.
45. Dalmia describes the 1882 Hindi novel *Pariksha Guru*, by Shrinivasdas, as similarly groundbreaking in its innovative use of "new devices," including the use of everyday speech and "signs directing the reader how to read the text," to create "a new realism." *Hindu Pasts*, 234.
46. Kaviraj, *The Unhappy Consciousness*, 133. It is important to note that this particular literary device is not unique to Bankim. Magic realist fiction, such as Alejo Carpentier's 1949 novel *El reino de este mundo* (*In the Kingdom of This World*), frequently reimagines historical events as "usable" in the present by means of their narrative "revitalization." See Lois Parkinson Zamora, *The Usable Past: The Imagination of History in Recent Fiction of the Americas* (Cambridge University Press, 1997), 39.
47. Hunter, quoted in Mukherjee, "Yet Was It Human?" 244.
48. Mukherjee, "Yet Was It Human?" 244–5.
49. Ibid., 245–6.
50. See Lipner, "Introduction," 63.
51. Sudipto Kaviraj, "The Two Histories of Literary Culture in Bengal," in *Literary Cultures in History: Reconstructions from South Asia*, edited by Sheldon Pollock (University of California Press, 2003), 503–66, 541.
52. Chakrabarty, *Provincializing Europe*, 162. On Chakrabarty's discussion of modern nostalgia for Hindu village life, see "Remembered Villages: Representation of Hindu-Bengali Memories in the Aftermath of the Partition," *Economic and Political Weekly* 31, no. 32 (August 10, 1996), 2143–51.
53. Tagore, quoted in Kaviraj, "The Two Histories," 541.
54. There were, in fact, several rebellions that historians have variously labeled the Sannyasi Rebellion. See David N. Lorenzen, "Warrior Ascetics in Indian History," *Journal of the American Oriental Society* 98, no. 1 (January–March 1978), 61–75.
55. Ibid., 73.
56. Julius J. Lipner, "Appendix C: History of the Sannyasi Rebellion," in *Anandamath; or The Sacred Brotherhood*, translated and edited by Julius J. Lipner (Oxford University Press, 2005), 293–6, 296.
57. Lipner notes that the historical rebellions included, besides *fakirs*, "starving and desperate villagers," "cashiered soldiers," and those from the lower classes, particularly disaffected ryots, or peasant farmers. Lipner, "Introduction," 29–30; and see Lorenzen, "Warrior Ascetics," 74–5.
58. Lorenzen, "Warrior Ascetics," 71.
59. Lipner, "Introduction," 63.

60. Ibid., 65.
61. Ibid.
62. For a comment on the use of the term neo-Hindu, as well as neo-Vedantic, see Lipner, "Introduction," n14, 8–9.
63. Paul Greenough, "Hunter's Drowned Land: An Environmental Fantasy of the Victorian Sunderbans," in *Nature and the Orient: The Environmental History of South and Southeast Asia*, edited by Richard H. Grove (Oxford University Press, 1998), 237–72, 238. On the "imperial picturesque," see Nigel Leask, *Curiosity and the Aesthetics of Travel Writing, 1770–1840* (Oxford University Press, 2002), Chapter 4, 157–202.
64. Greenough, "Hunter's Drowned Land," 263.
65. W. W. Hunter, *Annals of Rural Bengal*, 5th ed. (Smith, Elder, 1872).
66. Ibid., 1–3, 14.
67. Ibid., 3, 91.
68. Ibid., 89.
69. Lipner, "Introduction," 60. Lipner notes in his introduction that Bankim's location of the rebellion in Birbhum (which he excised from later editions of the novel) was both because of its ruins and its thick forests (39–41). Lipner points out that this "history" is quite contemporary, as exemplified by the bandit Phadke, a contemporary of Bankim who sought to rise against the British and was captured in 1879, and a possible model for the novel's *santan* leader (31). But as Lipner observes, trying to find correspondences between the novel's setting and Bengal's physical topography is a fool's errand, since Bankim's forest is as much symbolic as anything—as indicated by Bankim's deletion of geographical forest references in later editions. See Lipner, "Introduction," 46, 60, 68.
70. Upamanyu Pablo Mukherjee notes, for example, that by exposing the double standard of European colonialist historicity, Bankim's novel assumes an agency that Hunter's account denies to Indians. I do not agree with Mukherjee, however, that this move in the novel effectively invalidates Hunter's rendering of modernity, for Bankim's own assumptions about a pure Aryan past rely on the same oppositional logic as Hunter's. See Mukherjee, "Yet Was It Human?"
71. Lipner, "Introduction," 56.
72. Ibid.
73. Bankim, in an essay quoted by Raychaudhuri, *Europe Reconsidered*, 173.
74. This point is made by Banwari in his adulatory overview of Vedic characterizations of India's trees and forests, a book that bears the marks of a devotee: *Panchavati: Indian Approach to Environment*, translated by Asha Vorha (Shri Vinayaka Publications, 1992), 42.
75. See Chatterjee, *Nationalist Thought*, 58.
76. See Raychaudhuri, *Europe Reconsidered*, 161.
77. Ibid., 134.
78. Lipner, "Introduction," 51.
79. Ibid., 55.
80. Ibid., 66.
81. Sandipan Sen, "Sanskritisation of Bengali, Plight of the Margin and the Forgotten Role of Tagore," *Journal of the Department of English Vidyasagar* University 11 (2013–14), 51–8, 51.
82. Nair, *Translating Wisdom*, 6.
83. Ibid., 18. Nair comments that works and lives like those of Bullhe Shah exemplify "the over thirteen hundred years of variegated historical interactions between Hindus and Muslims" (4).

84. Sen, "Sanskritisation of Bengali," 51–2.
85. Nair, *Translating Wisdom*, 6.
86. See Supriya Chaudhuri, "Chapter 6: The Bengali Novel," 104, on nineteenth-century novelists' debts to both popular (including oral) and classical narratives, including Mukunda's *Chandimangal*, in *The Cambridge Companion to Modern Indian Culture*.
87. Ibid., 104.
88. Edward M. Yazijian, "Introduction," in *The Chandimangal of Kavikankan Mukundaram Chakravarti*, translated by Edward M. Yazijian (Penguin India, 2015), vii–xviii.
89. Kumkum Chatterjee, "Goddess Encounters: Mughals, Monsters and the Goddess in Bengal," *Modern Asian Studies* 47, no. 5 (September 2013), 1435–87, 1448.
90. David L. Curley, "'Voluntary' Relationships and Royal Gifts of *Pan* in Mughal Bengal," *Poetry and History: Bengali* Maṅgal-Kābya *and Social Change in Precolonial Bengal* (Western Washington University Open Access Books, [1999] 2008), 16, accessed February 12, 2021, https://cedar.wwu.edu/cgi/viewcontent.cgi?article=1004&context=cedarbooks.
91. Yazijian, "Introduction," xiii. The Portuguese are described in the last of the work's three stories, the "Book of the Merchant," where the eponymous merchant and his ship must traverse seas near Lanka controlled by Portuguese pirates (253).
92. Curley, "'Voluntary' Relationships," 17.
93. Ibid., 23–4.
94. Ibid., 49.
95. Dilip Chakrabarti, quoted in Lipner, "Introduction," 40.
96. Ibid., 43.
97. Mrinalini Chakravorty, *In Stereotype: South Asia in the Global Literary Imaginary* (Columbia University Press, 2017), 9.
98. Ranajit Guha's discussion of nineteenth-century Bengali literary responses to the colonial city's "official time" is instructive in this regard (see especially 348–51), "A Colonial City and Its Time(s)," in *The Indian Postcolonial: A Critical Reader*, edited by Elleke Boehmer and Rosinka Chaudhuri (Routledge, 2011), 334–54.
99. Kaviraj, *The Unhappy Consciousness*, 155.
100. Lipner, "Introduction," 60.
101. Bankim, quoted in Lipner, "Introduction," 87–8.
102. Raychaudhuri, *Europe Reconsidered*, 187.
103. Kaviraj, *The Unhappy Consciousness*, 133.
104. Sarkar, *Hindu Wife, Hindu Nation*, 141.
105. Jonathan Lehne, "An Opium Curse? The Long-Run Economic Consequences of Narcotics Cultivation in British India," June 10, 2018, accessed November 1, 2020, http://barrett.dyson.cornell.edu/NEUDC/paper_364.pdf, 2.
106. Raychaudhuri, *Europe Reconsidered*, 186.
107. British colonialism's various transformations of Indian topography were inaugurated, as mentioned previously, by Da Gama's arrival, which introduced a more systematized, worldwide commerce in natural products. Europe, a latecomer to South Asia's millennia-old network of maritime trade, eventually tore it to pieces, in part by monopoly capitalism funded through wars. For example, as Philip Curtin tells us, the Dutch East India Company, or VOC, "created a genuine monopoly over nutmeg and cloves production" in Southeast Asia "by controlling production itself," thanks to soldiers sent from the Netherlands to chop down healthy trees and so confine production to a smaller, controllable number in order to raise prices.

Indian writers knew this well: their works alternate between lamenting lost lands and celebrating regional ones that have so far escaped colonial exploitation. See Curtin, *Cross-Cultural Trade*, 149, 154. Also see Richard R. Grove, "Indigenous Knowledge and the Significance of South-West India for Portuguese and Dutch Constructions of Tropical Nature," *Modern Asian Studies* 30, no. 1 (1996), 121–43, 122, 137.
108. J. F. Richards, "The Indian Empire and Peasant Production of Opium in the Nineteenth Century," *Modern Asian Studies* 15, no. 1 (1981), 59–82, 64.
109. Bayly, *Indian Society*, 139–40.
110. Ibid., 144.
111. Ibid., 141.
112. Ibid., 139.
113. Ibid.
114. William Logan, *Malabar, Vol. I* (Government Press, 1887), 542; Bayly, *Indian Society*, 172.
115. Bayly, *Indian Society*, 139.
116. Indian farmers had been growing indigo for centuries before British planters arrived, as, for example, the Italian traveler Niccolao Manucci recorded in the late 1600s. Chetan Singh, "Forests, Pastoralists and Agrarian Society in Mughal India," in *Nature, Culture, Imperialism: Essays on the Environmental History of South Asia*, edited by David Arnold and Ramachandra Guha (Oxford University Press, 1996), 21–48, 35.
117. Raychaudhuri, *Europe Reconsidered*, 142; Bayly, *Indian Society*, 176.
118. Julius J. Lipner, "Critical Apparatus," in *Anandamath, or The Sacred Brotherhood*, translated and edited by Julius J. Lipner (Oxford University Press, 2005), 233–89, 233.
119. [Dinabhandhu Mitra], *Nil Darpan, or The Indigo Planting Mirror, A Drama*, translated by Anonymous ["A Native"] (C. H. Manuel, 1861), 16, 30.
120. See Ranajit Guha, *Elementary Aspects of Peasant Insurgency*, 175; and Bayly, *Indian Society*, 21.
121. Lakoff and Johnson, *Metaphors We Live By*, 29.
122. Bayly, *Indian Society*, 144.
123. Lipner, "Introduction," 70.
124. Ibid., 74.
125. See Lipner's fine discussion of Bankim's attitude to, and representations of, Indian Muslims, in "Introduction," 60–122; and see Sarkar's excellent analysis in *Hindu Wife, Hindu Nation,* 139ff. and 164ff.
126. Although Bankim had, in fact, composed the song's initial verses earlier, in the mid-1870s, he did not publish them, and it was only after the completed version appeared in *Anandamath* that the song's fame spread. See Ramaswamy, *The Goddess and the Nation*, 117.
127. The singer proclaims, to cite the most pertinent words, that he "revere[s] the Mother" who is "Rich in waters, rich in fruit,/Cooled by the southern airs … / Radiant with foliage and flowers in bloom." The Mother has "the strength of [Seventy millions]" who hold "sharpened swords." She is "Durga … wealth's Goddess, dallying on the lotusflower." The Mother is "Spotless" and "Darkly green," embodying "This ever-plenteous land of grace." See Lipner's full translation in the novel, 145–6.
128. Ramaswamy, *The Goddess and the Nation*, 98, 134, 156.
129. Ibid., 99.

130. Ibid., 107–8; also see Wendy Doniger, *Splitting the Difference: Gender and Myth in Ancient Greece and India* (University of Chicago Press, 1998), 388; and Lipner, "Introduction," 104.
131. Bankim, quoted in Lipner, "Introduction," 96.
132. Ibid., 97.
133. Sarkar, *Hindu Wife, Hindu Nation*, 275.
134. Lipner, "Critical Apparatus," 245.
135. See Günther D. Sontheimer, "All the God's Wives," in *Images of Women in Maharashtrian Literature and Religion*, edited by Anne Feldhaus (SUNY Press, 1996), 116–32, 117), in which he observes that the headstrong Banu, being from the Dhangar forest-dwelling people, represents the world beyond the polis. She balances the higher-caste wives of Khandoba, as well as the city and the forest. Banu likely derives from *ban*, or *van*, meaning forest.
136. See Lipner, "Introduction," 89, n136.
137. Bignami, "The Indian Huntresses," 392.
138. Lipner, "Introduction," 94–5.
139. This is from Sontheimer's translation in his essay "All the God's Wives," 122.
140. Ibid., 117.
141. Ibid.
142. Ibid., 116.
143. Ibid., 118.
144. Ibid., 122.
145. Ibid., 126–7.
146. Ibid., 127.
147. The legend, and the songs, describe, for example, how one wife embroiders Khandoba's shawl with an image of Mhalsa on one side and of Banu on the other. Ibid., 130.
148. Ibid., 120.
149. Ibid., 123.
150. Mirabai, song translated by John Hawley and Mark Jurgensmeyer, *The Songs of the Saints of India* (Oxford University Press, 2004), 135. Apropos of this verdant setting, the celebrant cowherding women, or *gopis*, have gathered in Lord Krishna's forest of Vrindavan, the "garden … where the basil grows" (ibid.).
151. Mirabai, Hawley and Jurgensmeyer, *The Songs of the Saints*, 132.
152. Sontheimer, "All the God's Wives," 119.
153. Lipner, "Introduction," 45. Lipner argues here that the title more accurately translates as "Monastery of the Anandas," as Jibananda calls the *santans*.
154. J. J. Roy Burman, "Shivaji's Myth and Maharashtra's Syncretic Traditions," *Economic and Political Weekly* 36, nos. 14/15 (April 14–20, 2001), 1226–34, notes that in the temple complex of Jejuri, the Khandoba pilgrimage site, "a Muslim family traditionally keeps the horses of the god" (1227).
155. M. N. Srinivas in 1952 coined the term Sanskritization to mean "a low-caste adoption of values or practices typically seen as upper-caste or Brahmanical," to use Seth Schoenhaus's words. "Usually," notes Schoenhaus, "this is undertaken with the aim of gaining acceptance among high caste members and therefore gaining access to the resources that come with membership in the upper echelon of Hindu society. In practice, this generally takes the form of low-castes collectively adopting vegetarianism or teaching Sanskrit in order to emulate upper caste practices." Yet "while the intended effect among low-caste groups as a whole is to promote the

idea of caste fluidity and the eventual breakdown of caste through the ease of social changes, an unintended consequence of such upward movement has been to solidify upper-caste values as definitive Hindu practices." Schoenhaus quotes Badri Narayan (2009) to note that this "has 'strengthened the Hindu hierarchic caste-based socio-cultural system'" (60). Seth Schoenhaus, "Indian Dalits and Hindutva Strategies," *Denison Journal of Religion* 16, no. 1 (2017), 55–67.
156. Ibid., 73.
157. Ibid.
158. Kaviraj, *Unhappy Consciousness*, 113.
159. Catherine B. Asher and Cynthia Talbot, *India Before Europe* (Cambridge University Press, 2006), 109–10.
160. Ibid., xvi.
161. A. K. Ramanujan, "Talking to God in the Mother Tongue," *India International Centre Quarterly* 19, no. 4 (Winter 1992), 53–64, 55.
162. Lewis Hyde, *Trickster Makes This World: Mischief, Myth, and Art* (Farrar, Straus and Giroux, 2010), 74.
163. Ibid., 71–2.
164. Ibid., 290.
165. Halbfass, for example, notes Bankim's interest in *bhakti*. But this emotional form of devotion, he believed, had to be balanced with intellectual cultivation, or *anushilana*. Halbfass, *India and Europe*, 243, 336.
166. Ibid., 92. For a sampling of *bhakti* poems in English translation, see Surdas, "song," in Hawley and Jurgensmeyer, *The Songs of the Saints*, 107.
167. Lipner informs us that

> at the time the novel was being written, Bankim was moving towards an understanding of bhakti which suggested a commitment that integrated the different kinds of human faculties—physical, intellectual, volitional and aesthetic—in a focus on the highest human goal. Love of self, of family, of society, of country, and of all sentient beings was to be incorporated in one's love of God.

Lipner "Critical Apparatus," 235.
168. Hyde, *Trickster Makes This World*, 286, 290.
169. Sugata Ray, *Climate Change*, 101. Grove, in *Green Imperialism* (75), notes that already by the 1550s, global botanical knowledge had expanded with European exploration and colonialism.
170. For example, Sahibdin was a prominent Muslim painter in the service of eighteenth-century Hindu Rajput kings of Mewar, in present-day Rajasthan. See Partha Mitter, *Indian Art* (Oxford University Press, 2001), 146.
171. Lipner, "Introduction," 53.
172. Ibid., 53. Lipner writes: "It is [the] darkness of the forest which generates insecurity and fear," which are representations of *tamas*, the "constraining force, resisting physical and spiritual growth" (52).
173. Molly Emma Aitken, "The Heroine's Bower: Framing the Stages of Love," in *A Celebration of Love: The Romantic Heroine in the Indian Arts*, edited by Harsha V. Dehejia (Roli Books, 2004), 105–19, 111.
174. Ibid., 111–12.
175. Lipner, "Introduction," 106.
176. Ibid., 107.

177. Kaviraj, *Unhappy Consciousness*, 133.
178. Ibid., 105.
179. Lipner, "Introduction," 97.
180. Ibid.
181. Ibid., 99.
182. Ibid., 88, 96.
183. Ibid., 48.
184. Ibid., 50.
185. Ibid., 48, 50.
186. Ibid., 51. Lipner explains here that in likening the forest's darkness to that of the "bowels of the earth," Bankim uses a term that can also mean "womb," making the association "very clear."
187. Romesh Chunder Dutt, *Lays of Ancient India: Selections from Indian Poetry Rendered into English Verse* (Kegan Paul, Trench, Trübner, 1894), 203–4.
188. Lipner, "Critical Apparatus," 288, n4.
189. Lipner, "Introduction," 151, n36; and "Critical Apparatus," 247.
190. Vandana Shiva, *Staying Alive: Women, Ecology and Survival in India* (Zed Books, 1988), quoting the Chipko women's activist Itwari Devi (198); and see 51, n1.
191. Ramaswamy, *The Goddess and the Nation*, 102; and Maria Mies and Vandana Shiva, *Ecofeminism* (Zed, 2014), 209.
192. Asher and Talbot, *India Before Europe*, 110–11.
193. Tanika Sarkar, for example, writes that Chaitanya's form of bhakti maintained a fairly orthodox view of caste. *Hindu Wife, Hindu Nation*, 106.
194. Raychaudhuri, *Europe Reconsidered*, 152.
195. Sarkar, *Hindu Wife, Hindu Nation*, 118, 160.
196. Ibid., 143.
197. Kalidasa, *Abhijnanashakuntalam: The Recognition of Shakuntala*, translated and edited by Vinay Dharwadker (Penguin India, 2016), 39.
198. Lipner notes that "dwelling on various features of feminine beauty is a trait of classical Sanskrit literature," so as to "show generally the subordinate social position of women with regard to men, and to closely identify women with various features of the natural world. This traditional gender contrast was reinforced in the minds of nineteenth-century Bengali literati by its Victorian parallels." Lipner, "Introduction," 12.
199. Sarkar, *Hindu Wife, Hindu Nation*, 160.
200. Kaviraj, *Unhappy Consciousness*, 91.
201. Sarkar, *Hindu Wife, Hindu Nation*, 160–1.
202. Kaviraj, *Unhappy Consciousness*, 152.
203. Lipncr, "Introduction," 14.
204. Mirabai, in Hawley and Jurgensmeyer, *The Songs of the Saints*, 134.
205. Ibid., 138.
206. Mirabai, like Kabir and other bhakti poet-saints, approvingly sings of indigenous women and non-Hindus who call to God. See Hawley and Jurgensmeyer, *The Songs of the Saints*, 137.
207. Parkhill, *The Forest Setting*, 8–9.
208. Lipner, "Introduction," 56.
209. Marjorie B. Garber, *Vested Interests: Cross-Dressing and Cultural Anxiety* (Penguin, 1993), 11.
210. Ibid.

211. See Adnan Hossain, "Beyond Emasculation: Being Muslim and Becoming Hijra in South Asia," *Asian Studies Review* 36 (December 2012), 495–513, 496.
212. As Lipner observes, "Theologically for Bankim there is but One, though she has many historical forms. She is the personification of power or *s[h]akti* in its various manifestations, and is both constitutive of (as *prakr[i]ti*) and protective of the earth. Here Bankim makes use of traditional Hindu teaching, imagery and liturgy." "Introduction," 102.
213. Hyde, *Trickster Makes This World*, 292.
214. Tanika Sarkar discusses Bankim's "unresolvable" conception of women, arguing that this stemmed from his simultaneous wish to maintain their ostensibly traditional domestic roles and also emancipate them from encrusted social trappings. See Sarkar, *Hindu Wife, Hindu Nation*, 148–9. It seems to me that *Anandamath* embodies this contradiction in its figuring of Shanti and Kalyani, as well as of the Mother Goddess.
215. Chatterjee, *The Nation and Its Fragments*, 9, 35.
216. Sarkar, *Hindu Wife, Hindu Nation*, 43.
217. Kaviraj, *Unhappy Consciousness*, 19, 21.
218. Ibid., 91–2. Bankim instead stressed Krishna's "rationalism" in the hope that it could serve as a "practical" inspiration for a national "future." This explains why Shanti and Kalyani firmly reject the advances of leering men, both santan and English. More importantly, as mentioned previously, the santans' forest retreat is evocative of Krishna's forest home of Vrindavan, where he and the *gopis* engage in their erotic play. But if Bankim in this way seeks to transpose elements of the Krishna biography and topos to *Anandamath*'s nationalist, warrior-ascetic context, what happens to Radha? See Kaviraj, *Unhappy Consciousness*, 102–3.
219. Ibid., 2–3.
220. Ibid., 22–3.
221. Lipner, "Introduction," 58.
222. Lipner discusses these roles in the same death-and-rebirth context; see "Introduction," 58.
223. See Kaviraj, *The Unhappy Consciousness*, 21.
224. Doniger, *Splitting the Difference*, 261.
225. Ibid., 266.
226. Ibid., 267–71.
227. Lipner, "Introduction," 56.
228. Kaviraj, *Unhappy Consciousness*, 2, 15.
229. Lipner once again provides a gloss on the novel's "interplay between darkness and light," observing that the classical Hindu texts on which Bankim drew are "replete with references to both these negative and positive forms of darkness." The latter is a "luminous darkness that presages a fresh dawn" of radiant truth. Lipner, "Introduction," 52.
230. Ibid., 68.
231. Bankim, quoted in Lipner, "Introduction."
232. Sudipta Kaviraj, "Foreword," in *Gita-Govinda: Love Songs of Radha and Krishna*, translated by Lee Siegel (NYU Press and JJC Foundation, 2009), xvii–xxiii, xxi. Also see Doniger, *The Hindus*, 479.
233. Kaviraj, "Foreword," xxii. Kaviraj, *The Unhappy Consciousness*.
234. Kaviraj, *The Unhappy Consciousness*, 103.
235. Ibid., 94.

236. Sarkar, *Hindu Wife, Hindu Nation*, 159.
237. While the young ascetic is also described as a "heavenly form" (191), it seems very unlikely that Captain Thomas would appreciate this, given his character and the ethos of the hunt.
238. As Lipner puts it, "Just as the forest is able to change form itself, so it is the locus of changing identities in others." "Introduction," 43.
239. Ibid., 57.
240. Ramaswamy, *The Goddess and the Nation*, "Chapter 3: Vande Mataram," 117–49.

3 Premchand's Forest, Bibhutibhushan's *Aranyak*, and the Progressive Era

1. Mohandas K. Gandhi, *Hind Swaraj*, quoted in Toral Jatin Gajarawala, *Untouchable Fictions: Literary Realism and the Crisis of Caste* (Fordham University Press, 2012), 102.
2. Gajarawala, *Untouchable Fictions*.
3. Ibid., 118.
4. Kaviraj, *The Unhappy Consciousness*, 161.
5. For a discussion of the All-India Progressive Writers' Association at this time, see, for example, Snehal Shingavi, "When Pen Was a Sword: The Radical Career of the Progressive Novel in India," in *A History of the Indian Novel in English*, edited by Ulka Anjaria (Cambridge University Press, 2015), 73–87.
6. Krupa Shandilya, "The Widow, the Wife, and the Courtesan: A Comparative Study of Social Reform in Premchand's *Sevasadan* and the Late Nineteenth-Century Bengali and Urdu Novel," *Comparative Literature Studies* 53, no. 2 (2016), 272–88, 274.
7. Vasudha Dalmia, "Introduction to the New Edition," in *The Gift of a Cow*, 2nd ed., translated by Gordon C. Roadarmel (Indiana University Press, [1968] 2002), v–xvii, xiv.
8. Miranda Eberle Shaw, *Buddhist Goddesses of India* (Princeton University Press, 2006), 51.
9. Gajarawala, *Untouchable Fictions*, 72.
10. Rosie Thomas, "Melodrama and the Negotiation of Morality in Mainstream Hindi Film," in *Consuming Modernity: Public Culture in a South Asian World*, edited by Carol A. Breckenridge (University of Minnesota Press, 1995), 157–82.
11. Ibid., 166.
12. Ibid., 165.
13. Premchand, quoted in Gordon Roadarmel, introduction to his translation of *Godaan, The Gift of a Cow*, translated by Gordon Roadarmel, reprint (Indiana University Press, [1968] 2002), 20.
14. Ashis Nandy, "The Defiance and Liberation for the Victims of History: Ashis Nandy in Conversation with Vinay Lal," in "Plural Worlds, Multiple Selves: Ashis Nandy and the Post-Columbian Future," special issue, Emergences, nos. 7–8 (1995–6), 37.
15. Gajarawala, *Untouchable Fictions*, 43.
16. Sudhir Chandra, "Premchand and Indian Nationalism," *Modern Asian Studies* 16, no. 4 (1982), 601–21, 613–14.
17. Shashi Bhushan Upadhyay, "Premchand and the Moral Economy of Peasantry in Colonial North India," *Modern Asian Studies* 45, no. 5 (September 2011), 1227–59, 1247, 1257.

18. Gajarawala, *Untouchable Fictions*, 45.
19. Ibid., 10.
20. Premchand, *Godaan* [Hindi], *Sahitya Chintan*, accessed June 11, 2021, http://sahityachintan.com/books-library/hindi/godan/page4.html.
21. Premchand, quoted in Roadarmel, introduction to his translation of *Godaan [The Gift of a Cow]*, xx.
22. Dalmia, "Introduction to the New Edition," xiv.
23. Upadhyay, "Premchand and the Moral Economy," 1235.
24. Gajarawala, *Untouchable Fictions*, 72.
25. Chakrabarty, *Provincializing Europe*, 10. Chakrabarty adds that "this tension is akin to the tension between the two aspects of nationalism that Homi Bhabha has usefully identified as the pedagogic and the performative."
26. In fact, it is the character Govindi, the wife of the industrialist Khanna, who exhibits many of the traits of a classical-ideal wife.
27. On Premchand's "fable-like" presentation of unambiguous "ethical and moral issues," see Mukherjee, *Realism and Reality*, 148.
28. Chatterjee, *The Nation and Its Fragments*, 9–13, passim.
29. Indrani Mitra, "'I Will Make Bimala One with My Country': Gender and Nationalism in Tagore's *The Home and the World*," *MFS: Modern Fiction Studies* 41, no. 2 (Summer 1995), 243–64, 252.
30. Ulka Anjaria, *Realism in the Twentieth-Century Indian Novel: Colonial Difference and Literary Form* (Cambridge University Press, 2012), 16.
31. Ibid., 37. Premchand's strategy illustrates the point that nationalist elites tried to secularize—which some critics see as a modern European universalizing of value—as well as localize their expressions of Indian self-identity (ibid., 14).
32. Bibhutibhushan Bandyopadhyay, *Aranyak: Of the Forest*, translated by Rimli Bhattacharya (Seagull Books, 2017). The novel was serialized in the 1930s and first published in book form in 1976. Subsequent parenthetical page references will be to this translation.
33. As with Bankim, Bibhutibhushan is commonly referred to by his single given name, as I do here.
34. These three films by Ray are called the *Apu Trilogy* and considered "among the finest films ever made." See, for example, SatyajitRay.org, "The Apu Trilogy," accessed June 15, 2021, https://satyajitray.org/apu-trilogy/.
35. Rimli Bhattacharya, trans., "The Thrice-Borne Text: Out of Bengal—A Note on the Translation," in *Aranyak* (Seagull Books, 2017), xiv–xvii, xiv.
36. Ibid., xiv–xvii.
37. Ranajit Guha, "A Colonial City," 343.
38. Vidya Sarveswaran, "The Forest as a Sacramentalized Ecosystem in *Aranyak: Of the Forest*," *Indian Journal of Ecocriticism* 1 (August 2008), 83–92, 84, 86.
39. The novel's translator, Rimli Bhattacharya, implies that the original Bangla text, too, interchanges terms for forest and jungle, noting in her "Note on Translation" prefacing the work that "the two most frequent adjectives in *Aranyak* are 'janamanbheem' (bereft of human beings) and 'bonyo' (from sanskrit [sic] vanya, which has been variously rendered in English as rude, rustic, wild, savage and uncivilized": Bhattacharya, "The Thrice-Borne Text" (xiv).
40. Forests that came within the ambit of settled societies were "purified," or sanctified, an outlook whose vestiges remain today, as the news story indicates. The forest can therefore be said to represent, in both premodern and modern narratives, an in-between

meeting space of "two contrasting ecologies," the *vana* and the *kshetra* (settlement), as Romila Thapar observes. In fact, the *Brihadaranyaka Upanishad*, an important late Vedic work whose Sanskrit title translates to "great forest" (in this case a rough synonym for "wilderness"), and which famously elucidates the four *ashramas*, says that a man who has lived righteously is "carried to the forest by the priests for the funeral ceremony." This "journey from the village to the forest" posthumously repeats the man's third *ashrama*, *Vanaprastha*. The settled societies that produced these narratives clearly viewed the forest as both a site of conflict and conciliation. See Aloka Parasher-Sen, "Of Tribes, Hunters and Barbarians: Forest Dwellers in the Mauryan Period," in *India's Environmental History: A Reader: Vol. 1: From Ancient Times to the Colonial Period*, edited by Mahesh Rangarajan and K. Sivaramakrishnan (Orient Blackswan, 2011) 127–52, 130; Thapar, "Perceiving the Forest," 111; and Swami Madhavananda, trans., *Brihadaranyaka Upanishad* (Advaita Ashrama, [1934] 1950), 839.
41. Sarveswaran, "The Forest as a Sacramentalized Ecosystem," 88, adduces this as one interpretation of the novel.
42. Bankimchandra Chattopadhyay, *Kapalkundala*, in *The Bankimchandra Omnibus, Volume 1*, translated by Radha Chakravarty (Penguin, 2005), 1–95, 17.
43. See "Selections from *Premsagar* by Lallulal," accessed June 15, 2021, http://www.columbia.edu/itc/mealac/pritchett/01glossaries/busch/premsagar.htm.
44. Ironically, forest products from elsewhere, such as areca nut for chewing *paan*, become habit-forming and expensive for some of the local characters. Dhautal Sahu, a moneylender who is "indifferent to … property," admits to Satya that his betelnut chewing "makes for quite a daily expense" (44). The house "walls" of another character, Rashbehari, are "streaked with juice from betel nuts" (90).
45. Chatterjee, *The Nation and Its Fragments*, 114–15.
46. Chakrabarty, *Provincializing Europe*, 88.
47. Kohn, *How Forests Think*, 199.
48. Ibid., 90.

4 History, Nation, and Forest in Salman Rushdie and Amitav Ghosh

1. Hunter, quoted in Greenough, "Hunter's Drowned Land," 249.
2. Ibid., 247.
3. Julia Kristeva, *Powers of Horror: An Essay on Abjection*, translated by Leon S. Roudiez (Columbia University Press, 1982), 2. Kristeva writes that "abjection … is the other facet of religious, moral, and ideological codes" (209).
4. See, for example, Jayashree Vivekanandan, "Scratches on Our Sovereignty?: Analyzing Conservation Politics in the Sundarbans," *Regions & Cohesion* 11, no. 1 (Spring 2021), 1–20.
5. Priyamvada Gopal, *The Indian English Novel: Nation, History, and Narration* (Oxford University Press, 2009), 97.
6. Salman Rushdie, *Midnight's Children* (Penguin, [1980] 1991). Subsequent page references, appearing in parentheses, refer to this edition.
7. Gopal, *The Indian English Novel*, 91.
8. Some scholars believe that the *sundri* (or *sundari*) tree gave its name to Sundarbans, while others—a majority, as far as I can tell—say that the name derives from the

Bengali word for beautiful, *shundor*. In both cases, the "bans" comes from the Sanskrit *van*, "forest," which in Bengali is *bon*, the same as in many other languages, as we have seen. See Annu Jalais, *Forest of Tigers: People, Politics and Environment in the Sundarbans* (Routledge, 2011), 18, n1.

9. Chatterji, *Anandamath*, 154.
10. Besides the *Ramayana*, see for instance Malcolm Davies, "The Roots of Folly," *Studi Classici e Orientali* 49 (2003), 159–63, 161; K. M. Briggs, "Folklore in Nineteenth-Century English Literature," *Folklore* 83, no. 3 (Autumn, 1972), 194–209, 198; and "Māra," *Encyclopedia Britannica*, May 20, 2013, accessed June 20, 2021, https://www.britannica.com/topic/Mara-Buddhist-demon.
11. Dalley, *The Postcolonial Historical Novel*, 11.
12. Rabindranath Tagore, "My Golden Bengal," accessed June 20, 2021, https://en.wikisource.org/wiki/My_Golden_Bengal.
13. Amitav Ghosh, *The Great Derangement: Climate Change and the Unthinkable* (University of Chicago Press, 2017), 5.
14. Ibid., 6.
15. Ibid.
16. Ibid., 3.
17. Kohn, *How Forests Think*, 17, 23–5.
18. Jalais, *Forest of Tigers*, 3.
19. Ibid., 4–5.
20. Ibid., 8.
21. Annu Jalais, "Dwelling on Morichjhanpi: When Tigers Became 'Citizens', Refugees 'Tiger-Food,'" *Economic and Political Weekly* 40, no. 17 (April 23–9, 2005), 1757–62, 1757.
22. See Torgovnick, *Gone Primitive*, 19.
23. Upamanyu Pablo Mukherjee, *Postcolonial Environments: Nature, Culture and the Contemporary Indian Novel in English* (Palgrave Macmillan, 2010), 124.
24. Ibid., 125; and Asher and Talbot, *India before Europe*, xvi, 82.
25. Mukherjee, *Postcolonial Environments*, 126.
26. Shulman, *Tamil: A Biography*, 113–15.
27. Ibid., 51.
28. Ibid., 49–53.
29. Ghosh, *The Great Derangement*, 4–5.
30. A particularly troubling event for Piya is the burning to death of a tiger at the hands of angry villagers in the last quarter of the novel, which causes her to question the insights she has gained thus far. Kanai addresses her shock at Fokir's involvement: "But what did you expect, Piya? … Did you think he was some grassroots ecologist? He's not. He's a fisherman—he kills animals for a living" (245). Yet it is Fokir who, in the cyclone he and Piya are caught in near the book's conclusion, spots a tiger "pulling itself out of the water and into a tree." The tiger "watched them for several minutes" (321), establishing a link with Piya and Fokir that counterbalances the earlier tiger-killing episode.
31. From *The Baburnama: Memoirs of Babur, Prince and Emperor*, translated by Wheeler M. Thackston (Modern Library, 2002), c. 1530, published in Persian in 1590; cited in Sudipta Sen, Ganges: The Many Pasts of an Indian River (Yale University Press, 2019), 261.
32. Kohn, *How Forests Think*, 114–15, 199.
33. As noted in my introductory chapter. See Chakrabarty, *Provincializing Europe*, 178.

34. Ghosh, *Sea of Poppies*. Page numbers referring to this edition will hereafter appear parenthetically in my discussion.
35. The other two novels are *River of Smoke* (Picador, 2011) and *Flood of Fire* (Picador, 2015).
36. Historian Michael N. Pearson urges us to see that the "history of an ocean needs to be amphibious, moving easily between land and sea." *The Indian Ocean* (Routledge, 2003), 5. Also see Sugata Bose, *A Hundred Horizons: The Indian Ocean in the Age of Global Empire* (Harvard University Press, 2006), 156.
37. Quoted in Sunil S. Amrith, *Crossing the Bay of Bengal: The Furies of Nature and the Fortunes of Migrants* (Harvard University Press, 2015), 81. South Asian teak and hardwood held great commercial value in this period. A French administrator in the French East India Company commented in 1757, "Everybody knows that [teak] is ... better than oak for shipbuilding." M. de Saint-Muan, quoted in Richard H. Grove, *Green Imperialism*, 181–2.
38. Eck, *Darśan*, 9.
39. *Sindoor* is traditionally applied by a married Hindu woman along the crease in her hair. Deeti's application of it to the mango leaf could be viewed as establishing a connection between her and the arboreal world. Such a connection would associate Deeti with figures like the forest goddess Banu, discussed in Chapter 2, who adorns herself with *sindoor*. While possible, this reading would equate Deeti with divine figures, a conclusion that is not supported elsewhere in the novel.
40. The ship's namesake bird, and more specifically the Indian variety, the red-naped or black ibis, is not primarily a water bird, suggesting that the schooner, like its passengers, is moving into uncharted spaces. For more on the ibis, see https://ebird.org/species/renibi1. Accessed February 1, 2022.
41. See Dosabhai Framji Karaka, *History of the Parsis, Including Their Manners, Customs, Religion, and Present Position* (Macmillan and Co., 1884), 51, 61, 63.
42. Zachary is a young mixed-race man for whom the sea offers a chance to escape American racism and who proves to be a valuable "link between the two parts of the ship"—that is, the upper, or quarter, deck of the officers to the rear and the lower, forward fo'c'sle for the crew (13). Zachary befriends and depends upon Serang Ali, the experienced, ranking lascar, the name for a non-European sailor in the service of European merchant vessels. These two exemplify the "linkisters," as another key character, Neel Rattan Halder, will later call those who, like himself, link cultures together (533). Space prohibits a discussion of these and other important characters.
43. The ship's mobility has perhaps already suggested to Deeti a means of moving beyond the limits of her socially ordained dharma. The link between dharmic duty and sight/insight is a long-standing one, most famously described in Krishna's divine revelation to Arjuna in the *Bhagavad Gita*.
44. Kohn, *How Forests Think*, 33.
45. See, for example, Tara Leverton, in "Gender Dysphoria and Gendered Diaspora: Love, Sex and Empire in Amitav Ghosh's *Sea of Poppies*," *English Studies in Africa* 57, no. 2 (2014), 33–44, 35; and Anupama Arora, in "'The Sea Is History': Opium, Colonialism, and Migration in Amitav Ghosh's *Sea of Poppies*," *Ariel: A Review of International English Literature* 42, nos. 3–4 (2012), 21–42, 26.
46. Ananda Coomaraswamy, *The Dance of Shiva: Fourteen Essays* (Rupa, [1918] 2013), 21.
47. Chakrabarty, *Provincializing Europe*, 176–7.
48. Ibid., 14.
49. Ibid., 16.

50. Ilanko Atikal, *The Cilappatikaram: The Tale of an Anklet*, translated and edited by R. Parthasarathy, Canto 25, line 197, p. 226, and Canto 28, line 139, p. 352.
51. Ibid., Canto 24, Stanza 19, p. 216. The trope is also seen in Kalidasa's *Shankuntala*, where early in the play King Dushyanta hides among forest trees while watching the alluring Shakuntala.
52. For instance, Rushdie concludes that the "strength" of Somali writer Nuruddin Farah's novel *Maps* is its "web of leitmotifs drawn from folktales and from dreams," which enables a "remaking of history" that "meshes with nightmare and myth" to offer us "new maps" of the world. Salman Rushdie, "Nuruddin Farah," in *Imaginary Homelands: Essays and Criticism, 1981–1991* (Granta/Penguin, 1991), 201–2, 202.

5 Indigeneity, Forestry, and the State in C. K. Janu, Mahasweta Devi, and Easterine Kire

1. Shiva, *Staying Alive*, 55. *Mahua*, the spelling most commonly used by environmental historians and that I have elected to use, is also sometimes rendered in English as *mohwa* or *mahul*. For variant spellings, and more on the importance of the *mahua* tree for Adivasis, see for instance Anita Agnihotri, *Forest Interludes: A Collection of Journals and Fiction*, translated by Kalpana Bardhan (Kali for Women, 2001), 204; and Spivak's translations of Mahasweta Devi's fiction, some of whose works I have cited previously, as I also do below.
2. Shiva, *Staying Alive*, 55.
3. Roger Jeffrey et al., "A Move from Minor to Major: Competing Discourses of Nontimber Forest Products in India," in *Nature in the Global South: Environmental Projects in South and Southeast Asia*, edited by Paul Greenough and Anna Lowenhaupt Tsing (Duke University Press, 2003), 79–99, 79. Ajay Skaria similarly emphasizes that Bhil and the Dangi communities today are clearly "not trying to master the forests" in the way that the state aims to do. One reflection of this is the communities' preservation of sacred groves that are in effect "symbolic representations of the jungle." Skaria, *Hybrid Histories*, 59, 61.
4. Jacques Pouchepadass, "British Attitudes Towards Shifting Cultivation in Colonial South India: A Case Study of South Canara District, 1800–1920," in *Nature, Culture, Imperialism: Essays on the Environmental History of South Asia*, edited by David Arnold and Ramachandra Guha (Oxford University Press, 1997), 123–51, 135. Pouchepadass notes the similar rationale with which the British regarded the supposedly "lazy" Irish who had come to depend on the "easy subsistence" of potato farming, a dependence, as we know, resulting from the British Government's extractive polices.
5. Ibid.
6. Ibid., 149.
7. K. S. Singh, "Transformation of Tribal Society: Integration vs Assimilation," *Economic and Political Weekly* 17, no. 34 (August 21, 1982), 1376–84, 1377, 1380.
8. Shiva, *Staying Alive*, 55.
9. Jeffrey et al., "A Move from Minor to Major," 79.
10. Richard P. Tucker, "The Depletion of India's Forests under British Imperialism: Planters, Foresters, and Peasants in Assam and Kerala," in *The Ends of the Earth: Perspectives on Modern Environmental History*, edited by Donald Worster (Cambridge University Press, 1989), 118–40, 119.

11. Singh, "Forests, Pastoralists and Agrarian Society," 25, 27.
12. Tucker, "The Depletion of India's Forests," 120, 140. It is important to add that Indian kings, whether Rajput, Chola, or Mughal, often treated certain forests in their realms as personal hunting grounds, so that killing tigers, for instance, became a frequent metaphor for courage and self-control in early accounts of Mughal emperors. The sixteenth-century Persian *Akbarnama* lauds Akbar's disciplined restraint, likening it to a "stalking … lion in the forest of the heart" and describes his military leaders as "tigers of valour's forest." Rajput and Maratha royals enjoyed forest hunts as much as the Mughals and harvested timber in some areas. Yet as I have previously noted, these kings were generally unable or unwilling to deal with "densely forested areas which usually surrounded" indigenous communities, in contrast to their British successors' zeal for "penetrating even remote mountain and jungle lands, turning forests into commodities." See Singh, "Forests, Pastoralists and Agrarian Society," 32, 47; and H. Beveridge, trans., *The Akbarnama of Abu Faz'l*, reprint (Asiatic Society, [1907] 2000), 52, 367.
13. Ramachandra Guha cautions us that to view Chipko as resulting spontaneously out of villagers' "natural" closeness to nature is to reproduce universalized romantic biases that preclude an appreciation of the villagers' keen historical sense. He argues that comparing Chipko participants to the Bishnoi sect of Rajasthan, which famously began saving their trees from a local king in 1763 by sacrificing their lives, and which is habitually invoked as an exemplar of "natural" group-think, is a similarly romantic move. Guha, *The Unquiet Woods*, 173.
14. Vandana Shiva is a prominent intellectual and activist whose deeply informed, sustained exposure of the ravages of corporate agro-business is justifiably famous. Her work has thus been indispensable to environmental activism and consciousness both in India and abroad, especially the anti-GMO movement. She was one of the first public intellectuals to write about the famous Chipko—literally, "hugging"—Andolan (or Movement) of the early 1970s, when tribal (mostly Bhotia) women ringed tree trunks to prevent them from being cut by logging interests. The tactic succeeded, and has since then become an exemplar of ecofeminist movements. For more on the Bhotia community that led the initial Chipko protests, see Sameera Maiti, "Question of Rights: A Case Study of the Bhotia of Uttarakhand (India)," *Anthropology in Action* 16, no. 3 (2009), 55–66, 60, 65 n3.
15. Shiva, *Staying Alive*, xv–xvi, 37–9. Shiva sees *Prakriti*, whose manifestation is embodied as "Shakti, the feminine and creative principle of the cosmos," as representing "the primordial … source of abundance." "*Prakriti*," she concludes, "far from being an esoteric abstraction, is an everyday concept which organises daily life. There is no separation here between the popular and elite imagery or between the sacred and secular traditions"—a statement that, of course, begs the question of whose daily life is being organized and which demographic groups produce and consume the popular. While it is true that many of the local Chipko activists adhere to Hindu traditions, Shiva implies that all indigenous groups do, overlooking the diversity of their belief systems across India.
16. Guha, *The Unquiet Woods*, 56, 152.
17. Bhaskaran and C. K. Janu. *Mother Forest: The Unfinished Story of C. K. Janu*, translated by N. Ravi Shanker (Women Unlimited and Kali for Women, 2004). Subsequent parenthetical page references are to this edition.
18. Arundhati Roy, "Arundhati Roy Supports Tribals' Cause" [letter to Kerala Chief Minister A. K. Antony], February 27, 2003, in Bhaskaran and Janu, *Mother Forest*, 63–6.

19. In *Aranyak*, Bibhutibhushan more than once notes such exploitation by the colonial state, such as the "mining" of the Santal forestland "for copper ore" (237).
20. N. Ravi Shanker, trans., "Translator's Note," in *Mother Forest: The Unfinished Story of C. K. Janu* (Women Unlimited and Kali for Women, 2004), ix–xii.
21. Ellen Turner, "An Unfinished Story: The Representation of Adivasis in Indian Feminist Literature," *Contemporary South Asia* 20, no. 3 (September 2012), 327–39, 336.
22. Arundhati Roy, *Walking with Comrades* (Penguin, 2011), 38.
23. Ibid., 39.
24. Ibid., 74–5.
25. Ibid., 170–2.
26. As with other Bengali writers, I use her given, or in English "first," name, as is more common in India. Outside of India, she is usually referred to as Devi.
27. For example, see Jennifer Wenzel, "Epic Struggles over India's Forests in Mahasweta Devi's Short Fiction," in "Post-Colonial Discourse in South Asia," special issue, *Alif: Journal of Comparative Poetics*, no. 19 (1998), 127–58; Gabrielle Collu, "Adivasis and the Myth of Independence: Mahasweta Devi's 'Douloti the Bountiful,'" *ARIEL: A Review of International English Literature* 30, no. 1 (January 1999), 43–57; and Harveen Sachdeva Mann, "Woman in Decolonization: The National and Textual Politics of Rape in Saadat Hasan Manto and Mahasweta Devi," *Journal of Commonwealth Literature* 33, no. 2 (June 1998), 127–41.
28. The effect of Mahasweta's unusual devices on a reader accustomed to a certain kind of modernist realism is something like Brecht's concept of "alienation effect" in theater, which eschews realism's supposed transparency of presentation by instead highlighting the performance's artifice. The aim is to have an audience see and question their social assumptions. See Bertolt Brecht, "Short Description of a New Technique of Acting Which Produces an Alienation Effect," in *Critical Theory: A Reader for Literary and Cultural Studies*, edited by Robert Dale Parker (Oxford University Press, 2012), 442–9.
29. Jennifer Wenzel, "Epic Struggles over India's Forests," 136.
30. Parama Roy, *Alimentary Tracts: Appetites, Aversions, and the Postcolonial* (Duke University Press, 2010), 141.
31. Ibid.
32. Chakrabarty, *Provincializing Europe*, 37, 49; Skaria, *Hybrid Histories*, 6.
33. Lutgendorf, "City, Forest, and Cosmos," 283–5.
34. Simon Schama, *Landscape and Memory* (Vintage, 1996), 96.
35. Harrison, *Forests*, 222.
36. The virtues of such an arboreal regard is one reason, I believe, that Thoreau cites from the *Upanishads* and *Bhagavad Gita* in *Walden; or, Life in the Woods* (1854). Henry David Thoreau, *Walden and "Civil Disobedience,"* reissue ed. (Signet, 2012), 10, 36, 134, 136.
37. The iconic 1957 Hindi film *Mother India* (dir. Mehboob Khan) invokes the same image to inform its Nehruvian nation-building message, signified for example when the protagonist, Radha (played by Nargis), rubs dirt on her face, linking herself to the earth for whose sake she has suffered. She is given the honor of symbolically opening the sluice that feeds the reservoir created by the new dam. Also see Ramaswamy, *The Goddess and the Nation*, 67. Similarly, India's first prime minister, Jawaharlal Nehru, told audiences in the 1950s that as children of the soil, they were themselves "Bharat Mata [Mother India]." Skaria notes the paradox of this analogy for the new

nation-state, since it is premised on primitivism even as it looks forward to the industrialization in which Nehru believed, as opposed to Gandhi's agrarian vision. See Ajay Skaria, "Cathecting the Natural," in *Agrarian Environments: Resources, Representation, and Rule in India*, edited by Arun Agrawal and K. Sivaramakrishnan (Duke University Press, 2000), 265–76.
38. Skaria, *Hybrid Histories*, xi–xii.
39. Mahasweta Devi, "Dhowli," in *Of Women, Outcastes, Peasants, and Rebels: A Selection of Bengali Short Stories*, translated by Kalpana Bardhan (University of California Press, 1990), 185–205, 192, 194.
40. Mahasweta Devi, "The Witch-Hunt," *Of Women, Outcastes, Peasants, and Rebels: A Selection of Bengali Short Stories*, translated by Kalpana Bardhan (University of California Press, 1990), 242–71.
41. Skaria, *Hybrid Histories*, xi.
42. Major Anthony Gilchrist McCall, India Office Library and Records (IOLR): Mss Eur E361. Papers of Major A. G. McCall, Indian Civil Service 1921-4. McCall Collection, memoir.
43. Howard Anderson Musser, *Jungle Tales: Adventures in India* (George H. Doran Co., 1922), v, 36. IOLR collection.
44. Mikhail Bakhtin, "Forms of Time and of the Chronotope in the Novel," in *The Dialogic Imagination: Four Essays*, edited by Michael Holquist, translated by Caryl Emerson and Michael Holquist (University of Texas Press, 1981), 84–259, 91, 99.
45. Mahasweta Devi, "Draupadi," translated by Gayatri Chakravorty Spivak, *Critical Inquiry* 8, no. 2 (Winter 1981): 381–408. All subsequent page references appear parenthetically and refer to this translation.
46. Lipner, *Anandamath*, 126.
47. Chinua Achebe, *Things Fall Apart* (Anchor, [1958] 1994), 394.
48. Roy, *Walking with Comrades*, 38, 43, 49.
49. Mahasweta Devi, "The Author in Conversation," in *Imaginary Maps: Three Stories*, translated and edited by Gayatri Chakravorty Spivak (Routledge, 1995), ix–xxii, x.
50. Ranajit Guha's well-known exposition of British counterinsurgent rhetoric applies equally to Senanayak's almost identical postcolonial perspective: "Insurgency is regarded as external to the peasant's consciousness and Cause is made to stand in as a phantom surrogate for Reason, the logic of that consciousness." Rebellion of this kind, in other words, is viewed as irrational. Ranajit Guha, "The Prose of Counter-Insurgency," in *Culture/Power/History: A Reader in Contemporary Social History*, edited by Nicholas B. Dirks, Geoff Eley, and Sherry B. Ortner (Princeton University Press, 1994), 336–71, 337.
51. Linda Hogan, "The Kill Hole," in *This Sacred Earth: Religion, Nature, Environment*, 2nd ed., edited by Robert S. Gottlieb (Routledge, 2004), 42–5, 40.
52. Mahasweta Devi, "The Hunt," in *Imaginary Maps: Three Stories*, translated by Gayatri Chakravorty Spivak (Routledge, 1995), 1–17; and see Hansda Sowvendra Shekhar, *The Mysterious Ailment of Rupi Baskey* (Aleph Book Co., 2014). All subsequent parenthetical page references to Mahasweta's story are to this edition.
53. Chakrabarty, *Provincializing Europe*, 26.
54. Hogan, "The Kill Hole."
55. Chakrabarty, *Provincializing Europe*, 24.
56. For more on "multiple modernities," see Saurabh Dube, *Subjects of Modernity: Time-space, Disciplines, Margins* (Manchester University Press, 2017).

57. Jane Bennett, *The Enchantment of Modern Life: Attachments, Crossings, and Ethics* (Princeton University Press, 2016), 8.
58. Chakrabarty, *Provincializing Europe*, 37.
59. My understanding and use of the terms "modern" and "modernity" in this case are captured in Chakrabarty's definition of "political modernity," which helpfully supplements, and rearticulates, my provisional use of "modernity" as described in my Introduction: "The rule by modern institutions of the state, bureaucracy, and capitalist enterprise" that "is impossible to think of anywhere in the world without invoking certain categories and concepts, the genealogies of which go deep into the intellectual and even theological traditions of Europe." These concepts, he notes, include "citizenship, the state, civil society, public sphere, human rights, equality before the law, the individual, distinctions between public and private, the idea of the subject, democracy, popular sovereignty, social justice, [and] scientific rationality" and are governed by an "unavoidable," "indispensable … universal and secular vision of the human" (*Provincializing Europe*, 4).
60. Harrison, *Forests*, 155–64.
61. Sudipta Kaviraj, "Laughter and Subjectivity: The Self-Ironical Tradition in Bengali Literature," *Modern Asian Studies* 34, no. 2 (May 2000), 379–406.
62. Linda Hutcheon, *Irony's Edge: The Theory and Politics of Irony* (Routledge, 1994), 17, 31.
63. Chakrabarty observes that the supposed transition from a premodern to a modern society, such as India is said to have experienced, "cannot any longer be seen simply as a sociological problem of historical transition … but as a problem of translation" as well. He goes on to remark on the disinclination of many Indian writers to translate every piece of vernacular speech that they transliterate, just as Mahasweta does. As Chakrabarty observes, "The English-language monograph in area studies … was a classic embodiment of [the process of translating diverse forms, practices, and understandings of life into universalist political-theoretical categories of deeply European origin." For this reason, "A standard … and least-read feature of the [area studies] monograph … was a section called the 'glossary' … No reader was ever seriously expected to interrupt their pleasure of reading by having to turn pages frequently to consult the glossary. The glossary reproduced a series of 'rough translations' of native terms, often borrowed from the colonialists themselves. These colonial translations were rough not only in being approximate (and thereby inaccurate), but also in that they were meant to fit the rough-and-ready methods of colonial rule. To challenge that model of "rough translation" is to pay critical and unrelenting attention to the very process of translation" (*Provincializing Europe*, 17).
64. Hogan, "The Kill Hole," 39.
65. See Serenella Iovino and Serpil Oppermann, eds., introduction to *Material Ecocriticism* (Indiana University Press, 2014), x, xii.
66. Wendy Wheeler, "Natural Play, Natural Metaphor, and Natural Stories: Biosemiotic Realism," in *Material Ecocriticism*, edited by S. Iovino and S. Oppermann (Indiana University Press, 2014), 67–79, 69. Wheeler rightly cautions that following "a materialist view to the exclusion of all other perspectives is assuming the features of a dogma and is working much as … theological" dogma did in the past. I would simply add that religious dogma is of course still very much with us—the obverse, in a sense, of positivist doctrine (69 and passim). See also Kate Rigby, "Spirits that Matter: Pathways toward a Rematerialization of Religion and Spirituality," in *Material*

Ecocriticism, edited by S. Iovino and S. Oppermann (Indiana University Press, 2014), 283–90. Rigby advocates a "materialist spirituality ... in which contemporary forms of knowledge are ... brought into conversation with non-modern (and frequently non-Western) religions and philosophies" (289–90).
67. Chakrabarty, *Provincializing Europe*, 37.
68. Dove, "The Dialectical History of 'Jungle' in Pakistan," 242.
69. Chakrabarty, *Provincializing Europe*, 16.
70. See Wendy B. Faris, "The Question of the Other: Cultural Critiques of Magical Realism," *Janus Head* 54, no. 2 (2002), 101–19, 113.
71. Harrison, *Forests*, 80, 110, 169.
72. Ibid., 110.
73. Saurabh Dube, "Introduction: 'Enchantments of Modernity,'" *South Atlantic Quarterly* 101, no. 4 (Fall 2000), 729–55, 729. Also see Bennett, *The Enchantment of Modern Life*, 7.
74. Bruno Latour, *We Have Never Been Modern* (Harvard University Press, 1993).
75. Jalais, *Forest of Tigers*, 72.
76. For example, Shekhar, in his acknowledgments at the end of the novel, thanks his editor for helping to transform "Rupi Baskey's story from an 'insulated fable' into a proper novel." See *The Mysterious Ailment of Rupi Baskey*, 210.
77. Hogan, "The Kill Hole."
78. Greg Garrard, "Teaching Education for Sustainable Development," *Pedagogy* 7, no. 3 (Fall 2007), 359–83, 373.
79. Naomi Klein, "Let Them Drown: The Violence of Othering in a Warming World," *London Review of Books* 38, no. 11 (May 2016), n.p., accessed June 7, 2017, http://www.lrb.co.uk/v38/n11/naomi-klein/let-them-drown.
80. Timothy Clark, *Ecocriticism on the Edge: The Anthropocene as a Threshold Concept* (Bloomsbury Academic, 2015), 140.
81. Kaviraj, "The Two Histories," 548.
82. Alex Tickell, "Some Uses of History: Historiography, Politics, and the Indian Novel," in *A History of the Indian Novel in English*, edited by Ulka Anjaria (Cambridge University Press, 2015), 237–50, 240–1.
83. Sethi, *Myths of the Nation*, 67.
84. Ibid., 65, 68–9.
85. Ibid., 184.
86. Ibid., 64, 69.
87. Devi, "The Author in Conversation," xi, xvii.
88. Ibid., xix.
89. As Mahasweta says in her interview with Spivak, "the [tribal] hands that fell the tree are not the hands responsible for deforestation all over India. Big money is involved ... The railways cooperate by carrying this illegally felled timber." "The Author in Conversation," xix.
90. One can read an additional irony in this reference to Hema Malini since in the 1970s when the story was published, Malini was a superstar, particularly notable for the iconic Hindi film *Sholay* in which she plays a rebellious rural beauty: Ramesh Sippy, dir., *Sholay* (Sippy Films, 1975).
91. I thank Bénédicte Meillon for noticing the sexualized association.
92. One could argue that the reading and rereading of the text vicariously reenacts the hunt's ritual repetition.
93. Devi, "The Author in Conversation," xviii.

94. Walter Burkert, *Creation of the Sacred: Tracks of Biology in Early Religions* (Harvard University Press, 1998), 44.
95. Ibid., 44.
96. Ibid., 46.
97. Chakrabarty, *Provincializing Europe*, 83.
98. For a summary of the debate about historical "rupture," see Robert A. Yelle, *The Language of Disenchantment: Protestant Literalism and Colonial Discourse in British India* (Oxford University Press, 2013), 12–18.
99. For an insightful analysis of how the practice of history as such fails to account for any kind of behavior, including labor, that is entails, for instance, gods and spirits—that is, a very different "labor" than what modernity envisages—see Chakrabarty, *Provincializing Europe*, chapter 3.
100. Kavita Daiya, "Ecologies of Intimacy: Gender, Sexuality, and Environment in Indian Fiction," in *A History of the Indian Novel in English*, edited by Ulka Anjaria (Cambridge University Press, 2015), 221–36, 233.
101. Sethi, *Myths of the Nation*, 137–8.
102. For a revealing study of the Mother India image, see Ramaswamy, *The Goddess and the Nation*, 2010.
103. Anima Pushpa Toppo, quoted in "Proceedings: First Global Meeting of the Indigenous Peoples' Forum at IFAD, February 11–12, 2013," 3–53, 25, accessed June 9, 2022, https://www.iwgia.org/es/documents-and-publications/documents/publications-pdfs/english-publications/338-ifad-iwgia-proceedings-first-global-meeting-of-the-indigenous-peoples%E2%80%99-forum-at-ifad-2013-eng/file.html.
104. For more on the growth of Northeast Indian writing, see, for example, Mark Bender, "Ethnographic Poetry in North-East India and Southwest China," in "Border Crossing," special issue, *Rocky Mountain Review* 66 (Summer 2012), 106–29.
105. Easterine Kire, *When the River Sleeps* (Zubaan, 2014). My subsequent parenthetical page numbers refer to this edition.
106. "Nagaland Population 2011–22," accessed June 30, 2021. https://www.census2011.co.in/census/state/nagaland.html.
107. See Kohn, *How Forests Think*.
108. Ibid., 119.
109. Gilles Deleuze and Felix Guattari, *A Thousand Plateaus: Capitalism and Schizophrenia*, translated by Brian Massumi (University of Minnesota Press, 1987), 233.
110. Donna J. Haraway, *When Species Meet* (University of Minnesota Press, 2013), 27.

Conclusion: The City in the Forest

1. Sunil Khilnani, *The Idea of India* (Farrar, Straus and Giroux, 1997), 141–6.
2. See M. Madhava Prasad, *Ideology of the Hindi Film: A Historical Construction* (Oxford India, 2000), 160–87.
3. Sunil Gangopadhyay, *Days and Nights in the Forest* (*Aranyer Din Ratri*), translated by Rani Ray (Penguin, [1968] 2010).
4. Satyajit Ray, dir., *Aranyer Din Ratri* (*Days and Nights in the Forest*). Bengali, 1970.

5. I use the spelling of the city's name both to defer to the translator's orthography and because the official transliteration "Kolkata" was not officially used until 2001. The same point applies to my spelling of the name when discussing Upamanyu Chatterjee's novel *English, August* below.
6. See, for example, Suranjan Ganguly, "No Moksha: Arcadia Lost in Satyajit Ray's *Days and Nights in the Forest*," *Film Criticism* 19, no. 2 (Winter 1994–5), 75–85.
7. Chatterjee, *The Nation and Its Fragments*, 145, 147; Skaria, *Hybrid Histories*, vii.
8. See, for example, the Central Cottage Industries Emporium (website), accessed April 14, 2021, http://www.cottageemporium.in.
9. Ibid.
10. Upamanyu Chatterjee, *English, August: An Indian Story* (Rupa & Co., 1989). Parenthetical page references that follow are to this edition.
11. India's urban population, like that of many countries in recent times, has mushroomed since independence, with 35 percent of the country's population of 1.4 billion residing in urban centers today. In 1947, with India's population at 340 million—a number complicated by the Partition—about 17 percent lived in cities; and in 1881, when the first census was taken and when Bankim was writing *Anandamath* (in the year before it appeared), the percentage was just nine. While this trend has flattened, and even dipped, amid the pandemic health crisis, it is projected to soon climb again. World Economic Forum White Paper, "Indian Cities in the Post-Pandemic World," published January 7, 2021, accessed February 7, 2022, https://www.weforum.org/whitepapers/indian-cities-in-the-post-pandemic-world. Also see The World Bank, "Urban Population (% of Total Population): India," accessed February 7, 2022, https://data.worldbank.org/indicator/SP.URB.TOTL.IN.ZS?locations=IN. Thirty-five percent of 1.4 billion is about 490 million; and Ashish Bose, "Trends and Implications of Urbanization in India During the 20th Century," in *The Asian City: Processes of Development, Characteristics and Planning*, edited by A. K. Dutt et al. (Springer, 1991), 353–68, 354, accessed March 20, 2022, https://doi.org/10.1007/978-94-011-1002-0_23.
12. World Economic Forum White Paper, "Indian Cities."
13. Donna J. Haraway, *A Cyborg Manifesto: Science, Technology, and Socialist-Feminism in the Late Twentieth Century* (University of Minnesota Press, 2016), 59–60.
14. Such works, in Haraway's view, assume "the drama of life to be individuation, separation, the birth of the self, the tragedy of autonomy, the fall into writing, alienation." Ibid., 58.
15. Aravind Adiga, *The White Tiger: A Novel* (Free Press, 2008); Indra Sinha, *Animal's People* (Simon & Schuster, 2007); Karan Mahajan, *The Association of Small Bombs* (Penguin, 2016). Subsequent parenthetical page references are to these editions.
16. For suggestive analysis of the relationship between ideas of whole and part, see Caroline Levine, *Forms Whole, Rhythm, Hierarchy, Network* (Princeton University Press, 2015), 40.
17. The bomb "crater," for instance, soon fills with "trash blended in with the roots of a tree trying desperately to hold on to sinking soil" (241); and years later, a grieving Mr. Khurana still notices "little bits of shattered leaf getting stuck in blisters of tar" on a street (72). Similarly, as a now-adult Mansoor walks through the grounds of a Delhi court, it seems to him that the branches of "dead trees" are extending "searching blind fingers" (135). And among members of a radical group he joins is a young, urban graduate of "a forest management institute" who "obviously hated forests" (143).

18. Arundhati Roy, *The God of Small Things* (Random House, 1997), 3. Subsequent parenthetical page references are to this edition.
19. This includes, for instance, an "old mangosteen tree" familiar to the twin protagonists (16).
20. Anuradha Roy, *An Atlas of Impossible Longing* (Hachette India, 2008). Subsequent parenthetical page references are to this edition.

Bibliography

Achebe, Chinua. *Things Fall Apart*. 1958. Reprint, Anchor, 1994.
Adiga, Aravind. *The White Tiger: A Novel*. Free Press, 2008.
Agnihotri, Anita. *Forest Interludes: A Collection of Journals and Fiction*. Translated by Kalpana Bardhan. Kali for Women, 2001.
Ahmed, Siraj. *Archaeology of Babel: The Colonial Foundation of the Humanities*. Stanford University Press, 2017.
Ahmed, Siraj. *The Stillbirth of Capital: Enlightenment Writing and Colonial India*. Stanford University Press, 2012.
Aitken, Molly Emma. "The Heroine's Bower: Framing the Stages of Love." In *A Celebration of Love: The Romantic Heroine in the Indian Arts*. Edited by Harsha V. Dehejia, 105–19. Roli Books, 2004.
Alam, Muzaffar. "World Enough and Time: Religious Strategy and Historical Imagination in an Indian Sufi Tale." In *Tellings and Texts: Music, Literature and Performance in North India*. Edited by Francesca Orsini and Katherine Butler Schofield, 107–36. Open Book Publishers, 2015.
Alam, Muzaffar, and Sanjay Subrahmanyam. "Love, Passion and Reason in Faizi's *Nal-Daman*." In *Love in South Asia: A Cultural History*. Edited by Francesca Orsini, 109–41. Cambridge University Press, 2006.
Amrith, Sunil S. *Crossing the Bay of Bengal: The Furies of Nature and the Fortunes of Migrants*. Harvard University Press, 2015.
Ananda Apothecary (website). https://milled.com/ananda-apothecary/what-rea lly-is-a-pure-essential-oil-74qJEQzSHY2uei9x. Accessed May 31, 2022.
Anderson, Benedict. *Imagined Communities: Reflections on the Origin and Spread of Nationalism*. 1983. Reprint, Verso, 2006.
Anjaria, Ulka. *Realism in the Twentieth-Century Indian Novel: Colonial Difference and Literary Form*. Cambridge University Press, 2012.
"The Apu Trilogy." SatyajitRay.org. https://satyajitray.org/apu-trilogy/. Accessed June 15, 2021.
Aravamudan, Srinivas. *Tropicopolitans: Colonialism and Agency, 1688–1804*. Duke University Press, 1999.
Arnold, David. *The Problem of Nature: Environment, Culture and European Expansion*. Blackwell Publishers, 1996.
Arnold, David. *The Tropics and the Traveling Gaze: India, Landscape, and Science, 1800–1856*. University of Washington Press, 2014.
Arnold, David, and Ramachandra Guha, eds. *Nature, Culture, Imperialism: Essays on the Environmental History of South Asia*. Oxford University Press, 1995.
Arora, Anupama. "'The Sea Is History': Opium, Colonialism, and Migration in Amitav Ghosh's *Sea of Poppies*." *Ariel: A Review of International English Literature* 42, nos. 3–4 (2012): 21–42.
Asher, Catherine B., and Cynthia Talbot. *India Before Europe*. Cambridge University Press, 2006.

Atikal, Ilanko. *The Cilappatikaram: The Tale of an Anklet*. Translated and edited by R. Parthasarathy. 1993. Reprint, Penguin, 2004.

Atken, Albert. "Peirce's Theory of Signs." *Stanford Encyclopedia of Philosophy*. Updated November 15, 2010. https://plato.stanford.edu/entries/peirce-semiotics/#SigVeh. Accessed July 30, 2020.

Baburnama: Memoirs of Babur, Prince and Emperor. Translated by Wheeler M. Thackston. Modern Library, 2002.

Baindur, Meera. *Nature in Indian Philosophy and Cultural Traditions*. Springer India, 2015.

Bakhtin, Mikhail. "Forms of Time and of the Chronotope in the Novel." In *The Dialogic Imagination: Four Essays*. Edited by Michael Holquist. Translated by Caryl Emerson and Michael Holquist, 84–259. University of Texas Press, 1981.

Balaev, Michelle. *The Nature of Trauma in American Novels*. Northwestern University Press, 2012.

Banabhatta. *The Hars[h]a-C[h]arita of Bana*. Translated by E. B. Cowell and F. W. Thomas. Royal Asiatic Society, 1897.

Banabhatta and Bhushanabhatta. *The Kadambari of Bana*. Translated by C. M. Ridding. Royal Asiatic Society, 1896.

Bandyopadhyay, Bibhutibhushan. *Aranyak: Of the Forest*. Translated by Rimli Bhattacharya. Seagull Books, 2017.

Banerjee, Pompa. "Milton's India and *Paradise Lost*." *Milton Studies* 37 (1999): 142–65.

Banker, Ashok K. *Prince of Ayodhya: Book One of the Ramayana*. Penguin, 2005.

Banwari. *Panchavati: Indian Approach to Environment*. Translated by Asha Vohra. Shri Vinayaka Publications, 1992.

Barton, Gregory Allen. *Empire Forestry and the Origins of Environmentalism*. Cambridge University Press, 2002.

Bate, Jonathan. *Romantic Ecology: Wordsworth and the Environmental Tradition*. Routledge, 2013.

Bayly, C. A. *Empire and Information: Intelligence Gathering and Social Communication in India, 1780–1870*. Cambridge University Press, 2000.

Bayly, C. A. *Indian Society and the Making of the British Empire*: The New Cambridge History of India. Rev. ed. Cambridge University Press, 1990.

Bender, Mark. "Ethnographic Poetry in North-East India and Southwest China." In "Border Crossing," special issue. *Rocky Mountain Review* 66 (Summer 2012): 106–29.

Benjamin, Walter. "Thesis XVII: Theses on the Philosophy of History." In *Illuminations*. Translated by Hannah Arendt, 264. Harcourt, Brace & World, 1968.

Bennett, Brett M. "The El Dorado of Forestry: The Eucalyptus in India, South Africa, and Thailand, 1850–2000." Supplement, *IRSH* 55 (2010): 27–50.

Bennett, Jane. *The Enchantment of Modern Life: Attachments, Crossings, and Ethics*. Princeton University Press, 2016.

Bennett, Jane. "The Force of Things: Steps toward an Ecology of Matter," *Political Theory* 32, no. 3 (June 2004): 347–72.

Berger, John. *Ways of Seeing*. Penguin, 1990.

Beveridge, H., trans. *The Akbarnama of Abu Faz'l*. 1907. Reprint, Asiatic Society, 2000.

Bhagavata Purana. Translated by Anonymous. Vol. IV.6.26. 1950. Reprint, Motilal Banarsidas, 1999.

Bhaskaran and C. K. Janu. *Mother Forest: The Unfinished Story of C. K. Janu*. Translated by N. Ravi Shanker. Women Unlimited and Kali for Women, 2004.

Bhatnagar, Rashmi, and Rajender Kaur. "South Asian Realisms and Its Futures." *South Asian Review* 32, no. 1 (2011): 13–38.

Bhattacharya, Rimli, trans. "The Thrice-Borne Text: Out of Bengal—A Note on the Translation." In *Aranyak*, xiv–xvii. Seagull Books, 2017.

Bignami, Cristina. "The Indian Huntresses: Nymphs or Goddesses?" *Rivista degli Studi Orientali* 84 (December 2011): 385–404.

Blomley, Nicholas. "Making Private Property: Enclosure, Common Right and the Work of Hedges." *Rural History* 18, 1 (2007): 1–21.

Bod, Rens. "Introduction: The Dawn of Modern Humanities." In *The Making of the Humanities, Vol. II: From Early Modern to Modern Disciplines*. Edited by Rens Bod, Jaap Maat, and Thijs Weststeijn, 3–19. Amsterdam University Press, 2012.

Bose, Ashish. "Trends and Implications of Urbanization in India During the 20th Century." In *The Asian City: Processes of Development, Characteristics and Planning*. Edited by A. K. Dutt, F. J. Costa, Surinder Aggarwal, and A. G. Noble, 353–68. Springer, 1991. https://doi.org/10.1007/978-94-011-1002-0_23. Accessed March 20, 2022.

Bose, Sugata. *A Hundred Horizons: The Indian Ocean in the Age of Global Empire*. Harvard University Press, 2006.

Bourdieu, Pierre. *Outline of a Theory of Practice*. Translated by Richard Nice. Cambridge University Press, 1977.

Brecht, Bertolt. "Short Description of a New Technique of Acting Which Produces an Alienation Effect." In *Critical Theory: A Reader for Literary and Cultural Studies*. Edited by Robert Dale Parker, 442–9. Oxford University Press, 2012.

Briggs, K. M. "Folklore in Nineteenth-Century English Literature." *Folklore* 83, no. 3 (Autumn 1972): 194–209.

Britannica, "Māra." *Encyclopedia Britannica*, 20 May 2013. https://www.britannica.com/topic/Mara-Buddhist-demon. Accessed June 20, 2021.

Britannica, The Editors of *Encyclopaedia*. "Chaitanya." *Encyclopedia Britannica*, 20 May 2013. https://www.britannica.com/biography/Chaitanya. Accessed June 12, 2021.

Broadbent, John. *Paradise Lost: Introduction*. Cambridge University Press, 1972.

Brodbeck, Simon, and Brian Black. "Introduction." In *Gender and Narrative in the Mahabharata*. Edited by S. Brodbeck and B. Black, 1–34. Routledge, 2007.

Buchanan-Hamilton, Francis. *A Journey from Madras through the Countries of Mysore, Canara and Malabar Performed Under the Orders of the Most Noble the Marquis Wellesley, Governor General of India*. Vol. 1 of 3. W. Bulmer & Co., 1807.

Burkert, Walter. *Creation of the Sacred: Tracks of Biology in Early Religions*. Harvard University Press, 1998.

Burman, J. J. Roy. "Shivaji's Myth and Maharashtra's Syncretic Traditions." *Economic and Political Weekly* 36, no. 14/15 (April 14–20, 2001): 1226–34.

Busch, Allison. "Listening for the Context: Tuning In to the Reception of Riti Poetry." In *Tellings and Texts: Music, Literature and Performance in North India*. Edited by F. Orsini and K. B. Schofield., 249–82. Open Book Publishers, 2015.

Camões, Luís Vaz de. *The Lusiads (Os Lusíadas)*. Translated from the Portuguese by Landeg White. Oxford University Press, 1997.

Canetti, Elias. *Crowds and Power*. Farrar, Straus and Giroux, 1984.

Casanova, Pascale. *The World Republic of Letters* Translated by M. B. Debevoise. Harvard University Press, 2007.

Census of India. *Vol. X, Part IV: Bombay—History*. Times of India Press, 1901.

Central Cottage Industries Emporium (website). https://cottageemporium.in. Accessed April 14, 2021.

Chakrabarty, Dipesh. *Provincializing Europe: Postcolonial Thought and Historical Difference*. Princeton University Press, 2000.

Chakrabarty, Dipesh. "Remembered Villages: Representation of Hindu-Bengali Memories in the Aftermath of the Partition." *Economic and Political Weekly* 31, no. 32 (August 10, 1996): 2143–51.

Chakravarty, Sumit, S. K. Ghosh, C. P. Suresh, A. N. Dey, and Gopal Shukla. "Deforestation: Causes, Effects and Control Strategies." In *Global Perspectives on Sustainable Forest Management*. Edited by Clement Okia, 3–28. InTech, 2012.

Chakravorty, Mrinalini. *In Stereotype: South Asia in the Global Literary Imaginary*. Columbia University Press, 2017.

Chandra, Sudhir. "Premchand and Indian Nationalism." *Modern Asian Studies* 16, no. 4 (1982): 601–21.

Chatterjee, Kumkum. "Goddess Encounters: Mughals, Monsters and the Goddess in Bengal." *Modern Asian Studies* 47, no. 5 (September 2013): 1435–87.

Chatterjee, Partha. *The Nation and Its Fragments: Colonial and Postcolonial Histories*. Princeton University Press, 1994.

Chatterjee, Partha. *Nationalist Thought and the Colonial World: A Derivative Discourse?* University of Minnesota Press, 1986.

Chatterjee, Upamanyu. *English, August: An Indian Story*. Rupa, 1989.

Chatterji, Bankimcandra. *Anandamath, or The Sacred Brotherhood*. Translated and edited by Julius J. Lipner. 1882. Reprint, Oxford University Press, 2005.

Chattopadhyay, Bankimchandra. *Kapalkundala*, In *The Bankimchandra Omnibus, Volume 1*. Translated by Radha Chakravarty, 1–95. Penguin, 2005.

Chaudhuri, Rosinka. "'Young India: A Bengal Eclogue': Or Meat-Eating, Race, and Reform in a Colonial Poem." *Interventions: International Journal of Postcolonial Studies* 2, no. 3 (2000): 424–41.

Chaudhuri, Supriya. "The Bengali Novel." In *The Cambridge Companion to Modern Indian Culture*. Edited by Vasudha Dalmia and Rashmi Sadana, 101–23. Cambridge University Press, 2012.

Cherian, P. J., and Giulia Rocco. "Excavations in Kerala's Pattanam Reaffirm Its Trade Links with Rome." *Frontline Magazine*, October 9, 2020. https://frontline.thehindu.com/arts-and-culture/heritage/the-roman-connection/article32588974.ece. Accessed June 6, 2021.

Clark, Timothy. *Ecocriticism on the Edge: The Anthropocene as a Threshold Concept*. Bloomsbury Academic, 2015.

Collu, Gabrielle. "Adivasis and the Myth of Independence: Mahasweta Devi's 'Douloti the Bountiful.'" *ARIEL: A Review of International English Literature* 30, no. 1 (January 1999): 43–57.

Coomaraswamy, Ananda. *The Dance of Shiva: Fourteen Essays*. 1918. Reprint, Rupa, 2013.

Cowen, D. V. *Flowering Trees and Shrubs in India*. 6th ed. Thacker and Co., 1950.

Curley, David L. "'Voluntary' Relationships and Royal Gifts of *Pan* in Mughal Bengal." *Poetry and History: Bengali* Maṅgal-kābya *and Social Change in Precolonial Bengal*. 1999. Reprint, Western Washington University Open Access Books, 2008. https://cedar.wwu.edu/cgi/viewcontent.cgi?article=1004&context=cedarbooks. Accessed February 12, 2021.

Curtin, Philip D. *Cross-Cultural Trade in World History*. Cambridge University Press, 1984.
Daiya, Kavita. "Ecologies of Intimacy: Gender, Sexuality, and Environment in Indian Fiction." In *A History of the Indian Novel in English*. Edited by Ulka Anjaria, 221–36. Cambridge University Press, 2015.
"*Dalbergia sissoo*, Shisham Tree Uses, Research, Side Effects." https://www.easyayurveda.com/2015/10/15/dalbergia-sissoo-sisham-shimshapa/. Accessed March 20, 2021.
Dalley, Hamish. *The Postcolonial Historical Novel: Realism, Allegory, and the Representation of Contested Pasts*. Palgrave Macmillan, 2014.
Dalmia, Vasudha. *Hindu Pasts: Women, Religion, Histories*. SUNY Press, 2017.
Dalmia, Vasudha. "Introduction to the New Edition." In *The Gift of a Cow*. 2nd ed. Translated by Gordon Roadarmel, v–xvii. 1968. Reprint, Indiana University Press, 2002.
Das, Hemant Kumar, "The Origin of Oriya Jatra." *Indian Literature* 50, no. 1 (231) (January–February 2006): 166–71.
Das, Pallavi V. "Railway Fuel and Its Impact on the Forests in Colonial India: The Case of the Punjab, 1860–1884." *Modern Asian Studies* 47, no. 4 (July 2013): 1283–309.
Davies, Malcolm. "The Roots of Folly." *Studi Classici e Orientali* 49 (2003): 159–63.
Davis, Coralynn. *Maithil Women's Tales: Storytelling on the Nepal–India Border*. University of Illinois Press, 2014.
Deleuze, Gilles, and Felix Guattari. *A Thousand Plateaus: Capitalism and Schizophrenia*. Translated by Brian Massumi. University of Minnesota Press, 1987.
Demske, Dieter, Pavel E. Tarasov, Christian Leipe, Bahadur S. Kotlia, Lalit M. Joshi, and Tengwen Long. "Record of Vegetation, Climate Change, Human Impact and Retting of Hemp in Garhwal Himalaya (India) During the Past 4600 Years." *The Holocene* 26, no. 10 (2016): 1661–75.
Devi, Mahasweta. "The Author in Conversation." In *Imaginary Maps: Three Stories*. Translated and edited by Gayatri Chakravorty Spivak, ix–xxii. Routledge, 1995.
Devi, Mahasweta. "Dhowli." In *Of Women, Outcastes, Peasants, and Rebels: A Selection of Bengali Short Stories*. Translated by Kalpana Bardhan, 185–205. University of California Press, 1990.
Devi, Mahasweta. "Draupadi." Translated by Gayatri Chakravorty Spivak. *Critical Inquiry* 8, no. 2 (Winter 1981): 381–408.
Devi, Mahasweta. "The Hunt." In *Imaginary Maps: Three Stories*. Translated by Gayatri Chakravorty Spivak, 1–17. Routledge, 1995.
Devi, Mahasweta. *Imaginary Maps: Three Stories*. Translated and edited by Gayatri Chakravorty Spivak. Routledge, 1995.
Devi, Mahasweta. "Why Eucalyptus?" *Economic and Political Weekly* 78, no. 32 (August 6, 1983): 1379–81.
Devi, Mahasweta. "The Witch-Hunt." In *Of Women, Outcastes, Peasants, and Rebels: A Selection of Bengali Short Stories*. Translated by Kalpana Bardhan, 242–71. University of California Press, 1990.
Dharwadker, Vinay. "Translator's Note." In Kalidasa's *Abhijnanashakuntalam: The Recognition of Shakuntala*. Translated and edited by Dharwadker, 51–4. Penguin India, 2016.
Donald, Diana. *Picturing Animals in Britain, 1750–1850*. The Paul Mellon Center for Studies in British Art and Yale University Press, 2007.
Dongria Kondh Tribe. "India Forest Rights Act [Under Threat]." Survival International. org. https://www.survivalinternational.org/about/fra. Accessed March 17, 2021.

Doniger, Wendy. "God's Body, or, The Lingam Made Flesh: Conflicts over the Representation of the Sexual Body of the Hindu God Shiva." In "The Body and the State: How the State Controls and Protects the Body, Part I," special issue. *Social Research* 78, no. 2 (Summer 2011): 485–508.

Doniger, Wendy. *The Hindus: An Alternative History*. Penguin, 2010.

Doniger, Wendy. *Splitting the Difference: Gender and Myth in Ancient Greece and India*. University of Chicago Press, 1998.

Douglas, Mary. *Purity and Danger: An Analysis of Concepts of Pollution and Taboo*. 1966. Reprint, Routledge Classics, 2002.

Dove, Michael R. "The Dialectical History of 'Jungle' in Pakistan: An Examination of the Relationship between Nature and Culture." *Journal of Anthropological Research* 48, no. 3 (Autumn 1992): 231–53.

Dube, Saurabh. "Introduction: 'Enchantments of Modernity.'" *South Atlantic Quarterly* 101, no. 4 (Fall 2000): 729–55.

Dube, Saurabh. *Subjects of Modernity: Time-Space, Disciplines, Margins*. Manchester University Press, 2017.

Dubrow, Jennifer. "Space for Debate: Fashioning the Urdu Novel in Colonial India." *Comparative Literature Studies* 53, no. 2 (2016): 289–311.

Dudley, Arthur. "*Chandrakanta* by Devaki Nandan Khatri." http://www.columbia.edu/itc/mealac/pritchett/01glossaries/busch/chandrakanta.htm. Accessed February 3, 2021.

Duncan, Ian. *Scott's Shadow: The Novel in Romantic Edinburgh*. Princeton University Press, 2007.

Dutt, Romesh Chunder. *Lays of Ancient India: Selections from Indian Poetry Rendered into English Verse*. Kegan Paul, Trench, Trübner, 1894.

Eaton, Richard, ed. *India's Islamic Traditions, 711–1750*. Oxford University Press, 2003.

Eck, Diana L. *Darśan: Seeing the Divine Image in India*. 3rd ed. Columbia University Press, 1998.

Eck, Diana. *India: A Sacred Geography*. Three Rivers Press, 2012.

Edney, Matthew. *Mapping and Empire: The Geographical Construction of British India, 1765–1843*. University of Chicago Press, 1997.

Falk, Nancy E. "Wilderness and Kingship in Ancient South Asia." *History of Religions* 13, no. 1 (August 1973): 1–15.

Fanon, Frantz. *The Wretched of the Earth*. Translated by Richard Philcox. 1961. Reprint, Grove Press, 2004.

Faris, Wendy B. "The Question of the Other: Cultural Critiques of Magical Realism." *Janus Head* 54, no. 2 (2002): 101–19.

Farooqi, Musharraf Ali. "Translator's Note to the Nineteenth-Century Urdu *Dastan* Narrative *Tilism-e-Hoshruba*." In *Words Without Borders*. December 2009. https://www.wordswithoutborders.org/article/tilism-e-hoshruba. Accessed February 3, 2021.

Feldhaus, Anne. "The Image of the Forest in the Mahatmyas of the Rivers of the Deccan." In *The History of Sacred Places in India as Reflected in Traditional Literature: Papers on Pilgrimage in South Asia*. Edited by Hans Bakker, 90–102. E. J. Brill, 1990.

Ferris, Ian. "'Before Our Eyes': Romantic Historical Fiction and the Apparitions of Reading." *Representations* 121, no. 1 (Winter 2013): 60–84.

Fisher, H. H. "Origin and Uses of Ipecac." *Economic Botany* 27, no. 2 (April–June 1973): 231–4.

Fisher, Michael H. *An Environmental History of India: From Earliest Times to the Twenty-First Century*. Cambridge University Press, 2018.

Gadgil, Madhav, and Ramachandra Guha. *This Fissured Land: An Ecological History of India*. University of California Press, 1993.

Gajarawala, Toral Jatin. *Untouchable Fictions: Literary Realism and the Crisis of Caste*. Fordham University Press, 2013.

Gangopadhyay, Sunil. *Days and Nights in the Forest (Aranyer Dinratri)*. Translated by Rani Ray. 1968. Reprint, Penguin, 2010.

Ganguly, Suranjan. "No Moksha: Arcadia Lost in Satyajit Ray's *Days and Nights in the Forest*." *Film Criticism* 19, no. 2 (Winter 1994–5): 75–85.

Garber, Marjorie B. *Vested Interests: Cross-Dressing and Cultural Anxiety*. Penguin, 1993.

Garrard, Greg. "Teaching Education for Sustainable Development." *Pedagogy* 7, no. 3 (Fall 2007): 359–83.

Ghalib, Mirza Asadullah Khan. "A Desertful of Roses: The Urdu Ghazals of Mirza Asadullah Khan 'Ghalib.' " http://www.columbia.edu/itc/mealac/pritchett/00ghalib/index.html. Accessed April 4, 2021.

Ghosh, Amitav. *The Great Derangement: Climate Change and the Unthinkable*. University of Chicago Press, 2017.

Ghosh, Amitav. *Sea of Poppies*. Penguin, 2008.

Gikandi, Simon. *Maps of Englishness: Writing Identity in the Culture of Colonialism*. Columbia University Press, 1996.

Gombrich, Richard F. *How Buddhism Began: The Conditioned Genesis of the Early Teachings*. 2nd ed. Routledge, 2011.

Goodyear, Sara Suleri. *The Rhetoric of English India*. University of Chicago Press, 1992.

Gopal, Priyamvada. *The Indian English Novel: Nation, History, and Narration*. Oxford University Press, 2009.

Goswami, Manu. *Producing India: From Colonial Economy to National Space*. University of Chicago Press, 2004.

Greenough, Paul. "Hunter's Drowned Land: An Environmental Fantasy of the Victorian Sunderbans." In *Nature and the Orient: The Environmental History of South and Southeast Asia*. Edited by Richard H. Grove, 237–72. Oxford University Press, 1998.

Grove, Richard H. *Green Imperialism: Colonial Expansion, Tropical Island Edens and the Origins of Environmentalism, 1600–1860*. Cambridge University Press, 1996.

Grove, Richard H. "Indigenous Knowledge and the Significance of South-West India for Portuguese and Dutch Constructions of Tropical Nature." *Modern Asian Studies* 30, no. 1 (1996): 121–43.

Guha, Ramachandra. "Prehistory of Community Forestry in India." In "Forest History in Asia," special issue. *Environmental History* 6, no. 2 (April 2001): 213–38.

Guha, Ramachandra. *The Unquiet Woods: Ecological Change and Peasant Resistance in the Himalaya*. Expanded ed. University of California Press, 2000.

Guha, Ranajit. "A Colonial City and Its Time(s)." In *The Indian Postcolonial: A Critical Reader*. Edited by Elleke Boehmer and Rosinka Chaudhuri, 334–54. Routledge, 2011.

Guha, Ranajit. *Elementary Aspects of Peasant Insurgency in Colonial India*. Oxford University Press, 1992.

Guha, Ranajit. "The Prose of Counter-Insurgency." In *Culture/Power/History: A Reader in Contemporary Social History*. Edited by Nicholas B. Dirks, Geoff Eley, and Sherry B. Ortner, 336–71. Princeton University Press, 1994.

Gupta, Manju, trans. "About This Novel." in *In the Mysterious Ruins* [*Chandrakanta* by Devakīnandana Khatrī]. Star Publications, 2004.

Haberman, David L. *People Trees: Worship of Trees in Northern India*. Oxford University Press, 2013.

Halbfass, Willhelm. *India and Europe: An Essay in Philosophical Understanding*. SUNY Press, 1988.

Handelman, Don, and David Shulman. *Śiva in the Forest of Pines: An Essay on Sorcery and Self-knowledge*. Oxford University Press, 2004.

Haraway, Donna J. *A Cyborg Manifesto: Science, Technology, and Socialist-Feminism in the Late Twentieth Century*. University of Minnesota Press, 2016.

Haraway, Donna J. *When Species Meet*. University of Minnesota Press, 2013.

Harder, Hans. "Nostalgia and Autobiographies: Reading Rabindranath Tagore's *Jībansmr[i]ti* (1912) and *Chelebelā* (1937)." In *HerStory: Historical Scholarship between South Asia and Europe: Festschrift in Honour of Gita Dharampal-Frick*. Edited by Rafael Klöber and Manju Ludwig, 189–209. XAsia Ebooks, 2018.

Harrison, Robert Pogue. *Forests: The Shadow of Civilization*. University of Chicago Press, 1993.

Hawley, John, and Mark Jurgensmeyer. *The Songs of the Saints of India*. Oxford University Press, 2004.

Hawley, John Stratton. *At Play with Krishna: Pilgrimage Dramas from Brindavan*. Princeton University Press, 2014.

Hecht, Susanna, Kathleen Morrison, and Christine Padoch, eds. *The Social Lives of the Forests: The Past, Present, and Future of Woodland Resurgence*. University of Chicago Press, 2014.

Heise, Ursula K. "The Hitchhiker's Guide to Ecocriticism." *PMLA* 121, no. 2 (March 2006): 503–16.

Hewitt, David. "Scott, Sir Walter (1771–1832)." *Dictionary of National Biography* (2004; 2008). https://doi-org.libpublic3.library.isu.edu/10.1093/ref:odnb/24928. Accessed February 3, 2022.

Hindustan Times. "Centre's Nod for Mining in 170,000 Hectares of Forest in Chhattisgarh." March 21, 2019. https://www.hindustantimes.com/india-news/centre-s-nod-for-mining-in-170khectares-of-forest/story-F60Pb7W8ybegHntaQ9YBwK.html. Accessed July 28, 2020.

Hobsbawm, Eric. *Bandits*. Penguin, 1985.

Hogan, Linda. "The Kill Hole." In *This Sacred Earth: Religion, Nature, Environment*. 2nd ed. Edited by Robert S. Gottlieb, 42–5. Routledge, 2004.

Homer. *The Odyssey*. Translated by Emily Wilson. W. W. Norton & Co., 2018.

Hooker, Joseph Dalton. *Himalayan Journals*. 2 Vols. John Murray, 1854.

Hooker, Joseph Dalton. *Life and Letters of Sir Joseph Dalton Hooker, Vol. I*. Edited and annotated by Thomas Huxley. John Murray, 1916.

Hossain, Adnan. "Beyond Emasculation: Being Muslim and Becoming Hijra in South Asia." *Asian Studies Review* 36 (December 2012): 495–513.

d'Hubert, Thibaut. "Patterns of Composition in the Seventeenth-Century Bengali Literature of Arakan." In *Tellings and Texts: Music, Literature and Performance in North India*. Edited by F. Orsini and K. B. Schofield, 423–43. Open Book Publishers, 2015.

Hunter, W. W. *Annals of Rural Bengal*. 5th ed. Smith, Elder, 1872.

Hutcheon, Linda. *Irony's Edge: The Theory and Politics of Irony*. Routledge, 1994.

Hyde, Lewis. *Trickster Makes This World: Mischief, Myth, and Art*. Farrar, Straus and Giroux, 2010.

"India's Ancient Tribes Battle to Save Their Forest Home from Mining." *The Guardian*, February 10, 2020. https://www.theguardian.com/environment/2020/feb/10/indias-ancient-tribes-battle-to-save-their-forest-home-from-mining. Accessed July 28, 2020.

Iovino, Serenella, and Serpil Oppermann, eds. *Material Ecocriticism*. Indiana University Press, 2014.

Jalais, Annu. "Dwelling on Morichjhanpi: When Tigers Became 'Citizens', Refugees 'Tiger-Food.'" *Economic and Political Weekly* 40, no. 17 (April 23–9, 2005): 1757–62.

Jalais, Annu. *Forest of Tigers: People, Politics and Environment in the Sundarbans*. Routledge, 2011.

Janu, C. K., and Bhaskaran. *Mother Forest: The Unfinished Story of C. K. Janu*. Translated by N. Ravi Shanker. Women Unlimited and Kali for Women, 2004.

Jayadeva. *Gita Govinda*. Translated by Colin John Holcombe. Ocaso Press, 2008.

Jeffrey, Roger, Nandini Sarkar, Abha Mishra, Neeraj Peter, and Pradeep J. Tharakan. "A Move from Minor to Major: Competing Discourses of Nontimber Forest Products in India." In *Nature in the Global South: Environmental Projects in South and Southeast Asia*. Edited by Paul Greenough and Anna Lowenhaupt Tsing, 79–99. Duke University Press, 2003.

Jharkhand Tourism (website). https://tourism.jharkhand.gov.in. Accessed December 11, 2016.

Johnson, Alan. "'Going Jungli': Flora Annie Steel's Wild Civility." In *Flora Annie Steel: A Critical Study of an Unconventional Memsahib*. Edited by Susmita Roye, 123–60. University of Alberta Press, 2017.

Jones, Sir William, trans. "Preface." In *Institutes of Hindu Law, or, The Ordinances of Menu, According to the Gloss of Cullúca*. iii–xvi. n.p., 1796.

Jonsson, Fredrik Albritton. "Adam Smith in the Forest." In *The Social Lives of the Forests: The Past, Present, and Future of Woodland Resurgence*. Edited by Susanna Hecht, Kathleen Morrison, and Christine Padoch, 45–54. University of Chicago Press, 2014.

Jonsson, Fredrik Albritton. "Rival Ecologies of Global Commerce: Adam Smith and the Natural Historians." *The American Historical Review* 115, no. 5 (December 2010), 1342–63.

Joshi, Priya. *In Another Country: Colonialism, Culture, and the English Novel in India*. Columbia University Press, 2002.

Jussay, P. M. "A Jewish Settlement in Medieval Kerala." *Proceedings of the Indian History Congress* 57 (1996): 277–84.

Kalidasa. *Abhijnanashakuntalam: The Recognition of Shakuntala*. Translated and edited by Vinay Dharwadker. Penguin India, 2016.

Karaka, Dosabhai Framji. *History of the Parsis, Including Their Manners, Customs, Religion, and Present Position*. Macmillan and Co., 1884.

Karve, Irawati. *Yuganta: The End of an Epoch*. Translated by Norman W. Brown. n.p., 2006. https://ia800203.us.archive.org/7/items/Yuganta-TheEndOfAnEpoch-IrawatiKarve/yuganta.pdf. Accessed June 12, 2019.

Kautilya. *Arthaśāstra*. Translated by R. Shamasastry. Sri Raghuveer Press, 1951.

Kaviraj, Sudipta. "Foreword." In *Gita-Govinda: Love Songs of Radha and Krishna*. Translated by Lee Siegel, xvii–xxiii. NYU Press and JJC Foundation, 2009.

Kaviraj, Sudipta. "The Imaginary Institution of India." In *Subaltern Studies VII: Writings on South Asian History and Society*. Edited by Partha Chatterjee and Gyanendra Pandey, 1–39. Oxford University Press, 1993.

Kaviraj, Sudipta. "Laughter and Subjectivity: The Self-Ironical Tradition in Bengali Literature." *Modern Asian Studies* 34, no. 2 (May 2000): 379–406.

Kaviraj, Sudipta. "The Two Histories of Literary Culture in Bengal." In *Literary Cultures in History: Reconstructions from South Asia*. Edited by Sheldon Pollock, 503–66. University of California Press, 2003.

Kaviraj, Sudipta. *The Unhappy Consciousness: Bankimchandra Chattopadhyay and the Formation of Nationalist Discourse in India*. Oxford University Press, 1995.

Khair, Tabish. *Babu Fictions: Alienation in Contemporary Indian English Novels*. Oxford University Press, 2001.

Khan, Pasha M. "What Storytellers Were Worth in Mughal India." *Comparative Studies of South Asia, Africa and the Middle East* 37, no. 3 (2017): 570–87.

Khan, Pasha M. "A Handbook for Storytellers: The *Ṭirāz al-akhbār* and the *Qissa* Genre" In *Tellings and Texts: Music, Literature and Performance in North India*. Edited by Francesca Orsini and Katherine B. Schofield,185–207. Open Book Publishers, 2015.

Khatrī, Devakīnandana. *Chandrakanta*. Translated by Manju Gupta as *In the Mysterious Ruins*. Star Publications, 2004.

Khilnani, Sunil. "Gandhi and Nehru: The Uses of English." In *A History of Indian Literature in English*. Edited by Arvind Krishna Mehrotra, 135–56. Hurst, 2003.

Khilnani, Sunil. *The Idea of India*. Farar, Straus and Giroux, 1997.

Kire, Easterine. *When the River Sleeps*. Zubaan, 2014.

Kishwar, Madhu. "Yes to Sita, No to Ram!: The Continuing Popularity of Sita in India," *Manushi* 98 (January–February 1997): 20–31.

Klein, Naomi. "Let Them Drown: The Violence of Othering in a Warming World." *London Review of Books* 38, no. 11 (May 2016): n.p. http://www.lrb.co.uk/v38/n11/naomi-klein/let-them-drown. Accessed June 7, 2017.

Kohn, Eduardo. *How Forests Think: Toward an Anthropology Beyond the Human*. University of California Press, 2013.

Kolodny, Annette. *The Lay of the Land: Metaphor as Experience and History in American Life and Letters*. University of North Carolina Press, 1975.

Khusrau, Amir. *The Book of Amir Khusrau: Selected Poems and The Tale of the Four Dervishes*. Translated by Paul Smith. New Humanity Books, 2015.

Khusrau, Amir. *India as Seen by Amir Khusrau*. Edited by R. Nath and Faiyaz "Gwaliori." 1933. Reprint, Historical Research Documentation Program, 1981.

Krishna Ayyar, K. V. *The Zamorins of Calicut: From the Earliest Times Down to A.D. 1806*. 1938. Reprint, University of Calicut, 1999.

Krishnan, Murali. "A Bridge that Lord Ram Built—Myth or Reality?" *Deutsche Welle* (*DW*). https://www.dw.com/en/a-bridge-that-lord-ram-built-myth-or-reality/a-41797 300. Accessed July 28, 2020.

Kristeva, Julia. *Powers of Horror: An Essay on Abjection*. Translated by Leon S. Roudiez. Columbia University Press, 1982.

Kumar, K. Pradip, T. K. Hrideek, Jaison Paul, and K. M. Kuruvilla. "Shade Trees and Its Importance in Cardamom Plantations." *Indian Journal of Arecanut, Spices & Medicinal Plants* 14, no. 4 (October 2002): 22–26.

Lakoff, George, and Mark Johnson. *Metaphors We Live By*. University of Chicago Press, 2003.

Latour, Bruno. *We Have Never Been Modern*. Harvard University Press, 1993.

Leask, Nigel. *Curiosity and the Aesthetics of Travel Writing, 1770–1840*. Oxford University Press, 2002.

Lee, David. "The Natural History of the Ramayana." In *Hinduism and Ecology: The Intersection of Earth, Sky and Water*. Edited by Gred Chapple and Mary Evelyn Tucker, 245–68. Harvard University Press, 2000.

Lehne, Jonathan. "An Opium Curse? The Long-Run Economic Consequences of Narcotics Cultivation in British India." June 10, 2018. http://barrett.dyson.cornell.edu/NEUDC/paper_364.pdf. Accessed November 1, 2020.

Leverton, Tara. "Gender Dysphoria and Gendered Diaspora: Love, Sex and Empire in Amitav Ghosh's *Sea of Poppies*." *English Studies in Africa* 57, no. 2 (2014): 33–44.

Levine, Caroline. *Forms Whole, Rhythm, Hierarchy, Network*. Princeton University Press, 2015.

Lewandowski, Susan J. "Changing Form and Function in the Ceremonial and the Colonial Port City in India: An Historical Analysis of Madurai and Madras." *Modern Asian Studies* 11, no. 2 (1977): 183–212.

Lipner, Julius J. "Appendix C: History of the Sannyasi Rebellion." In *Anandamath; or The Sacred Brotherhood*. Translated and edited by Julius J. Lipner, 293–96. Oxford University Press, 2005.

Lipner, Julius J. "Critical Apparatus." In *Anandamath, or The Sacred Brotherhood*. Translated and edited by Julius J. Lipner, 233–89. Oxford University Press, 2005.

Lipner, Julius J. "Introduction." In *Anandamath, or The Sacred Brotherhood*. Translated and edited by Julius J. Lipner, 3–124. Oxford University Press, 2005.

Liulevicius, Vejas G. *War Land on the Eastern Front: Culture, National Identity, and German Occupation in World War I*. Cambridge University Press, 2000.

Logan, William. *Malabar, Vol. I*. Government Press, 1887.

Lorenzen, David N. "Warrior Ascetics in Indian History." *Journal of the American Oriental Society* 98, no. 1 (January–March 1978): 61–75.

Lutgendorf, Philip. "City, Forest, and Cosmos: Ecological Perspectives from the Sanskrit Epics." In *Hinduism and Ecology: The Intersection of Earth, Sky and Water*. Edited by Christopher Key Chapple and Mary Evelyn Tucker, 245–68. Oxford University Press, 2000.

Lutgendorf, Philip. "The Secret Life of Ramchandra of Ayodhya." In *Many Ramayanas: The Diversity of a Narrative Tradition in South Asia*. Edited by Paula Richman, 217–34. University of California Press, 1991.

Macaulay, T. B. "'Minute' on Indian Education," February 2, 1835; n.p. http://oldsite.english.ucsb.edu/faculty/rraley/research/english/macaulay.html. Accessed June 9, 2022.

Mahajan, Karan. *The Association of Small Bombs*. Penguin, 2016.

Mahdihassan, S. "Three Important Vedic Grasses." *Indian Journal of History of Science* 22, no. 4 (1987): 286–91.

Maiti, Sameera. "Question of Rights: A Case Study of the Bhotia of Uttarakhand (India)." *Anthropology in Action* 16, no. 3 (2009): 55–66.

Malinar, Angelika. "Arguments of a Queen: Draupadi's View on Kingship." In *Gender and Narrative in the Mahabharata*. Edited by Simon Brodbeck and Brian Black, 79–96. Routledge, 2007.

Mann, Charles. *1491: New Revelations of the Americas Before Columbus*. Vintage, 2006.

Mann, Harveen Sachdeva. "Woman in Decolonization: The National and Textual Politics of Rape in Saadat Hasan Manto and Mahasweta Devi." *The Journal of Commonwealth Literature* 33, no. 2 (June 1998): 127–41.

Markham, Clements R. "Journal: India 18 October–25 November, 1860 (Vol. 4)," November 25, 1861, Royal Geographical Society, Clements R. Markham Collection, CRM/67, Scott Polar Research Institute Archives, University of Cambridge.

Markham, Clements R. "On the Effects of the Destruction of the Forests in the Western Ghauts of India, on the Water Supply," 1868, Royal Geographical Society, CRM Collection, Scott Polar Research Institute Archives, University of Cambridge.

Markham, Clements R, trans. "Introduction." In *Colloquies on the Simples and Drugs of India*, vii–xvi. 1563. Reprint, Henry Sotheran and Co., 1913.
Márquez, Gabriel García. *One Hundred Years of Solitude*. Translated by Gregory Rabassa. 1970. Reprint, Harper Perennial, 2006.
Martins, Xavier Mariona. "Portuguese Shipping and Shipbuilding in Goa, 1510–1780." PhD diss., Goa University, 1994.
Marx, Leo. *The Machine in the Garden: Technology and the Pastoral Ideal in America*. 35th Anniversary ed. 1964. Reprint, Oxford University Press, 2000.
Mathew, K. S., ed. "Calicut, the International Emporium of Maritime Trade and the Portuguese During the Sixteenth Century." *Proceedings of the Indian History Congress* 67 (2006–2007): 251–70.
Mathew, K. S., ed. *Imperial Rome, Indian Ocean Regions and Muziris: New Perspectives on Maritime Trade*. Routledge, 2016.
Mathew, K. S. "Introduction." In *Imperial Rome, Indian Ocean Regions, and Muziris: New Perspectives on Maritime Trade*. Edited by K. S. Mathew, 9–30. Routledge, 2016.
Mawdsley, Emma. "Hindu Nationalism, Neo-Traditionalism and Environmental Discourses in India." *Geoforum* 37 (2006): 380–90.
McCall, Major Anthony Gilchrist. India Office Library and Records (IOLR): Mss Eur E361. Papers of Major A. G. McCall, Indian Civil Service 1921–47. McCall Collection, memoir.
Mies, Maria, and Vandana Shiva, *Ecofeminism*. Zed, 2014.
[Mitra, Dinabhandhu]. *Nil Darpan, or The Indigo Planting Mirror, A Drama*. Translated by "A Native." C. H. Manuel, 1861.
Mitra, Indrani. " 'I Will Make Bimala One With My Country': Gender and Nationalism in Tagore's *The Home and the World*." *MFS: Modern Fiction Studies* 41, no. 2 (Summer 1995): 243–64.
Mitter, Partha. *Indian Art*. Oxford University Press, 2001.
Mohan, Anupama. "Maritime Transmodernities and The Ibis Trilogy." *Postcolonial Text* 14, nos. 3 & 4 (2019): 1–24.
Moore, Donald. "Beyond Blackmail: Multivalent Modernities and the Cultural Politics of Development in India." In *Regional Modernities: The Cultural Politics of Development in India*. Edited by K. Sivaramakrishnan and Arun Agrawal, 165–214. Stanford University Press, 2003.
Morey, Peter, and Alex Tickell. "Introduction." In *Alternative Indias: Writing, Nation and Communalism*. Edited by Morey and Tickell, ix–xxxviii. Rodopi, 2005.
Morrison, Kathleen. "Environmental History, the Spice Trade, and the State in South India." In *Ecological Nationalisms: Nature, Livelihoods, and Identities in South Asia*. 2nd ed. Edited by Gunnel Cederlöf and S. Sivaramakrishnan, 43–64. 2005. Reprint, Permanent Black, 2012.
Morrison, Kathleen D. "Pepper in the Hills: Upland–Lowland Exchange and the Intensification of the Spice Trade." In *Forager-Traders in South and Southeast Asia: Long-Term Histories*. Edited by K. D. Morrison and Laura L. Junker, 122–38. Cambridge University Press, 2003.
Morrison, Kathleen D., and Mark T. Lycett. "Constructing Nature: Socionatural Histories of an Indian Forest." In *The Social Lives of Forests: Past, Present, and Future of Woodland Resurgence*. Edited by Susanna B. Hecht, Kathleen D. Morrison, and Christine Padoch, 148–60. University of Chicago Press, 2014.
Mother India, dir. Mehboob Khan. Mehboob Productions, 1957.

Mukherjee, Meenakshi. "Epic and Novel in India." In *The Novel, Volume 1: History, Genre, and Culture*. Edited by Franco Moretti, 596–631. Princeton University Press, 2006.

Mukherjee, Meenakshi. *Realism and Reality: The Novel and Society in India*. Oxford University Press, 1996.

Mukherjee, Upamanyu Pablo. *Postcolonial Environments: Nature, Culture and the Contemporary Indian Novel in English*. Palgrave Macmillan, 2010.

Mukherjee, Upamanyu Pablo. " 'Yet Was It Human?': Bankim, Hunter and the Victorian Famine Ideology of *Anandamath*." In *Victorian Environments: Acclimatizing to Change in British Domestic and Colonial Culture*, 237–58. Palgrave, 2018.

Musser, Howard Anderson. *Jungle Tales: Adventures in India*. George H. Doran Co., 1922. IOLR collection.

Muziris Heritage Project (website). https://www.muzirisheritage.org/. Accessed July 8, 2021.

"Nagaland Population 2011-22." https://www.census2011.co.in/census/state/nagaland.html. Accessed June 30, 2021.

Nair, M. V., V. Selvakumar, and P. K. Gopi. "Excavation of a Unique Sailboat at Kadakkarappally, Kerala." *Current Science* 86, no. 5 (March 10, 2004): 709–12.

Nair, Shankar. *Translating Wisdom: Hindu-Muslim Intellectual Interactions in Early Modern South Asia*. University of California Press, 2020.

Nanda, Meera. *Prophets Facing Backward: Postmodern Critiques of Science and Hindu Nationalism in India*. Rutgers University Press, 2003.

Nandy, Ashis. *An Ambiguous Journey to the City*. Oxford University Press, 2001.

Nandy, Ashis. "The Defiance and Liberation for the Victims of History: Ashis Nandy in Conversation with Vinay Lal." In "Plural Worlds, Multiple Selves: Ashis Nandy and the Post-Columbian Future," special issue. *Emergences*, nos. 7–8 (1995–6): 3–76.

Nandy, Ashis. *The Intimate Enemy: Loss and Recovery of Self under Colonialism*. Oxford University Press, 1983.

Narayan, R. K. "Under the Banyan Tree." In *Under the Banyan Tree and Other Stories*, 187–92. Penguin, 1985.

Narayan, R. K. Waiting for the Mahatma, University of Chicago Press, 1981.

Narayana Rao, Velcheru. "A *Ramayana* of Their Own: Women's Oral Tradition in Telugu." In *Many Ramayanas*. Edited by Paula Richman, 113–34. University of California Press, 1991.

Narayanan, Vasudha. "Religious Vocabulary and Regional Identity: A Study of the Tamil *Cirappuranam* ('Life of the Prophet')." In *India's Islamic Traditions, 711–1750*. Edited by Richard M. Eaton, 393–410. Oxford University Press, 2003.

Narlekar, Anjali. *Bombay Modern: Arun Kolatkar and Bilingual Literary Culture*. Northwestern University Press, 2016.

Nehru, Jawaharlal. *The Discovery of India*. 1946. Reprint, Oxford University Press, 1989.

Ngũgĩ wa Thiong'o. *Petals of Blood*. Heinemann, 1977.

[Dinabhandhu Mitra]. *Nil Darpan, or The Indigo Planting Mirror, A Drama*. Translated by "A Native." C. H. Manuel, 1861.

Noehden, George Henry. "Account of the Banyan-Tree, or Ficus Indica, as Found in the Ancient Greek and Roman Authors." *Transactions of the Royal Asiatic Society of Great Britain and Ireland* 1, no. 1 (1824): 119–32.

Norton, Anne. *Bloodrites of the Post-structuralists: Word, Flesh, and Revolution*. Routledge, 2002.

Novetzke, Christian Lee. *The Quotidian Revolution: Vernacularization, Religion, and the Premodern Public Sphere in India*. Columbia University Press, 2016.
Online Etymology Dictionary. "Forest." https://www.etymonline.com/word/forest. Accessed May 12, 2021.
Oppenheimer, Paul. "Goethe and Modernism: The Dream of Anachronism in Goethe's 'Roman Elegies.'" *Arion: A Journal of Humanities and the Classics* 6, no. 1 (Spring-Summer 1998): 81–100.
Oppermann, Serpil. "From Ecological Postmodernism to Material Ecocriticism: Creative Materiality and Narrative Agency." In *Material Ecocriticism*. Edited by Iovino Serenella and S. Oppermann, 21–36. Indiana University Press, 2014.
Orsini, Francesca, and Katherine Butler Schofield. Introduction. In *Tellings and Texts: Music, Literature and Performance in North India*, edited by F. Orsini and K. B. Schofield, 1–27. Open Book Publishers, 2015.
d'Orta, Garcia. *Colloquies on the Simples and Drugs of India (Colóquios dos simples e drogas he cousas medicinais da Índia*; 1563). Translated by Sir Clements R. Markham. Henry Sotheran and Co., 1913.
Oxford Reference. "Sādhāraṇa Dharma." https://www.oxfordreference.com/view/10.1093/oi/authority.20110803100436176. Accessed May 2, 2021.
Pandey, Gyanendra. *The Construction of Communalism in Colonial North India*. Oxford University Press, 1992.
Parasher-Sen, Aloka. "Of Tribes, Hunters and Barbarians: Forest Dwellers in the Mauryan Period." In *India's Environmental History: A Reader: Vol. 1: From Ancient Times to the Colonial Period*. Edited by Mahesh Rangarajan and K. Sivaramakrishnan, 127–52. Orient Blackswan, 2011.
Parker, Grant. *The Making of Roman India*. Cambridge University Press, 2011.
Parkhill, Thomas. *The Forest Setting in Hindu Epics: Princes, Sages, Demons*. Edwin Mellen Press, 1995.
Parpia, Shaha. "Mughal Hunting Grounds: Landscape Manipulation and 'Garden' Association." *Garden History* 44, no. 2 (Winter 2016): 171–90.
Parthasarathy, R. "Introduction." In *The Cilappatikaram: The Tale of an Anklet*. Translated and edited by R. Parthasarathy, 1–16. 1993. Reprint, Penguin, 2004.
Parthasarathy, R. "Postscript." In *The Cilappatikaram: The Tale of an Anklet*. Translated and edited by R. Parthasarathy, 279–369. Penguin, 2004.
Pearson, Michael N. *The Indian Ocean*. Routledge, 2003.
Pearson, Michael N. *The New Cambridge History of India, Vol. I: The Portuguese in India*. Cambridge University Press, 2008.
Peirce, C. S. "On the Algebra of Logic: A Contribution to the Philosophy of Notation." *American Journal of Mathematics* 7, no. 2 (January 1885): 180–96.
Phule, Mahatma Jyotirao. *Slavery (In the Civilised British Government Under the Cloak of Brahmanism)*. Translated by P. G. Patil. 1885, Reprint, Government of Maharashtra, 1991.
Picart, Bernard. *Cérémonies et coutumes religieuses de tous les peuples du monde*, 9 volumes (1723–43). Translated anonymously from French as *Ceremonies and Religious Customs of the Various Nations of the Known World*. Claude du Bosc, 1786. Archive.org. https://archive.org/details/ceremoniesreligi05pica/page/n5/mode/2up. Accessed May 22, 2021.
Pollock, Sheldon. "Introduction." In *Ramayana Book Three: The Forest, by Valmiki*. vol. 15. Translated by S. Pollock, 13–34. Clay Sanskrit Library, 2006.

Pouchepadass, Jacques. "British Attitudes Towards Shifting Cultivation in Colonial South India: A Case Study of South Canara District, 1800–1920." In *Nature, Culture, Imperialism: Essays on the Environmental History of South Asia*. Edited by David Arnold and Ramachandra Guha, 123–51. Oxford University Press, 1997.

Prange, Sebastian R. "'Measuring by the Bushel': Reweighing the Indian Ocean Pepper Trade." *Historical Research* 84, no. 224 (May 2011): 212–35.

Prasad, M. Madhava. *Ideology of the Hindi Film: A Historical Construction*. Oxford India, 2000.

Premchand. *The Gift of a Cow*. Translated by Gordon Roadarmel. 1968. Reprint, Indiana University Press, 2002.

Premchand. *Godaan* (Hindi). Open access at *Sahitya Chintan*. http://sahityachintan.com/books-library/hindi/godan/page4.html. Accessed June 11, 2021.

Quint, David. *Epic and Empire: Politics and Generic Form from Virgil to Milton*. Princeton University Press, 1993.

Rajagopal, Krishnadas. "What Is Forest Rights Act?" *The Hindu*, March 2, 2019. https://www.thehindu.com/sci-tech/energy-and-environment/what-is-forest-rights-act/article26419298.ece. Accessed May 6, 2021.

Raman, Shankar. *Renaissance Literature and Postcolonial Studies: Renaissance Literatures and Postcolonial Studies*. Edinburgh University Press, 2011.

Ramanujan, A. K. "Afterword." In *The Interior Landscape: Classical Tamil Love Poems*. Translated and edited by A. K. Ramanujan, 79–102. NYRB Poets, 2014.

Ramanujan, A. K. "Afterword." In *The Oxford India Ramanujan*. Edited by Molly Daniels-Ramanujan, 231–97. Oxford University Press, 2004.

Ramanujan, A. K. "Three Hundred *Ramayanas*: Five Examples and Three Thoughts on Translation." In *Many* Ramayanas: *The Diversity of a Narrative Tradition in South Asia*. Edited by Paula Richman, 22–49. University of California Press, 1991.

Ramanujan, A. K. "Talking to God in the Mother Tongue." *India International Centre Quarterly* 19, no. 4 (Winter 1992): 53–64.

Ramaswami, Geetha, and Suhel Quader. "The Case of the Confusing Kanikonna Trees." *The Wire*, June 26, 2018. https://thewire.in/environment/the-case-of-the-confusing-kanikonna-trees. Accessed October 27, 2020.

Ramaswamy, Sumathi. *The Goddess and the Nation: Mapping Mother India*. Duke University Press, 2010.

Ramaswamy, Sumathi. *The Lost Land of Lemuria: Fabulous Geographies, Catastrophic Histories*. University of California Press, 2004.

Ramaswamy, Sumathi. *Passions of the Tongue: Language Devotion in Tamil India, 1891–1970*. University of California Press, 1997.

Ramnath, Madhu. *Woodsmoke and Leafcups: Autobiographical Footnotes to the Anthropology of the Durwa*. Harper Litmus, 2015.

Rangarajan, Mahesh. "Forest as Faunal Enclave: Endangerment, Ecology, and Exclusion in India." In *The Social Lives of Forests: Past, Present, and Future of Woodland Resurgence*. Edited by S. B. Hecht, K. D. Morrison, and C. Padoch, 192–98. University of Chicago Press, 2014.

Rangarajan, Swarnalatha. "Ecological Dimensions of the Ramayana: A Conversation with Paula Richman." *The Trumpeter* 25, no. 1 (2009): 22–33.

Rangarajan, Swarnalatha. "Women Writing Nature in the Global South: New Forest Texts from Fractured Indian Forests." In *Handbook of Ecocriticism and Cultural Ecology*. Edited by Hubert Zapf, 438–58. De Gruyter Mouton, 2016.

Rao, Raja. Author's foreword in *Kanthapura*, vii–viii. New Directions, 1967.
Ray, Romita. "Inscribing Asymmetry: Johann Zoffany's Banyan and 'The Extension of Knowledge.'" *South Asian Studies* 27, no. 2 (2011): 185–98.
Ray, Romita. *Under the Banyan Tree: Relocating the Picturesque in British India*. Paul Mellon Centre for Studies in British Art, 2003.
Ray, Satyajit, dir. *Aranyer Din Ratri* (*Days and Nights in the Forest*). Bengali, 1970.
Ray, Sugata. *Climate Change and the Art of Devotion: Geoaesthetics in the Land of Krishna, 1550–1850*. University of Washington Press, 2019.
Raychaudhuri, Tapan. *Europe Reconsidered: Perceptions of the West in Nineteenth Century Bengal*. Oxford University Press, 1988.
Reynolds, Holly Baker. "Madurai: *Kōyil Nakar*." In *The City as a Sacred Center: Essays on Six Asian Contexts*. Edited by Bardwell L. Smith and Holly Baker Reynolds, 12–44. E. J. Brill, 1987.
Richman, Paula. "Introduction: 'The Diversity of the *Ramayana* Tradition.'" In *Many Ramayanas*. Edited by Paula Richman, 3–21. University of California Press, 1991.
Richards, J. F. "The Indian Empire and Peasant Production of Opium in the Nineteenth Century." *Modern Asian Studies* 15, no. 1 (1981): 59–82.
Riehl, Wilhelm Heinrich. "Field and Forest" (1853). Translated by Frances H. King. *The German Classics of the Nineteenth and Twentieth Centuries: Masterpieces of German Literature*. vol. VIII (of 20). Project Gutenberg, [1914] 2004. http://www.gutenberg.org/cache/epub/12573/pg12573.html. Accessed April 22, 2019.
Rigby, Kate. "Spirits That Matter: Pathways toward a Rematerialization of Religion and Spirituality." In *Material Ecocriticism*. Edited by S. Iovino and S. Oppermann, 283–90. Indiana University Press, 2014.
Robbins, Bruce. "The Politics of Theory." *Social Text* 6 (Winter, 1987–88): 3–18.
Robbins, Paul. "Policing and Erasing the Global/Local Border: Rajasthani Foresters and the Narrative Ecology of Modernization." In *Regional Modernities: The Cultural Politics of Development in India*. Edited by K. Sivaramakrishnan and Arun Agrawal, 377–403. Stanford University Press, 2003.
Roy, Anuradha. *The Atlas of Impossible Longing*. Hachette India, 2008.
Roy, Arundhati. "'Arundhati Roy Supports Tribals' Cause'" [Letter to Kerala Chief Minister A. K. Antony], February 27, 2003." In *Mother Forest: The Unfinished Story of C. K. Janu*, 63–66. Women Unlimited and Kali for Women, 2004.
Roy, Arundhati. *The God of Small Things*. Random House, 1997.
Roy, Arundhati. *The Ministry of Utmost Happiness*. Knopf, 2017.
Roy, Arundhati. *Walking With Comrades*. Penguin, 2011.
Roy, Parama. *Alimentary Tracts: Appetites, Aversions, and the Postcolonial*. Duke University Press, 2010.
Roy, Rajah Rammohun. *Exposition of the Practical Operation of the Judicial and Revenue Systems of India, and of the General Character and Condition of Its Native Inhabitants, as Submitted in Evidence to the Authorities in England)*. Smith, Elder, 1832.
Rushdie, Salman. *Imaginary Homelands: Essays and Criticism, 1981–1991*. Granta/Penguin, 1991.
Rushdie, Salman. *Midnight's Children: A Novel*. 1981. Reprint, Random House, 2021.
Said, Edward W. *Orientalism*. Vintage, 1979.
Salih, Tayeb. *Season of Migration to the North*. Translated by Denys Johnson-Davies. 1969. Reprint, New York Review of Books, 2009.

Salopek, Paul. "Millions of Indigenous People Face Eviction from Their Forest Homes." NationalGeographic.com, May 15, 2019. https://www.nationalgeographic.com/culture/article/millions-india-indigenous-people-face-eviction-from-forests?loggedin=true. Accessed June 30, 2020.

Sarkar, Tanika. *Hindu Wife, Hindu Nation: Community, Religion, and Cultural Nationalism.* Indiana University Press, 2002.

Sarveswaran, Vidya. "The Forest as a Sacramentalized Ecosystem in *Aranyak: Of the Forest.*" *Indian Journal of Ecocriticism* 1 (August 2008): 83–92.

Sastri, Nilakanta. *History of Southern India from Prehistoric Times to the Fall of Vijayangar.* Oxford University Press, 1958.

Satia, Priya. *Empire of Guns: The Violent Making of the Industrial Revolution.* Penguin, 2018.

Schama, Simon. *Landscape and Memory.* Vintage, 1996.

Schlegel, Friedrich. "To Camões." Translated by Nora Goerne. In "Annex" to "Camões in Germany and Romantic Discourses of Decline in the 19th and 20th Century," special issue. *Revista de Filología Alemana* 23 (2015): 1–15.

Schoenhaus, Seth. "Indian Dalits and Hindutva Strategies." *Denison Journal of Religion* 16, no. 1 (2017): 55–67.

Schofield, Katherine Butler. "Learning to Taste the Emotions: The Mughal Rasika." In *Tellings and Texts: Music, Literature and Performance in North India.* Edited by Francesca Orsini and Katherine B. Schofield, 407–22. Open Book Publishers, 2015.

Schwab, Raymond. *The Oriental Renaissance: Europe's Rediscovery of India and the East, 1680–1880.* Translated by Gene Patterson-Black and Victor Reinking. Columbia University Press, 1984.

Scott, Sir Walter. *Waverley; or, 'Tis Sixty Years Since.* Adam and Charles Black, 1897.

"Selection from *Premsagar* by Lallulal." http://www.columbia.edu/itc/mealac/pritchett/01glossaries/busch/premsagar.htm. Accessed June 15, 2021.

Sen, Amartya. "The Argumentative Indian." In *The Argumentative Indian: Writings on Indian History, Culture and Identity*, 3–33. Picador, 2006.

Sen, Amartya. *The Idea of Justice.* Belknap Press, 2011.

Sen, Sandipan. "Sanskritisation of Bengali, Plight of the Margin and the Forgotten Role of Tagore." *Journal of the Department of English Vidyasagar University* 11 (2013–14): 51–8.

Sen, Sudipta. *Ganges: The Many Pasts of an Indian River.* Yale University Press, 2019.

Sethi, Rumina. *Myths of the Nation: National Identity and Literary Representations.* Clarendon Press, 1999.

Shandilya, Krupa. "The Widow, the Wife, and the Courtesan: A Comparative Study of Social Reform in Premchand's *Sevasadan* and the Late Nineteenth-Century Bengali and Urdu Novel." *Comparative Literature Studies* 53, no. 2 (2016): 272–88.

Shanker, N. Ravi, trans. "Translator's Note." In *Mother Forest: The Unfinished Story of C.K. Janu*, ix–xii. Women Unlimited and Kali for Women, 2004.

Sharma, Sunil. *Amir Khusraw: The Poet of Sufis and Sultans.* Oneworld, 2005.

Shaw, Miranda Eberle. *Buddhist Goddesses of India.* Princeton University Press, 2006.

Shekhar, Hansda Sowvendra. *The Mysterious Ailment of Rupi Baskey.* Aleph Book Co., 2014.

Shingavi, Snehal. "When Pen Was a Sword: The Radical Career of the Progressive Novel in India." In *A History of the Indian Novel in English.* Edited by Ulka Anjaria, 73–87. Cambridge University Press, 2015.

Shiva, Vandana. "Everything I Need to Know I Learned in the Forest." *The NAMTA [North American Montessori Teachers' Association] Journal* 38, no. 1 (Winter 2013): 273–6.

Shiva, Vandana. "Reductionist Science as Epistemological Violence." In *Science, Hegemony and Violence: A Requiem for Modernity*. Edited by Ashis Nandy, 232–56. Oxford University Press, 1988.

Shiva, Vandana. *Staying Alive: Women, Ecology and Survival in India*. Zed Books, 1988.

Sippy, Ramesh. *Sholay*. dir. Sippy Films, 1975.

Shrikumar, A. "Where Once Stood a Forest of Kadamba Trees …" *The Hindu*, December 7, 2018. https://www.thehindu.com/life-and-style/homes-and-gardens/tamil-lit erature-refers-to-madurai-as-kadambavanam-but-today-less-than-20-kada mba-trees-are-found-in-the-city/article25689117.ece. Accessed December 1, 2019.

Shulman, David. *Tamil: A Biography*. Harvard University Press, 2016.

Sidebotham, Steven E. *Berenike and the Ancient Maritime Spice Route*. University of California Press, 2011.

Sims, James H. "Christened Classicism in *Paradise Lost* and *The Lusiads*." *Comparative Literature* 24, no. 4 (Autumn 1972): 338–56.

Singh, Chetan. "Forests, Pastoralists and Agrarian Society in Mughal India." In *Nature, Culture, Imperialism: Essays on the Environmental History of South Asia*. Edited by David Arnold and Ramachandra Guha, 21–48. Oxford University Press, 1995.

Singh, K. S. "Transformation of Tribal Society: Integration vs Assimilation." *Economic and Political Weekly* 17, no. 34 (August 21, 1982): 1376–84.

Sinha, Amita. "The Sacred Landscape of Braj, India: Imagined, Enacted, and Reclaimed." *Landscape Journal: Design, Planning, and Management of the Land* 33, no. 1 (2014): 59–75.

Sinha, Indra. *Animal's People*. Simon & Schuster, 2007.

Sinha, Subir, Shubhra Gururani, and Brian Greenberg, "The 'New Traditionalist' Discourse of Indian Environmentalism." *The Journal of Peasant Studies* 24, no. 3 (1997): 65–99.

Sivaramakrishnan, K., and Arun Agrawal. "Regional Modernities in Stories and Practices of Development." In *Regional Modernities: The Cultural Politics of Development in India*. Edited by K. Sivaramakrishnan and Arun Agrawal, 1–61. Stanford University Press, 2003.

Skaria, Ajay. "Cathecting the Natural." In *Agrarian Environments: Resources, Representation, and Rule in India*. Edited by Arun Agrawal and K. Sivaramakrishnan, 265–76. Duke University Press, 2000.

Skaria, Ajay. "Gandhi's Politics: Liberalism and the Question of the Ashram." *South Atlantic Quarterly* 101, no. 4 (Fall 2002): 955–86.

Skaria, Ajay. *Hybrid Histories: Forests, Frontiers and Wildness in Western India*. Oxford University Press, 1999.

Smith, Brian K. "Classifying Animals and Humans in Ancient India." *Man* (New Series) 26, no. 3 (September 1991): 527–48.

Sontheimer, Günther D. "All the God's Wives." In *Images of Women in Maharashtrian Literature and Religion*. Edited by Anne Feldhaus, 116–32. SUNY Press, 1996.

Southey, Robert. *The Curse of Kehama*. Excerpted in *The Poets and Poetry of the Nineteenth Century: Robert Southey to Percy Bysshe Shelley*. Edited by Alfred H. Miles, 25–34. George Routledge & Sons, 1905.

Spivak, Gayatri Chakravorty. "Can the Subaltern Speak?" In *Marxism and the Interpretation of Culture*. Edited by Cary Nelson and Lawrence Grossberg, 271–313. University of Illinois Press, 1988.

Spivak, Gayatri Chakravorty. *A Critique of Postcolonial Reason: Toward a History of the Vanishing Present*. Harvard University Press, 1999.

Srinivas, M. N. *The Remembered Village*. Oxford University Press, 1979.
Stewart, Jon. *Hegel's Interpretation of the Religions of the World: The Logic of the Gods*. Oxford University Press, 2018.
Subrahmanyam, Sanjay. *The Career and Legend of Vasco da Gama*. Cambridge University Press, 1998.
Sullivan, Bruce M. "Chapter 10: Theology and Ecology at the Birthplace of Krishna." In *Purifying the Earthly Mother of God: Religion and Ecology in Hindu India*. Edited by Lance E. Nelson, 247–68. SUNY Press, 1998.
Swami Madhavananda, trans. *Brihadaranyaka Upanishad*. 1934. Reprint, Advaita Ashrama, 1950.
Tagore, Rabindranath. *Glimpses of Bengal*. Macmillan, 1921.
Tagore, Rabindranath. "Letter to Prashanta Chandra Mahalanobis." In *Tagore: An Anthology*. Edited by Krishna Dutta and Andrew Robinson, 176–7. 1921. Reprint, St. Martin's Press, 1997.
Tagore, Rabindranath. "My Golden Bengal" [*Amar Sonar Bangla*]. Wikisource. https://en.wikisource.org/wiki/My_Golden_Bengal. Accessed June 20, 2021.
Tagore, Rabindranath. "From *My Reminiscences*." In *Tagore: An Anthology*. Edited by Krishna Dutta and Andrew Robinson, 55–83. St. Martin's Press, 1997.
Tagore, Rabindranath. "Santiniketan Song." Tagoreweb.in. https://www.tagoreweb.in/Verses/collected-poems-and-plays-197/she-is-our-own-2609. Accessed November 27, 2020.
Tagore, Rabindranath. "The Religion of the Forest." In *Creative Unity*, 45–68. Macmillan, 1922.
Tagore, Rabindranath. "A Vision of History." 1903. Reprinted in *Journal of Studies in History & Culture*. http://jshc.org/a-vision-of-indias-history/. Accessed June 30, 2020.
Thakur, Renu. "Urban Hierarchies, Typologies and Classification in Early Medieval India: c. 750–1200." *Urban History* 21, no. 1 (April 1994): 61–76.
Thapar, Romila. "Perceiving the Forest: Early India." In *Environmental History of India Vol. 1: From Ancient Times to the Colonial Period: A Reader*. Edited by Mahesh Rangarajan and K. Sivaramakrishnan, 105–25. Permanent Black, 2012.
Thengane, S. R., S. V. Bhosle, S. R. Deodhar, and K. D. Pawar. "Micropropagation of Indian Laurel (*Calophyllum inophyllum*), a Source of Anti-HIV Compounds." *Current Science* 90, no. 10 (May 25, 2006): 1393–7.
Thomas, Keith. *Man and the Natural World: Changing Attitudes in England, 1500–1800*. New ed. Penguin, 1991.
Thomas, Rosie. "Melodrama and the Negotiation of Morality in Mainstream Hindi Film." In *Consuming Modernity: Public Culture in a South Asian World*. Edited by Carol A. Breckenridge, 157–82. University of Minnesota Press, 1995.
Thoreau, Henry David. *Walden and "Civil Disobedience."* Reissue ed. Signet, 2012.
Tickell, Alex. "Some Uses of History: Historiography, Politics, and the Indian Novel." In *A History of the Indian Novel in English*. Edited by Ulka Anjaria, 237–50. Cambridge University Press, 2015.
Tobin, Beth Fowkes. *Colonizing Nature: The Tropics in British Arts and Letters, 1760–1820*. University of Pennsylvania Press, 2004.
Toppo, Anima Pushpa. "Proceedings: First Global Meeting of the Indigenous Peoples' Forum at IFAD, February 11–12, 2013," 3–53. https://www.iwgia.org/es/documents-and-publications/documents/publications-pdfs/english-publicati ons/338-ifad-iwgia-proceedings-first-global-meeting-of-the-indigenous-peoples%E2%80%99-forum-at-ifad-2013-eng/file.html. Accessed June 9, 2022.

Torgovnick, Marianna. *Gone Primitive: Savage Intellects, Modern Minds*. Reprint ed. University of Chicago Press, 1991.

Trumpener, Katie. *Bardic Nationalism: The Romantic Novel and the British Empire*. Princeton University Press, 1997.

Tucker, Richard P. "The Depletion of India's Forests Under British Imperialism: Planters, Foresters, and Peasants in Assam and Kerala." In *The Ends of the Earth: Perspectives on Modern Environmental History*. Edited by Donald Worster, 118–40. Cambridge University Press, 1989.

Turner, Ellen. "An Unfinished Story: The Representation of Adivasis in Indian Feminist Literature." *Contemporary South Asia* 20, no. 3 (September 2012): 327–39.

Turner, Victor. *The Ritual Process: Structure and Anti-Structure*. 1969. Reprint, Cornell University Press, 1991.

Tzoref-Ashkenazi, Chen. "India and the Identity of Europe: The Case of Friedrich Schlegel." *Journal of the History of Ideas* 67, no. 4 (October, 2006): 713–34.

Upadhyay, Shashi Bhushan. "Premchand and the Moral Economy of Peasantry in Colonial North India." *Modern Asian Studies* 45, no. 5 (September 2011): 1227–59.

Vaidya, Anand. "Woh Jungle Hamara Hai." *Seminar* 690 (February 2017): 68–71.

Valmiki. *Ramayana, Book Three: The Forest*. Translated by Sheldon Pollock. Clay Sanskrit Library, 2006.

Venkatachalapathy, A. R. *The Province of the Book: Scholars, Scribes, and Scribblers in Colonial Tamilnadu*. Permanent Black, 2012.

Viswanathan, Gauri. *Masks of Conquest: Literary Study and British Rule in India*. Columbia University Press, 1989.

Vivekanandan, Jayashree. "Scratches on Our Sovereignty?: Analyzing Conservation Politics in the Sundarbans." *Regions & Cohesion* 11, no. 1 (Spring 2021): 1–20.

Wenzel, Jennifer. "Epic Struggles over India's Forests in Mahasweta Devi's Short Fiction." In "Post-Colonial Discourse in South Asia," special issue. *Alif: Journal of Comparative Poetics*, no. 18 (1998): 127–58.

Wheeler, Wendy. "Natural Play, Natural Metaphor, and Natural Stories: Biosemiotic Realism." In *Material Ecocriticism*. Edited by S. Iovino and S. Oppermann, 67–79. Indiana University Press, 2014.

Wikipedia. "Jharkhand." https://en.wikipedia.org/wiki/Jharkhand. Accessed December 11, 2016.

Williams, Raymond. *The Country and the City*. Oxford University Press, 1975.

Wohlleben, Peter. *The Hidden Life of Trees: What They Feel, How They Communicate— Discoveries from a Secret World*. Translated by Jane Billinghurst. Penguin India, 2016.

Wood, James. *How Fiction Works*. Picador, 2008.

Wordsworth, William. "Preface to Lyrical Ballads" (1802). University of Pennsylvania website. https://web.english.upenn.edu/~jenglish/Courses/Spring2001/040/preface1802.html. Accessed June 20, 2021.

Yazijian, Edward M., "Introduction." In *The Chandimangal of Kavikankan Mukundaram Chakravarti*. Translated by Edward M. Yazijian, vii–xvi. Penguin, 2015.

Yelle, Robert A. *The Language of Disenchantment: Protestant Literalism and Colonial Discourse in British India*. Oxford University Press, 2013.

Zamora, Lois Parkinson. *The Usable Past: The Imagination of History in Recent Fiction of the Americas*. Cambridge University Press, 1997.

Zarrilli, Phillip B. *Kathakali Dance-Drama: Where Gods and Demons Come to Play*. Routledge, 1999.

Zimmermann, Francis, trans. *The Jungle and the Aroma of Meats: An Ecological Theme in Hindu Medicine* [in French]. University of California Press, 1987.
Zipes, Jack. *The Brothers Grimm: From Enchanted Forests to the Modern World*. 1988. Reprint, Palgrave Macmillan, 2022.
Zvelebil, Kamil. "The Book of Lofty Wisdom." In *The Smile of Murugan: On Tamil Literature of South India*, 155–71. E. J. Brill, 1973.

Index

Abu'l Fazl 79, 227 n.12
Achebe, Chinua: *Things Fall Apart* 65
Adiga, Aravind: *The White Tiger* 49, 186–8
Adivasi 12, 20, 29, 32–3, 44, 48–9, 71, 93, 99, 120, 126, 145, 153–4, 155, 159–63, 167–8, 171, 175, 182, 184, 189–90
Agastya Sen character in *English, August* 184
Agastya, sage 25, 72
Agni 54, 73
Agnihotri, Anita: *Forest Interludes* 226 n.1
Ahmed, Siraj 5, 206 n.46
Aitken, Molly Emma 103–4
Ajmer 37
akam 54, 66
Akbar, Mughal Emperor 39
Akbarnama of Abu Faz'l 69
akil tree 68
Alam, Muzaffar 39
All-India Radio 166
Allahabad 32
allegory, and realism 162
  of history 150
Aman, Zeenat 118
Ambedkar, B. R. 119
Amber 39
Amina character in *Midnight's Children* 133, 150
Amrith, Sunil S. 225 n.37
Amritsar 155
Anandamath 7, 11, 13, 18, 22, 23, 42, 43, 46, 61, 71, 73, 79, 81, 82, 83, 84, 86, 90, 94, 146, 150, 158, 163, 186
  See also Chattopadhyay, Bankimchandra
Ananthamurthy, U. R. 181
Angami people 176
Anglo-Chinese (Opium) War 147, 150
Animal character in *Animal's People* 188
Animal's People 186, 188
  See also Sinha, Indira

Anjaria, Ulka 122
Anthropocene 33, 170
anupa forest 45, 46
Aparajito 123
Aparna character in *Days and Nights in the Forest* 183
Apu Trilogy films of Satyajit Ray 222 n.34
aranya 4, 30, 31, 45, 158
  Aranyak 124
Aranyak: Of the Forest 48, 145–6, 155, 183, 186
Aranyaka, Forest Book 6, 25, 123
Aravamudan, Srinivas 14
areca nut 37, 59, 63, 93, 99, 157
  See also betel nut
areca palm 1, 37, 51, 54
Aristotle 4
Arjun tree 125
Arjuna 25
Arthashastra 31, 204 n.2
  See also Kautilya
Arya 54
Aryan 20, 33, 36, 73, 81, 89, 90, 92, 129, 158
asceticism 108, 116, 135
ashan tree 129
Ashoka tree 18, 66
ashrama 30, 35, 43, 46, 73
ashramic forest retreat, detachment, education 43, 100, 103, 106, 116, 182–3
Assamese language and literature 181
Association of Small Bombs, The 186–8
  See also Mahajan, Karan
Athens, ancient 12
Atikal, Ilanko 55, 57, 59, 61–3, 66, 84
  See also The Cilappatikaram: The Tale of an Anklet
Aurobindo Ghose 22, 98
Awadh (Oudh) 77
Ayodhya 24, 30

Babu figure 79, 83, 110
Babur 144
Baburnama: Memoirs of Babur, Prince and Emperor 144, 224 n.31
Badra people 78
Bakhtin, Mikhail 163
Balaev, Michelle 192 n.26
Balram character in *The White Tiger* 187
bamboo tree, forest 51, 184
Banabhatta and Bhushanabhatta: *Kadambari* 58
Banaras 29, 55, 58
Bande Mataram 48, 79–80, 91, 97–9, 101
Bandhyopadhyay, Bibhutibhushan: *Aranyak: Of the Forest* 160, 183
Bangladesh, Bangladeshi 130
Banker, Ashok K. 20
  Prince of Ayodhya: Book One of the Ramayana 36, 40, 42, 73
Bankim (Bankimchandra)
  See also Chattopadhyay, Bankimchandra
Banu 99, 100, 101
Banwari: *Panchavati: Indian Approach to Environment* 1
banyan tree 14–15, 45, 91–2, 167
  geography of India 15
Bastar forests 158
Bay of Bengal 59
Bayly, C. A. 69, 96
Belgian Congo Forest 134
Bengal 11, 18, 35, 42–3, 47–9, 64–5, 75, 79–80, 82–3, 87–90, 92–9, 104, 110, 124, 126, 131, 136–7, 140, 165, 171, 181, 200 n.216, 211 n.12, 214 n.69, 215 n.98
  forests of 13, 18, 47–8, 65, 84, 90, 95, 101, 105, 110, 114, 124, 214 n.69
  landscape 90
  partition of 124
Bengali language, literature, writers 18, 20, 22, 26, 33, 36, 40, 44, 46, 49, 79, 82–3, 85, 87, 92–9, 106, 117–18, 122, 124, 141, 145, 156, 161, 166, 168, 181–2, 200 n.216, 203 n.288, 223–24 n.8
  Bengali writers, activists, and nationalists 7–8, 11, 13, 18, 26, 65, 80, 82, 84, 87–8, 97, 123, 126, 153, 161, 181–2, 215 n.98, 219 n.198, 228 n.26

Benjamin, Walter 9
Bennett, Jane 170
Berger, John: *Ways of Seeing* 11
betel nut 37, 39–40, 59, 92–3, 100
  See also areca nut
Bhabananda character in *Anandamath* 97–8, 100
bhadralok 79, 95, 140, 182
Bhagalpur 125, 130
Bhagavad Gita 103, 110, 185
Bhagavata Purana 29
Bhairava 69, 99
Bhakti movement 39, 70, 102–3, 107–9, 113, 140–1, 201 n.241, 218 nn.165, 167, 219 nn.193, 206
Bhanmati 126, 128–30
Bharati, Subramania 25
Bharatvarsha 129
Bhaskaran 156
Bhatnagar, Rashmi 84
Bhoodhan movement 32
Bhopal Gas Disaster 188
Bhotia people 154
Bibhutibhushan
  See Bandhyopadhyay, Bibhutibhushan
Bihar 182
Bimala character in *The Home and the World* 122
bioregional 25
Birbhum 89–90, 99
Black Forest, Germany 16, 69
Blake, William 14, 15
Bodhi tree 134–5
Bombay 133, 185
Bon Bibi 138–40, 145–6
boundaries, natural and forest 4, 186
  blurred 147
Bourdieu, Pierre 27
bourgeois 182–3
Brahmin 36, 52, 63–4, 69, 74, 82, 111, 183
Braj 30, 103
Brahmaputra River 142
Braudel, Fernand 7
Brihadaranyaka Upanishad 222–3 n.40
Brindavan
  See Krishna; Vrindavan
Buchanan-Hamilton, Francis 39, 75–6
Buddha 31, 114, 118, 134–5
Buddhism 34

Burke, Edmund 14, 43, 167
Burkert, Walter 174
Busch, Allison 39

Calcutta 22, 29, 35, 79, 111, 125, 128–9, 138, 140–1, 148, 166, 182–5
Calicut 57, 75, 82, 203 n.282, 205 n.23, 209 n.131
Camões, Luís Vaz de: *The Lusiads* (*Os Lusíadas*) 46, 75, 82, 86, 186
canafistula tree 57–8
Canetti, Elias: *Crowds and Power* 2
capitalism 15
cardamom 57, 63, 77
Casanova, Pascale 50, 156
Cenkuttuvan, King 54, 62, 65
Chaitanya 103, 107, 113, 219 n.193
Chakrabarty, Dipesh 7–11, 41, 44, 84, 87, 121, 145–9, 167–9, 171–4
  Provincializing Europe: Postcolonial Thought and Historical Difference 203 n.1, 222 n.25, 230 nn.59, 63, 232 n.99
Chakradhar 69
Chakravarti, Kavikankan Mukundaram: *Chandimangal* 40, 92–3
Chakravorty, Mrinalini 94
champa (Champak) tree 39, 66
Chandi goddess 40, 93
Chandimangal 40, 92–3
Chandra, Sudhir 119
chapati, indexical 9–10
Chattan 63
Chatterjee, Kumkum 93
Chatterjee, Partha 16, 26, 83, 129, 184
Chatterjee, Upamanyu 49
  English, August: An Indian Story 184–5
Chattisgarh 44, 54–5, 58–9, 62–3
Chattopadhyay, Bankimchandra 7–8, 11–13, 18, 22–3, 25, 31, 35, 37, 43, 46, 61, 71, 75, 77, 79, 81–4, 86–90, 94, 97, 114, 118, 126, 146–7, 155, 158, 160, 163, 165, 186
  negative and complex portrayal of Muslim Indians in *Anandamath* 80–1, 83–4, 86–90, 92, 94–5, 97–8, 101, 108–11, 113, 115, 212 n.29
Chattopadhyay, Tarinicharan: *History of India* 83

Chaudhuri, Supriya 92
Chera kings 54–5, 58–9, 62–3
chhatim tree 128
Chipko movement 154, 227 nn.13, 14, 15
chinar tree 128, 134
Chishti, Mu'in al-Din 37
Chishti, 'Abd al-Rahman 39
Chola kings 45–6, 54, 58, 205 n.29
Chota Nagpur 93
Cilappatikaram, The: The Tale of an Anklet 6, 52–6, 58–60, 64–5, 74, 150
cinnamon 57–8
city 3, 49, 57–8, 61–2, 74, 84, 93, 100, 116, 119–20, 182–3, 185–7
  vis-à-vis village 118
Clarissa Dalloway character in Woolf, Virginia 168
Clark, Timothy 170
classical literary era and tropes 27, 46, 54, 56, 81, 92, 101, 150
cloves 75
colonial discourse 87
colonialism, primarily British 5, 9, 13, 16, 28, 36, 41, 44, 52, 68, 70, 75, 81, 154, 173–5, 181–2
Columbus 126
Comtean-positivism 81
Conrad, Joseph 3
Cooper, James Fenimore: *The Pathfinder* 105
CPM (Communist Party of Party [Marxist]) 156–7
creepers (forest vine) feminine trope 29, 54, 60, 85, 89, 115, 127, 188, 204 n.8
critical-historicist 27
Curley, David L. 93
Curtin, Philip D. 7, 215–16 n.107
Curzon, Lord 87

Da Gama, Vasco 6–7, 46, 57, 75–6, 82, 86
dacoit 119
Daiya, Kavita 175
Dalhousie, Lord 76–7
Dalit 32–3, 117, 119
Dalley, Hamish 9, 22–3, 146
  "allegorical realism" 136, 146
Dalmia, Vasudha 44, 121, 213 n.45
Dandaka Forest (*Dandakaranya*) 1, 24, 73, 158–9

Dante 3, 169
dargah 37
darshan 11, 27, 73, 84, 100, 104, 141, 145, 148–9
   darshanic vision 8, 11, 48, 123, 125, 130, 145–8, 150–1, 181, 187, 190
Darukavana (Daruvana) 18, 66–7
Das, Pallavi V. 28
dastan 85
Davis, Coralynn 60, 206 n.38
Deccan 96
deciduous trees, forest 1, 24, 153
Deeti character in *Sea of Poppies* 123, 130, 147–8, 190
deforestation 12, 24, 28, 30, 76–7, 124, 155, 177, 231 n.89
Deleuze, Gilles and Felix Guattari 179
Derozio, Henry 25
Descartes, René 169
desert literary motif 63, 66, 68, 142, 147
   Arabian 68
Deveneyan, G. 65
Devi, Mahasweta 26, 44, 48–9, 153, 155–7, 160–8, 170–5, 178, 181, 184, 228 n.28, 231 n.89
Dhangar people 99–100, 217 n.135
dharma 63, 225 n.43
   dharmic 63, 81
Dharwadker, Vinay 4
"Dhowli"
   See Devi, Mahasweta
Dhurwa people 43
dialogic, dialogism 149
Diderot, Denis 7
Discovery of India, The 21
   See also Nehru, Jawaharlal
disenchantment of world concept 150, 167–9
   See also enchantment
DMK Party (Dravida Munnetra Kazhagam) 65
Dokkhin Rai 139
Dol-Purnima festival 125
domesticity 22, 72, 107, 109, 111, 119, 129, 156, 161, 163, 220 n.214
Dopdi character in "Draupadi" 164–7
Doulouti character in "Douloti the Bountiful" 160–1, 165
d'Orta, Garcia 75

Douglas, Mary 2
Dove, Michael R. 24, 45–6, 70, 169
"Draupadi" story
   See Devi, Mahasweta
Dravida 34, 65, 72
Dube, Saurabh 170
Dubrow, Jennifer 85
Duli character in *Days and Nights in the Forest* 182–3
Duncan, Ian 13
Durga 42, 92–3, 95, 97–9, 10, 105, 110, 122, 148
Duryodhana 70, 136
Dushyanta 4, 70, 73, 98, 100
Dutch East India Company (VAC) 7, 215 n.107
Dutt, Michael Madhusudan 20, 25, 97
Dyer, General 155

East India Company 5, 33, 76–7, 79–80, 86, 88, 95–6, 111, 113, 148
Eck, Diana L. 37, 72
ecocriticism 138, 168, 170, 230 n.66
   material 168
ecology 1, 24–5, 62, 66, 141, 162
ecology of selves 138, 178
emplacement concept 161–2
enchantment of world concept 167–9
   re-enchantment 168
   ecology of selves 178
   See also disenchantment
English language, ambivalent regard for 118
English, August: An Indian Story 184–5
   See also Chatterjee, Upamanyu
Enlightenment, European 13, 43, 68–9
environmental justice 141
epic 5, 40, 73, 75, 86
eucalyptus tree 20, 36, 42
explorers, European 126

fable, fable-like 32, 40, 48, 62, 81, 120, 122, 133, 178, 222 n.27, 231 n.76
famine, Bengal 80, 90, 98, 104, 110, 153
Fanon, Frantz 12
faqir 139
Feldhaus, Anne 200 n.211
femininity tropes 63, 109, 111, 135
   forest 63, 111
   See also forest nymph or maiden trope

Ferris, Ina 23
feudalism 119, 126
First War of Independence (1857–8) 77
Flaubert, Gustave 13
Fokir character in *The Hungry Tide* 138, 140, 142, 144–6
folk 16–17, 25, 29, 48, 53, 70–1, 74, 85, 92, 94, 100–1, 103, 105, 107, 109, 116, 138–41, 162, 170, 177, 184
   commodified by dominant culture 184
folk songs 48, 53, 86, 100, 138
folklore 20, 49, 68, 74, 175
folktale 3, 5, 18, 62, 68–9, 95, 123, 135, 138
forest, assemblage of motifs 147
   balancing city and nature 100
   barren 2
   culture, cultural mythos 2, 45
   duality 30, 61
   educative 90, 100, 114
   enchanted 16, 46, 111, 167, 169, 173, 188
   fecund 2, 70
   feminized, virginal, pure 63, 135, 172, 184
   historyless 48, 90, 131–2, 134
   idealized 186
   interconnectedness 145
   jungle 32, 46, 83, 112, 222 n.39
   liminal 110, 166
   maternal 63, 158
   mysterious 3
   natural boundary 4–5
   primordial 4
   "protected" 77
   "reserved" 77
   retreat 34
   rite of passage 20, 56, 134
   scientific, commercial 32, 44, 155, 168, 172
   tropical 7
   "village" 77
   womb-like 91–2, 122
   See also ashramic; Dove; Michael R.; hunting; index, indexical; jungle; kingship; liminality; Mother Forest
Forest Acts, Indian 28, 77–8
Forestry Department 32, 76–8, 157, 159, 166, 176, 184
"Forest of Pines" 66

forest nymph or maiden trope 118, 121–2, 135
Forest Service, Indian 44, 184–5
forestry, modern 78
   See also forest, scientific; Indian Forest Service
Forests: The Shadow of Civilization
   See Harrison, Robert Pogue
foris 4
Fraser, James Bailie 76
French East India Company 225 n.37
fuzzy concepts 32, 61, 101

Gadgil [Madhav] and [Ramachandra] Guha 78
Gajarawala, Toral Jatin 118
Gandhi, Mohandas K. 11, 17, 117, 119, 228–9 n.37
Gandhi, Indira 132
Gandhian movement 98, 119, 171
   Gandhian "romance" 118
Gandopadhyay, Sunil 49, 160, 182, 185
   See also Days and Nights in the Forest (Aranyer Dinratri)
Ganesh 148
Ganga (Ganges) River 55, 65, 91, 142
Gangetic dolphin 138, 144
Ganguly, Suranjan 183
Garber, Marjorie B. 109
garden, material and motif 39, 61, 74, 182
Garrard, Greg 170
gender 6, 67, 70–1, 102, 110, 112, 124, 162, 165, 182, 219 n.198
   cross-dressing 109
   See also femininity; *hijra*; masculinity; women
genre, Indian 13, 26, 40, 66, 68, 71, 84–5, 92–3, 105, 117, 123, 169, 178, 198 n.166, 200 n.211, 208 n.109
   mixing of 93, 117
   romance 11, 85
geo-body 32–3, 98
geo-piety 32
geography 15, 20, 22, 24, 32–3, 37, 67, 83, 96, 98
   Bengali 83
   sacred 37, 68, 98
   Tamil 96 n.122
   See also Mother India

Germany 69, 81
  forest 8, 16, 22, 81
  German "unity" 169
Ghalib 85
Ghose, Aurobindo
  See Aurobindo
Ghosh, Amitav 10–11, 36, 48, 123, 130–50, 154, 178, 181, 186, 188, 190
  The Great Derangement 137
  The Hungry Tide 48, 132, 136–46, 178
  Sea of Poppies 11, 48, 130, 146–50, 186
Gikandi, Simon 210–11 n.162
Gilgamesh 3, 43, 58, 169
Gir Forest 133
Gita Govinda 29–30
global literature 126
Goa 75, 82
Godaan 48, 117–19, 122–3
  Premchand
golaka 74
Gond people 128, 130
  Gondi language 124
Gopal, Priyamvada 133
gopis 29–30, 60, 74, 92, 102, 114, 202 n.218, 217 n.150
Goswami, Indira 181
Goswami, Manu 68
Grammar of Stolen Love 66
gramya (village) 30
Greenough, Paul 89, 131
grihastha 129
Grimm Brothers 3, 16, 69, 81–2, 169
Grove, Richard H. 218 n.169
grove, sacred 61
groves 18, 20, 23, 29, 31, 39–40, 51, 60–1, 63, 74, 89, 103–4, 190, 226 n.3
  sacred 89, 226 n.3
  Simsapa Grove and tree 31, 199 n.200
Guha, Ramachandra 77–8, 155, 227 n.13
Guha, Ranajit 9–10, 215 n.98, 229 n.50

Haberman, David L. 15
habitus 27–8
  of forest 167, 177
Halbfass, Willhelm 211 n.18, 218 n.165
Haraway, Donna J. 179, 186
Harrison, Robert Pogue 3–4, 12–14, 16, 43, 167, 169, 195 n.102

Hasdeo Anand Forest 44
Hawley, John Stratton 29, 219 n.206
Hawley, John and Mark Jurgensmeyer 217 n.150, 218 n.166
healer 81, 89
Heidegger, Martin 13
Heise, Ursula K. 27
Herder, Johann Gottfried 16
hero, epic, and heroic qualities 2, 6, 21, 25, 53–5, 65, 69–73, 82, 92, 102, 105, 135, 162, 174, 182, 208 n.109
  modern literary and historical 16, 22, 54, 65, 108, 110
  kingship
heroine 67, 98, 108, 126–7, 165, 174
Hewitt, David 197 n.139
hijra 102, 109, 158–9
Hill Dwellers 55, 57–9, 205 n.23
Himalaya 1, 18, 24–5, 28, 41, 54–5, 66, 72, 76, 78, 116, 161
  Kumaon 78
  Terai 41
Hindi 44–8, 65, 74, 85, 102, 117–18, 120, 122, 124, 127, 134, 181, 212 n.27, 213 n.45
Hindu 14, 26, 30, 37, 55, 68, 80–1, 83–4, 87, 94, 101, 127, 154, 211 n.12
  Hinduism 15, 32–3, 39, 40, 43, 58
Hindutva 20, 41–2
historical romance novel 23
history 11, 26, 30–1, 48, 95, 130, 134, 149, 168, 174
  and fictive present 124
  global 126
  historicize 78, 89, 164
  historicizing gaze 125
  mythic 104
  narrative of 138
Hogan, Linda 167, 170
Home and the World, The (Ghare Baire)
  See Tagore, Rabindranath
Homer, *The Odyssey* 25
Hooker, Joseph Dalton 210 n.162
Hori character in *Godaan* 119, 121, 123
houris 135
Hungry Tide, The
  See Ghosh, Amitav
"Hunt, The"
  See Devi, Mahasweta

Hunter, W. W.: *Annals of Rural Bengal* 86, 90, 93–4, 135, 150
hunting, forest 5, 46, 70, 101, 172–3
Hyde, Lewis 102, 109
hyle (forest) 4

Ibis ship in *Sea of Poppies* 11, 147, 149–50, 186
Ibis Trilogy, Ghosh's 147
Ilanko
  See Atikal, Ilanko
Imaginary Maps: Three Stories
  See Devi, Mahasweta
indentured labor 150, 160–1
Independence of India, 1947 2, 33, 41, 53, 181, 203 n.1, 228 n.27, 233 n.11
index, indexical 8, 76, 83, 125, 149–50, 181, 186–7, 189
Indian Forest Acts
  See Forest Acts, Indian
indigenous cultures 170
  denigration of 153–4, 158
  indigeneity 153–4
  romanticizing of 148, 163, 182, 184
  space 160
  See also Adivasi; Chipko movement; tribal
indigo 96–7
Indra 54
Inspector General of Forests 77
irony, modern and narrative 13–14, 17, 25, 32, 43, 78, 87, 95, 120, 142, 154, 162, 167–8, 174, 179, 183, 185–6, 189–90, 231 n.90
itihas 72, 171

jackfruit tree 52, 66, 189
Jafar, Mir 90, 94–7
Jain 46, 58, 63
Jaipur 39
Jalais, Annu 138
Jallianwala Bagh 155
"Jana, Gana, Mana" national anthem 33–4
  See also Tagore, Rabindranath
Jangal Desh 45
jangala 30, 45–6
Janu, C. K.: *Mother Forest* 26, 48, 155–8, 160, 162–3
jasmine 4, 39–40, 54, 66, 85, 128, 141

Jasminum 4
  See also *sambac*
jatra 140–1
Jayadeva: *Gita Govinda* 29
Jharkhand 164, 168, 182
Jiban, Jibananda 80
  character in *Anandamath* 106–9, 111, 116, 217 n.153
Jivaka 46
Jivakacintamani 46
Jones, Sir William 40, 43, 72
Joshi, Priya 22–3, 79, 85, 197 n.149, 213 n.42
Joyce, James 50
jungle 30, 32, 46, 57–8, 63, 68, 71, 83–4, 165, 189
  changeable 182
  forest 32, 46, 83, 112, 222 n.39
  home 166
  "jungle folk" 120, 157
jungli 84

Kabutri character in *Sea of Poppies* 148
Kadamba Forest 30, 58, 64, 128
kadamba (*cadamba*) tree 51
Kali 80, 135
Kali Yuga 103
Kalidasa 4, 17, 53, 72–3, 82, 90, 98, 100, 107, 113, 119, 125
  See also *Shakuntala*; *Abhijnanashakuntalam: The Recognition of Shakuntala*
Kalua character in *Sea of Poppies* 149
Kalyani character in *Anandamath* 80, 89, 135
Kampan (Kamban) 68–9
Kanai character in *The Hungry Tide* 139–46
Kannada language and literature 182
Kannaki character in *The Cilappatikaram* 6, 51, 53–65, 73
Kannauj 39
Kanthapura
  See Rao, Raja
Kapoor, Raj 118–19
Kapoor, Shashi 118
Karve, Irawati: *Yuganta* 208 n.116
Kathakali 27
Kaur, Rajender 84
Kauravas 54, 62, 70, 72, 103, 136, 164

Kautilya: *Arthashastra* 31, 204 n.2
Kaveri River 55, 65
Kavunti character in *Cilappatikaram* 61–2
Kaviraj, Sudipta 7, 32, 36, 87, 95, 171
kavya 198 n.166
kelikadamba tree 128
Kerala 48, 58, 153, 156
   See also Malabar
Khair, Tabish 79
Khandava Forest 59, 73, 188
Khari-boli dialect of Hindi 127
Khatrī, Devakīnandana: *Chandrakanta* (*In the Mysterious Ruins*) 85
Khusrau, Amir 37
kingship (moral leadership) 2, 30, 53–4, 65, 68–71, 73, 90, 162
kino tree 55, 66
Kire, Easterine: *When the River Sleeps* 48, 175, 178
Kishwar, Madhu 206 n.35
Kohn, Eduardo 27, 149, 177–8
Kol people 74
kolatan songs 74
Kolatkar, Arun 58
Kolodny, Annette 200–1 n.223
Kovalan character in *The Cilappatikaram* 6, 51, 53–64, 73, 204 n.8
Krishna 29–30, 50, 61, 67, 74, 92, 100, 148, 164, 166
Krishna Ayyar, K. V. 203 n.282
Kristeva, Julia 223 n.3
Kshatriya 63, 70–1, 74
Kumar, Sanjeev 166
kunj (*kunja*) 30, 74, 104, 106
kurinji, flower and topography 1, 61, 66–8 *tinai*
Kuru people 72
Kurujangala 45
Kusum character in *The Hungry Tide* 140–4

Laila-Majnun 127
Lakoff, [George] and [Mark] Johnson 97
Lakshmana 23, 30
Lakshmi 97
landscape 72
   changeable 142
   feminized 160–1
   and language 141
   local 53–4
   maternal 99
   sacred 29
   Tamil 54, 56, 65, 67, 99
Latour, Bruno 170
laurel tree, Indian 72
Laws of Manu 82
leadership
   See kingship
Lee, David 24
Lemuria 67
lila 30
Lilacaritra 69
liminal, liminality of forest 8, 10–11, 20, 46, 87, 91, 94, 97, 101–3, 110, 116, 162, 166, 186
   of jungle 112
   and rite of passage 46, 56, 135, 186
   spaces 10, 30, 46, 90, 160, 162–3
Lipner, Julius J. 18, 89–92, 98–9, 101, 103–5, 107–9, 112–13, 192 n.43, 203 nn.287, 288, 211 n.6, 212 n.29, 213 n.57, 214 n.69, 217 n.153, 218 n.167, 219 nn.186, 198, 220 nn.212, 220, 229, 221 n.238
   Anandamath, or The Sacred Brotherhood
Lorenzen, David N. 88
Lucknow 119
Lukács, Georg 27
Lusiads, The
   See Camões, Luis Vaz de
Lusibari 141, 143
Lutgendorf, Philip 70, 74, 209 n.123

Macaulay, Thomas B. 7
Madna 184–5
Madurai (Maturai) 52–7, 60, 63
magic realism 10, 169
Mahabharata 6, 20, 23, 37, 59, 70–3, 83, 90, 103, 164, 188
Mahajan, Karan: *The Association of Small Bombs* 49, 187–8
Maharashtra 69, 99
Mahasweta Devi
   See Devi, Mahasweta
mahatmya 68
Mahendra character in *Anandamath* 80, 88, 90, 97–9, 103–7, 110–15, 135
mahua tree and forest type 78, 128, 153–4, 172, 175, 183, 226 n.1

Maithil, Maithili 59–60, 73
Malabar 39, 57, 75–6, 96, 147, 209 n.131
Malayalam language and literature 156, 182
Malti character in *Godaan* 120, 122
Man Singh 39
mangalkavya 40, 92–3
mango tree 40, 67, 85, 90, 112, 136, 189–90, 234 n.19
    mango leaf 148, 225 n.39
mangrove forest 18, 48, 89, 131–5, 137–8, 142, 145–6, 150–1, 170, 210 n.162
    See also Sundarbans
Mansoor character in *The Association of Small Bombs* 187
Maoist guerillas 158, 184
mapping, cartographic 32–3, 65, 107
Mara goddess 135
Marathi 50, 100, 182
Markham, Clements R. 210 n.162
Márquez, Gabriel García: *One Hundred Years of Solitude* 12
Mary Oraon character in "The Hunt" 171, 175, 178
masculinity 111
Matavi character in *The Cilappatikaram* 61, 204 n.8
matavi plant 60–1
math (abbey) 80
Mathew, K. S. 57
Maturai
    See Madurai
Maturaikanchi 63–4
Mauritius 147
Mauryan kings 21, 204 nn.2, 9
Mayadevi 118
Mayasabha, hall of illusions 131
Medina 139
Mehta character in *Godaan* 71, 120, 123
Midnight's Children 48
    See Rushdie, Salman
migration 146, 153, 157
Milton, John: *Paradise Lost* 75, 82–3
mining in forests and tribal rights 159
Mirabai 100, 102, 108–9, 217 n.151
Mr. Khurana character in *The Association of Small Bombs* 187
miswak (*ukaay*) tree 5, 51
Mitra, Indrani 122
Mitter, Partha 170

modernity, modern outlook 2, 8, 12–13, 15, 23, 25–7, 32, 36, 40–1, 43, 50, 64, 71, 157, 160, 162, 167, 169, 173–5, 177–8, 181–5
    discourse of 169
    multiple modernities 41, 179
monastery, Hindu 89, 94
    Buddhist 112
Morichjhapi massacre 138, 141–2
Mother Forest
    See Janu, C. K.
Mother India goddess and trope 18, 22, 33, 35, 42, 48, 53, 65, 80–2, 88, 97–9, 100–1, 104, 161, 164, 175
    See also geography
Mughal dynasty and culture 39–41, 68–70, 78, 87, 92, 94, 97, 103, 144, 154, 185
Mukherjee, Meenakshi 72, 85–6, 208 n.109
Mukherjee, Upamanyu Pablo 86, 139–40
mullai blossom and topography 1, 54, 61, 66
multilingualism
    See polyvocal; and polyglot
Muslim Indians 12, 25, 33, 37, 47, 67–8, 80–1, 83–4, 86–90, 92–5, 97–8, 101, 108–11, 113, 115–16, 124, 138, 203 n.287, 204 n.20, 212 n.29, 214 n.83, 216 n.125, 217 n.154, 218 n.170
    See also Chattopadhyay, Bankimchandra, portrayal of Muslims in *Anandamath*
Muziris 57, 59, 62–3
myth, mythic 11, 86, 136, 140, 162, 173

Naga people, Naga literature and writers, Nagaland 49, 153, 175–9
    See also Kire, Easterine
Nair, Shankar 68, 92
Nandy, Ashis 2
Narayan, R. K. 118
Narayana Rao, Velcheru 71
Narayanan, Vasudha 68
Narlekar, Anjali 50
nation-state, modern Indian 7, 17, 43, 171
    postcolonial state
national anthem: "*Jana Gana Mana*" 33–4, 56
nationalism, European 116
nationalism, Indian, and nationalist activists and writers 1–2, 5–6, 8,

11–30, 32–3, 35–7, 41–7, 51–3, 55, 62, 65, 69, 74–5, 78–88, 98, 105, 107–8, 118–19, 122, 155, 161, 163, 171, 175, 181, 200 n.223, 203 n.1, 222 n.31
nation as family trope 119, 187
national identity 163, 177
nationhood, future ideal 149
romanticism 64, 78
See also regionalism
nature-culture dualism 186
Naxalite movement 159, 184
neem tree 1, 21, 40, 147
Nehru, Jawaharlal 17, 21, 36, 133, 228–9 n.37
  Nehruvian 132
  The Discovery of India 17, 21, 228 n.37
neocolonial 50, 170
neo-traditionalism 42–4
New Delhi (Delhi) 39, 158, 186–7
Ngũgĩ wa Thiong'o: *Petals of Blood* 12
Nidhuban Forest 30
Nikhil character in *The Home and the World* 122
Nikunjaban Forest 31
Nil Darpan 96, 97
Nilgiri Hills 20, 44, 78
Nilima character in *The Hungry Tide* 137–8, 141, 144
Nirmal character in *The Hungry Tide* 138, 141–3, 146
niti 70
Novetzke, Christian Lee 69
nutmeg tree 75, 189
nyaya 70

oak tree 3, 24–5, 76
opium, opium trade 90, 94–6, 148
  See also Anglo-Chinese (Opium) War
d'Orta, Garcia: *Colloquies on the Simples and Drugs of India* 75, 209 n.131
Orientalism, Orientalist 15, 26, 87
oral tradition 58, 65, 68, 92, 153, 205 n.29
Oraon people 49, 156, 172
  See also Mary Oraon

paan 37, 42, 93–4, 100, 140, 223 n.44
Padma character in *Midnight's Children* 133
Pal, Bipin Chandra 21
Palamau Forest 182

Panchavati
  See Banwari
Pandavas 37, 71–2, 103, 136, 164
Pandyan kings 54, 57–60, 62–3, 72–3
paradise, cultural concepts of 12, 35, 37, 39, 70, 135, 188
Paradise Lost
  See Milton, John
Paripatal Tamil Sangam poetry collection 141
Parkhill, Thomas 46, 90, 109
Parsi shipbuilders 148
Parthasarathy, R. 6, 55–6, 60, 62–3, 204 n.9, 205 n.29
  See also *Cilappatikaram, The*
Partition of India 136, 233 n.11
Passions of the Tongue
  See Ramaswamy, Sumathi
pastoralist 20, 48, 101, 183
Pather Panchali 123
  See also Ray, Satyajit
Pathupattu, Sangam poetry collection 64, 206 n.49
Pearson, Michael N. 225 n.36
peasant farmer 96, 121
Peirce, Charles Sanders 9, 27
pepper 37, 39, 55, 57–9, 63, 75–6, 157
Persian
  landscape 39
  language 39–40, 69, 124, 227 n.12
  poetry 37, 39
Persian-Islamic 87
  Persianate 39, 92
philology, comparative 43, 64
Phule, Jyotirao 33
Phule, Savatribai 33
Picart, Bernard 14–15
pilgrimage 1, 24, 29–30, 37, 59, 72, 88, 206 n.38, 208 n.109, 217 n.154
  See also tirthayatra
Pillai, Nellaiyappa 18
Pillai, Thakazhi Sivasankara 181
pine tree, forest 24–5, 39, 66, 76, 78
pipal (peepul) tree 39–40, 90, 190
Piya character in *The Hungry Tide* 142–6
plantain tree, leaf 51, 60, 75, 176
plantations 75, 96, 102, 154, 174, 189
Plato 12
Pollock, Sheldon 24, 69

polyglot, polyvocal (multilingualism) 25, 40, 48, 50, 67, 150, 156, 183
polysemy 70, 183
ponna tree 72
Portuguese 7, 46, 75, 82, 86, 93, 138
post-independence era 65
  generation 49
  trade 189
post-1991 Indian writers 185–90
postcolonial
  literature 168, 175
  state 154–69
Pouchepadass, Jacques 226 n.4
prakriti 21, 84, 99, 104, 120, 227 n.15
Prayag 29
pre-independence Indian writers 73, 181
predation motif 178
Premchand 48, 119, 122–3, 126, 222 nn.27, 31
  See also *Godaan* 71, 117–23
Premsagar 127
primitive 445, 71, 83
  primitive-civilized polarity 36
primitivism, modern concept of 17, 238–9 n.37
  in modern literature 81
primordial, primeval, forest 57, 91, 126
printing press 64
  print-based cultures 149
progress, narrative of 130
progressive writers 117
  era 123
Progressive Writers' Association 221 n.5
Provincializing Europe
  See Chakrabarty, Dipesh
Pukar (Puhar) 6, 52–3, 55–8, 63–4
Punjab 28
puram 54, 66
puranas, puranic 18, 29, 37, 57–8, 68, 98, 129, 171

Radha 29–30, 74, 101–3, 106, 113–14, 122, 220 n.218
Rai, Amrit: *Māncarit* 39–40
Rai Sahib character in *Godaan* 71
railway 12, 20, 28, 117, 154, 174, 231 n.89
rainforest 18, 133
Rajagopal, Krishnadas 210 n.147
Rajput 39, 103, 227 n.12

Rakshasa 30, 33, 73
Rama 23–5, 30, 59–60, 69, 72, 74, 97, 104, 135, 158
Ramacharitmanas 74
Raman, Shankar 82
Ramanujan, A. K. 9, 20, 67, 102, 208 n.109
Ramaswamy, Sumathi 20, 32, 42, 55–6, 64–5, 67, 98, 116, 206 n.58
Ramayana 1, 6, 18, 20, 23–4, 36, 40, 53, 59, 68–9, 71–3, 91, 111, 123, 135, 158, 170, 186, 198 n.166, 202 n.254, 208 n.109, 209 n.123
Ramlila 71, 73
Rao, Raja: *Kanthapura* 18, 85, 118, 171, 175
rasa theory 25, 27, 70, 125
Ravana 24, 29, 59, 72
Ray, Bharatchandra: *Anandamangal* 92
Ray, Romita 15
Ray, Satyajit 181, 183
  Days and Nights in the Forest (Aranyer Din Ratri) 182
Ray, Sugata 218 n.169
Raychaudhuri, Tapan 95, 194 n.81, 211 n.10
Raza, Rahi Massom: *Adha Gaon* 44
real, reality, realistic 27, 67, 84, 99, 195 n.113
realism, literary 10–11, 23, 27, 46, 84–6, 91, 104, 117, 119, 122, 147, 149, 178, 228 n.28
  and allegory 136, 146, 162
  romanticism 46
  See also Dalley, Hamish, allegorical realism; magic realism
real, reality and forest 125, 141, 146
  changing 128
  vis-à-vis unreality (illusion) 127, 177, 189
refugees, Bangladeshi 130, 138
regional, regionalism 18, 20, 31, 53–4, 58, 61, 71, 79, 82–3, 87, 90, 93, 98–9, 136
"Religion of the Forest" 33
  See also Tagore
Revathy character in *The Ministry of Utmost Happiness* 158–60
revivalism, nineteenth-century Hindu 26, 32, 43, 84
  Hindu, Hinduism
Reynolds, G. W. M. 22

Reynolds, Holly Baker 64, 206 n.49
rhetoric
　classical Indian 82
　colonial 78
　demotic 181
　formal 181
　of improvement, nineteenth-century European 76
　of loss and recovery 22
　modern 36, 42
　of progress 22
　religious-political 83
　rhetorical contradiction in Bankim 82, 87
　rhetorical strategy in Bankim 87
　rhetorical strategy in Mahasweta 161
　rhetorical strategy in Premchand 123
Ribbentropp, Berthold 77
Riehl, Wilhelm Heinrich 36
Rig Veda 24
Rigby, Kate 230–1 n.66
Roadarmel, Gordon C. 122
Robi character in *Days and Nights in the Forest* 182–3
Robin Hood 169
Romanticism, European 11–13, 15–17, 22, 46, 183
　influence on Indian writers 13, 16, 22, 69, 82–3
　Indian sources 15, 17
　Romantic poetry, English and European 10, 13, 15, 168
Rome, Romans 4–5, 63
Roy, Anuradha 26, 49
　An Atlas of Impossible Longing 189–90
Roy, Arundhati 49, 155, 158–60, 165, 189
　The God of Small Things 189
　The Ministry of Utmost Happiness 158–60
　Walking with Comrades 159
Roy, Parama 162
Roy, Rammohun 7, 21, 87
rubber tree 189
Rumi: *Masnavi* 92
Rushdie, Salman 48, 132–8, 142–3, 150, 226 n.52

Sadharana 46
sal tree 24, 78, 105, 125, 145, 147, 172, 183

Saleem Sinai character in *Midnight's Children* 48, 132–3
Salih, Tayeb: *Season of Migration to the North* 12
sambac 4
　See also jasmine
Samudri Raja 82
sandalwood 24, 55, 58–9, 66, 68, 98, 184, 188
Sangam era and poetry, Tamil 1, 12, 51, 53–4, 56, 64–7, 141, 206 n.49
sannyasi in *Anandamath* 80, 86–8
　historical Rebellion 88, 213 n.54
　renunciative act 111
Sanskrit language and literature 4, 20, 23, 26, 30, 39, 40, 43, 45–6, 53, 55–6, 60, 70, 62, 74, 81–2, 114, 163
Sanskritization 101, 217 n.155
Santal people 89–90, 130, 156, 183
　Santali language 124
santan 23, 42, 80–2, 84, 87–93, 95, 97, 101–2, 104, 106–16, 135, 214 n.69, 217 n.153, 220 n.218
Sarkar, Tanika 95, 99, 108, 114, 216 n.125, 219 n.193, 220 n.214
Sarveswaran, Vidya 126
Satyacharan (Satya) character in *Aranyak: Of the Forest* 125–30
Satyam Shivam Sundaram film 118
Satyananda character in *Anandamath* 81, 88–9
Savarkar, V. D. 20, 47
scepter, wooden 63–4
Scheduled Tribes and Other Traditional Forest Dwellers, government designation 36, 77
Schiller, Friedrich: *The Robbers* 17
Schlegel, Friedrich 17, 211 n.20
science, modern 5, 17, 26, 43, 67, 83, 89, 103, 169, 181, 202 n.254, 210 n.162
Scott, James 121
Scott, Sir Walter 13, 150
　Waverley 22, 83
Sea of Poppies
　See Ghosh, Amitav
semiotics 144
Sen, Amartya 40
Senanayak character in "Draupadi" 164–7
serissa tree 51

Sethi, Rumina 85, 171
sexuality 26, 109-10, 112, 119
   queer 110
Shah, Bullhe 92
Shah Jongoli 139
Shah, Majnu 86
shakti 86, 95, 99, 154
Shakuntala (also
   Abhijnanashakuntalam: The
   Recognition of Shakuntala) drama 4,
   17, 53, 60, 62, 73, 82, 85, 90, 98
   See also Kalidasa
Shakuntala character in Kalidasa's drama
   4-5, 73, 85, 98, 100, 107, 118-19,
   226 n.51
Shanker, N. Ravi 155-7
Shanti character in *Anandamath* 80, 89
Shantiniketan 29
Shaw, Miranda Eberle 118
Shekhar character in *Days and Nights in the*
   Forest 182, 184
Shekhar, Hansda Sowvendra 167
shikargarh 70
ships, shipbuilding 72, 75, 147-8
shisham tree 147
Shiva 25, 59, 64, 66-7, 69, 95, 99, 101
Shiva, Vandana 154, 200 n.215, 227
   nn.14, 15
shola rainforest 18, 66
Sholay film 231 n.90
Shulman, David 66-7, 72, 207 n.79
Shurpanaka 72
Simsapa Grove and tree
   See also groves
sindoor 100, 148, 225 n.39
Singh, Chetan 216 n.116, 227 n.12
Sinha, Indra: *Animal's People* 49, 186, 188
Siraj ud-Daulah 94
Sita 18, 24, 30, 43, 59-60, 73-4, 104, 184,
   206 n.38
Skaria, Ajay 17, 36, 184, 226 n.3, 228-9 n.37
Slovic, Scott 126
Sontheimer, Günther D. 100, 217 n.135
Southey, Robert 15
space, sacred 32, 33
   See also geography; landscape
spice trade 7, 52, 57
Spivak, Gayatri Chakravorty 10, 49, 155,
   157, 160-1, 171-3

Srinivas, M. N. 217 n.155
statecraft 72
stereotype in fiction 94
sthala-purana 58, 64, 85, 208 n.109
subaltern lives 9, 32, 145-7, 155-6
sublime, philosophical concept 14, 89
Sufi 25, 37, 39, 92
Sundarbans 18, 41, 48, 89, 131-9, 141-5,
   147, 150-1, 170, 210 n.161, 223-4 n.8
sundari tree 142, 224-5 n.8
surreal, surrealism of forest 132, 134, 136,
   142, 150, 188, 190
symbolic capital 28
syncretic 67, 80, 101, 116, 138

Tagore, Rabindranath 18, 29, 33-7, 42, 84,
   87, 98, 104, 122, 136, 150, 182, 185,
   200 n.216
tamarisk tree 121, 123
Tamil language, literature, writers 1, 4, 6,
   18, 20, 25-6, 45-6, 51, 54-5, 58-60,
   62-8, 72, 85, 102
   indigenous rights 26
   nationalism 51-4, 64-5
   Ramayana 72
   See also Sangam poetry; *Cilappatikaram,*
     The; Kampan
Tamil country 6, 18, 53-5, 57-9, 61-7
   landscape 56, 99
Tamil Nadu 18, 51, 65-6, 68
Tamilakam 54, 62, 65
Tamilpparru 56
Tamilttay goddess 65
Tamizh 64
tapovana 182
Tchsildar character in "The Hunt" 172
Telangana 158
Telugu language and literature 71, 74,
   85, 158
Thapar, Romila 30
therianthropy 177
Thiruvalluvar: *Tirukkural* 65
Thomas, Keith 25
Thomas, Rosie 119
Thompson, E. P. 121
Thoreau, Henry David 162
Tickell, Alex 171

tiger 7, 14, 130, 138
  killing of 145, 176
timber 58, 75–6, 89, 144, 147, 150–1, 154, 160, 174, 186, 189, 226 n.3, 227 n.12, 231 n.89
tinai 1, 12, 54, 61, 66–8, 141
Tiruttakkadevar 46
tirthayatra 37
  See also pilgrimage
Tobin, Beth Fowkes 13
Torgovnick, Marianna 210–11 n.162
tourism 130
transgression in literature 56, 60–1, 63, 72, 102–3, 107–11, 164
translation 4, 14, 17, 24, 49–50, 56, 82–3, 98, 123–4, 138, 156, 166, 168, 172, 192 n.43, 204 n.8, 208 n.109, 222 n.39, 226 n.1, 230 n.63
  as motif in *The Hungry Tide* 138
tribal communities 28, 32, 45, 77, 153, 156, 158–60, 164–72, 174, 176, 178, 182, 184–5, 203 n.282, 227 n.14, 231 n.89
  See also Adivasi; Chipko movement
trickster figure 102, 110–11
Trumpener, Katie 13
tulsi plant 29
Tulsidas 74
  See also *Ramacharitmanas*
Turner, Ellen 156
Turner, Victor 121, 123
  The Ritual Process 46, 109

Umaruppalavar 67–8
uncanny perspective and presence 10, 134, 136, 148, 185
Upadhyay, Shashi Bhushan 121
urban
  See city
Urdu language and literature 85, 117–18, 134
utilitarian colonial outlook 17, 77, 89, 175

Vaidya, Anand 32
Valmiki 1, 23–4, 68, 72, 84
van, vana 4, 29–31, 45
Van Gennep, Arnold 56
vanaprastha 129, 183
vanavasa 29
Vanchi 55, 59

Vande Mataram 42
  Bande Mataram
Vedas, Vedic 18, 20, 24, 26, 33–5, 40, 43, 66, 89, 91–2, 122, 126, 129, 161, 165, 183–4
Vellya Pappen character in *The God of Small Things* 189
Venkatachalapathy, A. R. 25, 85
vernacular literature 25, 28, 40, 46, 56, 68, 92, 168
Vico, Giambattista 3, 43
Vilie character in *When the River Sleeps* 176–9
village, Indian 2, 30, 159
  idealization of 82, 121, 159, 181
vision, perspective 10, 128, 142, 146, 189
  epiphany 145, 150, 161, 187, 190
  partial and fragmented vision 133
  problem of perspective 128
  See also *darshanic* vision
Vrindavan (Brindavan) 29–30, 32, 58, 60–1, 67, 74, 92, 102, 109, 147

waste, wasteland 32, 61, 76
Wayanad District of Kerala 155–7
Weberian concept of modernity 170
Wenzel, Jennifer 2
were-tiger 149, 175–9
West Bengal 49, 138, 170, 182
Western Ghats 1, 57, 72, 98
Wheeler, Wendy 169, 230 n.66
White Tiger, The
  See Adiga, Aravind
wild, wildness 3, 5, 32, 36, 45, 49, 130, 163, 166, 179, 182, 184, 189
wilderness 31
Williams, John 3
Williams, Raymond: *The Country and the City* 25, 41
Wilson, Emily 25
"Witch-Hunt, The"
  See Devi, Mahasweta
womb motif, ship as womb 147
  See also forest
women 22, 28, 49, 55, 60–3, 70–4, 87, 102, 106–8, 110–11, 113, 115, 118, 120–2, 126, 135, 140–2, 150, 154, 156–9, 162, 168, 172–3, 175–7, 182–3, 204 n.8,

206 n.35, 219 nn.198, 206, 219 n.198, 220 n.214, 227 n.14
Adivasi 49, 71, 120, 122, 165, 167, 175
rebels 108, 113, 164–5
rebellious 231 n.90
tribal 122, 126, 128, 168, 172–3, 175, 227 n.14
widows 141
See also Adivasi; *Anandamath*; Chipko movement; Devi, Mahasweta; "Draupadi"; femininity; forest nymph or maiden trope; *gopis*; Janu, C. K.; Sarkar, Tanika
Woolf, Virginia 168
Wordsworth, William 7, 34, 36
World of Apu film 123
See also Ray, Satyajit
writers, Indian, and literature, the novel 46–8, 85, 92, 122–3, 178, 215 n.86

See also nationalism, Indian; Bengali intellectuals

Yadava dynasty 69
Yavana 59, 63
Yazijian, Edward M. 202 n.250, 215 n.91
Yelle, Robert A. 232 n.98
Young, Arthur 76

Zachary Reid character in *Sea of Poppies* 148, 225 n.42
zamindar 5, 96
zamindari system 121, 123
Zamora, Lois Parkinson 213 n.46
Zarrilli, Phillip B. 26–7
Zimmermann, Francis: *The Jungle and the Aroma of Meats* 45
Zipes, Jack 82
Zoffany, Johan 15
zone of tension 46, 70, 169

www.ingramcontent.com/pod-product-compliance
Lightning Source LLC
Chambersburg PA
CBHW062121300426
44115CB00012BA/1767